LAST LAUGHS

Studies in Gender and Culture
A series edited by Wendy Martin, Queens College,
City University of New York

Volume 1 THE FEMALE IMAGINATION AND THE MODERNIST
AESTHETIC
edited by Sandra M. Gilbert and Susan Gubar

Volume 2 LAST LAUGHS
Perspectives on Women and Comedy
edited by Regina Barreca

This book is part of a series. The publisher will accept continuation orders which may be cancelled at any time and which provide for automatic billing and shipping of each title in the series upon publication. Please write for details.

LAST LAUGHS

Perspectives on Women and Comedy

Edited by

REGINA BARRECA
University of Connecticut

GORDON AND BREACH

New York London Paris Montreux Tokyo Melbourne

© 1988 by OPA (Amsterdam) B.V. All rights reserved.
Published under license by Gordon and Breach, Science Publishers, Inc.

Gordon and Breach Science Publishers

Post Office Box 786
Cooper Station, New York, New York 10276
United States of America

Post Office Box 161
1820 Montreux 2
Switzerland

Post Office Box 197
London WC2E 9PX
England

3-14-9, Okubo
Shinjuku-ku, Tokyo
Japan

58, rue Lhomond
75005 Paris
France

Private Bag 8
Camberwell, Victoria 3124
Australia

This material originally appeared as Volume 15, Issues 1-3 of the journal *Women's Studies*.

Library of Congress Cataloging-in-Publication Data

Last laughs.

  (Studies in gender and culture; v. 2)
  "This material originally appeared as volume 15 (1-3) of the journal Women's studies" — T.p. verso.
  Includes bibliographies.
  1. English literature — Women authors — History and criticism.   2. American literature — Women authors — History and criticism.   3. English wit and humor — Women authors — History and criticism.   4. American wit and humor — Women authors — History and criticism.   6. Feminist literary criticism. 7. Comic, The.   I. Barreca, Regina. II. Series.
PR111.L27 1988   820'.9'9287   88-21225
ISBN 0-677-22020-0
ISBN 0-677-22030-8 (pbk.)

No part of this book may be reproduced or utilized in any form or by any means, electronic or mechanical, including photocopying and recording, or by any information storage or retrieval system, without permission in writing from the publishers. Printed in Great Britain by Whitstable Litho Ltd., Whitstable, Kent.

Contents

I

Sylvia
Nicole Hollander   1

Introduction
Regina Barreca   3

Who Was That Masked Woman? The Prostitute and the Playwright in the Comedies of Aphra Behn
Catherine Gallagher   23

Life After Sex: The Fictional Autobiography of Delariver Manley
Janet Todd   43

Jane Austen: Irony and Authority
Rachel M. Brownstein   57

Austen's Laughter
Patricia Meyer Spacks   71

Deflation of Male Pretensions in Fanny Burney's *Cecilia*
Kay Rogers   87

II

Sylvia
Nicole Hollander   97

Frances Miriam Whitcher: Social Satire in the Age of Gentility
Linda A. Morris   99

Hate and Humor as Empathetic Whimsy in Anne Thackeray Ritchie
Carol Hanbery MacKay   117

Between Women: A Cross-Class Analysis of Status and
Anarchic Humor
   Regenia Gagnier   135

Slaying the Angel and the Patriarch: The Grinning Woolf
   Denise Marshall   149

(En)gendering Laughter: Woolf's *Orlando* as Contraband
in the Age of Joyce
   Judy Little   179

Truth-Telling: The Self and the Fictions of Humor
   Mary Ann Rorison Caws   193

III

Sylvia
   Nicole Hollander   201

Ironic Autobiography: From *The Waterfall* to *The Handmaid's Tale*
   Nancy Walker   203

Muriel Spark's *Unknowing* Fiction
   John Glavin   221

Metaphor-into-Narrative: Being Very Careful with Words
   Regina Barreca   243

Uncommon Woman: An Interview with Wendy Wasserstein
   Esther Cohen   257

Feminist Humor: Rebellious and Self-Affirming
   Lisa Merrill   271

Daughters of Anger/Material Girls: Con/Textualizing
Feminist Criticism
   Jane Marcus   281

Towards a Humorous View of the Universe
   Fay Weldon   309

About the Contributors   313
Index   317

Sylvia

NICOLE HOLLANDER

Introduction

REGINA BARRECA

Department of English, University of Connecticut

But I must confess I have never made any Observation of what I Apprehend to be true Humour in Women... Perhaps Passions are too powerful in that Sex to let Humour have its Course; or maybe by reason of their Natural Coldness, Humour cannot Exert itself to that extravagant Degree, which it does in the Male Sex.
William Congreve "Concerning Humor in Comedy" 1695

A difference of taste in jokes is a great strain on the affections.
George Eliot *Daniel Deronda* 1876

CONGREVE'S STATEMENT that women lack a sense of humor echoes through three hundred years of criticism of British literature.[1] The reasons Congreve supplies explaining his belief have reappeared in a variety of configurations from the seventeenth to the twentieth century. Recent critics have added their own speculations on why humor remains beyond the reach of women. Generally speaking, commentators on comedy continue to treat the subject as a necessarily all-male pastime, rather like writing in the snow.[2]

Eliot's claim, in contrast, can act as an emblem for the essays included in this collection. The citation and distinction of difference is the concern of the writers here; without apology, most deal with the issues of gender-specific readings. This is not to say that men have not written about comedy and the woman writer. However, a summary remark that might best serve to delineate traditional critical approaches to women and comedy was made by Reginald Blyth in *Humour in English Literature*, first published in 1959 and reprinted in 1970:

The truth is ... that women have not only no humour in themselves but are the cause of the extinction of it in others. This is almost too cruel to be true, but in every way women correspond to and are representative of nature. Is there any humour in nature? A glance at the zoo will answer this question ... [w]omen are the undifferentiated mass of nature from which the contradictions of real and ideal arose and they are the unlaughing at which men laugh (14).

Unfortunately this comment was not delivered as a joke.

As recently as 1976, J.B. Priestley wrote in *English Humor* that Jane Austen "frequently attends to what any man feels are feminine small potatoes" (126). When speaking of Elizabeth Gaskell's *Cranford*, Priestley felt obliged to point out that "the male reader knows what he is in for; many measures of indeed very small beer" (127). Priestley illustrates the accepted critical position with regard to women's humor. He asserts, with enormous conviction, that the "sort of humour essentially feminine in nature" is that characterised by "soft laughter and smiles" which "soon dissolve into tears" (138). Priestley put forth a view so traditional and so unenlightened as to be of help in determining why women's comedy has gone unrecognized. He offers us the following:

What my sex needs is an ample supply of first-rate women, who can look at us and listen to as not without sympathy but who are always prepared to laugh at us, knowing full well they have more sense than we have, so many thick-skinned pompous chaps (138).

If women are seen openly in this light it should not surprise us that they don't make too many jokes around Priestley. Faced with the prospect of women initiating humor, he is stern, dismissive and patronizing:

The movement generally called 'women's lib' does not seem likely to produce more and better feminine humor. If it should succeed, what it will probably offer us is a number of women who have been turned into second-rate men (138).

Obviously, much needs to be done. The essays in this collection work towards establishing a number of pathways into the uncharted regions where women laugh their hearts out.

Feminist criticism has generally avoided the discussion of comedy, perhaps in order to be accepted by conservative critics who found feminist theory comic in and of itself. Yet women writers have traditionally used comedy to subvert existing conventional structures: recent feminist criticism has acknowledged the power of rage in writings by women, but has as yet left unexamined the crucial roles of comedy paired with anger as shaping forces and feminist tools. Why this silence on a matter which is a characteristic manifestation of women's writing? It is of the utmost importance to raise, not to sweep aside, questions concerning the appropriation of comedy by women writers. What is needed at this point is an initial discussion of women and comedy from which other discussions can spring.

Although women authors have of course written comedies, some of the most important aspects of these comedies have been virtually ignored by critics who do not perceive the wide range of emotions raised by the texts. The critics quoted earlier tacitly acknowledge that women may attempt comedy but then argue that these attempts cannot be judged successful. They do not deny that women have tried to write comedy. They argue instead that women have not been able to do it nearly so well as men.

Regenia Gagnier quotes from a fascinating study testing the reactions of men and women to humorous stimuli under controlled circumstances. Under the findings of this study, men were found to be "objective" or "field independent" where women were found to be "subjective" or "field dependent" which means:

> that in public environments women look 'round to see who else is laughing and men immediately discern the absolute signification of ... hard core humor *per se*.[3]

Gagnier's use of sociological research to illuminate literary criticism is useful in several ways, not the least of which is establishing some of the cultural determinants involved in this issue. For example, the sociologically/anthropologically-based collection *Becoming Female: Perspectives on Development*, offers insight into the "clearly definable set of sex-role standards regarding humor which exists for males and females in our culture" (138). Is this why critics from Congreve to Priestley assert that women have no sense of the comic? Is it because you cannot see what you do not believe can exist?

Sociologists have concluded that: "... women are neither expected, nor trained, to joke in this culture ... [I]t seems reasonable to propose that attempting a witty remark is often an intrusive, disturbing and aggressive act, and within this culture, probably unacceptable for a female" (McGhee 225). It would appear from these studies that women who create comedy do so in order to intrude, disturb and disrupt; that comedy constructed by women is linked to aggression and to the need to break free of socially and culturally imposed restraints. If we agree with Theodor Adorno who argues in *Minima Moralia* that "femininity itself is already the effect of the whip"(96), then women's comedy also indicates the attempt to break free of the imposition of "femininity." The aggression and anger underlying comedic constructs (including works of literature) by women have been ignored almost completely. Yet, as the following essays will illustrate, anger and comedy are present as interlocking forces in many women's texts.

What expectations are awakened by women's narrative strategies which cause them to be misread? When Priestley asserts that Austen writes about "feminine small potatoes," he is summing up an important criticism of women's comedy: it appears to lack any significant content. Comedy written by women is perceived by many critics as trivial, silly and unworthy of serious attention. These reaction might appear understandable, given that women are writing outside the locus of power and authority. Writing about women's activities appears to many critics to have less purpose than writing about men's activities. When writing comedy, where the unofficial nature of the world is explored (to paraphrase Bakhtin), women are damned to insignificance twice over. They are the unofficial discussing the insignificant. Who but other women would listen?

For some critics, the fact that many women writers choose to write about the the so-called details of life (birth, death, marriage and sex) implies that women cannot master the universal (sports, politics and academics): "[m]ateriality is the favorite statement of feminine alliance with the concrete. It, in turn, implies masculine alliance with the abstract ..." (Ellmann 97). Schopenhauer, for example, believed that "[w]omen see what is immediately before them better than men can, because they never look at anything else." Ellman comments that the implication of Schopenhauer's statement is that "if a person does not see an object, it must follow that he sees something beyond or above the object" (97). We must notice that, in terms of comedy, women are neither permitted to initiate laughter or to laugh at the male/tradition-sanctified. Women have been shut out of the gender-specific domain of "true" comedy.[4]

When the occasional traditional critic such as Priestley deigns to discuss comedy by women he sees it as gentle, subtle and reconciling. He could not be more wrong. This mistaken concept is central to a misreading of women's comedic texts. Women are regarded as incapable of producing the very challenging, angry and subversive comedy that they in fact write. Aside from a few articles which raise the possibility for this uncommon interpretation, such as D.W. Harding's discussion of Jane Austen in terms of "Regulated Hatred," or Wilt's "The Laughter of Maidens, the Cackle of Matriarchs: Notes on the Collision between Comedy and Feminism," in addition to Judy Little's landmark book *Comedy and the Woman Writer: Woolf, Spark and Feminism*, there exists in the critical literature the conviction that those few women who write comedies write them only to provide mild entertainment. As Fay Weldon might say, "Ha. Ha."

Judith Wilt's trenchant argument is therefore immensely suggestive in underscoring the relationship between women's comedy and anger. There is, for women, a:

> boundary which comedy ceases to cheer and succor and becomes violent, destructive, murderous, [which] will tumble over the edge of myth into madness (Wilt 174).

This is a reaction to the growing awareness that comedy is an ideological construct. Men and women, Wilt claims, have different uses for comic constructs:

> Women are only just beginning to realise that male humour has various functions, but none of them is intended to please or benefit them. It can be a bonding device, assisting male solidarity (and excluding women). It can be a smoke-screen, set up to dissipate an aura of good humour (distracting and deceiving women). Finally, it can be a form of assault, a teasing attack (putting women in that mythical region, their place). In any event it is used to avoid, to impede, or to deride the possibility of free equal relationships between men and women (187).

Indeed, women do make use of humor and comedy in their writings, but often couple it with an incipient rage that may cloud the perception of the reader. The narrative strategies employed by women writers awaken certain types of reader expectations that do not conform to traditional views of comedy. It is my belief that comedy and anger are two fundamental mainstays of women's writing. There exists a general theory that suggests that laughter and smiling arise out of a primitive response to anger and fear; the baring of teeth to the enemy. Women writers' coupling of comedy and anger appears to be beyond the paradigmatic bounds set forth as acceptable when discussing comedy and when discussing feminism, making it appear to be subversive on several fronts. As a number of the essays included in this collection argue, women's comedy can in fact be characterised by the way it masks its own radical contradiction of accepted, patriarchal authority by the use of a comedic 'covert language'.

If we look at the ways in which theoreticians have discussed comedy as a genre, we see that they are concerned with a number of central ideas all regarded as necessary and proper defining 'comedy': comedy as celebration of fertility and regeneration; comedy as the vulgar and exaggerated presentation of the familiar; comedy as catharsis of desire and frustration; comedy as social safety valve; comedy as carnival; comedy as unconscious, psychological reaction to personal and social instabilities; comedy as happy ending, joyous celebration, and re-establishment of order.

What then are the defining features of comedy in women's writings in relation to the discussion of comedy in general? That women write comedies without "happy endings"; that despite the absence of such an ending, these works can indeed be classified as comedies; that they write comedies which destroy a social order, perhaps but not necessarily to establish a new and different order; that their comedies may contain very little joyous celebration; that they use comedy not as a safety valve but as an inflammatory device, seeking, ultimately, not to purge desire and frustration but to transform it into action. Rachel Blau DuPlessis has already drawn our attention to the ways women "write beyond the ending" of the prescribed "script" and has changed our perspectives on women's use of closure. In her discussion of the manner in which women writers "break the sentence" in order to construct narratives that go "beyond the teleological formulations of quest and romance," she provides the basis for an argument that posits a need for a redefinition of comedy along gender lines.[5]

In other words, how do twentieth-century women writers of comedy differ from their male counterparts? Is not the refusal to supply a happy ending indicative of modern and indeed post-modern literary works in general, and not just texts created by women? Judy Little provides an excellent discussion of the ways in which Woolf's comedy is far more subversive than that of Joyce, for example, in the essay included in this volume; Little raised the issue of "renegade" comedy in her earlier book. The question of women and modernism, as discussed by Gilbert and Gubar, Mary Ann Caws, Jane Marcus, Judy Little and a number of other feminists critics, is a complex one. Gilbert and Gubar argue that what appears to be the gender-neutral category of 'modernism' is in fact no more than a history of twentieth-century male writers (*Female Imagination* 9). The so-called black comedy associated with male writers of twentieth-century literature, while apparently rejecting the typical happy ending of conventional comedy nevertheless reaffirms what Little calls the "presumed ultimate importance of certain Western scripts" such as the universality of the male's quest for identity and the inevitable maleness of the hero in these texts ("Engendering Laughter" 17). Informing the male modernist comedy-of-despair is the presence of a number of "universals" or "givens" ultimately reaffirming rather than undercutting existing cultural systems.

Twentieth-century comedies by women shatter the very idea of the "universal." Even the existentialist male writer will write from within the dominant discourse in terms of his gender. The most economically oppressed of male writers nevertheless writes from a position of privilege awarded to him by a culture that equates value with maleness in much the same way that an Anglo writer writes from a position of privilege in the Western world. These observations may cause discomfort to the existentialist, economically depressed Anglo male writer — or critic — who regards his own oppression as unique. Yet even in the face of his discomfort, these observations remain valid.

A revised concept of comedy and women writers must be oriented toward values not usually associated with traditional views of humor in English literature. Certainly recent feminist criticism has accepted the challenge of providing new patterns and strategies to characterize women's narrative discourse. There is no reason comedy and humor should be excluded from this revisionist criticism. The interpretive applications for comedy written by women have been narrowed by the inherited critical structures which do not provide for the particularly insurgent strategies used by women writers. To explain further: without subverting the authority of her own writing by breaking down convention completely, the woman comic writer displays a different code of subversive thematics than her male counterparts. Her writing is characterised by the breaking of cultural and ideological frames. Her use of comedy is dislocating, anarchic and, paradoxically, unconventional. I say paradoxically because, of course, there is the constant problem of discussing works that must be grouped under a conventional heading such as "comedy" while simultaneously claiming that they subvert the elemental aspects of that convention. The discussion of women, comedy and aggression should proceed having established the following points:

a. In order to be read and for their comedy to be acknowledged as such, women writers have accepted the basic conventions associated with the genre. They have provided the signs which distinguish comedy from other literary forms in much the same way as they have used language that can be understood and have presented recognizable patterns establishing the works as fiction, novel, short story, etc., to the eyes of traditional critics.
b. Without stating it as such, the history of comedy has in fact been the history of male comedy. To consider and distinguish a tradition of female comedy must be regarded as a valid enterprise in light of this fact.
c. While providing the distinguishing signs of comedy, women writers still manage to undercut the conventions they employ by shifting the very framing devices used as definition. What can be regarded as a nominal happy ending might, for example, include a number of elements usually regarded as tragic. The refusal to provide a conventional happy ending might not in any way detract from the inclusion of the work as a comedy.
d. (1) Women's comedies have often been misread because the anger underlying the humor has disturbed the conservative conventions of comedy. If comedy written by women is meant to include certain elements (reconciling gentility, soft admonitions for social lapses, sweet mirth) and if these elements are markedly absent, the work might be misread as non-comedic. This might occur despite the fact that the work contains aspects of fiction usually associated with "traditional" i.e. men's comedy: irony, aggression, subtle and complex language constructions, for example.
(2) If you're not looking for it you are probably not going to find it. It doesn't mean that it's not there.
e. Although a number of elements included in a discussion of women's comedy can be applied to the discussion of comedy written by men or considered in the light of a broader, apparently gender-free discussion of, for example, modernism, it does not necessarily follow that the creation of a critical discourse concerning the unique relationship between women and comedy is invalid.
f. In the same way that Gilbert and Gubar argue that we must take note of "not only a male and female modernisms, but masculinist and feminist modernisms" (*Female Imagination* 2), so must we consider masculinist and feminist traditions of comedy.

There remains the additional and crucial complication that a figure of authority can say, with conviction, "that's not funny" to a subordinate who in turn is meant to alter his or her perception of the comic. Teachers say it to students who refuse to accept the solemnity of the classroom; parents say it to children who cannot hide their inability to accept their parents' viewpoint; older women say it to younger women in Jane Austen and George Eliot. And yet, when older people advise solemnity, we are on unsure footing in Austen and Eliot. Is their view of the world really so much more accurate? Austen's Emma and Eliot's Gwendolyn Harleth must learn to curb their wit because they might damage someone's sensibilities and because they must learn that their humor "just isn't funny." The voice of authority again: but there is no need to create such a ruling unless the possibility for transgression is imminent, unless there arises the immediate, unruly reaction which indicates that, yes, as a matter of fact, the situation is very funny indeed. If we were not disposed to laugh at Causabon and his "low wick," would Eliot's narrator need to remind us that he isn't as much a figure of fun as we might think he is? The narrator does not intercede to remind us that other characters should not be a source of the comic; why the didactic reminder if not to answer an expected reaction? We should not really be able to make sense of such a phrase; surely something is or is not funny. Surely it is not within anyone's power to decide whether something can be comic; the only control that an authority can exert in such a situation is to say whether the joke can be shared publically or whether it must be submerged into the realm of the text that is privately circulated and understood. Making it private sometimes makes it more powerful.

It is not revolutionary to claim that comedy raises questions concerning authority. Indeed, this principle has been demonstrated in works from Juvenalian satire onwards. Comedy has often been linked to man's (sic) ability to transcend his oppression by laughing at his chains, linked to his satiric facility which enables him to suggest changes for his society, and related to his natural cycles of regeneration and renewal. It is of paramount importance to note that these linkings are *well within* the boundaries of the established literary and social laws, for all their trafficking with subversion. Renewal implies the continuation of established patterns: new figures in unalterable positions. Regeneration has the same attendant sense of change-without-change, sons replacing fathers, daughters replacing mothers but without any drama, so to speak. Once the younger figures can achieve their new and rightful positions in the power structure, the tensions are released and so we have comedy.

This is not the case in comedies written by women. The woman writer forges a comedy that allows for complexity and depth without the generally oppressive didacticism so often found in the social satire of writers from Swift to Amis. The ending of comic works by women writers do not, ultimately, reproduce the expected hierarchies, or if they do it is often with a sense of dislocation even about the happiest ending. We could look, for example, at the final chapter of *Mansfield Park*. Austen refuses to provide a happy ending to the courtship between Edmund and Fanny. She refuses the reader's expectations for this couple; she refuses to state how long it took for them to fall in love, or how it happened. At best, she allows the reader only to impose a highly conscious, subjective fantasy on the process. "I purposely abstain from dates on this occasion, that everyone may be at liberty to fix their own ... I entreat everybody to believe that exactly at the time when it was quite natural that it should be so ... Edmund did cease to care about Miss Crawford ..." (Chap 48). It must be seen that Austen refuses to provide the final satisfaction of a even remotely believable happy ending and so, at some level, subverts the marriage plot. At best we have Fanny married to a man for whom she is "of course only too good." Is this a happy ending?

If men often misread women's comedy — in more than the Bloomian sense — then how do women read other women's comedy? Taking Annette Kolodny's arguments from "A Map for Rereading," we see that her points apply to comedic writings with a vengeance. Kolodny writes that it is:

> ... gender-inflected interpretive strategies [which are] responsible for our mutual misreadings ... [This allows us to] appreciate the variety of women's literary expression, enabling us to take it into serious account for perhaps the first time, rather than, as we do now, writing it off as caprice or exceptions, the irregularity in an otherwise regular design (259).

Women have traditionally been considered objects of comedy because they are perceived as powerless; they are perceived as humorless because it is assumed that they simply refuse to get the joke. Freud, seems to echo Eliot's comment from *Daniel Deronda* when he writes that "every joke calls for a public of its own." Freud goes on to say that successful comedy calls for "sufficient psychical accord" in order to be understood. In light of this, shouldn't the fact that women often seem "unlaughing" to men, when women are so often laughing in the company of their own sex, force us to inquire whether women have a comedy of their own?

Much of women's comedy, like many of the larger meaningful

aspects of women's writing — such as anger and rebellion — can only be viewed if one is prepared to deal with the covert narrative strategies employed by many women writers. This is where Gilbert and Gubar's "palimpsest" theory comes into play; the idea that there are hidden texts within texts in women's writing applies neatly to the writing of comedy. The hidden texts, the submerged texts, or the meta-texts of women's comedy often contain key features.

For example, Gilbert and Gubar propose that Austen called into question the entire relationship of women to fiction, forcing her female readers to question the rules governing their own lives: women who were "living lives regulated by the rules provided by popular fiction," were shown by Austen characters just "how very bankrupt that fiction is" (115). There is a seductive element in comedy, as Spacks has noted in a discussion of the emblematic eighteenth-century heroine:

As the creature of fantasy gets fleshed out, she becomes attractive, not just dangerous; the novel preaches subversive doctrine in the guise of supporting moral platitudes (129).

The books classified by writers like George Eliot as "silly novels by lady novelists" may, in light of these remarks, have more power than originally acknowledged. Even as recently as 1974, Rosalind Miles wrote in *The Fiction of Sex* that "novel writing is compatible with the conventional requirement of women that they should keep their heads down. The almost complete absence of women humorists from the scene may support this hypothesis" (39). To invert Miles' hypothesis is perhaps more useful once we see that women do not, in fact, keep their heads down: "novel writing is compatible with the subversive elements of women's writings, and the presence of humor in much writing by women supports this perspective." Miles' view that women kept their heads down and wrote humor-free prose is locked into a male-dominated critical discourse which did more than ignore women's comedy — it attempted to destroy it. Take, for example, Feibleman's discussion of Gertrude Stein's *Autobiography of Alice B. Toklas*:

Having nothing else to talk about, after years with gibberish, she talks about herself: her own life and her genius. And we long for the gibberish again, for that at least was self-contained. It is like looking inside a balloon after having for some time admired its shining surface, only to learn that there is nothing to it but surface. What a clever trick it was after all, and how amusing. For Miss Stein is a comedian and nothing else, and her words have a meaning only when she is talking nonsense (241).

Significantly, Judy Little claims that it is the very "lack of closure, this lack of resolution, [which] characterizes the feminist comedy..." (187). It is the lack of closure and the possibilities for freedom in Stein's humor that worry critics like Feibleman. In her introduction, Little states that the comedy of women writers "differs from rounded-off comic fiction in which the hero is ultimately reintegrated into society. The comedy [written by women] ... mocks the deepest possible norms" (1). In addition to Little, Wilt claims that the woman writer "hesitates, laughing at the edge, withholding fertility, humility, community" (180) — in other words, withholding every elemental aspect of comedy traditionally associated with women. Wilt asserts that:

No comedy is so obsessive, so hysterical, yet so pervasive, adds feminism, as that allotted to women. Not even comedy about women is so pervasive as comedy ... by women (177).

Perhaps the strongest argument for the importance of examining the complex relationship among women, comedy and subversion is initiated by Catharine Clement and Helene Cixous in *The Newly Born Woman* during their discussion of women's power to undo socio-cultural constructs.

Clement's polemical statement "all laughter is allied with the monstrous" could act as a banner for women and comedy. The last thing Clement and Cixous see as necessary for comedy is closure:

Laughter breaks up, breaks out, splashes over; Penthesileia could have laughed; instead, she killed and ate Achilles. It is the moment at which the woman crosses a dangerous line, the cultural demarcation beyond which she will find herself excluded (33).

In exploring laughter, women are exploring their own powers; they are refusing to accept social and cultural boundaries that mark the need or desire for closure as a "universal." Comedy is dangerous; humor is a weapon. Laughter is refusal and triumph. Is it any wonder, really, that Feibleman is nervous? Feminist comedy, according to Little, will say "truly dangerous things obliquely" (which echoes

Dickinson's "success in circuit lies") using complex liminal imagery (178). Women's comedy is "dangerous" because it refuses to accept the givens and because it refuses to stop at the point where comedy loses its integrative function. This comedy by women is about de-centering, dis-locating and de-stabilising the world. As Ellmann puts it: "Laugh and choose evil" (216).

The fixed idea of women as "the unlaughing at which men laugh" has been used as a weapon against both the "pretty little girls" and the "furious females" in order to negate whatever powers of humor they seem to possess. As Judith Wilt quotes from Mary Daly's argument concerning the trope of the unlaughing woman:

> Mary Daly ... offered an arresting metaphor for the mechano-smile which has routinized the always limited boundaries of comedy for women: "the cliche, 'she lacks a sense of humor' — applied by men to every threatening woman — is one basic 'electrode' embedded just deeply enough into the fearful foreground of women's psyches to be able to conduct female energy against the Self while remaining disguised." George Eliot ... touched this same insight when she smiled, ruefully, at her heroine-comic Gwendolyn Harleth for the revealing speed with which she "would at once have marked herself off from any sort of theoretical or practically reforming women by satirizing them" (177).

Fay Weldon's character Praxis mis-directs her humor in much the same way when, in the early days of "women's lib" she turns a meeting into "a joke, into a dinner-table story" and "presently could stop trembling when she thought about it" (237). "Comedy," cautions Wilt, "keeps turning against women ... even in our own hands" (177). In this, comedy again resembles anger: it is channelled through pathways not blocked by fear and authority and is therefore often mis-directed. Often it turns directly against the self as the simplest target, as Lisa Merrill argues in her essay "Feminist Humor: Rebellious and Self-Affirming."

Women's comedy is marginal, liminal, concerned with and defined by its very exclusion from convention, by its aspects of refusal and its alliance with subversive feminine symbols. The difference of women is viewed as a risk to culture. So it should be.

Mary Douglas writes that "each culture has its risks and its specific problems. It attributes a power to some image or another of the body, according to the situation of which the body is the mirror." This is crucial to the perceptions of and the place of women in the culture: "the things that defile are always wrong one way or another, they are not in their place or else they have crossed a line they never should have crossed and from this shift a danger for someone results".[6] Women can defile, spoil, and ruin because they derive power from their exclusion.

This leads us to the figure of the hysteric, the paradigmatic rebel against reality-testing, a central figure for the discussion of women and comedy. The hysteric, the most marginal of marginal figures, is "caught in the contradiction between cultural restraint and sorcerous repression." With her hidden "little implicit smile" she experiences "hell and pleasure at the same time" (Cixous and Clement 34). The hysteric refuses to acknowledge what others construct as reality. She has seen the boundaries created in order to delineate the real from the imaginary (easy from her exceedingly liminal position), and she has concluded that they do not in fact exist. Smiling through heaven and hell at the same time, and experiencing them both as much of the same, she is emblematic of the way women have been misread, and, by implication, the ways in which women's comedy has been misread. When pleasure is read as pain, there is bound to be misunderstanding. The hysteric often laughs even as she howls.

For women, there are a different set of endings, or non-endings, leading to pleasure. The pleasure of being the girl the boy "got" so that he can then found a nice little society around himself is *not* her happy ending. Instead, from a woman's:

own anarchic point of view, it is pleasure in breaking apart; but from the other's point of view, it is suffering, because to break apart is to aggress. The suffering is not originally hers: it is the other's which is returned to her, by projection (Cixous and Clement 34).

Smiling through an experience is different from undergoing catharsis: the experience remains potent, dangerous and enraging through the smile. The experience is put towards the impetus of destruction, not catharsis. It disables one from continuing as before, rather than enabling the continuation of the status quo. The pleasure derives not from the perpetuation of the familiar but from its destruction. This pleasure depends on surprises, disruptions, reversals, disunity and disharmony. The experience cannot be absorbed into the prefabricated cultural structures; it doubles on itself, not purged but strengthened.

No wonder woman's comedy has gone unseen or misread; pain is projected onto her pleasure, unhappiness onto her joy. The refusal to supply closure has been misread as an inability to do so, as a failure of imagination and talent on the part of the writer. Women's comedic writings depend on the process, not on the endings.

This sets the work of twentieth-century women writers apart from their male counterparts. According to Gilbert and Gubar, while male writers were exploring their disturbance at the breakdown of traditional structures, women writers were "expressing exuberance" at precisely the same phenomena (Female Imagination 3). The absence of a "normal" happy ending — as defined by the traditional critics of comedy discussed earlier — does not signal that the work is not a comedy. Far from it. As Cixous writes:

> there is a nonclosure that is not submission but confidence and comprehension; that is not an opportunity for destruction but for wonderful expansion (86).

What so often has appeared as submission is really refusal. What has been seen as solemnity is really the heartfelt, limitless nature of women's laughter.

Language explodes with meaning and by doing so explodes the structures of the system from within. This process is in itself duplicitous in that it destroys and creates simultaneously. Language also takes it upon itself for women writers to create the world; with no authority in an "otherly created" universe, without faith in a reality that reality-testing can verify, language returns to the boundary of the imaginary and the symbolic and appears as magical thinking, as creation itself. In comedy by women writers multiplicity replaces unity; the stylistic reflections of this perspective are significant.

For women writers of comedy recognition replaces resolution. Resolution of tensions, like unity or integration, should not be considered viable definitions of comedy for women writers because they are too reductive to deal with the non-closed nature of women's writings. As Ellmann asserts, the woman writer cares less for what is resolved than for what is recognized in all its conceivable diversions into related or, for that matter, unrelated issues. Once rules are suspended, admirable and remarkable "exceptions are released," recognised and embraced (229). The realization that rules can be suspended, that absolutes are only powerful when allotted power, when a unified, linear progression is given over to the recognition of multiplicity and diversion, all "else" becomes possible. Words play off many meanings rather than embodying one in such a way as to underscore women's unique relationship to patriarchal language. The presentation of "realism" is less meaningful if the concept of the real is open to question. Once "objectivity" is seen as simply the "non-controversial aspect of things" the "facade made up of classified data," as Adorno argues (69), then the concept of realism loses its own authority, and subjectivity — play — is given new significance. Although it would, of course, be incorrect to claim that male writers do not play with language in similiar fashions, it nevertheless remains true that such play is a consistent pattern in women's writings and *typical* of women's comedic texts.

It culiminates in the radical writings of authors such as Gertrude Stein who uses the language of non-sense and pun for de-struction and de-stabilization. We should keep in mind the statements quoted earlier concerning the terrifying fear that Stein was all surface, all boundary existing against an absence: in contrast to Feibleman, Carolyn Simpson celebrates Stein's multiplicity and her refusal to close off her narrative. Stein's refusal is framed as triumph by Simpson, not as a mistake.

That tantalizing hovering of [Gertrude Stein's] language then intensifies our sense of destabilization and subversively warns us against accepting the certainty of any text, Covertly arming the guerrilla war against certainty is any lack of scaffolding that Stein might have nailed up around her constructions so that we might stand around and measure them. The effect is to dislodge expectations that we can manage the text; that we can gain interpretative mastery without pain. So doing, no matter how remotely, Stein dislodges our trust in the smoothness, regularity, and uniformity of our dominant discourses ... (10).

Simpson's remarks indicate that a new reading which can encompass the dislodging of expectations, the disruption of regularity and the splintering of dominant discourse is in order that women's writing can avoid the mis-readings of critics who proclaim, with the history of critical thought behind them, that writings by women are of no use. The trap of such thought is difficult to avoid; it is like the accusations, discussed by Clement and Cixous, made against women considered witches. Under such accusations, the "perfect trap" was set since by laughing, or not laughing, crying, or not crying, being indifferent or not indifferent enough, a woman condemned herself (17). And, as Judith Wilt has shown, when we "have to do with women comics, matriarchal comics, we have to do with witches" (179). Since she inevitably faces condemnation, the woman writer of comedy decides to accept condemnation through laughter.

Women writers of comedy can acknowledge, by the very form of their expression, that accepted authority is not authoritative. They write comedies that deflate the language of the symbolic order. They structure their discourse so that it both escapes and appears to submit to the rules of the dominant discourse. Women writers must evade the traps set for them by systems wherein:

> self-possession and authority are functions of the father and communicable only in terms of the father; ultimately all language is that of the father. The images of independence ... all ultimately paralyzing, for they withdraw the power that they offer by means of the same language in which the offer is made (Scaldini 171).

Comedy is a way women writers can reflect the absurdity of the dominant ideology while undermining the very basis for its discourse. They can point to the emperor's new clothes. The creation of nonsense, puns, language play associated with eradicating the boundaries between the imaginary and symbolic reaffirms that women's use of language in comedy is different from men's. Most significantly, a discussion of women's comedy is necessary because, as Annette Kolodny has argued, "lacked familiarity with the woman's imaginative universe, that universe within which their acts are signs," men can neither read nor "comprehend the meanings of the women closest to them despite the apparent sharing of a common language." The author, Kolodny continues, must be able to:

> depend on a fund of shared recognitions and potential inference. For their intended impact to take hold in the reader's imagination, the author simply must ... be able to call upon a shared context with her audience. When she cannot, or dare not, she may revert to silence, to the imitation of male forms or ... madness (256).

If women appear 'unlaughing' at conventional masculinist humor, this might in part be because the directive to find something amusing is as inappropriate, even impossible, as the inverted directive not to find something funny. Charges of unlaughing and laughing inappropriately have been levelled at women, as we have seen, since women began to participate in the creation of literary works. These charges have also been brought against the female audience, of course expected to laugh at humor often based on the degradation and debasement of their sex. "The admonition to be happy," writes Adorno, "voiced in concert by the scientifically epicurean sanatorium-director and the high-strung propaganda chiefs of the entertainment industry" have about them the:

> fury of the father berating his children for not rushing joyously downstairs when he comes home irritable from his office. It is part of the mechanism of domination to forbid the recognition of the suffering it produces (62)

As we have seen, the women-have-no-sense-of-humor cliche is applied by men to every threatening women according to Mary Daly, and causes female energy to be directed "against the Self while remaining disguised.' Reflex action against this accusation — women laughing at something they do not find funny, or at a joke directed against their own values — can be characterized by Daly's phrase: 'smiling at the boss'.[7]

As Judy Little claims, the woman writer of comedy "realize[s] that she progresses not from rhetorical illusion to transcendent truth, but from one rhetorical illusion to another" ("Engendering Laughter" 18).

It is the inability of the critical tradition to deal with comedy by women rather than the inability of women to produce comedy that accounts for the absence of critical material on the subject. What follows in this collection is an attempt to explore the orienting strategies for women's comedic writing and to suggest instances in which these strategies are realised. A difference of tastes in jokes can provide, as these essays show, an important focus for feminist theory.

Notes

1. It should be noted that throughout this discussion the term 'humor' will be used to indicate an aspect of comedy; 'joke' to indicate a specific incident of condensed humor; 'laughter' to indicate the obvious manifestation of pleasure. The definition of comedy per se, since it is the very subject of the next eighteen essays (not to mention three cartoons), will be elaborated over the next hundred and fifty pages or so.
2. The major studies dealing exclusively with the role of comedy in British literature do not deal with women writers. Meredith may be the exception to the rule. Yet even his socially conscious and widely influential "An Essay on Comedy" emphasizes women as figures presented *in* comedy, more as passive generators of the comic spirit (since comedy is seen as a spirit of general freedom) than are their male counterparts. Ultimately, Meredith's broadly sweeping exhortation of

"good will towards all," while certainly welcome, does little to aid a discussion of women writers and comedy.
3. See Gagnier's article in this volume.
4. There have been, of course, numerous books and articles dealing with particular female writers as writers of comedy; many of them are excellent (see, for example, Wendy Martin's discussion on "The Satire and Moral Vision of Mary McCarthy" in Comic Relief: Humor in Contemporary American Literature, ed. by Sarah Blacher Cohen (Urbana: University of Illinois Press, 1978). However, few of these discussions explore the concept of a uniquely feminine use of the comic. The discussions are usually limited to the texts of one writer.
5. Du Plessis' *Writing Beyond the Ending: Narrative Strategies of Twentieth-Century Women Writers* (Indiana University Press: Bloomington, 1985) provides a number of provocative ideas concerning the relationship between modern women writers and narrative closure, as well as presenting ideas concerning the relationship between modernist and feminist discourse.
6. Mary Douglas. *Purity and Danger: An Analysis of Pollution and Taboo*. (London: Routledge and Kegan Paul, 1966). Quoted in Cixous and Clement, *The Newly Born Woman*, p. 33.
7. Quoted in Judith Wilt's "The Laughter of Maidens, the Cackle of Matriarchs: Notes on the Collision." *Women and Literature*. ed. Janet Todd. (New York: Holmes and Meier, 1980) 177.

Works Cited

Adorno, Theodor. Trans. E.F.N. Jephcott. *Minima Moralia*. London: Verso, 1974.
Bakhtin, Mikhail. *Rabelais and His World*. Bloomington: Indiana University Press, 1984.
Blyth, Reginald H. *Humor in English Literature: A Chronological Anthology*. Tokyo: The Folcroft Press Inc, 1959.
Caws, Mary Ann. *Reading Frames in Fiction*. Princeton: Princeton University Press, 1985.
Cixous, Helene and Catherine Clement. *The Newly Born Woman*. Trans. Betsy Wing. Minneapolis: University of Minnesota Press, 1986.
Congreve, William. "Concerning Humour in Comedy." *Theories of Comedy*. ed. Paul Lauter. Garden City: Doubleday, 1964.
Douglas, Mary. *Purity and Danger. An Analysis of Pollution and Taboo*. London: Routledge and Kegan Paul, 1966.
Du Plessis, Rachel Blau. *Writing Beyond the Ending: Narrative Strategies of 20th Century Women Writers*. Bloomington: Indiana University Press, 1985.
Eliot, George. *Daniel Deronda*. Baltimore: Penguin Books, 1967.
Ellmann, Mary. *Thinking About Women*. New York: Harcourt Brace and World Inc., 1968.
Feibleman, James K. *In Praise of Comedy*. New York: Horizon Press, 1939. 2nd ed. 1970.
Freud, Sigmund. *Jokes and their Relation to the Unconscious*. Trans. James Strachey. New York and London: W W Norton and Company, 1963.
Gagnier, Regenia. "The Limits of Humor and Hatred in Nineteenth Century Women's Autobiography: A Cross-class Analysis." *Last Laughs: Perspectives on Women and Comedy*. New York: Gordon and Breach, 1988.
Gilbert, Sandra and Gubar, Susan. "Introduction." *The Female Imagination and*

Modernist Aesthetic: Women's Studies. Vol 13. New York: Gordon and Breach, 1986.
——. *The Madwoman in the Attic*. New Haven and London: Yale University Press, 1979

Harding, D.W. "Regulated Hatred: An Aspect of Jane Austen." *Scrutiny* VIII, 1940.

Kolodny, Annette. "A Map for Rereading; or, Gender and the Interpretation of Literary Texts." *The (M)Other Tongue*. ed Shirley Nelson Garner, Claire Kahane, Madelon Sprengnether. Ithaca and London: Cornell University Press, 1985.

Kristeva, Julia. "Oscillation between Power and Denial", trans. Marilyn A. August, *New French Feminisms*, 91. quoted in Gilbert, Sandra and Susan Gubar. *Sexual Linguistics: Gender, Language, Sexuality. New Literary History*. Volume XVI #3. (Baltimore: The John Hopkins Press, 1983) 518.

Little, Judith. *Comedy and the Woman Writer: Woolf, Spark and Feminism*. Lincoln: University of Nebraska Press, 1983.

Marcus, Jane. "Daughters of Anger/Material Girls." *Last Laughs: Perspectives on Women and Comedy*. New York: Gordon and Breach, 1988.

McGhee, Paul. "The Role of Laughter and Humor in Growing Up Female." *Becoming Female: Perspectives on Development*. ed. Claire B. Kopp. New York: Plenum Press, 1979.

Merrill, Lisa. "Feminist Humor: Rebellious and Self-affirming." *Last Laughs: Perspectives on Women and Comedy*. New York: Gordon and Breach, 1988.

Miles, Rosalind. *The Fiction of Sex*. London: Vision Press, 1974.

Priestly, J.B. *English Humor*. New York: Stein and Day, 1970.

Scaldini, Richard. "Les Aventures de Telemaque, or Alienated in Ogygia," *Locus: Space, Landscape, Decor in Modern French Fiction*. ed. Philip H. Solomon. *Yale French Studies* 57, 1979.

Simpson, Catherine R. "Gertrude Stein and the Transposition of Gender." *The Poetics of Gender* ed. Nancy K. Miller. New York: Columbia University Press, 1986.

Weldon, Fay. *Praxis*. New York: Summit Books, 1978.

Wilt, Judith. "The Laughter of Maidens, the Cackle of Matriarchs: Notes on the Collison." *Women and Literature*. ed. Janet Todd. New York: Holmes and Meier, 1980.

Who was that masked woman? The prostitute and the playwright in the comedies of Aphra Behn

CATHERINE GALLAGHER

University of California, Berkeley

EVERYONE KNOWS that Aphra Behn, England's first professional female author, was a colosal and enduring embarrassment to the generations of women who followed her into the literary marketplace. An ancestress whose name had to be lived down rather than lived up to, Aphra Behn seemed, in Virginia Woolf's metaphor, to obstruct the very passageway to the profession of letters she had herself opened. Woolf explains in *A Room of One's Own*, "Now that Aphra Behn had done it, girls could go to their parents and say, You need not give me an allowance; I can make money by my pen. Of course the answer for many years to come was, Yes, by living the life of Aphra Behn! Death would be better! and the door was slammed faster than ever."[1]

It is impossible in this brief essay to examine all the facets of the scandal of Aphra Behn; her life and works were alike characterized by certain irregular sexual arrangements. But it is not these that I want to discuss, for they seem merely incidental, the sorts of things women writers would easily dissociate themselves from if they led pure lives and wrote high-minded books. The scandal I would like to discuss is, however, with varying degree of appropriateness, applicable to all female authors, regardless of the conduct of their lives or the content of their works. It is a scandal that Aphra Behn seems quite purposely to have constructed out of the overlapping discourses of commercial, sexual, and linguistic exchange. Conscious of her historical role, she introduced to the world of English letters the professional woman writer as a new-fangled whore.

This persona has many functions in Behn's works: it titillates, scandalizes, arouses pity, and indicates the vicissitudes of authorship and identity in general. The author-whore persona also makes of female authorship per se a dark comedy that explores the bond between the liberty the stage offered women and their confinement behind both literal and metaphorical vizard masks. This is the comedy played out, for example, in the prologue to her first play, *The Forced Marriage*, where she announces her epoch-making appearance in the ranks of the playwrights. She presents her attainment, however, not as a daring achievement of self-expression, but as a new proof of the necessary obscurity of the "public" woman.

The prologue presents Aphra Behn's playwrighting as an extension of her erotic play. In it, a male actor pretends to have escaped temporarily the control of the intriguing female play-wright; he comes on stage to warn the gallants in the audience of their danger. This was a variation on the Restoration convention of betraying the playwright in the Prologue with an added sexual dimension: the comic antagonism between playwright and audience becomes a battle in the war between the sexes. Playwrighting, warns the actor, is a new weapon in woman's amorous arsenal. She will no longer wound only through the eyes, through her beauty, but will also use wit to gain a more permanent ascendency. Here, woman's playwriting is wholly assimilated to the poetic conventions of amorous battle that normally informed lyric poetry. If the male poet had long depicted the conquering woman as necessarily chaste, debarring (and consequently debarred from) the act of sex itself, then his own poetry of lyric complaint and pleas for kindness could only be understood as attempts to overthrow the conqueror. Poetry in this lyric tradition is a weapon in a struggle that takes as its most fundamental ground-rule a woman's inability to have a truly *sexual* conquest: for the doing of the deed would be the undoing of her power.

Aphra Behn's first Prologue, stretches this lyric tradition to incorporate theatre. However, the woman's poetry cannot have the same *end* as the man's. Indeed, according to the Prologue, ends, in the sense of terminations, are precisely what a woman's wit is directed against:

Women those charming victors, in whose eyes
Lie all their arts, and their artilleries,
Not being contented with the wounds they made,
Would by new stratagems our lives invade.
Beauty alone goes now at too cheap rates
And therefore they, like wise and politic states,
Court a new power that may the old supply,
To *keep* as well as gain the victory:
They'll join the force of wit to beauty now,
And so *maintain* the right they have in you.[2]

Writing is certainly on a continuum here with sex, but instead of leading to the act in which the woman's conquest is overturned, playwriting is supposed to extend the woman's erotic power beyond the moment of sexual encounter. The prologue, then, situates the drama inside the conventions of male lyric love poetry but then reverses the chronological relationship between sex and writing; the male poet writes before the sexual encounter, the woman between encounters. She thereby actually creates the possibility of a woman's version of sexual conquest. She will not be immediately conquered and discarded because she will maintain her right through her writing. The woman's play of wit is the opposite of foreplay; it is a kind of afterplay specifically designed to prolong pleasure, rescucitate desire and keep a woman who has given herself sexually from being traded in for another woman. If the woman is successful in her poetic exchange, the actor warns the gallants, then they will no longer have the freedom of briskly exchanging mistresses: "You'll never know the bliss of change; this art Retrieves (when beauty fades) the wandring heart."

Aphra Behn, then, inaugurated her career by taking up and feminizing the role of the seductive lyric poet. The drama the audience is about to see is framed by the larger comedy of erotic exchange between a woman writer and a male audience. That is, this prologue does what so many Restoration prologues do, makes of the play a drama within a drama, one series of conventional interactions inside another. But the very elaborateness of this staging of conventions makes the love battle itself (the thing supposedly revealed) seem a strategic pose in a somewhat different drama. After all, what kind of woman would stage her sexual desire as her primary motivation? The answer is a woman who might be suspected not to have any: a woman for whom professions of amorousness and theatrical in authenticity are the same thing: a prostitute. Finally, just in case anyone in the audience might have missed this analogy, a dramatic interruption occurs, and the prologue stages a debate about the motivation behind all this talk of strategy. The actor calls attention to the prostitutes in the audience, who were generally identified by their masks, and characterizes them as agents of the playwright, jokingly using their masks to expose them as spies in the amorous war:

> The poetess too, they say, has spies abroad,
> Which have dispers'd themselves in every road,
> I' th' upper box, pit, galleries; every face
> You find disguis'd in a black velvet case.
> My life on't; is her spy on purpose sent,
> To hold you in a wanton compliment;
> That so you may not censure what she's writ,
> Which done they face you down 'twas full of wit.

At this point, an actress comes on stage to refute the suggestion that the poetess's spies and supporters are prostitutes. She returns, then, to the conceits linking money and warfare and thus explicitly enacts the denial of prostitution that was all along implicit in the trope of amorous combat. Unlike the troop of prostitutes, she claims,

> Ours scorns the petty spoils, and do prefer
> The glory not the interest of war.
> But yet our forces shall obliging prove,
> Imposing naught but constancy in love:
> That's all our aim, and when we have it too,
> We'll sacrifice it all to pleasure you.

What the last two lines make abundantly clear, in ironically justifying female promiscuity by the pleasure it gives to men, is that the prologue has given us the spectacle of a prostitute comically denying mercenary motivations. The poetess like the prostitute is she who "stands out," as the etymology of the word "prostitute" implies, but it is also she who is masked. Indeed, as the prologue emphasizes, the prostitute is she who stands out by virtue of her mask. The dramatic masking of the prostitute and the stagey masking of the playwright's interest in money are exactly parallel cases of theatrical unmasking in which what is revealed is the parallel itself: the playwright is a whore.

This conclusion, however, is more complex than it might at first seem, for the very playfulness of the representation implies a hidden "real" woman who must remain unavailable. The prologue gives two explanations for female authorship, and they are the usual excuses for prostitution: it alludes to and disclaims the motive of money; it claims the motive of love, but in a way that makes the claim seem merely strategic. The author-whore, then, is one who comically stages her lack of self-expression and consequently implies that her true identity is the sold self's seller. She thus indicates an unseeable selfhood through the flamboyant alienation of her language.

Hence Aphra Behn managed to create the effect of an inaccessible authenticity out of the very image of prostitution. In doing so, she capitalized on a commonplace slur that probably kept many less ingenious women out of the literary marketplace. "Whore's the like reproachful name, as poetess — the luckless twins of shame,"[3] wrote Robert Gould in 1691. The equation of poetess and "punk" (in the slang of the day) was inescapable in the Restoration. A woman writer could either deny it in the content and form of her publications, as did Catherine Trotter, or she could embrace it, as did Aphra Behn. But she could not entirely avoid it. For the belief that "Punk and Poesie agree so pat,/ You cannot well be *this*, and not be *that*"[4] was held independently of particular cases. It rested on the evidence neither of how a woman lived nor of what she wrote. It was, rather, an a priori judgement applied to all cases of female publication. As one of Aphra Behn's biographers, Angeline Goreau, has astutely pointed out, the seventeenth-century ear heard the word "public" in "publication" very distinctly, and hence a woman's publication automatically implied a public woman.[5] The woman who shared the contents of her mind instead of reserving them for one man was literally, not metaphorically, trading in her *sexual* property. If she were married, she was selling what did not belong to her, because in *mind and body* she should have given herself to her husband. In the seventeenth century, "publication," Goreau tells us, also meant sale due to bankruptcy, and the publication of the contents of a woman's mind was tantamount to the publication of her husband's property. In 1613, Lady Carey published (anonymously, of course) these lines on marital property rights, publication and female integrity:

Then she usurps upon another's right,
That seeks to be by public language graced;
And tho' her thoughts reflect with purest light

> Her mind, if not peculiar, is not chaste.
> For in a wife it is no worse to find
> A common body, than a common mind.[6]

Publication, adultery, and trading in one's husband's property were all thought of as the same thing as long as female identity, selfhold, remained an indivisible unity. As Lady Carey explained, the idea of a public mind in a private body threatened to fragment female identity, to destroy its integrated wholeness:

> When to their husbands they themselves do bind,
> Do they not wholly give themselves away?
> Or give they but their body, not their mind,
> Reserving that, tho' best, for other's prey?
> No, sure, their thought no more can be their own
> And therefore to none but one be known.[7]

The unique, unreserved giving of the woman's self to her husband is the act that keeps her whole. Only in this singular and total alienation does the woman maintain her complete self-identity.

We have already seen that it is precisely this ideal of a totalized woman, preserved because *wholly* given away, that Aphra Behn sacrifices to create a different idea of identity, one complexly dependent on the necessity of multiple exchanges. She who is able to repeat the action of self-alienation an unlimited number of times is she who is constantly there to regenerate, possess, and sell a series of provisional, constructed identities. Self-possession, then, and self-alienation are just two sides of the same coin; the alienation verifies the possession. In contrast, the wife who gives herself once and completely disposes simultaneously of self possession and self alienation. She has no more property in which to trade and is thus rendered whole by her action. She *is* her whole, unviolated womanhood because she has given up possessing herself; she can be herself because she has given up *having* herself. Further, as Lady Carey's lines make clear, if a woman's writing is an authentic extension of herself, then she cannot have alienable property in that without violating her wholeness.

Far from denying these assumptions, Aphra Behn's comedy is based on them. Like her contemporaries, she presented her writing as part of her sexual property, not just because it was bawdy, but because it was hers. As a woman, all of her properties were at least the potential property of another; she could either reserve them and give herself whole in marriage, or she could barter them piecemeal, accepting self-division to achieve self-ownership and forfeiting the possibility of marriage. In this sense, Aphra Behn's implied identity fits into the most advanced seventeenth-century theories about selfhood: it closely resembles the possessive individualism of Locke and Hobbes, in which property in one's self both entails and is entailed by the parcelling out and serial alienation of one's self. For property by definition, in this theory, is that which is alienable. Aphra Behn's, however, is a gender specific version of possessive individualism, one constructed in opposition to the very real alternative of staying whole by renouncing self possession, an alternative that had no legal reality for men in the seventeenth century. Because the husband's right of property was in the whole of the wife, the prior alienation of any part of her had to be seen as a violation of either actual or potential marital propriety. That is, a woman who, like Aphra Behn, embraced possessive individualism, even if she were single and never bartered her sexual favors, could only do so with a consciousness that she thus contradicted the notion of female identity on which legitimate sexual property relations rested.

Publication, then, quite apart from the contents of what was published, ipso facto implied the divided, doubled, and ultimately unavailable person whose female prototype was the prostitute. By flaunting her self-sale, Aphra Behn embraced the title of whore; by writing bawdy comedies, which she then partly disclaimed, she capitalized on her supposed handicap. Finally, she even uses this persona to make herself seem the prototypical writer, and in this effort she certainly seems to have had the cooperation of her male colleagues and competitors. Thus, in the following poem, William Wycherley wittily acknowledges that the sexual innuendos about Aphra Behn rebound back on the wits who make them. The occasion of the poem was a rumor that the poetess had gonorrhea. Wycherley emphasizes how much more public is the "Sappho of the Age" than any normal prostitute, how much her fame grows as she looses her fame, and how much cheaper is the rate of the author-whore than her sister punk. But he also stresses how much more power the poetess has, since in the world of wit as opposed to the world of sexual exchange, use increases desire, and the author-whore accumulates men instead of being exchanged among them:

> More Fame you now (since talk'd of more) acquire,
> And as more Public, are more Mens Desire;
> Nay, you the more, that you are Clap'd to, now,
> Have more to like you, less to censure you:
> Now Men enjoy your Parts for Half a Crown,
> Which, for a Hundred Pound, they scarce had done,
> Before your Parts were, to the Public known.[8]

Appropriately, Wycherley ends by imagining the whole London theatrical world as a sweating-house for venereal disease:

> Thus, as your Beauty did, your Wit does now,
> The Women's envy, Men's Diversion grow;
> Who, to be clap'd, or Clap you, round you sit,
> And, tho' they Sweat for it, will crowd your Pit;
> Since lately you Lay-in, (but as they say,)
> Because, you had been Clap'd another Way;
> But, if 'tis true, that you have need to Sweat,
> Get, (if you can) at your New Play, a Seat.

If Aphra Behn's sexual and poetic parts are the same, then the wits are contaminated by her sexual distemper. Aphra Behn and her fellow wits infect one another: the theatre is her body, their wits are their penises, the play is a case of gonorrhea, and the cure is the same as the disease.

Given the general Restoration delight in the equation of mental, sexual, and theatrical "parts," and its frequent likening of writing to prostitution and playwrights to bawds, one might argue that if Aphra Behn had not existed, the male playwrights would have had to invent her in order to increase the witty pointedness of their cynical self-representations. For example, in Dryden's prologue to Behn's *The Widow Ranter*, the great playwright chides the self-proclaimed wits for contesting the originality of one another's productions and squabbling over literary property. Drawing on the metaphor of literary paternity, he concludes:

> But when you see these Pictures, let none dare
> To own beyond a Limb or single share;
> For where the Punk is common, he's a Sot,
> Who needs will father what the Parish got.[9]

These lines gain half their mordancy from their reference to Aphra Behn, the poetess-punk, whose off-spring cannot seem fully her own, but whose right to them cannot be challenged with any propriety. By literalizing and embracing the playwright-prostitute metaphor, therefore, Aphra Behn was distinguished from other authors, but only as their prototypical representative. She becomes a symbolic figure of authorship for the Restoration, the writer and the strumpet muse combined. Even those who wished to keep the relationship between women and authorship strictly metaphorical were fond of the image: "What a pox have the women to do with the muses?" asks a character in a play attributed to Charles Gildon. "I grant you the poets call the nine muses by the names of women, but why so? ... because in that sex they're much fitter for prostitution."[10] It is not hard to see how much authorial notoriety could be gained by audaciously literalizing such a metaphor.

Aphra Behn, therefore, created a persona that skillfully intertwined the age's available discourses concerning women, property, selfhood and authorship. She found advantageous openings where other women found repulsive insults; she turned self-division into identity.

The authorial effect I'm trying to describe here should not be confused with the plays' disapproving attitudes toward turning women into items of exchange. *The Lucky Chance*, which I am now going to discuss, all too readily yields a facile, right-minded thematic analysis centering on women and property exchange. It has three plots that can easily be seen as variations on this theme: Diana is being forced into a loveless marriage with a fop because of her father's family ambition. Her preference for the young Bredwell is ignored in the exchange. Diana's father, Sir Feeble Fainwood, is also purchasing himself a young bride, Leticia, whom he has tricked into believing that her betrothed lover, who had been banished for fighting a duel, is dead. Julia, having already sold herself to another rich old merchant, Sir Cautious Fulbank, is being wooed to adultery by her former lover, Gayman. That all three women are both property and occasions for the exchange of property is quite clear. Diana is part of a financial arrangement between the families of the two old men, and the intended bridegroom, Bearjest, sees her merely as the embodiment of a great fortune; Leticia is also bought by "a great jointure," and though we know, interestingly, nothing of Julia's motives, we are told that she had played such a "prank" as Leticia. It is very easy, then, to make the point that the treatment of women as property is the problem that the play's comic action will set out solve. Whether she marries for property, as in the cases of Leticia and Julia or she is married *as property* (that is, given, like Diana, as the condition of a dowery), the woman's identity as a form of property and item of exchange seems obviously to be the play's point of departure, and the urge to break that identification seems, on a casual reading, to license the play's impropriety. One could even redeem the fact that, in the end, the women are all *given* by the old men to their lovers by pointing out that this is, after all, a comedy and hence a form that requires female desire to flow through established channels.

Such a superficial thematic analysis of *The Lucky Chance* fits in well with that image of Aphra Behn some of her most recent biographers promote: an advocate of "free love" in every sense of the phrase and a heroic defender of the right of women to speak their own desires. However, such an interpretation does not bear the weight of the play's structure or remain steady in the face of its ellipses, nor can it sustain the pressure of the play's images. For the moments of crisis in the play are not those in which a woman becomes property but those in which a woman is burdened with a selfhood that can be neither represented (a self without properties) nor exchanged. They are the moments when the veiled woman confronts the impossibility of being represented and hence of being desired and hence of being, finally, perhaps, gratified.

Before turning to those moments, I'd like to discuss some larger organizational features of the play that complicate its treatment of the theme of women and exchange. First, then, to the emphatic way in which the plots are disconnected in their most fundamental logic. The plots of Diana and Leticia rely on the idea that there is an irreversible moment of matrimonial exchange after which the woman is "given" and cannot be given again. Thus the action is directed toward thwarting and replacing the planned marriage ceremony, in the case of Diana, and avoiding the consummation of the marriage bed in the case of Leticia. Julia, however, has crossed both these threshholds and is still somehow free to dispose of herself. The logic on which her plot is based seems to deny that there are critical or irremediable events in female destiny. Hence in the scene directly following Leticia's intact deliverance from Sir Feeble Fainwood's bed and Diana's elopement with Bredwell, we find Julia resignedly urging her aged husband to get the sex over with and to stop meddling with the affairs of her heart: "But let us leave this fond discourse, and, if you must, let us to bed"

(p. 135). Julia proves her self-possession precisely by her indifference to the crises structuring Diana's and Leticia's experiences.

On the one hand, Julia's plot could be seen to undercut the achievement of resolution in the other plots by implying that there was never anything to resolve: the obstacles were not real, the crises were not crises, the definitive moment never did and never could arrive. Julia's would be the pervasive atmosphere of comedy that keeps the anxieties of the more "serious" love plot from truly being registered. But on the other hand, we could argue that the crisis plots drain the adultery plot not only of moral credibility but also of dramatic interest, for there would seem to be simply nothing at stake in Julia's plot. Indeed, Julia's plot in itself seems bent on making this point, turning as it so often does on attempts to achieve things that have already been achieved or gambling for stakes that have already been won. These two responses, however, tend to cancel one another, and we cannot conclude that either plot logic renders the other nugatory. *The Lucky Chance* achieves its effects, rather by alternately presenting the problem and its seeming nonexistence. The imminent danger of becoming an unwilling piece of someone else's property is at once asserted and denied.

The alternating assertion/denial emphasizes the discontinuity between the two "resolutions" of the woman's sexual identity that I discussed earlier: one in which the giving of the self intact is tantamount to survival; the other in which an identity is maintained in a series of exchanges. This very discontinuity, then, as I've already pointed out, is part of an overarching discursive pattern. The proof of self ownership is self sale; hence, Julia has no exculpating story of deceit or coercion to explain her marriage to Fulbank. But the complete import of what she does, both of what she sacrifices and what she gains, can only be understood against the background of a one-time exchange that involves and maintains the whole self.

The disjunction between the plot exigencies Leticia is subjected to and those that hold and create Julia, (our inability to perceive these plots within a single comic perspective) reveals the oppositional relationship between the two seventeenth-century versions of the female as property. Built into this very disjunction, therefore, is a complicated presentation of the seeming inescapability for women of the condition of property. In the play, the exchange of women as property appears inevitable, and the action revolves around the terms of exchange. The crisis plots, of which Leticia's is the most important, posit wholeness as the pre-condition of exchange and as the result of its successful completion. The unitary principle dominates the logic of this plot and also, as we are about to see, the language of its actors and its representational rules. Julia's plot, on the other hand, assumes not only the fracturing and multiplication of the self as a condition and result of exchange, but also the creation of a second order of reality: a reality of representations through which the characters simultaneously alienate and protect their identities.

This split in representational procedures can be detected in the first scene, where it is associated with the characters of the leading men. In the play's opening speech, Bellmour enters complaining that the law has stolen his identity, has made him a creature of disguise and the night. His various complaints in the scene cluster around a central fear of de-differentiation, of the failure properly to distinguish essential differences. Thus it is the "rigid laws, which put no difference/'Twixt fairly killing in my own defence,/And murders bred by drunken arguments,/Whores, or the mean revenges of a coward" that have forced his disguise, his alienation from his own identity. That is, the denial of the true, identity insuring, difference (that between duelers and murderers) necessitates false differences, disguises and theatrical representations that get more elaborate as the plot progresses. The comedy is this series of disguises and spectacles, but its end is to render them unnecessary by the reunion of Bellmour with his proper identity and his proper wife.

The very terms of Bellmour's self-alienation, moreover, are identitarian in their assumption that like must be represented by like. Bellmour has taken a life in a duel, and for that he is deprived of the life he thought he would lead. He has destroyed a body with his sword, and for that a body that belongs to him, Leticia's, will be taken from him also through puncturing. Even the comic details of Bellmour's reported death are consonant with this mode of representation:

RALPH: Hanged, Sir, hanged, at The Hague in Holland.
BELLMOUR: For what, said they, was he hanged?
RALPH: Why, e'en for high treason, Sir, he killed one of their kings.
GAYMAN: Holland's a commonwealth, and is not ruled by kings.
RALPH: Not by one, Sir, but by many. This was a cheesemonger, they fell out over a

bottle of brandy, went to snicker snee, Mr. Bellmour cut his throat, and was hanged for't, that's all, Sir. (p. 81)

The reductio ad absurdum of like representing like is the commonwealth in which everyone is a king. It is within this comically literalist system of representation that Bellmour is imagined to have had his neck broken for slitting the throat of a cheesemonger. It is no wonder that the climax of Bellmour's performance is a simulation of the exchange of like for like. As Sir Feeble Fainwood approaches the bed on which he intends to deflower Leticia, asking her, "What, was it ashamed to show its little white foots, and its little round bubbies?," Belmour comes out from between the curtains, naked to the waist. And, all the better to ward off that which he represents, he has Leticia's projected wound painted on his own chest and a dagger ready to make another such wound on Sir Feeble. The whole representational economy of this plot, therefore, has an underlying unitary basis in the notion that things must be paid for in kind. Even Leticia's self sale seems not to be for money but for the jewelry to which she is often likened.

Like Bellmour, Gayman also enters the first scene in hiding, "wrapped in his cloak," but the functional differences between the two kinds of self-concealment are soon manifested. The end of Gayman's disguises is not the retrieval of his property, but the appropriation of what he thinks is the property of others: "Are you not to be married, Sir," asks Bellmour. "No Sir," returns Gayman, "not as long as any man in London is so, that has but a handsome wife, Sir" (p. 77). His attempts are not to reestablish essential differences, but rather to accelerate the process of de-differentiation. "The bridegroom!" exclaims Bellmour on first seeing Sir Feeble. "Like Gorgon's head he's turned me into stone." "Gorgon's head," retorts Gayman, "a cuckold's head, 'twas made to graft upon" (p. 79). The dizzying swiftness with which Gayman extends Bellmour's metaphor speaks the former's desire to destroy the paired stability of exchanges. Looking at the bridegroom's head, Bellmour sees an image of destructive female sexuality, the Gorgon. Thus, the bridegroom represents the all-too-available sexuality of Leticia. Gayman's way of disarming this insight is to deck it with horns, to introduce the third term, taking advantage of Leticia's availability to cuckold Sir Feeble. But for Bellmour this is no solution at all, since it only further collapses the distinction between lover and husband, merging him with Sir Feeble at the moment he alienates his sexual property: "What, and let him marry her! She that's mine by sacred vow already! by heaven it would be flat adultery in her!" (p. 80). "She'll learn the trick," replies Gayman, "and practise it the better with thee." The destruction of the "true" distinctions between husband and lover, cuckold and adulterer, proprietor and thief is the state for which Gayman longs.

Bellmour's comedy, then, moves toward the re-establishment of true difference through the creation of false differences; Gayman's comedy moves toward the erasure of true differences through the creation of false and abstract samenesses. Gayman is in disguise because he cannot bear to let Julia know that he is different from his former self. He wishes to appear before her always the same, to hide the new fact of his poverty. He tries to get money from his landlady so that he can get his clothes out of hock and therefore disguise himself as himself in order to go on wooing Julia. On the same principle of the effacement of difference, Gayman later tries to pass himself off as Julia's husband when he, unbeknownst to her, takes the old man's place in bed.

Moreover, just as the false differences of Bellmour's comedy conformed to a unitary like-for-like economy of representation, the false samenesses of Gayman's plotting are governed by an economy of representation through difference. The most obvious example of this is the use of money. Money in this plot often represents bodies or their sexual use, and what is generally emphasized in these exchanges are the differences between the body and money. For example, in the scenes of Gayman's two prostitutions (the first with his landlady and the second with his unknown admirer), the difference between the women's bodies and the precious metals they can be made to yield is the point of the comedy. The landlady is herself metamorphosed into iron for the sake of this contrast: she is an iron lady who emerges from her husband's blacksmith's shop. She is then stroked into metals of increasing value as she yields 'postle spoons and caudle cups that then exchange for gold. However, Gayman's expletives never allow us to forget that this sexual alchemy is being practiced on an unsublimatable body that constantly sickens the feigning lover with its stink. Even more telling is the continuation of this scene in which Gayman receives a bag of gold as advance payment for an assignation with an anonymous woman. Here the desirability of the gold (associated with its very anonymity) immediately implies the undesirability of the woman who sends it: "Some female devil, old and damned to ugliness,/And past all hopes of courtship and address,/Full of another devil called desire,/ Has seen this face, this shape, this youth,/And thinks it's worth her hire. It must be so" (p. 94). Of course, as this passage emphasizes, in both cases the women's money stands for Gayman's sexual worthiness, but as such it again marks a difference, the difference in the desirability of the bodies to be exchanged. Hence the unlike substance, gold, marks the inequality of the like biological substances.

The freedom and the perils, especially the perils for women, that this comedy of representation through difference introduces into erotic life are explored in the conflict between Julia and Gayman. And this conflict returns us to the issue of authorial representation. Julia, like many of Aphra Behn's heroines, confronts a familiar predicament: she wishes to have the pleasure of sexual intercourse with her lover without the pain of the loss of honor. Honor seems to mean something wholly external in the play; it is not a matter of conscience since secret actions are outside its realm. Rather, to lose honor is to give away control over one's public representations. Hence, in the adultery plot, as opposed to the crisis plot, women's bodies are not the true stakes; representations of bodies, especially in money and language, are the focal points of conflict.

Gayman's complaint against Julia, for example, is that she prefers the public admiration of the crowd, which she gains through witty language ("talking all and loud" p. 99) to the private "adoration" of a lover, which is apparently speechless. Julia's retort, however, indicates that it is Gayman who will betray the private to public representation for the sake of his own reputation. It is Gayman who will "describe her charms," "Or make most filthy verses of me/Under the name of Cloris, you Philander,/Who, in lewd rhymes, confess the dear appointment,/What hour, and where, how silent was the night,/How full of love your eyes, and wishing mine." (We have just, by the way, heard Gayman sing a verse about Cloris's wishing eyes to his landlady.)

To escape being turned into someone else's language, losing the ability to control her own public presentation, Julia subjects herself to a much more radical severance of implied true self from self-representation than Gayman could have imagined. At once to gratify her sexual desire and preserve her honor, she arranges to have Gayman's own money (in some ways a sign of his desire for her) misrepresented to him as payment for sexual intercourse with an unknown woman. That is, Julia makes the anonymous advance earlier discussed.

Julia, then, is hiding behind the anonymity of the gold, relying on its nature as a universal equivalent for desire, universal and anonymous precisely because it doesn't resemble what it stands for and can thus stand for anything. But in this episode, she becomes a prisoner of the very anonymity of the representation. For, as we've already seen, Gayman takes it as a sign of the difference between the woman's desirability and his own. Apparently, moreover, this representation of her undesirability overwhelms the private experience itself, so that when the couple finally couples, Gayman does not actually experience Julia, but rather feels another version of his landlady. As he later reluctantly describes the sightless, wordless encounter to Julia (whom he does not suspect of having been the woman), "She was laid in a pavilion all formed of gilded clouds which hung by geometry, whither I was conveyed after much ceremony, and laid in a bed with her, where, with much ado and trembling with my fears, I forced my arms about her." "And sure," interjects Julia aside to the audience, "that undeceived him." "But," continues Gayman, "such a carcass 'twas, deliver me, so shrivelled, lean and rough, a canvas bag of wooden ladles were a better bedfellow." "Now, though, I know that nothing is more distant than I from such a monster, yet this angers me," confides Julia to the audience. "'Slife, after all to seem deformed, old, ugly." The interview ends with Gayman's final misunderstanding, "I knew you would be angry when you heard it" (p. 118).

The extraordinary thing about this interchange is that it does not matter whether or not Gayman is telling the truth about his sexual experience. The gold may have so overwhelmed his senses as to make Julia feel like its opposite: a bag of wooden ladles rather than precious coins; and, indeed, the continuity of images between this description and Gayman's earlier reactions to women who give him money tends to confirm his sincerity. The bag of ladles reminds us of the landlady, who was also a bag, but one containing somewhat more valuable table utensils: 'postle spoons and caudle cups. However, Gayman may be misrepresenting his experience to prevent Julia's jealousy. Either way, Julia was missing from that experience. Whether he did not desire her at all or desired her as someone else is immaterial; what Julia experiences as she sees herself through this doubled representation of money and language is the impossibility of keeping herself to herself and truly being gratified as at once a subject and object of desire.

By participating in this economy of difference, in which her representations are not recognizably hers, then, Julia's problem becomes her state of unexchangeability. The drive for self-possession removes her "true" self from the realms of desire and gratification. Because she has not given herself away, she finds that her lover has not been able to take her. Surprisingly, however, the play goes on to overcome this difficulty not by taking refuge in like-for-like exchanges, but by remaining in the economy of difference until Julia seems able to adjust the claims of self-possession and gratification.

The adjustment becomes possible only after Julia has been explicitly converted into a commodity worth three hundred pounds. The process leading up to this conversion merits our scrutiny. Gayman and Sir Cautious are gambling: Gayman has won 300 pounds and is willing to stake it against something of Sir Cautious's

Sir Cautious: I wish I had anything but ready money to stake: three hundred pound, a fine sum!
Gayman: You have moveables Sir, goods, commodities.
Sir Cautious: That's all one, Sir. That's money's worth, Sir, but if I had anything that were worth nothing.
Gayman: You would venture it. I thank you, Sir. I would your lady were worth nothing.
Sir Cautious: Why so, Sir?
Gayman: Then I would set all 'gainst that nothing.

Sir Cautious begins this dialogue with a comical identification of everything with its universal equivalent, money. Everything he owns is convertable into money; hence, he believes that money is the real essence of everything that isn't money. Hence, everything is *really* the same thing — money. For Sir Cautious the economy of difference collapses everything into sameness. The only thing that is truly different, then, must be "nothing," a common slang word for the female genitals. One's wife is this nothing because in the normal course of things she is not a commodity. As Sir Cautious remarks, "Why, what a lavish whoremaker's this? We take money to marry our wives but very seldom part with 'em, and by the bargain get money" (p. 126). Her normal nonexchangeability for money is what makes a wife different from a prostitute; it is also what makes her the perfect nothing to set against three hundred pounds. We could say, then, that Julia is here made into a commodity only because she isn't one: she becomes the principle of universal difference and as such, paradoxically, becomes exchangeable for the universal equivalent.

The scene provides a structural parallel for the scene of Gayman's prostitution, in which, as we have seen, money also marks difference. But the sequels of the two scenes are strikingly dissimilar. Gayman is once again back in Julia's bed, but his rather than her identity is supposedly masked. Whereas in the first encounter, Gayman went to bed with what he thought was an old woman, in the second, Julia goes to bed with what she thinks is her old husband. But the difference between these two scenes in the dark as they are later recounted stems from the relative inalienability of male sexual identity. Even in the dark, we are led to believe, the difference of men is sensible: Gayman says, "It was the feeble husband you enjoyed/In cold imagination, and no more./Shyly you turned away, faintly resigned. . . . Till excess of love betrayed the cheat" (p. 139). Gayman's body, even unseen, is not interchangeable with Sir Cautious's. Unlike Julia's, Gayman's body will undo the misrepresentation; no mere idea can eradicate this palpable difference and sign of identity, the tumescent penis itself. Hence, when Gayman takes Sir Cautious's place in bed, he does not really risk what Julia suffered earlier: "after all to seem deformed, old, ugly." Gayman's self will always obtrude into the sphere of representation, another version of the ladle, but one that projects from the body instead of being barely discernible within it.

This inalienable masculine identity, although it seems at first Gayman's advantage, is quickly appropriated by Julia, who uses it to secure at once her own good reputation and complete liberty of action. Once again we are given a scene in which the speaker's sincerity is questionable. When Gayman's erection reveals his identity, Julia appears to be outraged at the attempted deception: "What, make me a base prostitute, a foul adult'ress? Oh, be gone, dear robber of my quiet" (p. 139). We can only see this tirade as more deceit on Julia's part, since we know she tricked the same man into bed the night before. But since her deceit was not discovered and his was, she is able to feign outrage and demand a separation from her husband. The implication is, although, once again, this cannot be represented, that Julia has found a way to secure her liberty and her "honor" by maintaining her misrepresentations.

It is, then, precisely through her nullity, her nothingness, that Julia achieves a new level of self-possession along with the promise of continual sexual exchange. But this, of course, is an inference we make from what we suspect Julia of hiding: her pleasure in Gayman's body, her delight that she now has an excuse for separating from her husband, her intention to go on seeking covert pleasure. All of this is on the other side of what we see and hear.

It is this shady effect, I want to conclude, that Aphra Behn is in the business of selling. And it is by virtue of this commodity that she becomes such a problematic figure for later women writers. For they had to overcome not only her life, her bawdiness and the author-whore metaphor she celebrated, but also her playful challenges to the very possibility of female self-representation.

Notes

1. *A Room of One's Own* (London, 192), p. 67. Woolf here no doubt exaggerates the deterrent effects of Behn's scandal. We know that hundreds of women made some sort of living as writers in the late seventeenth and early eighteenth centuries. Indeed, there was no consensus that Behn was infamous until the second half of the eighteenth century. Nevertheless, in an age that loved scandal, she seems willingly to have obliged her audience's taste.
2. "Prologue," *The Forced Marriage or the Jealous Bridegroom* (London, 1671), n.p.
3. This quotation is from Robert Gould's *Satirical Epistle to the Female Author of a Poem called "Sylvia's Revenge"* (London, 1691). The poem acknowledges that the lines are a paraphrase from Rochester's "Letter from Artemisia in the Town to Chloe in The Country." The sentiment is presented as a commonplace.
4. Ibid.
5. This discussion is heavily indebted to Angeline Goreau's *Reconstructing Aphra. A Social Biography of Aphra Behn* (Oxford, 1980), especially pp. 144-162. Goreau has gathered much of the evidence on which I draw; however, we reach very different conclusions on the basis of the evidence. Goreau writes that Behn "savagely resented" the charge of immodesty and makes no references to the playwright's own sly uses of the author-whore metaphor. For a discussion of Behn's self-presentation that recognizes her use of this trope, see Maureen Duffy, *The Passionate Sheperdess. Aphra Behn 1640-89* (London, 1977), especially pp. 94-104.
6. Lady Elizabeth Carey, *The Tragedy of Mariam, the Fair Queen of Jewry* (London, 1613) Act III, unpaginated. Quoted in Goreau, p. 151.
7. Ibid.
8. William Wycherley, *Miscellany Poems*, vol. III, *The Complete Works of William Wycherley* (London, 1924), pp. 155-6.
9. "Prologue," *The Widdow Ranter or The History of Bacon in Virginia* (London, 1690),

n.p. The Prologue was, in fact, first spoken to Shadwell's comedy, *The True Widow*, in 1678, yet another reminder that the author–whore metaphor was ready-made for Behn's appropriation.
10. Quoted at the opening of Fidelis Morgan, *The Female Wits. Women Playwrights of the London Stage 1660-1720* (London, 1981), n.p.
11. *The Lucky Chance or An Alderman's Bargain* (performed first in 1686) in *The Female Wits*, p. 76. All further quotations are from this edition of the play, and page numbers are given in the body of the essay.

Life after sex: the fictional autobiography of Delariver Manley

JANET TODD

Sidney Sussex College, Cambridge University

MALE SATIRE of the Restoration and early eighteenth century was especially misogynist when it contemplated the disparity between what women appeared to be and what they should have been. These two constructions — the sordid "reality" and the unembodied ideal — had been influentially formulated by the Roman writer Juvenal whose sixth satire spoke powerfully of male disappointment and anger, outragedly proclaiming the harlot in the empress and the lady, all "driven by the dictates of their sex".[1]

The Juvenalian women did not much speak for themselves but in Restoration England women were increasingly turning author. In the satires of Gould, Rochester, Pope and Swift the writing woman took her place with the female wrestlers of Juvenal as a refinement of female horror; verbal antics became confounded with sexual ones, and the pen became a female instrument of lubriciousness.

The nastiness of women was supremely expressed in the sexual act and its aftermath; male disillusion, impotence and venereal disease. The only comfort in this situation was the consoling narrative of female distress following defloration, a much told tale of madness, disease and death. As the eighteenth century wore on women writers would themselves frequently glorify this female trajectory and give it an immense potency. But it was extremely rare for them to counter the narrative directly and uncover its assumptions, to demystify the sexual act that had taken on such immense proportions. Before the sentimental image of chaste, maternal, subordinate womanhood hardened into a prescription, however, Delarivier Manley was one woman who tried to give the conventional tale a subverting comic turn and provide sexualized female writing with a cheerful rather than horrific aim.

Manley enters history primarily on the periphery of the lives of her more remembered male colleagues, the Tory satirist and poet Jonathan Swift and the Whig essayist, Richard Steele. Her early years can be glimpsed only through her own creations. In her fictional autobiography, *The Adventures of Rivella* (1714) she tells the life of Rivella, a literary character who yet claims to have written Manley's works: *Rivella* is the *History of the Author of the Atalantis*, a book which by 1714 everyone knew to have come from the pen of the infamous Mrs Manley.

Rivella was the daughter of a gentleman whose absolute loyalty to Charles I was in due course rewarded by Charles II with the lieutenant-governorship of Jersey. Born unhandsome between two pretty sisters, plump and pockmarked, Rivella nevertheless gained a lifelong admirer who now tells her tale. She had a sheltered upbringing, one of those private virtuous educations that always spell ruin in Manley's novels and, on the death of her father, she was easily persuaded into marriage with her older kinsman, now her guardian. The marriage proved bigamous and Rivella was left alone, a fallen woman with an illegitimate son. Recovering her wits if not her reputation, she began writing for the stage, the most obvious outlet at the time for the woman writer.

Manley lived for a time with the Duchess of Cleveland, Charles II's former mistress, with whom she soon quarrelled. Later she took her revenge when she created the amorous Duchess de l'Inconstant in *The New Atalantis* out of her one-time friend and benefactor. Amorous entanglements followed including one with John Tilly, warden of the Fleet Street prison, as well as a rather sordid effort to gain money from another person's estate, an episode which, when fictionalized in *Rivella*, even the partisan biographer could not make wholesome. In her later years, Manley had a rather uneasy relationship with John Barber, a printer from the City of London. Despite personal disappointments, difficulties and illnesses, she continued writing until her death in 1724 at Barber's printing house.

Through her literary efforts, Manley enters history beside her creation, Rivella. She had a modest success with one play and a less modest one with the new genre into which she entered, the scandalous chronicle, familiar to French readers and already used with considerable success by the Restoration playwright and novelist, Aphra Behn. For her most famous work in this line, *Secret Memoirs and Manners of Several Persons of Quality, of both sexes. From the New Atalantis* (1709), Manley was briefly detained by the authorities, an affair made heroic in *Rivella* where she describes her spirited admission of guilt to save her publishers and sources. *The New Atalantis* became notorious in later centuries for its erotic depictions, rendered the more unsavoury by the knowledge that they were created by a woman. But, at the time, the work was considered primarily as political satire especially aimed at linking Whig public corruption with private indecency.

As a political pamphleteer on behalf of the conservative courtly faction (the party with which, unlike in the later eighteenth century, many early women writers were associated), as well as a scandal chronicler, Manley joined various literary and political battles with opponents like the Whig Richard Steele, as well as with sometime friends like Jonathan Swift, whom she followed into editorship of the Tory journal *The Examiner* in 1711. Steele who was already promoting the newer, more confined sentimental concept of womanhood in the *Tatler* and the *Spectator* condemned female political activity on aesthetic grounds, considering that "there is nothing so bad for the Face as Party-Zeal". While she remained immune to this kind of belittling advice, in *Rivella* Manley does appear to have succumbed to the notion that women should avoid political affairs when she admits that "Politicks is not the Business of a Woman". Considering the date, however — 1714 — the year that ended Tory influence in government and concluded Stuart rule, she might just as well have written that Tory politics was not good business for anyone. In her choice of genres and subject matter, Manley did make something of being a woman but she appears rarely to have been hindered by the notion, expressed by Steele and rapidly gaining ground, that there was a content and mode inappropriate for the female sex. Indeed at a time of uncertain authorship, several of her works were variously attributed to Swift and Defoe.[2]

In her works and the comments of others, Delarivier Manley's life emerges as energetic, disturbed and utterly involved. Without any sentimental views of female friendship and of romantic liaisons, she campaigned as vigorously against erstwhile friends like the Duchess of Cleveland, Richard Steele, and the feminist poet Sarah Fyge Egerton — who appears as the apple-pie toting termagent in *The New Atalantis* — as against established opponents like the immensely powerful Duchess of Marlborough, whose political energy, scandalously transformed into sexual appetite in the satires, Manley seems covertly to have admired. Often morally dubious in personal, financial and literary dealings, she rarely appears pathetic, despite the very real difficulties she faced in her life as an unprotected woman making a still unconventional literary living. Much is obviously unknowable about her activities and views, but one thing is sure, that she never achieved the elevated detachment from social and political matters that she attributed to her voyeuristic goddess in *The New Atalantis*; "I see the World without going into it, and hear so much, that I do not desire to see it" (I, 203).[3]

The women writers of the Restoration and early eighteenth century like Aphra Behn and Manley were still writing mainly for a male audience whatever their actual readership, and their images were formed to the presumed taste of men. They were writing in a world where it seemed just possible, if not necessarily desirable, for the energetic woman to flourish spectacularly, where clever women like the mistresses of Charles II or the Duchess of Marlborough could manipulate their way to power. In this society the loss of reputation was a social error but need not be a fatal disaster. But, as the anachronistic, romantic Stuarts gave way to the pedestrian Hanoverians and as women's cultural construction gradually changed into something less sexually distasteful for men and more morally and physically refined, the verve and gusto, the scandal and sexuality, the effrontery and puffing of the early writers seemed improper, and Behn and Manley became the very type of what a woman writer should not be. Much had always been made of Manley's scandalous life in opponents' accounts, but she had nonetheless been attacked as an equal by her major male contemporaries, still not entirely constrained by the sentimental rhetoric of the "fair sex" which would come to dominate literary relations between the sexes later in the century. But future ages found the conjunction of gender and scandal far more shocking and until very recently Manley, when considered at all, has been appearing in works with such titles as *Rogues and Scoundrels* (1924) and *Five Queer Women* (1929).[4] The life she insisted on bringing before the public was left as a cautionary tale to other women writers once the public itself had changed its manners and taste.

Delarivier Manley's view of herself as a young woman in her fictional autobiography, "Sweet, Clean, Witty, Friendly, Serviceable", is relayed through the medium of a male admirer. The same useful gentleman is given a quick justification for the older Manley's notorious public life with its sexual irregularities, political scandals, shady legal and financial dealings and naughty erotic writings: "Her Vertues are her own, her Vices occasion'd by her Misfortunes; and yet as I have often heard her say, If she had been a Man, she had been without Fault: But the Charter of that Sex being much more confin'd than ours, what is not a Crime in Men is scandalous and unpardonable in Woman" (p. 7).

Manley is acutely aware of the objections that can be made to her scandalous and sexy subject matter. Whether or not the foreword to her scandal novel *The Secret History of Queen Zarah and the Zarazians* (1705) is by her, it certainly conforms to her views and illustrates her frequent tendency to justify, excuse and boast all at once. As many detractors insisted and she could not deny, her main material was gossip about the great, secrets revealed of intimate happenings that people would rather have kept hidden. Inevitably the secrets that she told appealed to the prurient desires of the reader and could titillate the sophisticate and corrupt the innocent. Sometimes she glories in what she is doing and sometimes defangs it by declaring that her revelations are innocuous for the events are all far in the past. But in the preface to the second volume of *The New Atalantis*, after she has had the measure of hostile reaction and enthusiastic consumption, she makes greater claims, setting out grandly to turn her image from a female scandal monger into a male satirist in the line of Juvenal and Dryden; satire, she claims, was always personal or it would have had no bite, and the flailing of individual vice signified not a vicious gossip but a "lofty stedfast Soul."

In Manley's works, the driving force of humanity is desire; the most successful learn to manipulate this desire in others and to avoid being controlled by it themselves. Although a narrator might condescendingly admire the spontaneous gesture and the authentic emotion, she may also lament, with sophisticated melancholy, that the sincere and transparent are not fitted for a world in which survival means dissimulation and constant devotion to self-interest. Marriages for love may be the ideal, but marriages for interest are both common and appropriate, although ritually condemned. Women marry for reputation and maintenance, men marry to clear their mortgages; the success goes to the most manipulative and cunning. When equality is reached, there is an impasse, as happens in Defoe's *Moll Flanders* where the heroine fools and is fooled simultaneously or in the life of the fraudulent Restoration "princess" Mary Carleton who cheats and is cheated by her "lord". The answer to the rake, the male predator, who stalks through so much female fiction of this century is not the later, almost compulsory, demand for his destruction or for more male protection of women from other men, but the recommendation that women achieve more awareness, wit, and self-control.

The world of the scandal novels is quite openly sordid and debased. Yet, it is also energetic and vigorous. Luxury is both contemptible and attractive. There is much describing of elaborate clothes, coaches and expensive interiors, much detail of gold, lace and costly embroidery. Rich food and drink accompany the intimate bawdy talk on nights that are always oppressively hot, and they augment the sense of intricate social corruption. Sexuality is overwhelming and inevitably isolating through its expression in individual desire, but the sheer number and variety of the sexual scenes Manley describes makes physical enslavement a soothingly uniting predicament. As night comes in her tales, the copulations begin and the separate sins become a comfortable communal fall. To survive in the harsh, complicated society of *Zarah*, *The New Atalantis* and *Rivella* everyone must wear a mask. Social grace is wanted, not the sentimental virtues of chastity and compassion, so much preached for and to women, decorum not sincerity, good conversation and wordly sense: "The Knowledge which teaches Men to live among People of Civility and Manners".

Yet, although very much a lady as well as a goddess, one of the two onlookers of the scenes in *The New Atalantis* is nevertheless "Virtue". Her presence emphasizes the apparent need of society to define an ideal of virtue and to try to illustrate it in life — usually, it becomes apparent, at another person's (woman's) expense. Because of this need, education is especially problematic, although there is general unquestioning acceptance that it should be in virtue, particularly for young girls. Virtue is needed to guard a girl against premature indulgence in sex, and "virtuous" books must keep out titillating romances that encourage her seemingly natural desire for seduction. Despite a rhetoric of admiration, the purpose of a virtuous education in moral principles, sincerity and chastity seems to be the thwarting of nature, a necessity for existence in a civilized world.

Repeatedly, this education is revealed as socially inept, even dangerous for girls. By suppressing sexual expression, it merely delays and heightens it; as Astrea wearily remarks at the close of yet another story of seduction and betrayal, "we see the tender Sex, with all their Native-Timorousness, Modesty and Shame-fac'd Education, when stung by love, can trample under Foot the consideration of Virtue and Glory" (II. 192). For the older male seducer, a virtuous education simply renders the young girl a yet more delicious prey; it becomes a seductive attribute to femaleness, sought by men to enhance the charms of the victim and give piquancy to defloration.

Manley expresses the conventional distaste for the use of sexuality by artful women, and she condemns them for employing their sexual desirability to trap rich men into marriage. Yet she also gives them justification by asserting that the same desire for riches and power animates men and women; while men have many routes to attain them, women have only their sexual attractiveness.

Because of the different social effects of sexual indulgence on the two sexes, different narratives are inevitably provided for them, but the difference is not, as it would be later in the eighteenth century, that men may prey on women or guard and save them according to genre, while women must enter the archetypal stories of the virgin or the whore. Instead both sexes divide into the naive and the manipulative, and their stories evolve accordingly. Silly innocent women are fooled by men, who are in turn deceived by sophisticated scheming women. The female victim is always pitied at length, but she is given none of the spiritual significance she would acquire in the novels of Samuel Richardson a few years later. She suffers for her sexual activity far beyond men, but on the whole it is a social suffering and the sexual fall, largely demystified, does not bear the immense religious and moral weight it supports in sentimental literature.

One sexual narrative is repeated so frequently in Manley's tales that it assumes the status of a myth. It coincides with the developing intertwined stories of virtue in distress and of love betrayed, which will come to dominate literature about women and which are already being expressed in the woman-centred tragedies of Otway and Rowe.

A schematic outline will reveal its archetypal quality — as well as the autobiographical resonance its repetition also suggests. It is this story that *Rivella* so naughtily subverts.

A young innocent girl is unprotected by a sensible mother; she finds at puberty that her male guardian or father figure is displaced by or transformed into a lusty and destructive man bent on rape or seduction. The sad account of Charlot from Part I of *The New Atalantis* foreshadows the type. In this narrative Manley has ample opportunity to repeat her worldly points about the problematic nature of education and to illustrate the difficulty of constructing a viable self amidst conflicting influences of moral instruction, ambivalent literature, overwhelming personalities and natural sexual but socially destructive drives.

In the tale, the Duke educates his ward Charlot only in virtue, banishing from her environment all novels and poetry that might provoke lascivious feelings or teach dissimulation. She thus becomes a modest, silent, sincere young woman, a correct product of the education she has experienced. Then literature wickedly intrudes into her chaste scene and all becomes heated and obscure. First Charlot simply reads instructive moral poetry, which reinforces her virtuous inclinations. But her acting out for her guardian of scenes from the works, her assumption of roles despite her authenticity and innocence, has the effect of inflaming the Duke whose fatherly love is rapidly transformed into an altogether less proper emotion. Meanwhile he himself is a victim of literature in his assent to the notion of the amoral political author, Machiavelli, that greatness may be expressed in wickedness; he therefore finds himself lusting after the person whose purity he should guard, uninhibited by any restraint on his inclinations.

Preparing to seduce his ward, the Duke excites her mind with less elevated verse. Charlot has learnt to see the father where the Duke is now presenting the lover; consequently his signs of desire assume incestuous overtones for the reader. In due course, his disorder, his trembling and shortness of breath inject Charlot with "that new and lazy Poison." Certainly it is the birth of sexuality in her, but it is also the beginning of desire for social power, always a component of sexual feeling in Manley's works. The apparent need to please in women is, according to the author, often less the desire for sexual gratification than a claim to influence; other forms of empire seem "to be politically deny'd them, because the way to Authority and Glory is stop'd up" (I,55). Charlot is excited by a temporary sexual power that gives her social influence but which she does not adequately understand — "ignorant of the Power of Love, that Leveller of Mankind". So she cannot use this influence to promote her own interests.

Under the sway of the seductive Ovid, Petrarch and other licentious reading, "Books ... abominable for Virgins ... such as explain the Mysteries of Nature, the congregated Pleasures of Venus", her moral education melts into "Precepts of airy Virtue", and she desires and gains sexual fulfillment. The reader becomes the voyeur of the first seduction and is delivered the scene through the eyes both of the amorous Duke and of the naive daughterly girl. But the sexual climax, coming after the expected description of excessive heat, waiting bed, and dishabille, is, in literary and social terms, anticlimactic: while yet she was "doubtful of his designs, he took advantage of her confusion to accomplish 'em ... Thus was Charlot undone! thus ruin'd by him that ought to have been her Protector!" (I, 72)

Entering the new category of the fallen woman, Charlot finds her virtuous education valueless. Designed to guard virginity for social or moral ends, it has no purpose outside the sexual meaning and no relevance to the fallen woman's need to gain control over herself and her environment. Indeed such an education is now actually harmful, for it simply renders Charlot sincere and without disguise. A worldly wise Countess who "knew the Management of Mankind, and how to procure herself universal Love and Admiration", a lady who has been bred up in the "fashionable way of making Love, wherein the Heart has little or no part", gives Charlot new role models from literature of manipulative and powerful women who have understood men and gained power and influence. At the same time she tries to teach the young girl that love must be used by a woman as a tool with which to establish herself in the world. But the good Charlot cannot so quickly learn a new lesson; she fails to fix the Duke in marriage and watches her own passion grow as his declines, failing to understand that "the same unaccountable thing that cools the Swain, more warms the Nymph." The end is inevitable. Giving up the role of educator, the Countess concentrates on herself and her interest; she sets up the seductive sexual scene, and swiftly catches the Duke in marriage. Charlot is left to "Horror, Sorrow, and Repentance"; "She dy'd a true

Landmark: to warn all believing Virgins from shipwracking their Honour upon ... the Vows and pretended Passion of Mankind" (I, 83).

But of course the moral is not as clear as this. The repentance has few religious overtones, and the honour and virtue obtain no transcendental meaning. "Men may regain their Reputations," comments Astrea at the end of Charlot's story, "tho' after a Complication of Vices, Cowardice, Robbery, Adultery, Bribery, and Murder, but a Woman once departed from the Road of Virtue, is made incapable of a return; Sorrow and Scorn overtake her, and ... the World suffers her to perish loath'd, and unlamented" (I, 83-4). Vice is translated into sexual activity for a woman, and into murder, robbery and bribery for a man, and both translations are given social not moral significance. Indeed chastity for a woman is not really a virtue at all, but simply good social sense in the absence of consummate ability.

The story of Charlot gains some resonance in Manley's works from its equivocal use of the theme of virtue in distress or love betrayed, and it adds more through the autobiographical content. For a version of the tale of Charlot is so often told that, even without a knowledge of *Rivella*, it would be difficult not to discern that it held some special fascination for the author. Sometimes the story trails off into sorrow and exile, as it did in the narrative of Charlot and the Duke; sometimes it ends in the woman's suicide and the man's unperturbed reentry into society. But often it continues in the less dramatic sadness and sordidness of a woman's life outside respectable society. It is into the last narrative that Manley herself most clearly enters. In *Rivella*, the narrator claims that the story of Delia in *The New Atalantis* is actually the life story of the author of that work. Rivella, the famous writer, becomes the result of the sexual victimization of Delia, an innocent young orphan; Delia and Rivella unite in Delarivier.

Like Charlot and so many other women in Manley's works, Delia is poisoned by romantic tales. She is persuaded into marriage with her guardian, a man 23 years her senior. The marriage is simply a variation of seduction, since it proves bigamous. The effect is the usual social isolation of the woman and her realization at last that virtue is specific to gender. Men may sin and sin and be socially reclaimed, but women, even if only guilty in appearance, are irretrievably lost and cannot be reconciled to society: "Is it not this Inhospitality that brings so many unhappy Wretches to Distruction? Dispairing of Redemption, from one vile degree to another, they plunge themselves down to the lowest ebb of Infamy!" (II, 191)

In its use of the narrative of virtue in distress, the story of Delia highlights many of the difficulties Manley had encountered in the presentation of a public female image. The teller of Delia's story, aiming to arouse as much sympathy as possible in the reader, insists that the young girl is innocent of sexual longing despite her unwise perusal of romance and that she is precipitated into marriage through illness; her guardian cares for her and she is grateful. Such a timely collapse would come to many later heroines who find themselves married or compromised not through sexual desire but through physical weakness. Meanwhile the guardian, like Charlot's Duke, is tinged with incest, for he is associated with her father and was present at her birth. Yet, Astrea, goddess of justice, will have none of this special pleading and, in her critical comments, the narrative of virtue in distress becomes a less elevated tale of foolish love betrayed, and the heroine is transformed from a pure child into a silly sexual woman.

The usual narrative ending is withdrawal and death for distressed innocence, and suicide for betrayed passion. But of course Delarivier Manley does not kill herself or pine and die. Instead, she becomes a writer and she uses her infamy to her advantage. The sad story of Delia is continued in the robust *Rivella*, where the reader learns that a woman without reputation and honour may be freed for economic activity. In time she transforms herself from the deceived and confused object of desire into its subject. But although Rivella is sometimes described as a looker, an amorous gazer on others, far more strikingly she uses herself as a writing subject, to create in her inflaming works an image of herself as object of male desire. It is, after all, female desirability, not desire itself, that has social currency and gains social power in a patriarchal world.

In *Rivella* the assumed author creates the male eyes that will see her. The fictional autobiography is written as a conversation of two men, in which one details the author's life and arouses the other to appreciation of her charms, despite a frank admission of her bulky size, her advanced years and her tarnished reputation as "the Town Talk". Significantly for habitual readers of Mrs Manley, the story of her life is told on one of the hottest days.

In *Rivella* the author displays herself for her purchasing male readership and makes a direct link between authorship and seduction, literary consumption and sexual gratification. Her words dissolve her fatness, smooth her pock marks, light up her expressive eyes and give an "establish'd Reputation" to her neck and breasts. The final scene of the autobiography, echoing the many sexual and scandalous encounters in Manley's books, invites the fictional listener, with the reader, to hear the author's seductive conversation, sit at her well furnished table, and to repose with her "during the Heat of the Day" on her bed "nicely sheeted and strow'd with Roses, Jassamines or Orange-Flowers ... her Pillows neatly trim'd with Lace or Muslin, stuck round with Junquils, or other natural Garden Sweets" (p. 119).

Despite the amorous build-up and the many precedents in her tales, this scene will — just this once — not give way to the narrative of love betrayed, for, even beyond sexual cunning, the scene hints at a new power of women through their manipulation of literary language. The lady here is a literary woman who has weathered sexual and social disasters and has learnt the power of words. No sexual act that might objectify and victimize the female is written into her account, although sexual activity may be implied, and the end is not the rushed retreat of the satisfied man and the sorrow of the abandoned woman. Instead there is a companionable airing in the park or on the water when the heat of the day is gone.

Here in this ending of Manley's fictional autobiography, a mixture of imaginative history and scandalous exposure, desire is controlled and contained, and the reader is made to agree with the listener whom the author has created for herself, that she, a fallen woman who does not die, a maker of wicked romances, is the "only Person of her sex that knows how to Live".

Rivella is well aware of the identification of woman writer and whore in male writing and she comically plays with the convention. She uses the image of the literary lady for a verbal erotic seduction brought about through the special female ability of the author to please with scenes of love. The prose forms a kind of boudoir into which the reader and the listener in the tale must both expectantly penetrate. In this prose there is a sense of excitement at the power of language, a new social power to set beside or, indeed to manipulate and direct, sexual power. Words can control response and make and unmake desire. They alone can construct the meaning of the sexual act and they alone can create sex without pregnancy, venereal disease, or lifelong misery. They alone can form it into tragedy or comedy.

In *The New Atalantis*, Manley diffuses the criticism that she is corrupting the mind of the reader with the rather lame excuse that only vicious activity can harm, not the mere hearing of scandal. Yet she does not rest with such simplicity and, in common with the writers throughout the eighteenth century, she is both appalled and excited by the obvious and feared effect of literature on the mind. While declaring that stories of sexual excitement cannot by themselves corrupt and incite to sexual activity, she provides example after example of young girls inflamed into love by the rash perusal of romantic tales. But in *Rivella* she avoids this whole troubling nexus by moving her story into the sophisticated world of the older woman and the always privileged men. Rivella presents an image of herself as mistress of the titillating effect and there need be no pretence that literature does not often and deliciously nudge life: "After perusing her Inchanting Descriptions, which of us have not gone in Search of Raptures which she every where tells us, as happy Mortals, we are capable of tasting" (p. 4), remarks the obliging male. Men's often dangerous desire ends, where it ought, in the author herself; female desire need not result in distress but instead yield delight and money through its representation. The whore becomes storyteller of men's lust and historian of the comic history of "virtue in distress" made entertaining and profitable.

Notes

1. See *Juvenal: Sixteen Satires Upon the Ancient Harlot* transl. Steven Robinson (Manchester: Carcanet New Press, 1983) pp. 113-129.
2. For a description of Manley as political satirist, see G.B. Needham, "Mary de la Riviere Manley, Tory Defender," HLQ, 12, 1948-9, 253-88.
3. The quotations are taken from *The Novels of Mary Delariviere Manley*, 2 vols, ed. Patricia Koster (Gainesville: Scholars' Facsimiles & Reprints, 1971). Page numbers refer to the facsimiles in this work. I have retained original spellings but not the frequent italicization. Owing possibly to a confusion of sources, it was common until recently to refer to Mrs. Manley as "Mary", although her signed works, private letters, will and tombstone all bear the name "Delariviere" or "Delarivier"; for a discussion of the matter see Koster, pp. v-vi.
4. See Philip R. Sergeant, *Rogues and Scoundrels* (London: Hutchinson & Co., 1924) and Walter and Clare Jerrold, *Five Queer Women* (London: Brentano's Ltd., 1929). For a description of later critical obsession with Manley's personal reputation, see Jane Spencer, *The Rise of the Woman Novelist* (Oxford: Blackwell, 1986) and Dolores Palomo, "A Woman Writer and the Scholars: A Review of Mary Manley's Reputation," *Women & Literature*, 6, 1, (Spring, 1978).

Jane Austen: irony and authority

RACHEL M. BROWNSTEIN

Department of English, Brooklyn College, City University of New York

IT IS A TRUTH universally acknowledged, right now, that language is involved in giving and taking both power and pleasure. Whether we begin by asking if the pen is a substitute for the penis, or think about why we read stories of love and adventure, or consider, from any point of view, pornography or psychoanalysis, we end by analyzing ways people please themselves and assert authority over others by using words. (To observe that critics writing about pleasure and power have managed to get what measure of the good stuff they can is to state the merely inevitable.) Claiming that women writers are powerful — *i.e.* effective and influential — has been a focus of feminist critics concerned to dispute the canon, to rehabilitate forgotten writers, and to revise women's relation to the languages of power. That Jane Austen, unforgotten, canonized, and stunningly authoritative, has been a problem for feminists is not surprising: in the struggle for power between politically radical and conservative critics, she has for years been claimed by both parties. Her own interest in power is suggested as her uses of the word acknowledge there are different kinds: in *Pride and Prejudice*, for instance, Elizabeth says that "It is not in my power to accept" an invitation (211), and, "I do not know any body who seems more to enjoy the power of doing what he likes than Mr. Darcy," (183) and her friend Charlotte reflects that "all her friend's dislike [of Darcy] would vanish, if she could suppose him to be in her power." (181) Courtship as power play is the subject of all Austen's novels; playing with — or against — power is the substance of them. And through irony, by pointing to the limits of definitive and assertive language, Jane Austen suggests a powerful and pleasurable relation women in patriarchy may have to discursive authority.

The title page of *Sense and Sensibility*, the first novel Austen published, identified it as by "A Lady"; *Pride and Prejudice* is signed "By the Author of 'Sense and Sensibility,'" in other words by A Lady already published. The veiling signature insists on the dignity of femininity itself as "Currer Bell," "George Eliot," "Fanny Fern," or "Mrs. Humphry Ward" do not. It implies, as if modestly, that all ladies speak in the same voice — Austen was of course not the only one to write as one —, which with pointedly feminine obliqueness will avoid such blunt signifiers as proper names, and say precisely what one might expect it appropriately to say, and no more. "A Lady" insists like a post-modern critic on an author's gender and class, indeed identifies the writer simply as a representative, perhaps only a function, of gender and class. The word makes the titillating suggestion that sex is the subject, and also a promise that it will be avoided. (Austen obliges on both counts.) Finally, the signature indicates that the female author is an accepted kind of author, probably one who will make herself delightful and useful without going so far as to set up as an authority. As Mary Ellmann wrote decades before the body became a theme of cultural critics, "the male body lends credence to assertions while the female takes it away" (148). Signing herself "A Lady," even a published author promises to assert neither her (discreetly veiled) self nor any original idea of her own. This novelist will not, presumably, pit her literary capacity and performances against "the abilities of the nine-hundredth abridger of the History of England, or of the man who collects and publishes in a volume some dozen lines of Milton, Pope, and Prior, with a paper from the Spectator, and a chapter from Sterne, [which] are eulogized by a thousand pens;" she does not claim authority, merely, slyly, "genius, wit, and taste." (*NA*, 37)

On the other hand, precisely by coming on as A Lady the author is assuming a certain kind of authority: as Mary Poovey has argued, economic changes, together with anxieties about class and gender distinctions, created in eighteenth-century England the enthroned image of The Proper Lady, symbol of refinement and taste (and perhaps wit, if not genius), and with it, at considerable cost to themselves and their sex, some real power for ladies. It was largely limited to the drawing room. Austen's writing as such A Lady, her mode of assuming ladylike authority in ladylike language, provokes the questions about her social and political allegiances that have divided the critical authorities who have written on the most respected woman writer in English. Jane Austen's awesome respectability has alienated some of her readers, and inspired wrong-headed enthusiasm in others. Does she want women's power confined to drawing rooms? Does she sanction or mock the image of the authoritative proper lady, which confines as it defines feminine power?

As A Lady, Austen seems now to represent and speak for British civility, perhaps even civilization, at its toniest. In *The Counterlife*, the American novelist Philip Roth introduces a representative traditional Austen fan, an Englishwoman who rereads the novels each year because, she says, "The characters are so very good." More explicitly, she continues, "I'm very fond of Fanny Price, in *Mansfield Park*. When she goes back to Portsmouth after living down with the Bertrams in great style and grandeur, and she finds her own family and is so shocked by the squalor — people are very critical of her for that and say she's a snob, and maybe it's because I'm a snob myself — I suppose I am — but I find it very sympathetic. I think that's how one would behave, if one went back to a much lower standard of living." (270) Mrs. Freshfield is pleased that the characters are fastidious, and that the author is — that both dislike squalor, quite as she does. It is not fair to lump such a reader with the so-called Janeites; she is no idealizer of a gentle, genteel Jane; what she is is a Jane Austen snob. She imagines Jane Austen has the same standards of embattled gentility she has, that like her Austen values those standards above everything. Readers of *Mansfield Park* will allow that Mrs. Freshfield's confusion of standards *for* living with standards *of* living is something Jane Austen tempts one toward; the serious question is whether Austen is accountable for attracting snobs like her and encouraging them in snobbishness. I think she is. When we thrill to the way Mrs. Bennet is dispatched as "a woman of mean understanding, little information, and uncertain temper," or to the translucent, transcendent tact with which Mr. Bennet tells his daughter Mary, in company, "You have delighted us long enough," (101), we respond with approval to a snob's ruthless high standards, and to her high-handedness. Austen's novels set us at a little, pleasant, critical distance from the actual, inelegant, disorderly world her letters reveal she herself lived in just as we do. Furthermore, the twentieth-century reader who, while not an authentic member of the English gentry, enjoys the sublime confidence of *Pride and Prejudice* — famously one of the world's impeccable masterpieces — can congratulate herself on her superior taste with a smugness very like Mrs. Freshfield's. I suspect that even morally serious readers able to list the shortcomings of Sir Thomas and Lady Bertram, and prove Jane Austen knew they are no better than Fanny Price's Portsmouth parents, enjoy their own complicity with Austen's sure, exclusive Lady's tone.

This tone is, wonderfully, so authoritative as to enable Austen to put down titled ladies. Those of us who are not complacent about being snobs enjoy noting that titled ladies are not among the most admirable characters in the novels: that hypercorrected Lady Middleton and empty Lady Bertram are portrayed as patriarchy's mere creatures, and conventional Lady Russell and authoritarian Lady Catherine de Bourgh as its wrong-headed police. Nevertheless, it is as a lady — an untitled member of the gentry, "a gentleman's daughter," which is how Elizabeth Bennet appropriates the term for herself — that Jane Austen condemns them. Austen carefully shows that Lady Catherine's manners are no more than her aspirations better than Mrs. Bennet's. To mock Lady Catherine's "authoritative manner," (84) she reports in unexceptionably calm and decorous ladylike tones that, for instance, after dinner and cards at Rosings, "the party ... gathered round the fire to hear Lady Catherine determine what weather they were to have on the morrow. From these instructions they were summoned by the arrival of the coach. ..." (166) Austen's special interest in exposing the pomposities of a great Lady or the pretensions of a couple of would-be ones — for example, the "two elegant ladies" (41) who are the Bingley sisters' maids — are signs, if we need them, that she signs herself with irony. There are ladies and ladies; "A Lady," as a signature, claims to be generic and claims at the same time a certain classy distinction. How are the claims related?

About being A Lady writing, which is to say about writing as a member of the group of women novelists, Austen's irony is even clearer, and also more complex. Her position on women's novels is spelled out in *Northanger Abbey*: they are more original than most of what's published, she declares. Even though their characters are very often stereotyped and their plots are commonly implausible, she says, they are both pleasurable and accurate, works "in which the greatest powers of the mind are displayed, in which the most thorough knowledge of human nature, the happiest delineation of its varieties, the liveliest effusions of wit and humour are conveyed to the world in the best chosen language." (*NA*, 38) The emphasis falls on "chosen language." Choosing language, commenting on the stereotypes and formulas of novelists, and the language available for use in social life, is always Austen's subject. Of Emma's response to Mr. Knightley's proposal, the narrator writes: "What did she say? — Just what she ought, of course. A lady always does." (*E*, 431). Writing as A Lady, Austen savors the discrepancy between being a stable sign in her culture as well as a user and analyst of its signs.

A letter to her niece Fanny Knight suggests her relish of a woman writer's peculiar position and power. Fanny, evidently, had regaled her aunt by recounting an adventure rather wilder than a fictional Austen heroine might have had, a visit to a gentleman's room. Intending to be charmed, indeed excited, there, poor Fanny had ended up disgusted, like Swift's gentleman in the lady's squalid dressing room. Evidently she emerged with her sense of irony intact, and of this her aunt expressed approval: "Your trying to excite your own feelings by a visit to his room amused me excessively. — The dirty Shaving Rag was exquisite! — Such a circumstance ought to be in print. Much too good to be lost." (*Letters*, 412) A cluster of characteristic Austen values come together here: an appreciation of telling details; a pleasure in telling them, and in hearing tell; a clear sense of the connections between saying and feeling, and social and emotional life; and seriousness about getting into print. Austen admired women's novels that told stories like Fanny's, about the ironic self-awareness of a rational creature absurdly caught in a lady's place.

Her own novels, with their ostentatious embrace and sly mockery of the tropes of fiction for women, depend on her readers' familiarity with that fiction — on their having the thorough, easy knowledge of them that enables one to recognize social or literary conventions, and to relish them. The reader she counts on will respond to a turn of standard plot as if to the anthem of an outgrown school, and treasure a collegial allusion to such matters as the "telltale compression of the pages [that promises] ... we are all hastening together to perfect felicity" (*NA*, 250) — all of us together, characters and narrator and readers assembled in the same linguistic craft. Austen presents herself as a daughter of the novelists who formed her vision and her readers', and continued to inform it. Condescending, mocking, competitive, this attitude is also defensively and devotedly filial. Far from struggling in a Bloomian agon with awesome precursors she aims to overthrow, Austen keeps her mother and sister novelists always in mind to measure the ways she is like and yet unlike them. If we must have a psychological hypothesis to "explain" this with, the paradigm of female development elaborated by Nancy Chodorow will be more useful than the Oedipal model.

Austen wrote first of all for her intimate family, "great Novel-readers & not ashamed of being so" (*Letters*, 38), as she put it; Austen fans tend like a very close family to be clubby and even a little apologetic about a very personal taste (as opposed to a liking for George Herbert, say, or George Eliot). We relish a sense of the choosiness and the exclusiveness (the sad accident of there being only six novels enhances it) of our little community. The pronoun in the title of Lionel Trilling's last essay, "Why We Read Jane Austen," reveals something more than a magisterial critic's traditionalist, universalist attitude: the feeling that the culture we share with Jane Austen is beleaguered or not enough valued, that powerful people on the outside don't take it seriously, serves to bind us more tightly together, "we" snobs like Mrs. Freshfield, "we" readers of women's novels, "we" humanists in a dehumanizing world, even "we" wary students of how language determines our pleasures and power. Those others who take the truth to be whatever is universally acknowledged remain ever in the corner of Jane Austen's eye: by their limitations we measure our own sagacity, and also our snugness. As Katherine Mansfield remarked, "every true admirer of the novels cherishes the happy thought that he alone — reading between the lines — has become the secret friend of their author." Wayne Booth, quoting this in *The Rhetoric of Fiction*, adds — losing the connection with words on the page, but avoiding Mansfield's "he" — that the Austen reader has an "illusion of travelling intimately with a hardy little band of readers whose heads are screwed on tight and whose hearts are in the right place." (266) The illusion depends on the way the confident, confidential tones of A Lady are deployed so as to mock the accents of authoritative patriarchal discourse in the universe that contains her universe and her fictions.

The literary tradition in which Jane Austen was placed and/or placed herself — the tradition of Jane West and Mary Brunton — was not the dominant tradition; one of the most arduous projects of feminist scholars has been to retrieve and reevaluate eighteenth-century fiction by women. Everything Austen wrote about the novel (and perhaps everything in her novels too) indicates that she knew quite as well as we do that the genre she chose or was constrained to choose (rather as her heroines choose their husbands) was not universally esteemed — that Catherine Morland is representative if not accurate in her assumption that "gentlemen read better books" than novels (*NA*, 106), works, presumably, of greater heft and seriousness. Logically enough, while portraying authority figures and their discourse as in general not exemplary, Austen mocked women's novels most for their moralizing. The maxims that articulate the attitude of patriarchal authority on sex and marriage, the main subject of such novels, are parodied in *Pride and Prejudice*: Elizabeth lifts up her eyes in amazement as her sister Mary moralizes, after Lydia runs away, "that loss of virtue in a female is irretrievable — that one false step involves her in endless ruin — that her reputation is no less brittle than it is beautiful." (*P & P*, 289) Pointedly, Austen does not write down: she will not preach like pedantic Mary. Her Mr. Collins comically echoes the stentorian tones of the "learned doctors" who spell out the moral meanings of romantic actions in novels by, for instance, Charlotte Lennox and Fanny Burney. In his final letter to Mr. Bennet he warns "my cousin Elizabeth, and yourself, of what evils you may incur, by a precipitate closure with [Darcy's] proposals," and declares his amazement at the "encouragement of vice" that occurred with Lydia and Wickham were received by her parents. (363-4) Mr. Bennet rightly observes that this clergyman's attitude is less than Christian, but he himself is no more a reliable authority than his heir is. He is as Elizabeth's meditations on his character point out considerably less than ineffectual, not only pathetically hampered by the entail from disposing of his own patrimony, but worse than useless as a head of his household. Austen's shift from the explicit didacticism of her sister novelists is signalled by the absence of an authoritarian father figure from the novel: Mr. Gardiner, who has the tact to arrange some things, is a shadowy minor character. There is no one but the hero and heroine themselves to discuss, at the end, what "the moral" of their story might be (381). Hapless Mr. Bennet's comment on life itself meanwhile resonates: "For what do we live, but to make sport for our neighbours, and laugh at them in our turn?" (364) It is neither the moral of the whole novel nor one the whole novel repudiates.

Pride and Prejudice is about women's lives in relation to sexual roles and to marriage; therefore — that the connection is inevitable is Jane Austen's point — it is about power, and independence and authority. The novel opens, seductively, in the mode of the Johnsonian essayist: "It is a truth universally acknowledged that a single man in possession of a good fortune must be in want of a wife." On the face of it this sentence has an authoritative ring: as surely, it is the paradigmatic Jane Austen sentence, which was famously and enigmatically praised by Virignia Woolf as "a woman's sentence." Confronted by the sentence suitable for men writers, Woolf declared, Austen "laughed at it and devised a perfectly natural, shapely sentence proper for her own use and never departed from it." (80) The initiating philosophical-sounding premise of *Pride and Prejudice* is a good example. It laughs at authoritative sentence-making. As everyone has pointed out, it is full of logical holes: a truth universally acknowledged is probably less than true; the truth at issue here is not really that single men want girls (which "in want of" does not mean anyway) but that poor girls need husbands. And, far from describing the real state of things in society, the novel's first sentence expresses a gossip's fantasy that women exchange or traffic in men. The sentence acknowledges, by putting it first, Mrs. Bennet's view of things (or is it only what for her purposes Mrs. Bennet acts as if she believes?): that rich men want to be supplied with (even poor) wives. We are encouraged to reflect that although this is not the case, it may be operatively true when people act as if it's true. The power of discourse to determine action is suggested.

The last sentences of Chapter I, quite as authoritative as the first sentence is, complement it, by contrast. Far from entertaining Mrs. Bennet's point of view, the narrator here speaks from above, and decisively detaches herself from the woman: "She was a woman of mean understanding, little information, and uncertain temper. When she was discontented she fancied herself nervous. The business of her life was to get her daughters married; its solace was visiting and news." These dismissive declaratives crackling with the briskness that charms snobs are very different from the meditative voice that pronounces the ironic, pseudo-philosophical first sentence. But the conclusion of the chapter resembles its commencement in one important regard, that is, in claiming distance and authority — the authority a lady in a drawing room shares with a philosopher, a society epigrammatist shares with a judge. The reader is encouraged to reflect on the similarities and also the differences between ladies and philosophers, drawing rooms and the arenas of real power. And the limits of any authoritative statement are suggested when we look more closely and discover that the impressive balance and antithesis of the final sentence is factitious: Mrs. Bennet's solace, far from being a change from her business, is her mode of conducting that. "News," the narrator's last word on this first chapter, a simple word rather elaborately kinder to Mrs. Bennet than "gossip" might be, nicely labels the subject of the chapter. The cap suggests the chapter was substantive; but as Chapter 2 follows, the roundness and fullness the cap helps emphasize begin to seem illusory. We find that the scene between Mr. and Mrs. Bennet was by no means as crucial and conclusive as we thought when it turns out that Mr. Bennet visited Mr. Bingley before his wife asked him to.

The first sentence and the first chapter of *Pride and Prejudice*, integral, finished units in their different, equally forceful ways, mime so as subtly to mock the certainties of authoritative discourse; in the plot of the novel, such discourse becomes a theme. Proud Mr. Darcy sets the action going when he scrutinizes Elizabeth Bennet and pronounces her "Tolerable, but not handsome enough to tempt *me*!" To the feminist critic, that italicized pronoun recalls the sinister bar of the masculine "I" that Virginia Woolf described, in *A Room of One's Own*, as a shadow disfiguring male texts: as Darcy goes on to declare his opinions on female accomplishments and related matters, the egoism of the male authority is amusingly exposed. The action that devolves from his comment on Elizabeth proves his first judgment was false and the first step toward its own undoing. To begin with, Elizabeth mocks by repeating the line, telling the story on him; "she had a lively, playful disposition," the narrator explains, "which delighted in any thing ridiculous." (12) By talking so as to render him ridiculous she is deliberately manipulating her own psyche (rather in the manner of Fanny Knight visiting her gentleman's room); "he has a very satirical eye," she tells Charlotte, "and if I do not begin by being impertinent myself, I shall soon grow afraid of him." (24) In other words, by repeating his words to others she is talking for — in effect to — herself, choosing and using language not to express feeling but to create it, to make herself feel powerful. Darcy will accurately observe, much later, that she finds "great enjoyment in occasionally professing opinions which in fact are not your own" (174). Lest we think she does this just to flirt, we find her, very much later in the novel, doing the same thing in the very private precincts of her own mind, as she thinks about the question of whether Bingley will propose to Jane. At the conclusion of that gentleman's visit to Longbourn, toward the novel's end, the narrator tells us that, "Not a word passed between the sisters concerning Bingley; but Elizabeth went to bed in the happy belief that all must speedily be concluded, unless Mr. Darcy returned within the stated time. Seriously, however, she felt tolerably persuaded that all this must have taken place with that gentleman's concurrence." (346) Here again, talky Elizabeth is enjoying herself by professing — silently, but nevertheless as if to a drawing-room audience, in well-constructed, carefully timed sentences — an opinion that is not seriously — not in fact — her own. The remarkable sentence that begins "Seriously, however," as it remarks on the non-seriousness of the sentence that precedes it, raises interesting questions about the power of positive assertions — highly subversive questions about the seriousness of all definitive statements and sentences, in what is after all a tissue of words, a series of sentences. Austen invites us to consider that words and sentences might not be signs or containers of meaning after all, that playfulness rather than meanings might be what they represent: "My dearest sister," Jane says once her affairs are settled and Elizabeth's are at issue, "'now *be* serious. I want to talk very seriously. Let me know every thing that I am to know, without delay. Will you tell me how long you have loved him?'" Elizabeth answers, "'It has been coming on so gradually, that I hardly know when it began. But I believe I must date it from my first seeing his beautiful grounds at Pemberley.'" Jane can tell she doesn't mean it: "Another intreaty that she would be serious, however, produced the desired effect; and she soon satisfied Jane by her solemn assurance of attachment." (373).

Elizabeth could tell herself Darcy might ruin her sister's happiness only because she knew he would not, being ready by now to have his friend marry Jane. As she also knows, he was long before conquered by her own "lively" — he does not call them "satirical" — eyes, "bewitched" by her powers, so much so as to ask her to understand — she would have had to be either an impossibly rational creature or a very smug witch to do so — that he fell in love with her against his better judgment. But she does not say these things. Many chapters later, when they finally can both with dignity agree to marry, it is after a long talk which ends with Elizabeth biting her tongue: on the verge of making a caustic observation, she "checked herself," for "she remembered that he had yet to learn to be laught at, and it was rather too early to begin." (371) Since people are comical, quite as Mr. Bennet says, dignity is precarious, and silence helps better than words to maintain it. Darcy will eventually be made to learn to laugh: in the novel's nearly penultimate paragraph, which begins to detail the bliss of the married life of the Darcys at Pemberley, we are told that Darcy's sister Georgiana "at first ... listened with an astonishment bordering on alarm, at [Elizabeth's] lively, sportive, manner of talking to her brother. He, who had always inspired in herself a respect which almost overcame her affection, she now saw the object of open pleasantry. Her mind received knowledge which had never before fallen in her way. By Elizabeth's instructions she began to comprehend that a woman may take liberties with her husband, which a brother will not always allow in a sister more than ten years younger than himself." (388) In the happy end Georgiana will take the place at Elizabeth's side of Jane, the more feeling sister with whom Elizabeth shared the sisterly mockery of men Jane never could engage in either. She will be the female confidante and foil — the other woman to talk to — that is necessary to the happiness of even the mistress of Pemberley. Both Darcys, then, will be instructed by Elizabeth happily ever after. In other words, just as the marriage plot comes to triumphant closure it is neatly undercut: female bonding and women's laughter are elements of this novel's happy end. One woman will make a man the object of her pleasantries while another one listens and learns. This subtle subversion of the conventional romantic plot accords with the novel's attitude toward verbal tissues that appear to wrap things up once for all.

Like her heroine, Austen questions authoritative discourse through dialogue. Dialogue, Mary Ellmann wrote, "might be defined as the prevention of monologue" (xii); as such it is a critique of patriarchal absolutism in prose. There are many modes of dialogue in *Pride and*

Prejudice, the first of which is ironic narrative. When Austen refers to the "two elegant ladies" who wait on the Bingley sisters she means that these women absurdly pretend, like their mistresses, to elegance. Irony is an efficient mode: the description of the maids serves for the mistresses. Like an impatiently rude interlocutor, irony questions a statement as it is made; a single sentence becomes in effect two, assertion cum contradiction.

Literal dialogue between characters in the novel may also be a process of assertion and contradiction, sometimes of opinions, sometimes of the authority to state them. Although we tend to remember *Pride and Prejudice* as chock full of witty exchanges, some of the most interesting dialogue is between talk and the lack of it. There dialogue is as much the subject as the mode of discourse. The first chapter is a case in point: "My dear Mr. Bennet," his lady begins the action by saying to him one day, "have you heard that Netherfield Park is let at last?", to which "Mr. Bennet replied that he had not." The switch to indirect discourse signals the man's taciturnity; he is not quite responding to his wife. One is reminded of this marital lack of exchange when Elizabeth and Darcy talk together later: "'It is *your* turn to say something now, Mr. Darcy. — *I* talked about the dance, and *you* ought to make some kind of remark on the size of the room, or the number of couples.' He smiled, and assured her that whatever she wished him to say should be said." (19) Elizabeth is unlike her mother making deliberate, sophisticated conversation about conversing, but my point — aside from the small truths that voluble Elizabeth resembles her mother, and that Austen's egoistic young people both tend to italicize pronouns — is that Darcy is hardly a Benedick to Elizabeth's Beatrice, therefore the real exchange is between talking and not talking, and that that is one way Austen suggests the limits of discursive authority.

In her Lady's voice, which combines an authoritative ring with flexible self-mocking undertones, Austen can comment with varying degrees of explicitness on the limits of rhetorical and human authority. Through self-reflexive irony she can keep her distance from the discourse of authority, the patriarchal mode of imposing oneself through language. Except for ladies in domestic and literary circumstances (drawing rooms and fictions) circumscribed by the world of men, women have been denied such authority. Writing as A Lady and considering the constraints that determine her persona —

considering as a persona —, Austen reflected on the power of authoritative language. And on other kinds of power. When Elizabeth scrutinizes her third-volume feelings about Darcy, she acknowledges that it is she who has the power to provoke the words that will change her life: "She respected, she esteemed, she was grateful to him, she felt a real interest in his welfare; and she only wanted to know how far she wished that welfare to depend upon herself, and how far it would be for the happiness of both that she should employ the power which her fancy told her she still possessed, of bringing on the renewal of his addresses." (266) The rhythms are authoritative, magisterial. The novel reader knows the heroine must wait, and we with her, for a second proposal it is not in her power to make — but also that Elizabeth's struggle to turn fancy into knowledge and power is the significant action. The proposal, important though it is, will be a coda to the inner action of discriminating among thoughts and the words for them. Only if we ignore that sentence and its sisters can we read *Pride and Prejudice* as a mere romance. Which is not to gainsay the pleasure we take in the novelist's very romantically and conventionally uniting the lovers, in the very end — or, rather, in the Gardiners' having done so. Having been responsible for the mechanics of getting the couple together, Elizabeth's relatives are thrust forward in the novel's last sentence as the only legitimate claimants to agency. Does the emphasis fall on the fact that the hero and heroine are mere puppets of circumstances, or perhaps of the marriage plot? Are we meant to envy their prospect of happiness ever after in the paradise of Pemberley? Or to note with sly pleasure that these cultivated but rather dull middle-class Gardiners will be frequent guests at that monument to Lady Catherine's class? It is hard to decide, and this, I think, is what must be borne in mind when we write about Jane Austen, whose authoritative irony eludes, even mocks, our authoritative critical discourses.

Selected Bibliography

Austen, Jane. *The Novels of Jane Austen*, ed. R.W. Chapman (5 vols.) Oxford: Oxford University Press, 1933.
Austen, Jane. *Jane Austen's Letters*, collected and edited by R.W. Chapman. Oxford: Oxford University Press, 1979.

Booth, Wayne C. *The Rhetoric of Fiction.* Chicago: University of Chicago Press, 1961.
Chodorow, Nancy. *The Reproduction of Mothering.* Berkeley: University of California Press, 1978.
Ellmann, Mary. *Thinking about Women.* New York: Harcourt, Brace, Jovanovich, 1968.
Poovey, Mary. *The Proper Lady and the Woman Writer.* Chicago: University of Chicago Press, 1984.
Roth, Philip. *The Counterlife.* New York: Farrar, Straus, and Giroux, 1986.
Trilling, Lionel. "Why We Read Jane Austen." *The Times Literary Supplement,* 5 March 1976.
Woolf, Virginia. *A Room of One's Own.* New York and London: Harcourt Brace Jovanovich, 1957.

Austen's laughter

PATRICIA MEYER SPACKS

Yale University

IN 1985 the Long Wharf Theatre in New Haven mounted a production of "Pride and Prejudice," adapted by David Pownall, a British dramatist. It opened with Mr. Bennet, in his study, turning to the audience to observe, "It is a truth universally acknowledged. ..." Everyone laughed. Throughout the play, Mr. Bennet's voice, conflated with that of Austen's narrator, directed audience response. We knew that we should mock what he mocked; his laughter elucidated the play's moral order.

I didn't much like this play, but it called attention to intricate ways in which laughter and judgment relate to one another in Austen's novels. Alert readers understand that Mr. Bennet's laughter should not guide them: indeed, his suggestion that we live to laugh at our neighbors and to be laughed at by them makes us conscious of his moral insufficiency. On the other hand, everyone knows that Austen in her roles as novelistic narrator and as personal letter writer appears to enjoy laughing at others. John Halperin's biography suggests, in fact, that Austen's propensity for mocking other people's miscarriages and grand pianos indicates *her* moral inadequacy. I want to muse about connections between laughter as moral guide and as index of moral failure by looking at a sequence of novels that seriously engage the problem of what it means to laugh at other people: *Pride and Prejudice, Mansfield Park,* and *Emma.* I do not propose that each of Austen's novels shows a more subtle understanding of the dynamics of laughter than does its predecessor; I want to argue, rather, that each emphasizes different aspects of that dynamic and correspondingly demands the reader's comic response in different ways.

Pride and Prejudice abounds in laughter. It begins with Mr. Bennet laughing at Mrs. Bennet; it ends with Darcy's sister bewildered at why Elizabeth is allowed to laugh at her brother when she is not. Earlier, the alleged impossibility of laughing at Darcy has provoked Elizabeth's mockery. "'Mr. Darcy is not to be laughed at!' cried Elizabeth. 'That is an uncommon advantage, and uncommon I hope it will continue, for it would be a great loss to *me* to have many such acquaintance. I dearly love a laugh'" (*Pride* 57) Both Elizabeth and her father dearly love a laugh, and much of the novel's energy comes from their laughter. Often the reader joins in without discomfort. When Elizabeth asks about Mr. Collins, having read his letter, "Can he be a sensible man, sir?", and her father replies, "I have great hopes of finding him quite the reverse" (64), we surely share his wicked anticipation of the ridiculous. And Mr. Bennet's ridicule often conveys accurate moral judgments; the novel tempts us to accept him as guide.

Yet one soon realizes the defensive function of both Mr. Bennet's laughter and Elizabeth's. If Elizabeth overhears a handsome young man refusing to dance with her on grounds of her insufficient attractiveness, she will make the episode into a joke and tell it to her friends. When her aunt suggests that she may fall in love with Wickham, when Miss Bingley attempts to patronize her, when Jane tries to adjudicate the moral complexities of Wickham's story and Darcy's — Elizabeth finds material for laughter. Her father has survived twenty-odd years of unhappy marriage by turning everything into a joke. He steadily asserts his superiority to his intellectually limited wife by mocking her and everyone else in ways she cannot fathom. For father and for daughter, laughter helps fend off real social, psychological, and familial difficulties. We will not find here any invariable equation between laughter and clearsightedness.

Still, the characters who laugh at others often prove more attractive than those who do not. One can understand Mrs. Bennet's deadly seriousness about the business of getting her daughters married, but it's pretty hard to *enjoy* that seriousness except as Mr. Bennet does: by making it a target for mockery. Mary and Collins in their self-aggrandizing solemnities demonstrate their unawareness of a world outside themselves. Even Jane, admirable Jane, seems a trifle boring in her relative lack of humor. The social conditions of the small world these characters inhabit might make an objective observer weep — but laughter, defensive or not, surely offers a more satisfying response.

But the book also represents immediately unattractive kinds of laughter. Miss Bingley's assertions of superiority through mockery reveal unalloyed aggressiveness. "I could hardly keep my countenance," she says, about Elizabeth's bedraggled appearance after her walk through the mud (36); she enjoys claiming social superiority by laughing at deviations from strict propriety. Lydia and Kitty laugh constantly, their mindless, grating mirth a sign of their refusal to make distinctions. Lydia laughs when she buys an ugly bonnet, laughs when she lacks money to pay a reckoning, and laughs at every detail of her own morally reprehensible elopement and marriage. The emptiness of her good humor underlines the deficiencies of her consciousness. Increasingly as the novel continues, Mr. Bennet's laughter calls attention to his abnegation of responsibility. He makes fun of his daughters' failings instead of trying to correct them; he ridicules his wife instead of confronting her folly.

It is, apparently, too late for Mr. Bennet really to change, but not too late for Elizabeth. Her growth in self-knowledge and in sensitive awareness of others manifests itself partly in her new relation to laughter. Love and laughter, it turns out, are not at first compatible. In a comic but painful scene just before Darcy's proposal, Mr. Bennet invites his favorite daughter to laugh with him over Mr. Collins's suggestion that Elizabeth and Darcy might marry. "Mr. Darcy," Mr. Bennet exclaims, "who never looks at any woman but to see a blemish, and who probably never looked at *you* in his life!" (363). This interpretation of Darcy corresponds to Elizabeth's worst fears, but she feels obliged to try "to join in her father's pleasantry" as he dwells on every comic possibility of Collins's letter, finally inquiring, as a culminating joke, whether Lady Catherine had called to refuse her consent. Elizabeth replies with the expected laugh, but the narrator comments, "Elizabeth had never been more at a loss to make her feelings appear what they were not. It was necessary to laugh, when she would rather have cried. Her father had most cruelly mortified her, by what he said of Mr. Darcy's indifference..." (364).

No longer does laughter provide an adequate defense against painful feeling, given Elizabeth's new emotions. By her intelligence and wit she has dominated most situations; now she can only wait, trying "to make her feelings appear what they were not," trying to laugh when laughter no longer tells any truth about her beyond the truth of her effort to conceal. Even when Darcy proposes once more, elevating Elizabeth at once to happiness, she finds it necessary to restrain herself — this time, to restrain her comic impulse. Darcy reveals that he has given Bingley permission to woo Jane; the text comments, "Elizabeth longed to observe that Mr. Bingley had been a most delightful friend; so easily guided that his worth was invaluable; but she checked herself. She remembered that he had yet to learn to be laught at, and it was rather too early to begin" (371). If it is good for Darcy to learn to be laughed at, it is also good for Elizabeth to learn to check herself. Laughter can become dangerous self-indulgence.

In the witty and moving and altogether wonderful letter Elizabeth writes to Mrs. Gardiner, reporting her engagement, she claims, "I am the happiest creature in the world. Perhaps other people have said so before, but not one with such justice. I am happier even than Jane; she only smiles, I laugh" (382-3). The capacity for laughter that helped to differentiate Elizabeth from Jane in the first place has been transformed into a gift of joyfulness. Elizabeth retains her talent for irony and for self-mockery, as this letter shows. But she has also learned a new way of laughing. She is ready now to live happily ever after.

All this makes a fairly simple kind of sense. One can draw easy conclusions about the novel's position on the question of laughter. Laughter allows useful defensive transformations of pain into pleasure; it records the freedom and power of a kind of wit closely allied with intelligence. Its dangers are equally clear: it evades discrimination. As Elizabeth says to Charlotte, who has just expounded her view that "Happiness in marriage is entirely a matter of chance," "You make me laugh, Charlotte; but it is not sound" (23). To distinguish the "sound" from its opposite is the fundamental ethical responsibility.

Yet this clear scheme leaves the situation of the narrator and of the reader oddly indeterminant. *Pride and Prejudice*, as every reader knows, constantly invites *us* to laugh — to laugh even at the admirable heroine, and certainly to share her laughter at the ultimately admirable hero. When, for example, Elizabeth realizes that she has misjudged Darcy by too readily trusting Wickham's version of events, she condemns herself, commenting, "Had I been in love, I could not have been more wretchedly blind" (208).We can almost hear the narrator's snicker; by this time we strongly suspect what Elizabeth — who claims, "Till this moment, I never knew myself" — cannot yet allow herself to know: that she *is*, after all, in love. A much later example, among many: Darcy and Bingley come to call on the Bennets, their feelings and motives unknown. Mrs. Bennet, of course, pursues Bingley with "officious attention." Elizabeth reacts: "At that instant she felt, that years of happiness could not make Jane or herself amends, for moments of such painful confusion." But the narrator observes, "Yet the misery, for which years of happiness were to offer no compensation, received soon afterwards material relief, from observing how much the beauty of her sister rekindled the admiration of her former lover" (337). The narrator laughs, inviting her readers to join her, at universal human frailty: not even Elizabeth is exempt.

Generations of critics by now have called attention to the complexities of Austen's narratorial stance, the air of mocking superiority with which she locates the ubiquity of self-deception. For the omnipresence of self-deceiving fantasy, one of the novelist's central themes, mockery supplies an approriate response. Yet Austen's treatment of laughter in *Pride and Prejudice* raises questions about what, exactly, the laughter she invites finally means. Laughter cuts Elizabeth off from the possibility of romance and blinds her father to other people's feelings. As readers, we too must be careful not to laugh too much. When we accept the narrator's invitation to feel superior to the novel's characters, we find ourselves unable to comprehend those characters' emotional lives. We thus resemble Mr. Bennet, who at first cannot see Elizabeth's passionate love for Darcy, and Elizabeth, who long fails to recognize Darcy's feeling for her. While Elizabeth preserves her mocking stance, she perceives in Darcy only corresponding mockery. Laughter, protecting frail mortals, can also distort their vision.

At a low point in Elizabeth's fortunes, when she realizes that Darcy is just the man to make her happy, but thinks she has lost him forever, she begins "to comprehend that he was exactly the man, who, in disposition and talents, would most suit her." At least in a first reading, this appears to be a dark moment in the narrative. The narrator comments, however, "But no such happy marriage could now teach the admiring multitude what connubial felicity really was" (312). She teases Elizabeth for her romantic fantasies and for her pride even at this moment of despair: the young woman imagines not only blissful marriage, but admiring responses to it. Yet to laugh at romance is not enough: the novel tells us that too. When Elizabeth finally achieves the marriage she has imagined, we thrill to the happy ending in spite of the fact that the text has consistently denied the possibility of perfect felicity in human experience. As readers we have been educated like the lovers: not to reject romance despite our understanding that the desire for romance may constitute, as it does for Lydia, a trap; to laugh, but not too long. We must strike a delicate balance in order to allow full emotional and intellectual space for the happy ending.

Mansfield Park raises the stakes, intensifying issues implicit in the earlier novel. Every reader can recall much laughter in *Pride and Prejudice* and in the experience of reading it — but not in *Mansfield Park*. Fanny Price doesn't laugh; the laughter of the Crawford siblings is presented as morally dubious in the extreme; and the teasing narrator now has virtually disappeared. These facts, indeed, correspond to familiar sources of critical dissatisfaction with this novel. We may miss the Jane Austen we are used to and feel uncomfortable to find wit and spontaneity now associated with ethical ambiguity and solemnity converted to an apparent index of virtue. Thinking about laughter in the book helps to illuminate the novelist's purposes and the boldness of her enterprise.

Not only does Fanny Price rarely laugh, she actually *tries not to laugh*. The point is made at least twice. Once, talking to Edmund long before he has acknowledged any tender feeling for Mary Crawford, Fanny says of Mary, "She made me almost laugh" (*MP* 64). *But,* the sentence continues, to supply the moral reservation that makes Fanny believe laughter inappropriate. Again, Fanny, at a dance, is talking with Tom Bertram, who has just made a slanderous remark about Mrs. Grant when he sees her at his elbow — a materialization making "so instantaneous a change of expression and subject necessary, as Fanny, in spite of every thing, could hardly help laughing at" (119). Similarly, she keeps *almost* laughing at Henry Crawford's verbal maneuvers — but she usually manages to refrain. When Edmund comments that life around the family hearth seems drearier since his father's return, Fanny replies that the tone has always been the same in Sir Thomas's circle. "There was never much laughing in his presence," she observes. Edmund decides that she's right, but continues to regret the lost liveliness of the Crawfords' participation. "I suppose I am graver than other people," Fanny concludes. "The evenings do not appear long to me" (197). In other words, laughter does not for her mark social pleasure.

A digression. An old friend of mine, an English comic novelist, went on a lecture tour to Finland. Over and over he presented readings of his work in progress, which he had previously thought very funny, to stony-faced Scandinavian audiences. No one ever even chuckled. His self doubt mounted ferociously, until a woman came up to him after a reading and said, "It was really terribly funny — I had all I could do to keep from laughing."

The ethos behind that comment bewilders me; it's not so hard to understand Fanny's code. Her gravity registers her unfailing commitment to understanding rather than to enjoyment. She refuses to participate in the kind of frivolity that might obscure the proper grounds of judgment. Her reluctance to laugh, in other words, belongs to aspects of her character that one must judge admirable. Still, a reader may find it difficult not to respond in rather the way my friend did to his dour audiences — difficult not to feel irritated at the rigidity, the withholding, that make part of such a refusal.

But the laughter of other characters in *Mansfield Park* helps to encourage a more sympathetic view of Fanny. Over and over one must feel the link between laughter and moral weakness. The Crawfords present easy and obvious examples. Genuinely witty though they often are — the reader, less firmly controlled than Fanny, will probably laugh with them at least occasionally — they laugh at the wrong things. A famous instance is Mary Crawford's mockery in the family chapel at Sotherton: "It must do the heads of the family a great deal of good to force all the poor housemaids and footmen to leave business and pleasure, and say their prayers here twice a day, while they are inventing excuses themselves for staying away" (86-7). Shortly after this speech, Miss Crawford learns of Edmund's intention to become a clergyman. Fanny thinks Mary will now feel distressed at what she has said; but Miss Crawford's embarrassment is fleeting. She does not learn to refrain from making fun of the clergy. Her laugh characterizes her; as she approaches Fanny through the obscuring mazes of Sotherton, Fanny recognizes her presence by her laugh.

Henry eroticizes the theme of laughter. His seductive dialogue with Maria Bertram at Sotherton dwells on the subject. Maria observes, of his behavior during the drive, "I was glad to see you so well entertained. You and Julia were laughing the whole way" (98). Henry denies any memory of what they were laughing at, but concludes,

"Your sister loves to laugh," Maria — resentfully? regretfully? provocatively? — comments, "You think her more light-hearted than I" (99). Agreeing that Julia is "more easily amused," and hence "better company," Henry manages to convert the comparison to a compliment for Maria: "there are situations in which very high spirits would denote insensibility" (99). The dialogue becomes a discussion of Maria's current emotional situation, during which she proclaims her "feeling of restraint and hardship" in her engagement to Rushworth. This conversation leads to the crucial choice of Maria to play Agatha in the Mansfield Park production of "Lovers' Vows": Henry announces that Julia's playing the part would "be the ruin of all my solemnity," since "The many laughs we have had together would infallibly come across me, and Frederick and his knapsack would be obliged to run away" (133).

Henry's use of laughter as part of his erotic tease obviously says nothing about the intrinsic value of this form of human expression. He can turn laughter and its absence equally well to his own purposes; and in fact neither Julia's laughter nor Maria's "sensibility" is innocent. Emotional inauthenticity pervades Mansfield Park. Mrs. Norris's characterization of herself as too deep in mourning to tolerate a companion, Lady Bertram's conviction that she must have missed her husband, young Tom Bertram's way of dealing with Fanny by making her "some very pretty presents" and laughing at her (18) — such aspects of life in the Bertram household call attention to the dubiousness of conventional emotional indices. Fanny's weeping seems more authentic — although since it expresses the passivity which she must learn to surmount, perhaps we may be allowed a certain irritation at it. In any case, one enjoys laughter, and accounts of laughter-provoking situations, more readily than one enjoys the spectacle of a weeper. Jane Austen as novelist manifestly knows this. *Mansfield Park* deliberately thwarts readers' desires, refusing to provide easy satisfactions, forcing one to recognize the inadequacy of enjoyment as a criterion of excellence, demanding that we take pleasure (as perhaps our forebears more readily did) in the working out of narrative strategies controlled by moral intent. Laughter's moral contamination in this novel heightens the reader's uneasiness. One feels relief at the rare references to innocent and happy laughter: for instance, when the narrator, registering Fanny's thoughts, refers to "all the laughs of playfulness which are so essential to the shade of a departed ball" (284).

Mansfield Park suggests the rarity of "laughs of playfulness" and the possible corruptions of "playfulness" itself. The most crucial laugh in this novel is only half uttered. It occurs in Mary Crawford's final conversation with Edmund. As Edmund reports it: "I imagined I saw a mixture of many feelings — a great, though short struggle — half a wish of yielding to truths, half a sense of shame — but habit, habit carried it. She would have laughed if she could. It was a sort of laugh, as she answered, 'A pretty good lecture upon my word. Was it part of your last sermon?'" (458). The habit of laughter thus becomes not merely an index of failed discrimination, like Mr. Bennet's, but a sign of active refusal to allow oneself moral insight.

It is not surprising, given the consistent association here between laughter and ethical inadequacy, that the gently mocking narrator of Austen's earlier novels has almost entirely disappeared. She emerges occasionally, in references to the progress of romance. One familiar example, near the end of the book: "I purposely abstain from dates on this occasion, that every one may be at liberty to fix their own, aware that the cure of unconquerable passions, and the transfer of unchanging attachments, must vary much as to time in different people. — I only intreat every body to believe that exactly at the time when it was quite natural that it should be so, and not a week earlier, Edmund did cease to care about Miss Crawford, and became as anxious to marry Fanny, as Fanny herself could desire" (470). This joke declares the narrator's psychological penetration and invites the reader's. "Unconquerable passions" and "unchanging attachments" belong to fictions of romance, not to human experience; the narrator endorses the actual at the expense of the ideal. Her deflating laughter hints a moral norm and declares an end to the emotional extremities that have marked this novel.

But such jokes are rare in *Mansfield Park*. We may laugh at Mr. Rushworth, obsessed with his pink satin costume, at Mrs. Norris making off with the green baize from the stage curtain, at Lady Bertram in her unassailable moral and physical lassitude — laugh, in other words, at less benign follies than that of believing in "unconquerable passions" and "unchanging attachments." Yet the narrator's tone often sounds sharp in relation to such folly — which, after all, has for Fanny Price effects almost as destructive as vice could have.

The distinction between vice and folly, however, constitutes a crucial aspect of Austen's subject. Unlike the other novels, *Mansfield Park* places vicious impulse and behavior close to the center of the action and allows them more serious consequences than, say, Wickham's seductions have. "Let other pens dwell on guilt and misery," the narrator commands (461). But guilt and misery supply part of the subject here, as they have not done before. The new attitude toward laughter reflects this fact. If one allows oneself to laugh at other people, one runs the danger of laughing at the wrong things — of becoming not only a Mr. Bennet (who, after all, does not laugh at Lydia's elopement) but, far more seriously, a Mary Crawford. The novelist draws back from the danger. Without enjoying guilt and misery as subjects, she acknowledges their existence and that of the vice that generates them. Her moral alliance with Fanny Price as character expresses itself most vividly in the refusal she shares with Fanny: the refusal to risk laughing at what should be condemned. She thus textually dramatizes the central issues of *Mansfield Park*.

But she appears to have arrived at a narrative impasse. If laughter is too dangerous to be risked more than occasionally, what becomes of the comic novelist? Working out an answer to that question in *Emma*, she establishes a more complicated view of laughter, discriminating clearly between its acceptable and unacceptable modes.

"Universally," Thomas Hobbes writes, "the passion of laughter is sudden self-commendation resulting from a stranger's unseemliness. ... One doth not laugh, however, at the unseemliness of friends and kindred, since they are not strangers. Therefore there are three things conjoined that move one to laughter: unseemliness, strangers, and suddenness" (Hobbes 59). This view of laughter foretells Freud's theory of jokes, with its emphasis on the aggressive component of wit. But Hobbes also helps to locate Austen's new emphasis, in *Emma*, on laughter as self-aggrandizement. Friends' unseemliness, however, serves as well as strangers' to provoke laughter in and about Highbury.

Emma probably contains as much laughter as does *Pride and Prejudice* — though laughter of a less entertaining variety. The painful scene in which Emma laughs at Miss Bates, the novel's moral and dramatic climax, exists in a complex context of previous representations of social laughter. People laugh in *Emma* for diverse reasons. Not infrequently, Emma herself laughs when nothing funny has been said. She talks with Knightley about Harriet's refusal of Robert Martin; Knightley realizes that Emma has been matchmaking, suspects her of plotting about Mr. Elton, and warns her that "if Elton is the man, I think it will be all labour in vain" (*Emma* 66). Emma laughs before uttering her disclaimers. Similarly, when Harriet wonders why the charming Miss Woodhouse is not married or about to be, Emma laughs, then claims her disinclination for wifehood. Such episodes reveal laughter as emotional disguise. Emma's artificial and nervous mirth attempts to characterize as no more than a laughing matter the issue just raised. Her laughter insists that all situations remain under her control; often it signals her need to preserve hierarchy with herself at the apex.

The narrator often solicits readers' laughter at her characters in this novel: especially stupid Harriet, self-obsessed Mr. Woodhouse, the blind, smug Eltons. Moreover, we have abundant opportunities to laugh at Emma herself — also capable of blindness and smugness and of her own forms of stupidity and self-obsession. Consider, for example, the opening of Chapter 11: "Mr. Elton must now be left to himself. It was no longer in Emma's power to superintend his happiness or quicken his measures. ... She hardly wished to have more leisure for [the lovers: i.e., Elton and Harriet]. There are people, who the more you do for them, the less they will do for themselves" (91). As so often in this fiction, the narrator uses Emma's own language and point of view against her. The comic conjunction of the pragmatic verb *superintend* with the abstract noun *happiness*, the force of the self-congratulating cliche about people's unwillingness to help themselves: such devices make us chuckle at the sublime self-satisfaction of Emma's unawareness.

The Box Hill episode contains much laughter. Frank and Emma flirt ostentatiously, but Emma's gaiety, as she herself recognizes, is fraudulent. "She laughed because she was disappointed" (368): a typical form of disguise. In response to Mr. Knightley's penetrating question — "Is Miss Woodhouse sure that she would like to hear what we are all thinking of?" — Emma, also typically, laughs "as carelessly as she could" (369), claiming the ease and control that in fact she lacks. The game that Frank initiates turns on Emma's proclaimed willingness to laugh at what people say, and she finds "a great deal to laugh at and enjoy" in the "very indifferent piece of wit" that first issues from the participants' efforts (371). Her mockery of

Miss Bates belongs to an atmosphere in which laughter has been declared the sign of power.

As Mr. Knightley's rebuke makes clear, laughter in fact marks moral insufficiency. The semiotics of laughter keeps shifting in this novel, as various characters try to control it; and the reader is troublingly involved in unraveling the sign system. For we too have laughed at Miss Bates, and the narrator has repeatedly encouraged us to do so. Miss Bates's monologues perhaps provide the novel's most memorable comedy. Readers invariably remember them, not in detail (no one could remember what Miss Bates says in detail) but in the effect of abundant vitality her non-sequential outpourings create. And many readers confess to laughing also at Emma's insult.

Why is it all right for us to laugh at Miss Bates and not for Emma to do so? The answers may seem obvious. For one thing, Emma's sin depends on the actual presence of her victim. As Mr. Knightley has pointed out earlier in the novel, "We all know the difference between the pronouns he or she and thou, the plainest-spoken amongst us; we all feel the influence of a something beyond common civility in our personal intercourse with each other — a something more early implanted" (286). What we say *to* someone else can never have the freedom of what we say *of* the person in his or her absence. Yet more apparent is the distinction between characters in a book and people in real life: one hardly feels morally culpable for mocking those who exist only by virtue of words on a page. But Knightley's reminder of social class and status raises issues relevant to readers as well as to conversationalists. The use of laughter for "self-commendation," to return to Hobbes's phrase, involves subtle manipulations of power. The satisfactions of the text, when that text provides targets of mockery, include vicarious experience of power. Allowed to participate imaginatively both in Emma's ridicule and in Knightley's rebuke, the reader doubly enjoys an illusion of superiority. And Austen's narrator, in *Emma*, repeatedly directs attention to the reader's moral implication in problems worked out through the narrative.

Knightley's comment, like Hobbes's, invokes subtleties of the social contract. Because Emma already holds a position of power relative to Miss Bates, she must not call attention to it. And because she accepts the conventions of friendship as governing her relations with the tedious, impoverished woman, she must not react to Miss Bates as she might respond to a stranger, indulging in self-commendation at the expense of another. "Something ... early implanted" — something essential to the nature of civilized human beings — demands generosity and empathy, not just civility, in face-to-face contact. By laughing at Miss Bates, not only in her presence but in a situation where others will witness the woman's humiliation, Emma has violated fundamental human obligation.

She has also focused attention on a point that the novel emphasizes in various ways: laughter, often, gratifies selfish needs (for readers and writers as well as characters: and Emma, of course, in her passion for inventing and interpreting fictions, adumbrates both). The laughter of this novel does not typically, as in *Pride and Prejudice*, reflect failure to discriminate; nor does it resemble the worst laughter of *Mansfield Park*, that which betrays active refusal of moral obligation. It constitutes self-indulgence — dangerous, not evil. Unwillingness to laugh, on the other hand — Mr. Woodhouse's utter inability to see a joke — signals its own sort of self-indulgence: reluctance to exert oneself to appreciate another's playfulness or wit, to respond to a fresh perspective. To put the implications more generally: even the most apparently trivial emotional response or non-response, in Austen's universe, has moral meaning.

The new perception about laughter in *Emma* also consolidates thematic hints of the earlier novels. As in *Mansfield Park*, laughter here can constitute moral evasion; as in *Pride and Prejudice*, it can also indicate moral penetration. The danger lies in the human tendency to take self-flattering views: people believe themselves engaged in penetration (as Mr. Bennet often does) when in fact they use laughter as avoidance (as does Mr. Bennet). *Emma* demonstrates the extreme difficulty of avoiding self-deception.

Awareness of laughter's function as self-aggrandizement, a momentary declaration of control or of superiority, may suggest how Austen manipulates the subtle comic effects of this novel: for instance, in the climactic moment of the proposal scene: "What did she say? — Just what she ought, of course. A lady always does" (431). John Halperin refers to the "dreary technique" by which Austen tells rather than shows what happens; he observes, of this sequence, "Again the writer avoids the direct depiction of strong feelings; again an ending disappoints" (Halperin 278). It certainly doesn't disappoint *me*: I think it's funny. The three short sentences exemplify not Austen's refusal to satisfy her readers but her generosity in offering readers something they do not expect. The joke startles by its unexpectedness, and, like other jokes in *Emma*, it invites the responder's sense of superiority. It suggests that Emma, in a pinch, falls back on convention to govern her behavior. We laugh because we expect that a situation so intensely emotional as a proposal will elicit spontaneity, immediacy: not propriety. Imagining that we ourselves in similar circumstances would behave differently, we may fleetingly foster our own self-esteem at Emma's expense. Or possibly at the novelist's expense, for the joke also involves novelistic conventions and the narrator's awareness of their powerful grip.

The very end of *Emma* brings another joke about convention: Mrs. Elton's reaction to Emma's wedding. "Mrs. Elton, from the particulars detailed by her husband, thought it all extremely shabby, and very inferior to her own. — 'Very little white satin, very few lace veils; a most pitiful business! — Selina would stare when she heard of it'" (484). We laugh to hear a wedding judged by such superficial and conventional standards. But what are we to make of the sentence after this one, the novel's conclusion: "But, in spite of these deficiencies, the wishes, the hopes, the confidence, the predictions of the small band of true friends who witnessed the ceremony, were fully answered in the perfect happiness of the union"? "Perfect happiness" belongs also to the realm of convention: of romantic literary convention. John Halperin wants to know what Emma says when Mr. Knightley proposes partly because he has read other novels that provide such information. Readers in general want to believe in the perfect happiness of fictional characters because the possibility of perfect happiness is one of the satisfactions fiction uniquely offers. *Pride and Prejudice* encourages us to partake of this fantasy; but *Emma* calls new issues to the reader's attention. Having allowed us to achieve "self-commendation" by feeling superior to those who rely on convention, does Austen's narrator indulge in a final joke, allowing her own self-commendation at our expense: because we too like to rely on convention in fiction? One can never be sure, reading Jane Austen, where the next joke is coming from — or what, exactly, it means.

Works Cited

Austen, Jane. *Emma*. Volume 4 of The Novels of Jane Austen. Ed. R.W. Chapman. 3rd ed. Oxford: Oxford UP, 1933.

———. *Mansfield Park*. Volume 3 of The Novels of Jane Austen. Ed. R.W. Chapman. 3rd ed. Oxford: Oxford UP, 1934.

———. *Pride and Prejudice*. Vol. 2 of The Novels of Jane Austen. Ed. R.W. Chapman. 3rd ed. Oxford: Oxford UP, 1932.

Halperin, John. *The Life of Jane Austen*. Baltimore: Johns Hopkins UP, 1984.

Hobbes, Thomas. *De Homine*. Translated by Charles T. Wood. In *Man and Citizen*. Ed. Bernard Gert. Garden City: Doubleday, 1972.

Deflation of male pretensions in Fanny Burney's *Cecilia*

KAY ROGERS

Brooklyn College, City University of New York

THE FIRST SIGNIFICANT scene in Fanny Burney's *Evelina* shows the heroine sitting in a ballroom while men walk by, looking her over and deciding whether or not to ask her to dance; her choice, meanwhile, is between accepting the first man who offers or abstaining from dancing altogether. This scene accurately represents Evelina's situation throughout the novel, as she is eyed, seized, and coveted by men; as she waits, unable even to make inquiries, to learn whether Lord Orville loves her and whether her father will acknowledge her as his.

Burney placed her next heroine, Cecilia, in what seems to be an entirely different situation. Cecilia is extraordinarily independent for a young woman of the eighteenth century. She is twenty years old, accustomed to society, experienced enough to have reliable judgment — hence free of "the timid fears of total inexperience, and ... the bashful feelings of shamefaced awkwardness" (1:30) which inhibit Evelina. She has no parents or guardians to whom she has emotional ties and thus no one whom she feels obligated to obey. Most important, she has plenty of money; Burney subtitled the book *Memoirs of an Heiress*. Attractive as well as rich, she can marry as she likes, and she does not have to marry anyone. Early in the book, she resolves to take charge of her life and forms a rational plan: she will drop "all idle and uninteresting acquaintance," choose her friends, devote as much time as she likes to music and reading, and share her superfluous income with carefully chosen, deserving people in need

(1:73-74). Surely this is a young woman who, unlike Evelina, has the internal and external resources to control her own life.

But in fact her situation turns out to be essentially the same.

Her uncle, the Dean, left her plenty of money, but left control of it and of herself to three guardians. He chose them with care and the best intentions, but it did not occur to him to consult her, the person for whose benefit they were chosen. They are Mr. Harrel, a dissipated man of fashion; Mr. Briggs, a vulgar miser; and the Honorable Mr. Delvile, a haughty aristocrat. Briggs, who controls the money, refuses to advance her six hundred pounds of her own, because "girls knew nothing of the value of money, and ought not to be trusted with it." "Her uncle had left her a noble estate," and Briggs will conscientiously do his duty as guardian by taking "care to see it put in proper hands, by getting her a good and careful husband" (1:241-42). The other two guardians are equally intent on marrying her off — Harrel to a worthless friend who needs her money, and Delvile to an inane young lord. All three assume that she cannot wait to be married and cannot find her own man, and that her preferences, or indeed any personal qualifications of her prospective husband, are of no importance. The will further stipulates that she must live with one of her three guardians, all of whose life styles she detests; at Harrel's house, the least unpleasant of the three, she is perpetually involved in boring, empty socializing. The will also stipulates that she will lose her fortune if she marries a man who refuses to give up his surname for hers. Of course it turns out that the man she loves, Delvile's son, Mortimer, refuses to make this sacrifice. In the end, she gets the man but gives up the money; so the heiress is reduced to the same economic dependence as an ordinary woman. Burney's plot dramatizes the subjection of women — as they lose control of their money at marriage and are devalued in the family because inordinate importance was attached to the surname, which they could not carry. Cecilia is set up to do what most women could not do, to keep her name after marrying. The result? — she loses name as well as fortune.

It is a depressing fable — or it would be if Burney had not managed to turn hopelessness and frustration into humor. Prevented by internal as well as external inhibitions from rebelling openly against men's control of women's lives or from deconstructing the rationale for their authority, she turned to the perennial resource of a subject class — laughter. Making explicit what is implicit in patriarchal society —

namely, that women are reduced to being wards of men — she placed her mature, sensible heroine under three male guardians not one of whom is qualified to control anyone. Burney cannot realistically dispel their actual power, but she can relieve her own and her readers' feelings by showing how ludicrously undeserving they are.

Irresponsible Harrel is more contemptible than amusing. But Burney's deflation of pompous Delvile, the representative of a patriarchal aristocracy, is extremely funny. Delvile is sublimely convinced that he is an important, a superior, and a busy person. Why? — because he is accustomed to being deferred to. He talks constantly of being "overwhelmed with business," but that business typically consists of giving a few directions to his servants (3:65). He believes himself "surrounded by people who can do nothing without my orders" (2:268-69), when in fact everyone wishes he would stay out of their way. Burney misses no opportunity to contrast Delvile's pretensions to awe-inspiring power with his actual inability to impress anyone, nor to show his pomposity deflated by his own need to assert his dignity. When he descends upon a middle-class mother in hopes of discovering scandal about her son and Cecilia, he will not deign to divulge his name. When she lets drop some rumor about "old Mr. Delvile," he cuts her off with indignation — how can ordinary people presume to talk of him? She innocently protests, "I don't care for my part if I never mention the old gentleman's name again! I never heard any good of him in my life, for they say he's as proud as Lucifer, and nobody knows what it's of, for they say — " "*They* say?" he shouts, "and who are *they*?" "Lord, every body, Sir! it's his common character." All he can do is sputter, "Then everybody is extremely indecent ... to pay no more respect to one of the first families in England" (4:117).

Cecilia initially calls on Delvile to get him to intercede with Briggs so he will give her some of her own money to pay her bookseller's bill and cover a debt for a friend. As Delvile impresses on her how burdensome his guardianship is, because of his weighty social and business obligations, his "haughty affability" chills her into reserve. But since he interprets this as timid veneration, he is "equally pleased with himself for inspiring, and with her for feeling it" (1:130-31). When at last she gets an opportunity to mention her money, Delvile instructs her that a young lady has no need for books, since her future husband will have collected a library, and goes on to reprove her for taking on a debt without consulting him, for he had assured her his opinion was always at her service when she was "in any dilemma". Then, with gracious condescension, he points out that Briggs has always been in charge of her money and refers her right back to him (1:249-50).

Delvile is equally condescending and useless when Cecilia asks him to intervene with her other guardian, Harrel, who has been trying to push her into the arms of the odious Sir Robert Floyer. Her desperate appeal prompts him first to remark that Harrel's "father was the son of a steward of Mr. Grant, who lived in the neighbourhood of my friend and relation the Duke of Derwent," secondly to deplore the late Dean's impropriety in naming Harrel and Briggs as coadjutors with him, thirdly to congratulate himself on his readiness, in spite of this, to offer his counsel and instruction to the Dean's niece, and fourthly, to pronounce that Harrel, "ought certainly to have desired Sir Robert Floyer to acquaint me with his proposals before he gave to him any answer" (2:101-2). This is all the help he offers.

Delvile's self-importance is based on familial as well as social position: he expects the same awe-filled deference from wife and son as he does from the lower orders. Burney pointedly plays him off against Mrs. Delvile, who shares his social eminence but, unlike him, has corresponding natural qualities to support it. She too is arrogant, but she has reason to feel superior to everyone: for she *is* superior. Hence she is amenable to rational persuasion and comes to approve Mortimer's marriage to Cecilia. Because she is reasonable, but also because a woman cannot have the bland assured domination of the patriarch, she retains a sense of proportion: she can see comic incongruity in a situation which provokes her husband to simple outrage. Women can, of course, be as pompous as men; but society does not support their pretensions as it does those of the male ruling class.

Mrs. Delvile rigorously excludes stupid people from her company — except of course for the head of her household. She deals with him by avoiding him as much as possible, opposing "him in nothing when his pleasure was made known, but" forbearing "to enquire into his opinion except in cases of necessity" (2:314). And yet all the while, Mr. Delvile never doubts that he enjoys her unquestioning respectful obedience and that of their son. He is surprised even more than aggrieved when his wife urges him to consent to Mortimer's marriage: "I had been willing to hope the affair over from the time my disapprobation of it was formally announced." He threatens Mortimer with his "eternal displeasure" if he attempts to discuss this subject further: "it is no news, I flatter myself, to Mortimer Delvile or his mother, that I do nothing without reason" (4:167-68). In fact, he does nothing *with* reason: everyone around him can see that he is too governed by prejudice and emotion to be capable of clear thinking (see, e.g., his son's analysis, 4:169). Through Delvile, Burney undermines the moral foundation of patriarchy: namely, that senior males are more rational than women or young people, so that it is for everyone's good that they govern society.

Briggs, the third guardian, is a comic miser — overdrawn, unfortunately, since Burney never could contain herself when demonstrating her horror of vulgarity. But he is very funny when played off against Delvile. It takes his crudity to tell off Delvile as he needs to be told off. Cecilia has moved in with the Delviles and is about to leave with them for their castle in the country. Briggs stumps in, indignant because he has laid out a few shillings in preparation for her coming to stay with him. (She has told him plainly she cannot live in his squalid home, but of course he has not heard a word she said.) Mrs. Delvile soon figures out what is going on, is amused, and returns to her chair. But Mr. Delvile stands transfixed with contempt for Briggs's vulgarity. Briggs goes on to abuse him for expensive display which he cannot afford. Delvile will not lower himself to speak to Briggs, but gives him a look intended to petrify him. Briggs goes right on jeering at Delvile's absurd pride of family — "all them old grandfathers and aunts you brag of; a set of poor souls you won't let rest in their coffins." Though Delvile is enraged, he will not lower himself by continuing the argument. But since his "dignity, that constant object of his thoughts and his cares, had received a wound from this attack which he had not the sense to despise," he could talk of nothing, throughout the journey to the country, "but the extreme impropriety of which the Dean ... had been guilty, in ... leaguing him with a *person* so coarse and disgraceful" (2:303,306). Despite her hatred of vulgarity, Burney shows the self-made man, who has at least the ability to make money, coming off better than the man whose distinction comes from no intrinsic quality whatsoever.

Two additional male authority figures are deflated in the book, Mr. Albany, the moralist, and Mr. Hobson, the well-fed businessman. Hobson is totally pleased with himself because he has made a lot of money. He assumes that he has done so through outstanding ability, though his conversation reveals a decidedly limited intellect, and that women's minds are beneath consideration because they do not understand business. Thus Burney shows how modern commercial values, in a society that excludes women from business, lead to disparaging them as empty-headed. Hobson urges Cecilia to marry right away, for let a lady "be worth never so much, she's a mere nobody, as one may say, till she can get herself a husband, being she knows nothing of business, and is made to pay for every thing through the nose" (4:247). Convinced that the successful businessman is well qualified to speak at length on every subject, and equally convinced that everyone wants to hear his wisdom, he constantly treats the company with long-winded truisms like, "the best way to thrive in the world is to get money; but how is it to be got? Why, by business: for business is to money, what fine words are to a lady, sure road to success. Now I don't mean by this to be censorious upon the ladies, being they have nothing else to go by." They are not responsible for their ignorance of all that is important, he kindly acknowledges: "when they are taken in by rogues and sharpers, the fault is all in the law, for making no proviso against their having money in their own hands" (4:255). By making Hobson such a fool, despite his success and the occasional common sense of his remarks, Burney undermines confidence in the values of the world he represents, in which women could not claim competence. Being able to make money does not carry with it the rationality and moral worth which justify rule, any more than being born the heir to a noble family.

Albany is a philanthropist who constantly berates Cecilia for failing to do her duty; he has the highest possible motives, but he is sublimely oblivious to the practical constraints within which she must operate. Forced by her uncle's will to live with the Harrels, and forced by the Harrels into incessant socializing, she is also constrained by the general pressure on women to conform, to comply with the people around them. Women, especially young ones, were not only trapped in social circumstances they could not control, but blamed as unwomanly if they criticized or tried to change them. Yet men like Albany insisted on judging them by abstract standards of right. When he hails her, "why didst thou fail me? ... thou thing of fair professions! thou inveigler of esteem! thou vain, delusive promiser of pleasure!" (4:44), we recognize the familiar aggrieved tone of a man disappointed in his unrealistic expectations of woman. Albany is one of a long line of male critics who have reviled women for deceit and flattery in a society which forced them to accommodate to men.

When Albany catches Cecilia with a dissipated crowd in a public place, it does not occur to him to question whether she wants to be with them (she does not). He just shouts indignantly, "Canst thou not one short moment spare from the tumultuous folly which encircles thee?" When she whispers that she would be happy to listen to him if there were not so many witnesses, he declaims, "Whence ... these vain and superficial distinctions? Do you not dance in public? ... Do you not dress to be admired ...? Why then this fantastical scruple, unjustified by reason ...? Oh slaves of senseless contradiction! Oh feeble followers of yet feebler prejudice!" (2:81-82) He is much too idealistic to think about what happened to women who defied social prejudice. Albany's detachment from Cecilia's reality, and his self-centeredness, become even more apparent in a later scene. Just at the moment when Cecilia has given up hope of ever again seeing the man she loves, Albany arrives to demand her attention. Before long he is telling her that her sorrow is "extacy" compared to his and opening his wounds so that she will feel sorry for him instead of herself (4:8-9).

Finally, in one delightful scene, Burney brings these four wise mentors together — the traditional aristocrat, the preacher, and the two representatives of the rising power of money. Cecilia has come of age and is eager to conclude her business with her two remaining guardians. After keeping her in suspense for three days, Delvile finally appoints the exact time when Briggs must appear, as Delvile is much too busy "to stay above three minutes" (4:43). Briggs, who really is a man of business, arrives early, and seizes the opportunity to press Cecilia to let him manage her money until she marries. At this point Hobson comes in to inquire officiously about a mutual acquaintance, and soon he and Briggs are wrangling about the proper use of riches. Briggs takes pride in saving every penny he can, while Hobson takes equal pride in the comfortable living which his success has made possible.

As Briggs and Hobson quarrel over whether a successful businessman should or should not indulge in oysters, Albany bursts in: "Once more I come to prove thy sincerity; now wilt thou go with me where sorrow calls thee?" She cannot, of course, since she will not be able to get the guardians together again. But Albany notices only that she has failed him again: 'what wanton trifling!" he exclaims, "why shouldst thou thus elate a worn-out mind, only to make it feel its lingering credulity?" The bemused Hobson asks whether Albany has ever been on the stage — perhaps he is repeating a speech from a play. "'Is it but on the stage humanity exists?' cried Albany indignantly; "Oh, thither hasten, then, ye monopolizers of plenty! ye selfish, unfeeling engrossers of wealth ...' 'As to engrossing,' said Mr. Hobson, happy to hear at last a word with which he was familiar, 'it's what I never approved myself. My maxim is this: if a man makes a fair penny, without any underhand dealings, why he has as much a title to enjoy his pleasure as the Chief Justice. ... Though what I hold to be best of all, is a clear conscience with a neat income of two or three thousand a year" (4:68,71-72). For Hobson the two are closely, if not causally, related.

The three men go on debating the proper use of money, each one convinced his is the only sensible point of view. Albany's may be morally right, but it is rendered ridiculous by his high-flown language, especially as this is played against the prosiness of Hobson and the crudity of Briggs. Briggs would send every beggar to Bridewell and insists they break their own legs to cheat rich people of cash. Albany declaims, "Poor subterfuge of callous cruelty!" Hobson proses, "I am not a near man ... but ... I have as good a right to my own savings, as to my own gettings; and what I say is this, who'll give to *me*? let me see that, and it's quite another thing" (4:74).

Finally the busy Mr. Delvile arrives. Without greeting anyone or apologizing for his lateness, he advances in his usual stately manner and ponderously explains his motives for coming. His speech, Burney comments, "was directly addressed to no one, though meant to be attended to by every one, and seemed proudly uttered as a mere apology to himself for not having declined the meeting." Interpreting the resulting "silence as the effect of his awe-inspiring presence," Delvile is becoming more affable, until Briggs begins to bait him. He facetiously tells Hobson to go down on his knees before "'Squire High and Mighty," and Hobson solemnly explains why that would not be appropriate. Delvile and Briggs are practically coming to blows when Cecilia — who has been standing by during all these debates in helpless silence — begs Briggs to be appeased so they can finish their business. Albany declaims against "unmeaning dissension," and Hobson puts in a long speech to the effect that "quarreling's a thing I don't uphold, being it advances one no way" (4:76-79).

At last they leave, and Delvile and Briggs settle Cecilia's business in five minutes. But only after four male egos have expressed themselves for over an hour. Macaulay singled out this scene for praise, but criticized the contrivance that brought these "four old fools" into a room together (605). It *is* contrived on the realistic level, but there is symbolic justification for bringing together these various representatives of male power over women. Wildly different as they are, they agree in their priorities — as they pursue their preoccupations, oblivious to a woman's eagerness to complete business essential to her. This book dramatizes the subjection of women in a patriarchal society — and every man in it is undisciplined, irresponsible, wrong-headed, or stupid.

The male average is higher in Burney's other three novels, though they too have their share of foolish or irresponsible men. Those three, however, are dominated by worthy male mentors, who would seem to support patriarchy. These figures reflect Burney's idolization of her father, which had a pernicious effect on her art as well as her life. Even in *Cecilia*, her awe toward anyone resembling a good father often diverts her portrayal of Albany from the cutting satire it might have been into sentimental grandiosity. Some of Burney's contemporaries who shared her resentment of men who pass judgment on women and tell them what to do were able to express it with less ambivalence. Elizabeth Inchbald presents two admirable priests in *A Simple Story*, but she delicately ridicules both the self-righteousness and domineering of these holy men and their unawareness of these shortcomings. Charlotte Smith fills her books with stupid men who sneer at women because women lack professional training — from shyster lawyers who refuse to talk business with women to clergymen who expect to be venerated simply because they have got through the university and figured out how to please the local bishop. These writers were keenly aware of male patronage and domination, but in general not prepared to attack directly either the fact of male authority or its theoretical rationale. What they did do was notice the weaknesses of those who assumed they ruled by right of natural wisdom and virtue. Sober presentation of this theme could produce works that were powerful, but also depressing and flawed, such as Mary Wollstonecraft's *Maria: or The Wrongs of Woman* or Burney's own *The Wanderer*. It was more effective artistically to highlight comically the discrepancy between the pretensions of patriarchal theory and the inadequacies of actual individual patriarchs.

Works cited

Burney, Frances. *Cecilia: or, Memoirs of an Heiress*. London: T. Cadell, W. Davies, and T. Payne, 1809. 4 vols.

Macaulay, Thomas Babington. "Madame d'Arblay." *Critical and Historical Essays*. Everyman's Library. London: Dent, 1907.

Sylvia

NICOLE HOLLANDER

Frances Miriam Whitcher: social satire in the age of gentility

LINDA A. MORRIS

University of California, Davis

THE SENECA FALLS convention of 1848 is now widely regarded as the birthplace of the woman's rights movement in America. With only two weeks notice, 300 women and men traveled to this small village in upstate New York where they debated for two days the merits of a document — the Declaration of Sentiments and Resolutions — drawn up and introduced to the convention by Elizabeth Cady Stanton and Lucretia Mott. Echoing the Declaration of Independence, the Seneca Falls document responded to what its authors called the degradation of women in American society. The solutions they posited in their resolutions were overtly and specifically political — they called for changes in the political system, including the enfranchisement of women, and they declared of "no authority" all unjust laws that stood in the way of women's full equality with men. By the time the convention adjourned, 100 of the 300 present had signed the Declaration and agreed to convene again two weeks later in Rochester, New York. Much to the signers' surprise, the press greeted their actions with hostility and ridicule so disparaging that a number of women subsequently withdrew their endorsement for the Declaration; the majority, however, remained steadfast (Buhle and Buhle 97).

Five months later, in December of 1848, a different group of women also came in for harsh criticism in the press; this time, however, the women were not early feminists but rather the participants of a sewing society in Elmira, New York. The form this particular criticism took was a satiric story published anonymously in *Godey's Lady's Book* and written by Miriam Whitcher, the wife of an Elmira Episcopal minister. On the face of it, the events in Elmira had no connection to the earlier events in Seneca Falls, in spite of the geographical and temporal proximity of the two, but upon closer examination the two had much in common. Whitcher, in her satire, was responding to the same social ills that prompted the convening of the Seneca Falls convention: she was motivated by a similar desire to change society's ways, and her writing was charged with a deeply felt indignation.

Unlike the Seneca Falls participants, however, Miriam Whitcher did not perceive the social malaise to be a political problem with a potential political solution. Instead, she seemed to hold women responsible for their own degradation and to see social satire as a means through which she might make women aware of the foolishness of their behaviour; i.e., humor became a potential corrective for society's ills. Indeed, Whitcher was by no means a feminist — one of the targets of her humor in an early sketch is a woman's rights advocate — yet the personal indignation and frustration that inform her humor originated in the same quarter as did the feminist movement: women's increasingly restricted role in mid-nineteenth-century American society. These restrictions, which have received considerable scholarly attention in recent years, warrant only a brief summary here.[1]

As the predominant farming and mercantile modes of production in the Northeastern states began to give way in the 1820s and '30s to an industrial-capitalist economy, women were increasingly relegated to the private or domestic "sphere" and cut off from the public world of their fathers, husbands, sons and brothers.[2] Whereas women had once been central to the family economy, as farmers, as producers of essential commodities for the family, as workers in home industry, by mid-century many native-born women, especially those in towns and cities, no longer viewed themselves as significant contributors to their local or family economies. It was in this era that the "Cult of True Womanhood" emerged, and in this era that women's power began to reside chiefly in their ability to "influence" men. Newly deemed the moral superiors of men, they were increasingly charged with the responsibilities of rearing and educating children and creating homes that served as havens for their men when they returned each day from the admittedly tainted world of commerce. As men gained greater wealth, women became more active consumers, and their homes and their bodies became the show pieces for their family's financial success. The values of gentility began to conflict with the values of domesticity, and women became increasingly idle and peripheral. Ironically, then, but not coincidentally, women faced a world of shrinking opportunities at the very time when political and economic doors opened wider for white males from all classes of society.

One possible response to these restrictions was to attempt, through political activity, to change the conditions that gave rise to them in the first place; this was the alternative pursued by the woman's rights movement as symbolized by the Seneca Falls convention of 1848. Another response was the one introduced by Miriam Whitcher, who sought to change the *effects* of these restrictions by persuading women to alter their behavior. Her humor decried women's preoccupation with the latest fashions, their meanspiritedness, their lack of charity toward others, their propensity to fill their days with useless and malicious gossip, to name only a few of the targets of her satire.

Whitcher was not the first woman writer to focus on a manifestation of the society's ills rather than its origins in the political arena. Jane Austen, for example, was keenly critical of the frivolity of idle women's behavior, while George Eliot, in "Silly Novels by Lady Novelists," took to task a whole host of women novelists for their "busy idleness":

> The standing apology for women who become writers without any special qualification is, that society shuts them out from other spheres of occupation. Society is a very culpable entity, and has to answer for the manufacture of many unwholesome commodities, from bad pickles to bad poetry. But society, like "matter," and Her Majesty's Government, and other lofty abstractions, has its share of excessive blame as well as excessive praise. Where there is one woman who writes from necessity, we believe there are three women who write from vanity; and besides, there is something so antiseptic in the mere healthy fact of working for one's bread, that the most trashy and rotten kind of feminine literature is not likely to have been produced under such circumstances. "In all labour there is profit"; but ladies' silly novels, we imagine, are less the result of labour than of busy idleness. (218-19)

As surely as the women of Seneca Falls hoped through their political actions to correct the social and political inequalities they perceived, Miriam Whitcher used her social satire as a forum through which women might "see" themselves and mend their ways. As the feminists quickly learned, calling attention to a social wrong was no assurance that it would be cured; if one lone voice could have made such a difference, however, it might well have been Whitcher's.

Frances Miriam Berry (known to her family and friends as Miriam) was born November 1, 1813, in Whitesboro, New York, a small village in Oneida county in the midst of what has come to be called "the burned-over district," the setting for America's "Second Great Awakening" (Cross). One of eleven children (four others died in infancy), Whitcher remained a resident of her father's household for thirty five years, until 1847, when she married the pastor of the newly founded St. John's Episcopal Church, the Rev. Benjamin William Whitcher. The Whitesboro of Whitcher's childhood and young adulthood was extraordinarily lively, and the Berry family home, a popular inn that faced the village green, offered a perfect perspective from which to observe all the local activities. As the historian Mary Ryan has demonstrated, in the decade following the completion of the Erie Canal (1825-1835), Oneida County experienced great social turbulence. "It was in Oneida County, New York, that Charles Grandison Finney first practiced those 'new measures' that have come to identify the modern evangelical tradition. It was in Oneida County, and pre-eminently Whitestown and Utica, that the fires of revivalism kindled a fervent campaign to rid the world of intemperance, slavery, prostitution, profanity, Sabbath breaking, and nearly every sin a seventh-generation Puritan-turned-Victorian was capable of imagining" (*Middle Class* 11). In 1832, Whitcher herself became a convert at one of Finney's Whitesboro revivals and joined the local Presbyterian church (O'Donnell 13).

The women of the county and of the town of Whitesboro were unusually active during this period, with female moral reform societies of every persuasion abounding in the county. By 1835, even Whitesboro with its population of only 5,000 had at least one such society with 40 members (Ryan, *Middle Class* 117). Women steadily outnumbered men at revival meetings during this period (Johnson), while in their own single-sex societies or associations, they could "band together to defend their homes" against the perceived threats posed by rapid economic change and what Ryan calls a "morally suspicious commercial culture." Through these societies women could use their "influence" in a socially accepted manner — to the community's advantage — and they could recapture, at least temporarily, some of their lost sense of importance to the society at large. "It was in the association, in other words, that the Oneidans of the 1830s and 1840s worked out their (collective) family problems" (Ryan, *Middle Class* 237).

During these same tumultuous years, Whitesboro hosted meetings by representatives of every current fad or cause, from phrenology at the one extreme to abolition at the other. Whitcher herself became an active member in a literary group called "The Moeonian Society," and while she professed to being a shy and lonely person, she was bold enough to read her early burlesque sketches aloud to this society, then published them in the newspaper of nearby Rome, New York, under the title "The Widow Spriggins."[3] Toward the end of this period, she also began to publish her most famous stories in *Neal's Saturday Gazette*, a Philadelphia publication. These sketches, all presented through the Widow Bedott's perspective and in her own language, poke fun at nearly every facet of village life and at the widow herself in her relentless search for a husband. In an 1846 sketch, for example, the widow pursues the recently widowed Timothy Crane to a lecture by a traveling phrenologist named Mr. Vanderbump. Fascinated by Mr. Vanderbump's display of plaster heads, the widow offers this version of his phrenology lecture to a friend who arrives late:

But that are head that sets aside o' the commentater — the one that's got such a danglin' under lip and flat forrid and runs out to such a pint behind — that's old mother O'Killem, the Irish woman that murdered so many folks — she was an awful critter. He said 't wa'n't to be disputed though, that she'd done a master sight o' good to menkind — he reckoned they ought to raise a moniment tew her — 'cause any body that lookt at her head couldent persume no longer to doubt the truth o' phreenyology. He told us to observe the shape on 't perticlerly. Tou see the forrid's dretful flat — well, that shows how 't the intellectible faculties is intirely wantin'. But he dident call it *forrid*. He called it the *hoss frontis*. I s'pose that's 'cause its shaped more like a hoss than a human critter — animal propensitudes intirely predominates, you know. That's what makes it stick out so on the back side — that's the *hoss* hindis I s'pose — *hoss frontis* and *hoss hindis*, you know. I felt oncomonly interested when he was a tellin' about her, 'cause I've read all about her in "Horrid Murders" — a book I've got — it's the interestinest book I've read in all my life. (*Papers* 64-65)

In contrast to the Aunt Maguire sketches that followed, the Widow Bedott stories are more parodic than satiric, reflecting Whitcher's confidence that the widow's foolishness would speak for itself.

In her use of vernacular humor as a vehicle for social criticism, Miriam Whitcher was in the vanguard of the American humor tradition that ultimately included writers as diverse as Thomas B.

Thorpe, George Washington Harris, Marietta Holley, and Samuel Clemens. Her immediate and only female predecessor was Ann Stephens, who had created a fictive onion farmer named Jonathan Slick who commented on the foibles of the nouveau riche of New York society in a series of letters he ostensibly wrote to the folks back home in Connecticut. Like Whitcher, Stephens concerned herself with the behavior of would-be women of fashion, but from the point of view of a naïve male narrator whose innocence about high society made him as much a source of derision as were the women he observed. Stephens' immediate predecessor, in turn, was Seba Smith, whose male narrator, Jack Downing, also spoke (and wrote) in his native vernacular tongue. In contrast to Stephen's preoccupation with "society," Smith's primary concern was the politics of the Jacksonian era, at both state and national levels, and his humorous sketches generated a host of imitators in the nineteenth century, most of them male and most of them politically conservative.

All the other Northeast humorists familiar to modern scholars, such as James Russell Lowell and B.P. Shillaber, wrote after Miriam Whitcher began publishing her Widow Bedott sketches.[4] In the half century that followed, women humorists such as Sara Willis Parton (Fanny Fern) and Marietta Holley (Josiah Allen's Wife) would rediscover the remarkable versatility and authenticity a female persona afforded them in their humorous social criticism, but Miriam Whitcher's particular form of social satire represented groundbreaking work: she was the first vernacular humorist to create a female narrator, and the first to focus almost exclusively upon women's domestic sphere.[5]

In May, 1847, Whitcher moved with her husband, William, to Elmira, New York, where she encountered social expectations and community values suprisingly different from those of Whitesboro. A larger town than Whitesboro, Elmira was also experiencing more dramatic social and economic changes, accompanied by rapid social mobility, as the example of one man will illustrate. In 1819, a thirty-year-old itinerant salesman named John Arnot arrived in Elmira on what his admiring biographer called "a mercantile venture" (Towner 114-15; Mellor 1261-67). In the 1820s he married the daughter of his chief business rival, Stephen Tuttle, and by the end of the decade had established himself as the foremost merchant in the town. John Arnot had a hand in nearly every business enterprise of the time: he was a stockholder, director, then president of the Chemung Canal Bank; he brought the Erie Railroad into Elmira; he took over the local gas company; and he extended the Northern Central Railroad into the lucrative coal fields of northern Pennsylvania. By the 1860s, he had become arguably the most powerful and wealthy man in Elmira, and he passed that legacy on to his sons. Such a classic rags-to-riches story would certainly have taken place in Utica during the decades following the construction of the Erie Canal, but not in the village of Whitesboro, only a few miles away; its economic structure remained remarkably stable.

Unlike the women of Whitesboro, the women of Elmira in mid-century apparently had no tradition of community involvement in reform societies, no strong sense of allegiance with their churches, and little or no interest in literary matters, making them, as far as Whitcher was concerned, not especially "agreeable companions." Instead, according to Whitcher,

the women generally are pretty much occupied with cooking, fixing, scandal & quilting. The last named accomplishment is carried to an extent almost beyond belief (by the way my quilt was sent home the other day — I would not let them put nearly as much work on it, as they wanted to — it is thus — very pretty —) There seems to be a perfect passion for quilting among the ladies — & a great strife to have the most elaborate patterns. Mrs Luce has one that has more work on than any other that I ever saw — but she says it will bear no comparison with many in the village — & their stitches are the least — nay — less than the least you ever saw. I wouldn't dare have them see those I brought from home, yes I would too — for I wish them to know that I do'nt care for such things.[6]

Viewed from a political perspective, the women of Elmira as Whitcher depicted them in her humor illustrate precisely why their relegation to the private sphere denigrated women instead of elevating them to a superior status, as the apologists for the status quo argued. With no significant role to play in a community that was experiencing rapid social and economic change, many women found little better than gossip and scandal to occupy their time; however, without the political point of view of the suffragettes, Whitcher assumed that the women themselves were responsible for their own degradation. Focusing thus on the symptoms of the ills, Whitcher held women up to public scrutiny in her humor and in effect asked them to see their own reflections there and to reform accordingly.

Her humor recorded, too, her personal frustrations with Elmira society. Separated from her family and missing especially her sister Kate to whom she felt a life-long closeness, she also had to adjust to her new role as a minister's wife. Frustrated by her husband's inability to have more effect on his congregation, by the wretched condition of their small house, by their difficulty in managing on his small salary, Whitcher gave a prominent role to a minister and his wife in a new series of sketches she created at the request of Louis Godey for his *Lady's Book*.[7] She also created a new persona, Aunt Maguire.

Like her fictive sister, the Widow Bedott, Aunt Maguire spoke in a rustic tongue, unaided by any narrative intervention, but unlike her sister, Aunt Maguire was not herself the target of Whitcher's humor. The Widow Bedott, a recognizable if exaggerated humorous type, monopolized all conversations, relentlessly pursued every available widower in two seperate villages, gossiped unmercifully, especially about other widows, and laced her speech, unconsciously, with malapropisms that confirmed her foolishness. As a fool, as an object of humor, the Widow Bedott could personify Whitcher's sense of good-natured absurdity; however, when Whitcher became more acutely aware of the extent to which social pretentiousness had taken hold of many women's lives (and when those values that she labeled "genteel" increasingly impinged upon her own life) she needed a persona who could mediate between her own frustrations and her pointed and satiric observations about female society. What Whitcher needed, in short, was a more moderate voice and a woman endowed with greater common sense and compassion; she needed what Walter Blair has termed a "horse-sense philosopher." Thus Witcher created Aunt Maguire: she was at once a social commentator and an established, respected figure in her fictive community, Scrabble Hill. Aunt Maguire was not Miriam Whitcher, nor did she speak with her voice, but she was Whitcher's spokesperson and, as we shall see, her apologist.

From the beginning, the Aunt Maguire sketches enjoyed popular success with both Louis Godey and the readers of his *Lady's Book*, while they chronicle Whitcher's growing dissatisfaction with life in Elmira. The third sketch, for example, which Godey claimed "called forth a general burst of praise from one end of the Union to the other," was written in anxious anticipation of an event planned for the Whitchers during their first year in Elmira (311). Because ministers were paid so little (and had such difficulty collecting their salaries, at that), local church members frequently sponsored annual "donation parties" for the minister and his family, donating to the family commodities that would help see them through the year. In reality, Whitcher was pleasantly surprised at how well their donation party went, in spite of her expectations that it would be a "trying time" (Letters, Nov.8, 1847, 4). The parishioners were generous and inventive in their contributions: 11 loaves of cake, 24 lbs of coffee, 1 bottle of prunes, 1 lounge from the upholsterer, dozens of yards of fabric (mostly calico) but also 1½ yards "*yaller* flannel," and 2 pairs of baby shoes, to name only a few items. Never at ease in public gatherings, Miriam Whitcher nonetheless presented herself to advantage; as several people told her husband, they "were agreeably disappointed in his wife — had thought until that evening that she was distant and haughty" (Letters, Nov.29, 1847, 2).

The donation party Aunt Maguire narrates, however, is quite a different matter, revealing Whitcher's deep distrust of her new neighbors. In "Parson Scrantum's Donation Party," the parishioners bring only the most paltry gifts (ribbons, pins, a half round of cheese), consume most of the food they donate, and generally behave badly. Especially singled out for ridicule are "seminary gals" who throw sausages around the rooms and break dishes and lamps. In the end the donation party costs the minister and his wife so much money and anguish that he resigns and announces his intention to move his family to a different parish where he hopes they will never be given another donation party.

[Parson Scrantum]: "Brethren, since I come among you, I've done my best to be a faithful pastor — if I've failed I hope to be forgiven. At first I had an idee that I should be able to rub along, on my small salary; and I don't know, but I might a done it, if it had n't a ben for *one thing*." Here he paused. "What was *that?*" says Deacon Peabody. Mr. Scrantum continued — "I've ben here tew years, and you've had the kindness to give me tew donation parties. I've stood it so fur, but I can't stand it no longer; brethren, I feel convinced that *one more donation party* would completely *break me down.*" (*Papers* 271)

The next three sketches set off a raging controversy in Elmira, reflecting as they did not imaginary problems, as in the "Donation Party," but actual events and people of Elmira. With what must have been the best of intentions, the Rev. Whitcher urged his female parishioners to begin a sewing society as a means of raising money for charity; he also persuaded his reluctant wife to participate (Letters, Dec. 19, 1847, 5). The November 1848 issue of the *Lady's Book* carried Aunt Maguire's account of the founding of just such a society, while a story in the January 1849 issue told about the first two meetings of the group. One woman, Miss Samson Savage, dominated the society, (even in her absence), and she bore the brunt of Whitcher's satiric thrust:

> She was always a coarse, boisterous, high-tempered critter, and when her husband grow'd rich, she grow'd pompous and overbearin'. She made up her mind she'd rule the roast, no matter what it cost — she'd be the *first* in Scrabble Hill. She know'd she wa'n't a lady by natur nor by eddication, but she thought mabby other folks would be fools enough to think she was if she made a great parade. So she begun by dressin' more, and givin' bigger parties than any body else. Of course, them that thinks money's the main thing (and ther's plenty such here and every where), is ready to flatter her and make a fuss over her, and approve of all her dewin's. If ther's any body that *won't* knuckle tew her, I tell ye they have to take it *about east*. She abuses 'em to their faces and slanders 'em to their backs. (*Papers* 303)

Angered because the sewing society began when she was out of town, Miss Samson Savage "drops in" on a meeting to "see what they're up tew." She refuses the women's invitation to join the society until she knows its purpose, and when she learns that the women want "to arn enough to repair the meetin'-house and build a new pulpit," she expresses nothing but contempt:

> "I'd look purty wouldent I, a workin' to fix up that meetin'-house for Tuttle to preach in! ... He don't know nothin' — can't preach no mor'n *that stove-pipe*" — (she hates Parson Tuttle 'cause he hain't never paid no more attention to her than he has to the rest o' the congregation) — "he's as green as grass and as flat as a pancake. ... I despise Tuttle, and I'll tell him so tew his face when I git a chance. Ye don't ketch me a slanderin' folks behind ther backs and then soft-soapin' 'em to their faces, as some folks dew. ... And where's his wife, I'd like to know? Why ain't *she* here to work to-day? A purty piece o' bisness, I must say, for you all to be here a diggin' away to fix up Tuttle's meetin'-house when *she's* to hum a playin' *lady*." ... And from that she went on and blazed away about Miss Tuttle at a terrible rate. Miss Stillman and Polly Mariar, and a number more o' the wimmin, sot tew and helped her whenever they could git a word in edgeways; and such a haulin' over as Miss Tuttle and the parson got, I never heerd afore in all the days o' my life. (*Papers* 307-09)

Heretofore, Whitcher scholars have assumed that Miss Samson Savage was a wholly fictitious character, or at most a composite figure. Whitcher's letters, however, reveal that within days of the *Lady's Book* arriving in Elmira, she was identified as the author of the sketch, and

Mrs Arnot was recognised at once, to her infinite rage and that of her friends & *toadeaters*. As she is almost universally disliked of course there is a deal of crowing & triumphing at seeing her taken off. William's enemies are making a handle of it to injure him, & some of his friends are so much afraid of the miserable woman, & such worshippers of money, that they are dreadfully alarmed. There are some who are bold enough to stand by their minister & tell him to fear nothing, but let the "galled jade wince." It is not very pleasant for me, who have hitherto been so retired & unnoticed here, to be thus hauled into notoriety, & subjected to all sorts of mean insults from Mrs Arnot & her clique, as I shall be. (Letters, Dec 28, 1848, 2)

The complexities of the issue unfold in layers as one digs further into the details of history and biography that underlie the sketch and the characterization of Miss Samson Savage. Mrs. Arnot, Whitcher's life model, was the wife of the Horatio Alger figures mentioned previously; he, too, is described in the sketch:

When they first come to our place, he was a follerin' the tin-peddlin' bisness; he used to go rumblin' round in his cart from house to house, and the rich folks ruther turned up their noses at him, or he consated they did, and it made him awful wrathy; so he determined he'd be richer'n any on 'em, and pay 'em off in their own coin. Old Smith says he's heerd him time and agin make his boast that he'd ride over all their heads some day — dident seem to have no higher eend in view than to be the richest man in Scrabble Hill. He sot his heart and soul and body on 't, and knowin' how to turn every cent to the best advantage, and bein' wonderful sharp at a bargain, he succeeded; every thing he took hold of prospered, and without actilly bein' what you could call dishonest, afore many years every body allowed he was the richest man in the place. (*Papers* 302)

Whitcher transforms Mrs. Arnot into a Vermont-born seamstress, while the minister whom Miss Savage maligns in the sketch is given Mrs. Arnot's maiden name, Tuttle. With a clever but thinly disguised twist, Whitcher has Mrs. Arnot (Miss Samson Savage) malign her own family (Tuttle).

Whitcher could not have seriously expected to get away with her portrayal of Mrs. Arnot, nor could she have been seriously surprised to have her authorship revealed. She knew in advance that one of her neighbors had visited Whitesboro and learned there that she was the author of the Widow Bedott sketches, which was the only identification given to the author of the Aunt Maguire sketches, and her "Donation Party" story had been reprinted on the front page of the Elmira *Gazette* in May of 1848. She also had been forewarned that the characters in the "Sewing Society" sketch were too thinly veiled: "The first article I wrote, William wouldn't let me send — he thought the characters would certainly be recognized and make trouble. The last one too, he thought too personal, and would not consent to my sending it for some time. I tried a third time, but I was discouraged & gave it up in despair. So after suggesting some slight alterations he permitted me to send the second" (Letters, Oct. 12, 1848, 3).

As this letter suggests, Whitcher sent off her second version of the article knowing that it might ultimately expose her authorship, but she was willing to take that risk in order to satirize the behavior that so offended her; she also believed that its comic potential was too great to pass up. The Elmira *Gazette* fueled the rumors that "the author of these articles resides among us" by publishing the "Sewing Society" sketch in their December 28 issue, then reprinting two Widow Bedott stories in January and February of 1849. Neither Miriam nor William Whitcher could have anticipated, however, how fully the humor would hit home, and not only in Elmira:

> I wrote him [Godey] yesterday & gave him an account of the fuss here, & begged him to notice in the Dollar that several villages were contending for the honor of being the birth place of "Mrs Samson Savage," which is an amusing fact. A man from a village in Seneca county, came into one of our bookstores the other day to get some Lady's Books, saying that they were all alive about it in his place, because they had a Mrs Samson Savage there. And we have heard from Havana — a village twenty miles from here — they have fitted the coat to a woman there .... (Letters, Dec. 28, 1848, 3)

"The commotion caused by the article," Whitcher wrote her Whitesboro family, did not subside, partly because of the fury of the Arnots and their friends, and partly because the townspeople took great delight in indentifying their Elmira neighbors by the names given them in the sketches: "Every body insists upon applying Mrs Samson Savage to Mrs Arnot. She goes by the name every where, & her admirers or echoes, are called the 'Stillman family.' The young man Capt. Hasted of whom I spoke in a letter some time ago as being the beau of Mrs T ... is called universally 'Cappen Smalley,' & they say it cuts him to death" (Letters, Jan. 1, 1849, 1). Nor was the fire extinguished for many years to come. A resident of Elmira who was interviewed nearly half a century after the sketch was published still held a grudge against Miriam Whitcher, but for a curious mixture of reasons.

"Know her? Yes I did! She was an awful woman. She slandered everybody. It was awful. She put me and my sister in the book. We were the Peabodys." "But," [the interviewer] says, "she didn't say so much about the Peabodys did she?" "Of course she didn't! You'd a thought our family didn't amount to anything. But we were just as prominent as anybody and I guess we were thought as much of." (Palmer)

In large measure, however, the controversy remained alive because the humor was decidedly on target. Godey could not keep up with the demands for back orders for the January 1848 *Lady's Book,* and subscriptions to his magazine jumped to 40,000 copies monthly by June of the same year, an unprecedented high. Whitcher did acknowledge that it was "imprudent" for her to have written the piece, but, she said, "I could not help it. I thought it a good subject for ridicule...." (Letters, Jan. 1, 1849, 1)

By February the Whitchers were still at the center of controversy. Determined to leave Elmira at the first possible opportunity, and actively looking for a new church, they were equally determined not to appear to be driven out by their "enemies," a hope that was not entirely realized. William Whitcher called a vestry meeting at the request of parishioners who wanted him to resign, and summarized the proceedings in these terms:

I called upon the senior warden to state the object of the meeting ... but he could not tell any object; but that it [seemed] best to meet & talk over the state of the Parish. I then read to them my statement of its affairs which made two of them bite their lips, i.e. Mr Luce and Mr Hatch. Mr Hatch had appropriated $140, of the churches money to his own use, my allusion to this sealed his mouth effectually when he began his complaints. Mr Luce next began to complain of my unpopularity, and I convinced the rest of the vestry if not himself, that he had been the main cause of it, which shut him up for the rest of the evening ....' The conversation then became more general, and the merits of "Aunt Maguires" Article were fully discussed, both as to its local and literary merits, Mr Hatch thot it was silly, (an opinion in which I suppose all the Stillman family will agree) others thought it to the life, whether considered as local or general, and the grand result in regard to it was that it was a very small affair for ten grave men to talk seriously of allowing it to disturb the harmony of a Parish. (Letters, Feb.12, 1849, 4)

At the end of the meeting, William Whitcher asked for a vote of confidence from the vestry, which he received, then announced his intention to resign as soon as possible. "All went home apparently well satisfied" (Letters, Feb. 12, 1849, 5). Miriam Whitcher's opportunity to leave came almost immediately, for she was called home to Whitesboro in March to attend to her dying father. When she left Elmira, she vowed privately never to return again, and she did not.

Her husband stayed on for a few more months, then still unable to find a position in another church, nevertheless resigned his Elmira parish and joined his wife in Whitesboro.

From the greater security of Whitesboro, Whitcher wrote her final words on the Elmira events in a sketch that reflected a new understanding on Whitcher's part that the way women behaved in Elmira was symptomatic of a larger social malaise. Capitalizing on the fact that villages other than Elmira thought their own sewing societies had been satirized in the *Lady's Book*, Whitcher has Aunt Maguire travel to a neighboring village to visit her husband's relatives. While she is there, the latest issue of the *Lady's Book* arrives, and the village gossips have a field day because it contains a story that they think is based on *their* sewing society.

"Oh," says Miss Hawkins, "as true as I'm a live woman, it's got every one of our members in, and shows us all up shamefully, only jest me and Sary Ann. I can't see as ther's any body in it that resembles us a mite. But you're drawed out, Miss Teeters; and Cappen Sapley, he's down large as life; and the Bomans are in for 't; and so's Bill Sweezen's wife, and Samanthy Cooper, and Tom Baily's wife, and Miss Ben Curtis; and there's a Miss Stillman and her daughter, that's meant for the Longs. They're all fictitious names, to be sure, but it's easy enough to tell who's who. But the squire's wife ketches it the worst of all. I tell ye, it takes her off to fits. Nobody can mistake it."

"But how do you know it actilly means your Society?"

"Oh, that's plain enough," says Miss Hawkins, "for it tells things that was positively said and done at some o' the meetin's. Jest how the squire's wife went on; calls her 'Miss Samson Savage.' ... But the mystery to me is, how the minister's wife got hold on't. She wa'n't there. Somebody that *was* there must a told her. I wonder who't was?" (*Papers* 317-18)

As in Elmira, the local minister's wife is "blamed" for writing the story, only this time it is a different town where the minister's wife is in fact innocent. She is, however, maligned by the townspeople in much the same terms Whitcher was in Elmira:

"I say," says Miss Teeters, says she, "it's high time we got rid o' the minister; he ain't the man for us. A ginteel and intellectible congregation like our'n had ought to have a man o' great eloquential powers. And as for his wife, I never could bear her, with her old stripid dress that she wears every Sunday, rain or shine. I don't believe she was ever accustomed to ginteel society."

"Nor I neither," says Miss Hawkins. "I took a dislike tew her when they first come here. I don't like yer mum characters that never say nothin' about nobody. It seems she's ben savin' on 't up to let off in the newspapers. Bethiar Nobles says she told her she thought our congregation drest tew much; and I shouldent wonder if she did, for she' stuck to that old straw bunnit and everlastin' stripid dress all winter, and I s'pose it's to set an example o' plainness afore us, jest as if we'd foller *her* lead. For my part, I think she might better spend more time a dressin', and less a writin' for the newspapers. And they say he incourages her in it, and likes to have her write. I wish they was both furder off."

"I wish so tew," says Miss Teeters; "and I guess ther's a good many that wish so. She ain't popilar at all in our set. She never runs in sociably, as Miss Van Duzen used to. They say she goes a great deal more among the poor folks, than she does among the ginteel part o' the congregation. And that's a sure sign, *I think*, that she's ben more accustomed to minglin' with them sort o' folks, than with such as we be." (*Papers* 319-20)

Aunt Maguire's cousin comes to the minister's defense (after all the other neighbors have left, of course), giving Whitcher one more chance to blaze away at the hypocrisy of the villagers and to make a curious but familiar apology for her own writing — it brought in much-needed income:

As soon as they'd gone, Eunice burst out laughin', and says she: "Well, if that ain't the best piece o' news I've heerd this many a day. I've always heerd that that Sewin' Society was a reg'lar slander-mill, where the principal busines is to brew mischief against the minister; and I'm glad they've got showed up at last. The minister's a good man, and a smart man tew; but the biggest part o' the congregation is such a set of ignoramuses, that they don't know a smart man from a fool. They always make a great fuss over their minister when he first comes; but if he don't preach smooth things tew 'em all the time, they soon contrive to starve him out or quarrel him off. When they gin this one a call, they agreed to give him five hundred dollars a year, and pay it quarterly. And it is a solemn fact, that half on't hain't ben paid yet. Betsey Hall, a girl that used to wash for 'em sometimes, told me so. She said she'd often listened to the door, and heerd the minister and his wife a talkin' over their troubles; and she says that ther ain't more'n half a dozen in the congregation that pay their dues reglarly; and if 't wa'n't for what the minister's wife gits for writin' for the newspapers, they wouldent be able to pay their house-rent and keep out o' debt, no way." (*Papers* 320-21)

The story then takes a curious and improbable turn: Aunt Maguire suddenly realizes that she herself may be to blame for all the trouble because she once "told" Mr. Godey about her own sewing circle back in Scrabble Hill; she surmises that he wrote up her conversation in the form of a story and published it in his magazine. Ashamed of the harm she unintentionally caused the innocent minister's wife, she decides to seek her out and apologize for the trouble she has caused. The minister's wife immediately absolves her of all responsibility:

"Well, I'm glad you feel so," says I; "but ain't it curus that the Slabtown folks should take it all to themselves as they dew?"

"Not at all," says she; "human natur's the same every where."

"I guess so," says I. "Any how, your Sewin' Society must be wonderfully like our'n, or they wouldent be so determind it means them; but what hurts my feelin's is, that you should have to suffer for 't. I was so distrest when I heerd they was a layin' on't to you, and usin' on't to injure yer husband, that I felt as if I must come right over and see you, though you was a stranger. If any body's to blame, I'm willin' to bear it."

"O fie," says she, "don't you fret yourself a bit about it. If people choose to fit your coats to their own backs, 't ain't your fault; and if they fit nice and snug, perhaps they'll do as good service as if they were made expressly for 'em."

"Jest so," says I. "But it does seem tew bad that you should suffer for't. Ain't ther no way o' puttin' a stop tew it?"

"Never you mind," says she; "we minister's folks must have our trials, of one sort or another, wherever we go. If we hadent this perhaps we should have somethin' still worse."

"But," says I, "what if they should drive you away from here?"

She smiled, and dident say nothin'.

"Well," says I, "to judge from what I've seen o' Slabtown since I come here, I'm bold to say that, if they do drive you away, they can't possibly drive you to a worse place."

"Hush, Aunt Magwire," says she, "human natur's the same every where; we must expect trouble wherever we go. I feel prepared for almost any thing."...

I come away a few days after that, and I ruther guess it'll be a good while afore I go a visitin' to Slabtown agin. The place is tew awful *ginteel* to suit my taste. (*Papers* 342-44)

In spite of the Slabtown minister's wife's brave statements, Miriam Whitcher was not ultimately prepared for the fate that awaited them; during the next several years, the Whitchers suffered irreparable harm as a result of the events in Elmira. William Whitcher was unable to find another permanent position, as word of his wife's satiric writing preceded them at every available parish. Impoverished, Miriam Whitcher remained at home in Whitesboro with her mother, unmarried sisters, and infant daughter, while William accepted temporary assignments that kept them apart for long stretches of time. The letters that passed between them reveal the strains of the separation and the bitterness of their poverty, and Miriam Whitcher soon lost heart for satire; she wrote only a few more Widow Bedott stories for the *Saturday Gazette*, then turned all her energies to writing a pious novel that she never finished. In January of 1852, at the age of 39, Miriam Whitcher died of tuberculosis.

When modern feminists first encounter the humor of Miriam Whitcher, they often express impatience with her propensity to cast her satiric barbs almost exclusively at women. Aside from a pompous minister who marries the Widow Bedott, the only men who come in for sustained humorous criticism are reformers or faddists, such as the phrenologist, Mr. Vanderbump. Women were always at the heart of her work as both the subjects and objects of her humor, but they were held up to ridicule so they might "see" themselves and mend their ways. The growing harshness with which she judged other women was at once a reflection of her own experience of genteel society and her growing disappointment at the way women behaved in that society. Her humor, then, was not only an outlet for personal frustrations and disappointments but was also intended to serve as a social corrective.

In the last analysis, that Whitcher did not have the political perspective enjoyed by her contemporaries at Seneca Falls makes her no less a critic of the restricted role women occupied in mid-nineteenth-century American society. It would be a quarter century later before another American woman humorist, Marietta Holley, would add that political, feminist perspective to the rich legacy she inherited from Miriam Whitcher: a robust sense of humor; a primary focus on women and women's concerns; a strong-minded, common-sensical, outspoken female protagonist; and a clear sense that women's lives were demeaned by the tenets of gentility.

Notes

1. See, for example, Cott, Fetterley, Harris, Ryan, Sklar, Smith-Rosenberg, and Welter.
2. Mary P. Ryan, for example, notes that between 1820 and 1835 in Oneida County, "home manufacturing of textiles declined to one-fourth of its former volume" (*Middle Class* 64).
3. Rome *Democratic Sentinel* (April 30–August 20, 1839). This novella was posthumously reprinted in *Widow Spriggins, Mary Elmer, and Other Sketches*.
4. Lowell's first *Biglow Papers* was published in 1848, while Shillaber's popular Mrs. Partington appeared in book form first in 1854.
5. Although not strictly speaking a Northeast humorist, Caroline Kirkland did publish *A New Home — Who Will Follow?* in 1839, the year Whitcher published her Widow Spriggins series in the Rome newspaper; Kirkland is widely considered to be America's first woman prose humorist.
6. Letter of June 27, 1847, 1-2, to her sister. Whitcher Letters, Manuscript Collection, New York Historical Society. I am especially indebted to Jenny Lawrence for giving me a copy of the official typed transcription she prepared for the New York Historical Society. All further references are to the typed transcription.
7. For a discussion of the declining influence of the American clergy during this period, see Ann Douglas, especially Chapter 1.

Works Cited

Blair, Walter. *Horse Sense in American Humor, from Benjamin Franklin to Ogden Nash.* New York: Russell & Russell, 1962.

Buhle, Mari Jo and Paul Buhle, eds. *The Concise History of Woman Suffrage: Selections from the Classic Work of Stanton, Anthony, Gage and Harper.* Urbana: U of Illinois P, 1978.

Cott, Nancy F. *The Bonds of Womanhood: "Woman's Sphere" in New England, 1790-1835.* New Haven: Yale UP, 1977.

Cross, Whitney R. *The Burned-Over District: The Social and Intellectual History of Enthusiastic Religion in Western New York, 1800-1850.* Ithaca: Cornell UP, 1950.

Douglas, Ann. *The Feminization of American Culture.* New York: Knopf, 1977.

Eliot, George. *Essays and Uncollected Papers.* Boston: Houghton Mifflin, 1908. Vol. 22 of *The Writings of George Eliot.*

Fetterley, Judith, ed. "Introduction." *Provisions: A Reader from 19th-Century American Women.* Bloomington: Indiana UP, 1985. 1-40.

Godey, Louis. *Godey's Lady's Book* 36 (1848): 311.

Harris, Barbara J. "The Cult of Domesticity" in *Beyond Her Sphere: Women and the Professions in American History.* Westport: Greenwood P, 1978.

Johnson, Paul E. *A Shopkeeper's Millenium: Society and Revivals in Rochester, New York, 1815-1837.* New York: Hill & Wang, 1978.

Mellor, George A. "The Arnots of Elmira." *Chemung County Historical Journal* (1964): 1261-67.

O'Donnell, Thomas F. "The Return of the Widow Bedott: Mrs. F.M. Whitcher of Whitesboro and Elmira." *New York History* 55 (1974): 5-34.

Palmer, Mrs. George Archibald. *Elmira Telegram* 4 Nov. 1923.

Ryan, Mary P. *Cradle of the Middle Class: The Family in Oneida County, New York, 1790-1865.* Cambridge: Cambridge UP, 1981.

———. "Creating Woman's Sphere," in *Womanhood in America: From Colonial Times to the Present.* 2nd ed. New York: Watts, 1979.

Sklar, Kathryn Kish. *Catharine Beecher: A Study in American Domesticity.* New Haven: Yale UP, 1973.

Smith-Rosenberg, Carroll. *Disorderly Conduct: Visions of Gender in Victorian America.* New York: Oxford UP, 1985.

Towner, Asburn. *Our Country and Its People: A History of the Valley and County of Chemung from the Closing Years of the Eighteenth Century.* Syracuse: Mason, 1892.

Welter, Barbara. "The Cult of True Womanhood: 1820-1860." *American Quarterly* 18 (1966): 151-74.

Whitcher, F.M. Whitcher Letters. MS Collection. New York Historical Society, New York City.

———, *The Widow Bedott Papers.* New York: Mason, 1880.

———, *Widow Spriggins, Mary Elmer, and Other Sketches.* New York: Carleton, 1867.

Hate and humor as empathetic whimsy in Anne Thackeray Ritchie

CAROL HANBERY MACKAY

University of Texas, Austin

> There was something fierce, bright, good-humoured about her. ... It is a rare combination, for women are not often both gentle and strong.
> — Anne Thackeray [Ritchie], *The Village on the Cliff*

> It was impossible to be seriously angry.
> — Anne Thackeray [Ritchie], "Jack the Giant Killer," in *Five Old Friends and a Young Prince*

I

"THERE ARE 40,000,000 unmarried women in London alone!" So responds Anne Thackeray Ritchie to her brother-in-law, Leslie Stephen, according to an anecdote recollected by Stephen's daughter, Virginia Woolf (*CDB* 71).[1] By retorting with such obvious exaggeration, Ritchie thus handles her growing irritation with Stephen. Almost instinctively, she draws on multifariousness, an outrushing energy, which in this case disperses some of the anger she doubtless feels at the time. Transforming her own anger into a form of empathetic whimsy about the status of women in their nonrelation to men, Ritchie's humor undoubtedly deflates some of Stephen's expected exasperation as well.

Women more than men seem to have defined themselves in terms of multiple roles, and sometimes one's sense of self can get lost through the conflicting demands of these roles. Yet at the same time, the complex interrelationships of roles can become very powerful, even creative.[2] We see this process at work in Ritchie's need as a writer to transform anger into an aesthetic form that also communicates and serves others. She saves herself and others when she performs this creative act, for she sets an example by living out its implications. This special form of whimsy in effect creates a safe arena in which women can express the conjunction of contrasting — perhaps even dangerous — emotions. And unexpectedly, empathetic whimsy often implies a disarming intellectual perspective which is at once self-effacing and critical.

Denied immediate outlets for their hatred, women have often rechanneled hate through humor. Women authors tend to employ formal mechanisms — images, conceits, rhetorical devices — in order to express and deal with hate and humor in an empathetic way, as opposed to the aggressive humor characteristic of many male authors. In point of fact, women writers create images which embody both hate and humor, thus enabling the reader to experience the two emotions at once, in an altogether new way. In the writings of Anne Thackeray Ritchie we can recognize this creative consolidation in her unique brand of whimsy. What first appears as mere caprice or odd fancy enables Ritchie to critique stereotypes and conventions — especially those that have limited societal roles for women — with disarming success. In particular, the whimsical mode of her domestic fairytales dispels the hateful but familiar conventions perpetuated by literary expectations and unconsciously adopted by society. A survivor in life and art (she coped admirably with her father's fame and Leslie Stephen's temperament, becoming a noted novelist and essayist in her own right), Anne Thackeray Ritchie demonstrates how transforming hatred into whimsy makes it more accessible and ultimately more controllable.

Daughter of noted Victorian novelist William Makepeace Thackeray and by marriage aunt to Virginia Woolf, Anne Thackeray Ritchie (1837-1919) stands at the boundaryline between Victorianism and Modernism. Influenced by her father, Ritchie nonetheless developed her own impressionistic style, which in turn served as an example to the niece who would eventually depict her Aunt Anny as the eccentric central character, Mrs. Hilbery, in *Night and Day*.[3] Looking back toward her father, Ritchie could see the sentimental cynic torn by conflicting emotions yet seldom consolidating them — empathetic with the spirit of feminism in the depiction of some of his female characters (most notably Becky Sharp, Beatrix Castlewood, and Ethel Newcome) yet trapped by the delimited outlook of the Victorian male. Playful humor remains part of that picture, however, for Ritchie to imitate and make her own, in both art and life.

In *A Nineteenth-Century Childhood*, Mary MacCarthy records her impressions of Lady Ritchie as someone who focuses on minutiae in order to combine humor with serious commentary. MacCarthy cites the case of Samuel Butler not getting the joke when Ritchie informs him about her theory that Anne Hathaway was the author of Shakespeare's sonnets (126). Apparently he does not recollect the recent publication of his own book, *The Authoress of the Odyssey*, but perhaps, too, as evidenced by the embittered satire of *The Way of All Flesh*, his humor is narrowly ruled by unmitigated hatred of his Victorian upbringing. If Ritchie's wit is sometimes missed by the person at whom it is directed, it is also important to note that she often knowingly employs herself as the target — or rather half-target — of her own wit, as she does when she fusses over phony concoctions in the footnotes to her biographical introductions to Thackeray's works.[4] Here, as throughout her canon, Ritchie uses self-deprecating humor to comment more broadly on confining structures or conventions that have been largely male-determined.

II

For Ritchie, hatred — taking shape as anger — seems largely directed at social unfairness, often (though not always) focused on women. Usually she depicts such results in loneliness, failure, or the absence of opportunities to savor life's richness. Note, for example, how the opening frame to her "Beauty and the Beast" whimsically evokes the narrator and her spinster companion:

Poor H.! I am not sure but that she would have gladly looked in a mirror in which she could have sometimes seen the images of those she loved; but our chimney-glass, with its gilt moulding and bright polished surface, reflects only such homely scenes as two old women at work by the fire, some little Indian children at play upon the rug, the door opening and Susan bringing in the tea-things. (*FOF* 82)[5]

In the body of her domestic fairytales, Ritchie depicts victims bound in time and place by modern-day fairytale villains, but she shows this entrapment as partly their own fault — and perhaps this insight also disguises or modifies her anger. The difference between Ritchie and her victims is that they lack the transforming power represented by the author's multifarious energy, her predilection for the aesthetic, and her acute self-consciousness.

As a young writer, Ritchie is quick to discover the humorous possibilities inherent in exaggeration, and she enjoys piling up words and phrases for comic effect. Thus, we witness the titular character in "Cinderella" turned down by her stepmother in her aspirations to attend the Guildhall ball — "refused, scorned, snubbed, wounded, pained, and disappointed" (*FOF* 66); later, poor Ella works hard sewing for her stepsisters — "her little fingers quilled, fluted, frilled, pleated, pinned, tacked the trimmings on their dresses more dexterously than any dress-maker or maid-servant could do" (67). Multifarious image-making seems almost to arrest time, and it may also lead us to question — however lightheartedly — the reality of the story. Nonetheless, the evocation of a specific place is crucial to Ritchie's technique; the location of the ball is characterized, its importance and centrality clearly emphasized.

The merging of hate and humor to produce a unified example of whimsy characteristically involves what I term *espièglerie* — a focal point, a nexus — for the unity to be complete. Whimsy takes a high-spirited form in Ritchie, and *espièglerie*, or prankishness, captures that notion. Furthermore, the capriciousness implied by whimsy remains deceptive; its apparent accidentalness actually conceals rule-governed usage and formal structures. Ritchie's points of crystallization — such as the magic lamp and its slides in the preface to her second novel, *The Village on the Cliff* — tend to contain certain elements: they grow out of a negative emotion; they evoke a place; they combine reality and illusion; they suggest multifariousness; they include a sense of time (often reaching backward or outside of time); and they present an aesthetic or formal invocation (which may highlight or affect the *form* of the work). Instances of *espièglerie* act like templates for symbols — in effect, symbol-structures — which Ritchie uncovers and elaborates, with her characteristic qualities of intimate familiarity and generalized sensory detail. *Espièglerie* is thus her most elaborate mode of producing whimsy, while less complex methodology produces more modest forms of single images or phony footnotes.

Ritchie's first novel, *The Story of Elizabeth*, reveals many of the elements of *espièglerie* as yet undigested, but the pieces are beginning to come together. This novel tells the tale of a foolish young woman who, unlike her creator, lacks the ability to make whimsical the problems of her life. The Victorian woman is accustomed to seeing herself as a naive, whimsical object, but if she can gain creative power over this image, she can control and exercise her anger. Early in the novel, it takes the narrative voice to undermine the heroine's picture of herself as unique — "it was a commonplace little *tableau de genre* enough — that of a girl sitting at a window, with clasped hands, dreaming dreams more or less silly" (23) — but by novel's end Elizabeth acquires a perspective on her own muted happiness that shows her capable of sharing with the narrator an alternative vision of herself still trying to work out her hate and rage: "I could fancy Elizabeth a prisoner within those walls, beating like a bird against the bars of the cage, and revolting and struggling to be free" (264).[6]

Whimsy also surfaces intermittantly in Ritchie's second novel, *The Village on the Cliff*, where we witness instances of near-*espièglerie*. For example, soon after we meet the hero, Dick Butler, we learn that he has openly extricated himself from a marriage proposal that arose from false motives on his own part:

His curly head had stood him in stead of many a better quality; his confidence and good manners had helped him out of many a well-deserved scrape, but he was certainly no sinewy hero, no giant, no Titan, like those who have lately revisited the earth — (and the circulating libraries, to their very great advantage and improvement). (17)

Reversing our expectations, Ritchie renders contempt whimsical by (negatively) implying multifariousness in comparison with the absent "many a better quality." More prominent is Ritchie's foregrounding of artificiality; her commentary is often parenthetical, yet the effect of this sort of commentary is that of being thrust forward rather than being tucked back. Such mechanisms of containment — quotation marks, parentheses, footnotes — paradoxically let her highlight inner irony. Place, too, is highlighted humorously by her reference to circulating libraries, while time receives a mildly playful treatment as she toys with the reality and illusion of the heroic. The effect is less extreme that what full-fledged *espièglerie* offers, but once again the elements are present in embryonic form.

This same quality of hate and humor incompletely merged appears as well in one of Ritchie's early essays, "Toilers and Spinsters," first undertaken in 1860, when her father was still alive. At the outset, Ritchie announces "little sympathy" for unmarried ladies living in comfortable circumstances but "pining away in lonely gloom" (1). Anger and impatience characterize this depiction, as she sarcastically parodies the novels of solitary, heartbroken women who have spawned their own literary genre. As the passage goes on, however, we sense this bitterness giving way to the spirit of multifariousness. Form becomes accentuated in the use of capitals and rhetorical questions:

> Are unmarried people shut out from all theatres, concerts, picture-galleries, parks, and gardens? May not they walk out on every day of the week? Are they locked out all the summer time, and only let out when an east wind is blowing? Are they forced to live in one particular quarter of the town? Does Mudie refuse their subscriptions? (3-4)

In effect, Ritchie's long series of rhetorical questions amounts to a revelation of anger. Furthermore, reaching back in time through near-*espièglerie* allows her to contain negative emotions, for it adds the philosophical perspective that "it has ever been so." Ritchie is indeed well on her way to mastering a form that will permit her to engage in self-expression while still producing art.

III

Writing her first two novels allowed Ritchie to experiment with the techniques she later developed into *espièglerie*. By the time she published *Five Old Friends and a Young Prince* — her collection of domestic fairytales — she may well have found her ideal form. Modelling contemporary accounts on fairytale plotlines encouraged Ritchie to transform negative emotions into whimsical constructs. In this context, we frequently witness an isolated character for whom *espièglerie* coalesces a special or extraordinary moment. The reader, by contrast, feels an uplifting conjoinment with the narrative viewpoint. Ritchie uses overt reference to artifice to control the reader's experience, without necessarily altering the character's world — in a manner which recalls Thackerayan metafiction. Her *espièglerie* transforms scenes and emotions, not so much by containing them as by acting upon them from the outside, as it were — fixing a beam of light on a passage that follows, or into the dark mood of a surrounding passage. Separate from but illuminating its subject, *espièglerie* occurs most frequently in transitions, introductions, segués — in short, as frame.

The volume of fairytales and the introductions to her father's works — marking points early and late in her career — are especially appropriate for Ritchie's purposes.[7] She reveals a preference for short forms which can be yoked together through the use of frames — that can take the form of *espièglerie* — and in which she can use preexisting creations — fairytales, her father's works — as reference points. This sort of embedding enables Ritchie to modulate and control painful emotions; it is not a matter of merely stringing together a series of digressions. Ritchie may use instances of *espièglerie* as structural elements, interstices, or turning points, but she often creates a deliberate parallel with the stories or texts as a whole. This is especially the case in the frame already cited to "Beauty and the Beast." Toying with the fairytale format in her frame, Ritchie adapts it to everday reality in the body of her tale. So both form and analogy are evoked, then turned into something specific and "realistic." As readers, we "transist" in and out of the form — discovering parallels and partaking of emotional transformation through the rhetorical techniques of *espièglerie*.

Anger can congeal into depression, agedness, death-in-life. Ritchie recognizes this danger, and in "Beauty and the Beast" she presents the dire effects of anger for characters who cannot indulge in whimsicality. One of Belle's sisters, Anna, feels anger more than the others:

Indignant, injured, angry with her father, furious with the managers, the directors, the shareholders, the secretary, the unfortunate company, with the Bankruptcy Court, the Ogdens, the laws of fate, the world in general, with Fanny for sobbing, and with Belle for looking placid, she sat blankly staring out of [the] window as they drove past the houses where they had visited, and where she had been entertained as an honoured guest. . . . (*FOF* 96-97)

The multiplicity of Anna's targets alters our perspective on her anger; while we may have compassion for this anger, we must smile at it whimsically. Numbed by her negative emotions, Anna becomes speechless, and Ritchie reports "her face looked quite fierce and old."

Here is a victim who is unable to transform her anger through the whimsical magic of *espièglerie*. The implication is that if we cannot laugh as well, we may suffer the same fate of being frozen by anger. Anger is thus evoked, then transformed through *espièglerie* — and we are forced to witness the aftermath of a failure to engage in the transforming power of humor.

So, in effect, *espièglerie* often has author and reader whimsically viewing a character's negative emotions. This is the case as well in "Beauty and the Beast" with Guy Griffiths, who is described as beast-like as he looks at himself in the mirror:

He saw a great loutish, roundbacked fellow, with a shaggy head and brown glittering eyes, and little strong white teeth like a dog's; he gave an uncouth sudden caper of rage and regret at his own appearance. "To think that happiness and life itself and love eternal depend upon tailors and hair-oil," groaned poor Guy, as he went into his room to write letters. (*FOF* 129)

On this occasion we see *espièglerie* depicting a momentary pause, in which the character feels anger and bitterness, while we can experience a moment outside of time (in the fairytale evocations), a highlighting of aesthetic elements (in the exaggeration and similes), and a multifarious advent of energy in his reacting to the image by dancing (which can hardly fail to amuse us, even as it describes his suffering). Guy's mirror image, thus presented, evokes reality and illusion. And his final act is to focus his place, by going into his room and performing civilized obligations — so he doesn't even have the spatial and psychological freedom of the beasts with which he has just been compared.

In her essay on "Heroines and Their Grandmothers" Ritchie actually goes on to outline part of an aesthetic for women authors in the transforming of life's miseries. She criticizes the run of excessively sad heroines by her contemporaries, comparing them unfavorably with those of Jane Austen and Fanny Burney. Imagining some of these earlier characters coming to life again, Ritchie engages in *espièglerie*: playing with reality and illusion, as well as time travel, she unleashes an array of these characters with multifarious energy, letting us know just which ones would "faint with horror" (Evelina and Cecilia) or "burst out laughing" (Elizabeth Bennet) or "lose her temper" (Emma Woodhouse) or "turn scarlet and stop her little ears" (Fanny Price) (*T&S* 73). Ritchie is here clearly favoring "subjective" over "objective" novelists, *i.e.*, essentially women over men, and it is "penwomen," she says, who recognize the value of analyzing emotions rather than recording the history of events (77).[8] Emphasizing the importance of the writer-reader relationship as well, seeing it as both "subtle" and "strange" (94), Ritchie talks about it as the communication of good friends, an easing of isolation on both sides. Finally, she observes, "Novel-writing must be like tears to some women, the vent and the relief of many a chafing spirit" (95).

This essay reveals Ritchie using *espièglerie* to introduce her analysis and then proceeding to argue at least one possible purpose of fiction — a healing of emotional wounds, a nurturing, which she implies may be to a great extent the prerogative of women authors. At the same time, her own approach to fiction indicates some reservations about unalloyed sadness and disaster; she seems to know that unhappy endings may possess a higher quality than happy ones but feels they might be a strategical mistake on the part of the author. Thus we see how *espièglerie* helps Ritchie to mediate between her acknowledgment of the healing function of fiction — primarily a woman's prerogative, necessarily involving some emotional negativity — and her desire to make literature uplifting, if not completely painless.

IV

In "Beauty and the Beast," the beast-like Guy Griffiths tells Belle, "Yes, you shall go home, and I will stop here alone, and cut my throat if I find I cannot bear the place without you. I am only joking. I daresay I shall do very well" (*FOF* 145). Exaggerating negative emotion to the point of near-violence, Ritchie flirts with a more aggressive form of humor, perhaps parodying a male equivalent to *espièglerie*. Women writers seem more inclined to seek out the fluid style of *espièglerie*, within which they can handle and develop a sense of reconcilable dichotomies. Thus they have created vehicles for the expression of a wide range of turbulent emotions and often for structuring whole works, as Woolf has done with women's "organizing events" in the worlds of her novels.[9] It is consistent, too, with the effect of *espièglerie* that Woolf's novels may at first reading seem chaotic, consisting of the mere minutiae of existence.

Methods of whimsy utilized by women writers usually involve a crossing of conceptual or ontological boundaries: a fictional footnote is a metafictional device, commenting at once on fact and fiction; Marianne Moore's "imaginary gardens with real toads" (267) is a self-evident example of conjoining distinct — even opposite — realms of discourse; the most homely of creatures, the fly, paradoxically interrupts Emily Dickinson's advent of the eternal. In contrast, a male approach seems likely to magnify negative emotions or else to negate and collapse them. I am thinking here especially of one of Kurt Vonnegut's whimsies in *Breakfast of Champions* — "All of us were stuck to the surface of a ball, incidentally" (241). Male writers often negate boundaries — the same boundaries that female *espièglerie* highlights and then transcends. Intellectual or analytical women writers such as George Eliot and Mary McCarthy may employ a variant of *espièglerie* that resembles a male methodology, however; their technique in texts like *Impressions of Theophrastus Such* and *The Groves of Academe* seems to involve the freezing of boundaries and isolation of contained elements, around which abstractions are woven. McCarthy, in particular, tends to focus on well-bounded, discrete items; in her cold fictional world negative emotions are caught, as it were, in the form of *espièglerie*.

In the male version of *espièglerie*, we are more likely to encounter an abrupt shift to a larger frame of reference — a jarring effect which is often quite comical. The shift is also often spatial (rather than temporal) in nature — that is, we feel moved outside of something or drawn suddenly away. This is in fact the case in the Vonnegut example cited above, which radically breaks our sense of perspective, continuity, and emotional distance. (Contrast Vonnegut's statement, which is literally and comically true, with Ritchie's exaggerations.) The change occurs very quickly, too, making the male counterpart of *espièglerie* a more economical form of humor. Our sense of humor may involve the sudden release from a negative state — which is frequently shown as very negative indeed. So perhaps the notion that female writers are more flexible or fluid comes in part from an unconscious response to the complexity of their version of *espièglerie*: they can subtly alter and gradually cause changes in viewpoint, as Jane Austen and Anne Thackeray Ritchie do — as distinct from the quick, violent, spatially jarring, largely male version.

George Meredith, in his *Essay on Comedy*, sees comedy as essential — central — to civilization. In fact, Meredith, whose creations will shortly include the subtly comic heroine Clara Middleton (in *The*

Egoist), goes on to observe, "Comedy lifts women to a station offering them free play for their wit, as they usually show it, *when they have it*, on the side of sound sense" (*Comedy* 28; my emphasis). A century later, Robert Polhemus views comic faith as replacing religion and social structures with its own set of values, which are more generally oriented toward life and this world. His theory in part grows out of Austen's "comedy of union," and his first chapter, on *Emma*, begins by quoting Austen's famous opening — "Emma Woodhouse, handsome, clever, and rich, with a comfortable home and happy disposition, seemed to unite some of the best blessings of existence..." (37) — which certainly contains elements of *espièglerie*. And all along, Arthur Koestler has spoken of the bisociative mechanisms inherent in humor — effected by the creative enterprise of boundarycrossing in punning and word-play. For Koestler, humor is clearly a "creative act," producing "a new synthesis" (182) — something that should not be gender specific.

But do these observations and theories truly acknowledge or transcend gender-specific commentary? Are they not bound in the first place by androcentrism — an ethnocentrism perpetuated by patriarchal order?[10] Does it not take a woman (or at least another marginal figure or "outsider"), like Rachel Brownstein, responding to another woman writer, like Jane Austen, to begin to break down the barriers of perception about the full range of how humor can operate — and point to what we might call its ideal ends? For Brownstein and her undergraduate friends, Austen herself seemed a comic heroine: she "translated vitality into reason, wit, language"; "by reconciling opposites, transforming the complex into the simple...[the heroine] makes herself...complete"; "to take her view of life was to transcend life, to float far above a woman's place, inflated by irony" (14). Unimpeded by role-restrictions yet informed by their insights, the embedded humor of female *espièglerie* is unleashed from its *poly*-sociative sourcepoints.

In a section from Konrad Lorenz' book *On Aggression* entitled "An Avowal of Optimism," he suggests that humor will help compete with (*i.e.*, ameliorate) aggression. "Laughter produces, simultaneously, a strong fellow feeling among participants and joint aggressiveness against outsiders," he reports (284). But the continued emphasis on aggression, and even the choice of "fellow" feeling, reflects a male-oriented worldview, whereas to project a female viewpoint is to imagine a quieter, less physical, more internalized shared feeling from the outset. As Carol Gilligan observes in her book *In a Different Voice*, women perceive aggression as tied to "the fracture of human connection"; in contrast, their goal is to establish "activities that make the social world safe, by avoiding isolation and preventing aggression rather than by seeking rules to limit its extent" (43). Even their brand of humor shows women working to create "a feeling of connection, a primary bond between other and self" (47).[11]

Women authors utilizing *espièglerie* could be said to fall on a spectrum with regard to aggressiveness, however. At the more aggressive end, Sylvia Plath demonstrates that the techniques of *espièglerie* can be employed so as to magnify the negative emotion — in an almost complete reversal of the sort of balancing effect Ritchie utilizes. In general, the different elements — time, place, reality/ illusion, multifariousness, aesthetic invocation — are *imploded* or conflated violently. The result, of course, is the opposite of whimsy or of any ameliorating emotion. Plath inverts the technique of "female" amelioration of emotion, creating a devastating negativity — while still employing the elements of *espièglerie*:

I rocked shut

As a seashell.
They had to call and call
And pick the worms off me like sticky pearls.
Dying,
Is an art like anything else.
. . . . .
And I eat men like air. ("Lady Lazarus" 7-9)

It is all Hollywood, windowless,
The fluorescent light wincing on and off like a terrible migraine . . . ("Lesbos" 30)

In the above lines, note how the element of place becomes an utter entrapment. The intensity, or multifariousness, of the imagery takes over, and time becomes a horrific cycling. In both poems, there is a form of aesthetic reference or invocation (in "Dying/ Is an art" and "Hollywood"), but these invocations ultimately collapse inward on the poet, laying bare the emotional elements *espièglerie* usually transforms.

Much less aggressive, closer to the gentle brand of *espièglerie* evinced by Ritchie, is the work of another nineteenth-century woman novelist, Mary Cholmondeley.[12] The opening of *Red Pottage*, for example, reveals the usual elements of *espièglerie*. The epigraph and disorienting reference to Swift ("'I can't get out,' said Swift's starling, looking through the bars of his cage") foreground formal structures, and the reference to illusory captivity recalls illusion and reality (1). As the male protagonist thinks intensely about something he has been avoiding for a long time, we recognize time as both capricious and oppressive. The imprisonment motif has clear implications of negativity — anger, frustration, impatience (typically feminist) — and the overall effect approaches Ritchie's refined whimsicality. Here, too, may be some of the "glow" of multifariousness, energy, and brightness, as the character is briefly referred to as "the glass of fashion" — itself an aesthetic embedding.

So Cholmondeley employs *espièglerie*, after her own fashion. And as is so often the case, we see the technique beginning a work, setting its tone. *Espièglerie* is, for many women authors, a structural and transitional unit was well as a means of compressed expression and emotional manipulation. The reader characteristically finds herself both inside and outside the work, with a dazzling, double perspective on emotions or experiences which might be overwhelming if actually felt or presented in a straightforward manner.

Perhaps the contrast between male and female brands of *espièglerie* can be made more concrete by looking briefly at two whimsical poems about flies, one by Dickinson, the other by Robert Lowell. In "I heard a Fly buzz — when I died —" Dickinson's multifarious energy is focused on the fly itself, yet the mysterious, slightly humorous image of the fly becomes a still point of *espièglerie*:

I heard a Fly buzz — when I died —
The Stillness in the Room
Was like the Stillness in the Air —
Between the Heaves of Storm —

The Eyes around — had wrung them dry —
And Breaths were gathering firm
For that last Onset — when the King
Be witnessed — in the Room —

I willed my Keepsakes — Signed away
What portion of me be

Assignable — and then it was
There interposed a Fly —

With Blue — uncertain stumbling Buzz —
Between the light — and me —
And then the Windows failed — and then
I could not see to see — (111-12)

In contrast, in "Harriet," Lowell's kinetic fly comes up against the male rhetorician's aggression; killed, it becomes the image of death, rather than an evocation of the experience of death:

A repeating fly, blueblack, thumbthick — so gross,
it seems apocalyptic in our house —
whams back and forth across the nursery bed
manned by a madhouse of stuffed animals,
not one a fighter. It is like a plane
dusting apple orchards or Arabs on the screen —
one of the mighty ... one of the helpless. It
bumbles and bumps its brow on this and that,
making a short, unhealthy life the shorter.
I kill it, and another instant's added
to the horrifying mortmain of
ephemera: keys, drift, sea-urchin shells,
you packrat off with joy ... a dead fly swept
under the carpet, wrinkling to fulfillment. (FL&H 13)[13]

Dickinson's conflation of two planes of reference occurs beautifully in her last line, "I could not see to see." Whereas her poem concludes with the transcendence of time, Lowell's finishes with an assertion of ephemera — "the dead fly swept/under the carpet, wrinkling to fulfillment." The negative emotion is profound in Dickinson — having been confronted by the speaker, death has wrung out all grief — whereas Lowell's poem maintains its focus on the literal death of a fly. Finally, it is worth noting that Lowell's poem falls into the tradition of the sonnet, while Dickinson's is very much her own form, unique, invented. At the same time, Dickinson unconsciously draws on shared elements of *espièglerie* — the technique developed so fully in the works of Anne Thackeray Ritchie.

Notes

1. Stephen's first wife was Minny Thackeray, Ritchie's sister, who died in 1875. For a more detailed analysis of Ritchie's influence on Woolf, particularly in terms of

discovering and developing one's own voice and sense of humor, see my study, "The Thackeray Connection."
2. Elsewhere I have concentrated my analysis on the empowering function of multiple roles for Ritchie and other women writers. See my study, "'Only Connect.'"
3. Woolf's ambivalence toward her Aunt Anny remains predominantly friendly not only in this novel, published in the year of Ritchie's death, but also in her essay-review of Ritchie's selected letters, "The Enchanted Organ." Nonetheless, the anger that surfaces in works like *A Room of One's Own* could not always be mitigated by humor, as Jane Marcus so deftly argues in her own essay, "Art and Anger."
4. See, for example, the foonote for *Vanity Fair* in which Ritchie cites a German correspondent's pedantic questioning of the spelling of a name in one of Thackeray's letters (1: xxvi). Such playfulness is hardly self-deprecatory — something Jack Zipes fails to recognize in his partial analysis of only one of her fairytales (xxvi).
5. Citing Ritchie's work for future reference is tricky, largely because most publishing houses retained her maiden name of "Miss Thackeray" long after her marriage to Richmond Ritchie (seventeen years her junior) in 1877. Much of her work also first appeared separately in journals like *The Cornhill Magazine* before being revised for collections. And now most of her canon is unfortunately out of print.
6. The question of Ritchie's endings is a fascinating one, plagued by both her own ambivalence (see the discussion that follows on "Heroines and Their Grandmothers" in Section III) and Thackeray's possible interfering editorial role.
7. The first series of thirteen biographical introductions appeared in 1898-99; the second, consisting of eighteen revised and enlarged versions, appeared in 1910-11. AMS Press is currently publishing a two-volume edition of these prefaces, with a critical and historical introduction by MacKay.
8. Again the salient factor for Ritchie is empathetic identification. The contrasting styles look ahead to the contrast epitomized in the discussion of Lorenz and Gilligan in Section IV.
9. *Mrs. Dalloway* and *To the Lighthouse* are probably the two most obvious examples.
10. Ruthven provides a useful chapter on "Dismantling androcentric assumptions" (59-92).
11. See also Gilligan's discussion of how an act of assertion need not be an act of aggression but rather one of communication (61-63).
12. Another critic, Vineta Colby, has chosen to concentrate on the opposite view of Cholmondeley: "One is conscious always in her work of a tightly controlled restraint, from which at times fragments of violence, repressed sexuality, cold-blooded cruelty and sadism, burst out and scatter wildly" (217).
13. Lowell made two significant changes in this version of the poem compared to its earlier incarnation in *Notebook* — changes which show him becoming both less and more aggressive, in effect changes which cancel each other out. "Gunning potato bugs" becomes "dusting apple orchards," while "packratted off with joy" is changed to "you packrat off with joy" — now rendering Harriet more of a target.

Works Cited

Austen, Jane. *Emma.* Ed. and introd. Ronald Blythe. 1816. Harmondsworth: Penguin Books, 1966.
Brownstein, Rachel M. *Becoming a Heroine: Reading about Women in Novels.* 1982. Harmondsworth: Penguin Books, 1984.
Butler, Samuel. *The Authoress of the Odyssey.* London: Longmans, Green, 1897.
———. *The Way of All Flesh.* 1903. New York: New American Library, 1960.
Cholmondeley, Mary. *Red Pottage.* Introd. Elaine Showalter, 1899. New York: Viking-Penguin, 1985.
Colby, Vineta. "'Devoted Amateur': Mary Cholmondeley and *Red Pottage.*" *Essays in Criticism* 20 (1970): 213-28.
Dickinson, Emily. *Final Harvest: Emily Dickinson's Poems.* Ed. Thomas H. Johnson. Boston: Little, Brown, 1961.
Eliot, George. *Impressions of Theophrastus Such.* London: William Blackwood, 1879.
Gilligan, Carol. *In a Different Voice: Psychological Theory and Women's Development.* Cambridge: Harvard UP, 1982.
Koestler, Arthur. *The Act of Creation: A Study of the Conscious and Unconscious in Science and Art.* 1964. New York: Dell, 1967.
Lowell, Robert. *For Lizzie and Harriet.* New York: Farrar, Straus and Giroux, 1973.
———. *Notebook.* Rev. ed. 1971. New York: Farrar, Straus and Giroux, 1972.
Lorenz, Konrad. *On Aggression.* Trans. Marjorie Kerr Wilson. 1966. New York: Bantam, 1967.
MacCarthy, Mary [Warre Cornish]. *A Nineteenth-Century Childhood.* 1924. London: Martin Secker, 1929.
McCarthy, Mary [Therese]. *The Groves of Academe.* 1951. New York: New American Library, 1963.
MacKay, Carol Hanbery. "'Only Connect': The Multiple Roles of Anne Thackeray Ritchie." *The Library Chronicle of the University of Texas* n.s. 30 (1985): 83-112.
———. "The Thackeray Connection: Virginia Woolf's Aunt Anny." *Virginia Woolf and Bloomsbury: A Centennial Celebration.* Ed. Jane Marcus. Bloomington: Indiana UP; London: Macmillan, 1987. 66-95.
Marcus, Jane. "Art and Anger." *Feminist Studies* 4 (1978): 69-98.
Meredith, George. *The Egoist: A Comedy in Narrative.* 1879. London: Constable, 1915.
———. *An Essay on Comedy and the Uses of the Comic Spirit.* 1877. London: Constable, 1919.
Moore, Marianne. *The Complete Poems of Marianne Moore.* New York: Macmillan and Viking, 1967.
Plath, Sylvia. *Ariel.* Introd. Robert Lowell. 1961. New York: Harper & Row, 1965.
Polhemus, Robert M. *Comic Faith: The Great Tradition from Austen to Joyce.* Chicago: U of Chicago P, 1980.
[Ritchie] Anne, Thackeray. *Five Old Friends and a Young Prince* ("The Sleeping Beauty in the Wood," "Cinderella," "Beauty and the Beast," "Little Red Riding Hood," "Jack the Giant Killer," and "A Young Prince"). 1868. London: Smith, Elder, 1905.
———. *The Story of Elizabeth.* Leipzig: Bernhard Tauchnitz, 1863.
———. *Toilers and Spinsters and Other Essays.* London: Smith, Elder, 1874.
———. *The Village on the Cliff.* London: Smith, Elder, 1867.
Ruthven, K.K. *Feminist Literary Studies: An Introduction.* Cambridge: Cambridge UP, 1984.

Thackeray, William Makepeace. *The Centenary Biographical Edition of the Works of William Makepeace Thackeray*. Ed. and introd. Anne Thackeray Ritchie. London: Smith, Elder, 1910-11. 26 vols.

Vonnegut, Kurt, Jr. *Breakfast of Champions*. 1973. New York: Dell, 1975.

Woolf, Virginia. "Leslie Stephen." *The Times* 28 Nov 1932. Rpt. in *The Captain's Death Bed and Other Essays*. New York: Harcourt, Brace & World, 1950. 69-75.

———. *Mrs Dalloway*. New York: Harcourt, Brace, 1925.

———. "The Enchanted Organ: Anne Thackeray." *The Moment and Other Essays*. London: Hogarth, 1947. 156-58.

———. *Night and Day*. London: Duckworth, 1919.

———. *A Room of One's Own*. New York: Harcourt, Brace & World, 1929.

———. *To the Lighthouse*. New York: Harcourt, Brace, 1927.

Zipes, Jack. *Victorian Fairytales: The Revolt of the Fairies and the Elves*. New York: Methuen, 1987.

Between women: a cross-class analysis of status and anarchic humor

REGENIA GAGNIER

Stanford University

IN THIS ESSAY I shall provide an interdisciplinary summary of the current status of humor theory; inquire into its relationship to humor in women's writing; and in a cross-class analysis of humor in some Victorian women's autobiographies, examine the relation of status to humor generally.

It is commonly held by paleopsychologists and assumed by humor theorists in literature, anthropology, linguistics, psychology, and sociology that humor for humankind originated in the Laugh, generally represented as the primal roar-of-triumph over the Enemy. From this benign genesis evolved the humorous practices of ridiculing the Victim and wit at the Victim's expense. From this paleosocial base, three theories of humor have developed: the cognitive-perceptual, generally called incongruity theory; the social-behavioral, generally called disparagement theory; and the psychoanalytic, generally called the suppression-repression, or release, theory (see Raskin, 21-41). Historical proponents of incongruity theory included Kant in 1790, for whom "laughter is an affection arising from sudden transformations of a strained expectation into nothing" (177); Schopenhauer in 1819, for whom "the cause of laughter in every case is simply the sudden perception of incongruity between a concept and the real objects which have been thought through it" (76); and, in a refined form, Bergson in 1899, for whom "the incongruity gives rise to laughter when the mechanical is encrusted upon the living" (84).

Disparagement theory was perhaps best formulated by Hobbes in 1650 (with his customary generosity): "The passion of laughter is nothing else but the *sudden glory* arising from some ... *conception* of ... *eminency* in ourselves, by *comparison* with the *infirmity* of others" (46). But as far back as Plato, malice or envy was thought to be at the root of the Comic (*Philebus* 45-49); and Aristotle subordinates the incongruity of the mechanical, animal-like Ridiculous to disparagement: "Comedy is an imitation of men worse than the average; worse ... as regards one particular kind [of fault], the Ridiculous, which is a species of the Ugly" ("Poetics" 229). And for Hegel in 1835, laughter is little more than "an expression of self-satisfied shrewdness" (302). The third, release, theory was, of course, best stated by Freud: play breaks the bona-fide communication of earnest, serious information-carriers. The more inhibitions, for release theory, the better opportunity for humor, which is why so many jokes are about sex, race, and politics.

These three theories are at the base of everything that has followed.[1] Incongruity theory includes the script theory of linguists, in which a text is compatible with two different scripts, one of which is illicit (Raskin, ch. 4); and the frame theory and bisociation of psychologists, in which the collative properties of humor stimuli are relative to the perceiver's knowledge of them, and a situation or idea is perceived in two habitually incompatible frames of reference (McGhee 14 and Suls 40). A refined disparagement theory has by now confined the disparagement to the "unaffiliated" (that is, not self-identified) under the rubric of "disposition" theory, which claims (remarkably) that we are disposed to laugh with our friends at our enemies and we are not disposed to laugh with our enemies at our friends (Zillmann 91-2).[2] But — and this will be significant when we speak of women's humor — such disparagement theories have perplexed sociologists when applied to disempowered groups, as when black people in controlled situations have seemingly perversely laughed at anti-black jokes.[3]

It will come as no surprise that historically theorists of humor have been men, and they have seldom considered the role of gender in humor, although recent discussion of the function of sex in humor should not go unremarked. Some cognitive and neuropsychologists, for example, have viewed the perception of incongruities as an innate capacity of the brain. Thus the holistic processing capacities of the right hemisphere (the "male" side) produce awareness of incongruous relationships, whereas the left (the "female", or analytic, sequential, side) can barely comprehend incongruities, or jokes (McGhee 24-34). Thus neuropsychologists have discovered the "dual process" model, based upon the relative capabilities of the cerebral hemispheres and emotive environment: faced with humorous stimuli, males are "objective" or "field independent," whereas females are "subjective" or "field dependent" (Suls 50, Chapman 146):[4] which means that in public places women look 'round to see who else is laughing and men immediately discern the absolute signification of incongruity and thus the hard core of humor *per se*. Regarding this (until very recently) common topos of behavioral science research, the correlation of "field dependency" with female stereotypes and "field independency" with male stereotypes, a student of mine, Annie Tillery, observed that men are perceived in behavioral science as field insensitive, contextually unaware, and environmentally oblivious.

I pass over the debates over methodology among such physicalist theorists, such as the pros and cons of the Facial Action Coding System (La France 1-12). My point is that although there has been some research on biology and humor, there has in fact been very little, in any discipline, on *gender* and humor, that is, little research that analyzes women's humor in a male public domain or that accounts for masculine and feminine humor in the context of their historical power relations. There is some general agreement that male humor has been more aggressive, more akin to the primal roar, than female, and, correlatively, that roaring has been a more acceptable practice for men than women (see Chapman and Foot 361–78). As Nina Auerbach said in an earlier response to this paper, it seems that historically men have preferred women's tears to their more threatening laughter. The anthropologist Mahadev Apte has concluded from cross-cultural analysis that women's humor in the public realm is constrained by prevalent cultural values of male superiority and dominance and female passivity; that certain social factors like marriage and advanced age remove the constraints and reduce the differences between men's and women's humor; that men fear women's humor for much the same reason that they fear women's sexual freedom — because they encourage women's aggression and promiscuity and thus disrupt the social order; that therefore men desire to control women's humor just as they desire to control women's sexuality — to wit, in the public domain; and finally that women's humor among themselves may not be assimilable to any of these categories (Apte 67-81). If for male theorists humor is functional, promoting group cohesion and intergroup conflict through disparagement, and social control through momentary releases that only serve to reinforce the status quo (see Fine 173), women's humor may do none of the above.

With this female lacuna in the research in mind, I attempted to see what 19th- and early 20th-century British women — women in a classist and sexist, that is heavily stratified, society — found funny among themselves. My informants, as it were, are not Jane Austens, not women whose humor has won acclaim in the public arena: they are working-class and educated middle-class women who recorded lives that were either lived or well begun in the nineteenth century and whose expected audience was in most cases other women.[5] It is my thesis that however restricted they were in public, among themselves Victorian women used humor neither for disparagement nor temporary release, but rather as a prolonged anarchic assault upon the codes constricting them. This is to say that their humor primarily lay within the category of incongruity but that their use of incongruity had socio-behavioral implications for exploring difference rather than merely disparaging it and for prolonged critical action rather than momentary release.

In May of 1930 Virginia Woolf responded to Margaret Llewelyn Davies's request that she write the preface for a collection of working women's autobiographies. Woolf responded that books — real books — did not need prefaces, that the collection was not exactly a book, and that therefore she would write not a preface but "the following letter addressed not to the public but to you."[6] In this correspondence between two women about the correspondence of other women Woolf reflects upon the Congress of the Working Women's Co-Operative Guild of June 1913 in Newcastle, where she had first encountered the autobiographers, and registers two instances of humorous incongruity: first, the incongruity of working-class women, who are traditionally "hands" not "heads," giving speeches (an old joke employed by Monty Python, whose charladies discuss Jean-Paul Sartre), and, second, Woolf's incongruous presence among them. Woolf's description reduces the women speaking to automata, in Bergson's term, "mechanical." "A bell struck; a figure rose; a woman took her way from among us; she mounted a platform; she spoke for precisely five minutes; she descended. Directly she sat down another woman rose; mounted the platform; spoke for precisely five minutes and descended; then a third rose, then a fourth — and so it went on, speaker following speaker, one from the right, one from the left, one from the middle, one from the background — each took her way to the stand, said what she had to say, and gave place to her successor" (xvi).

In Aristotle's *Poetics*, humor, as distinguished from comedy — and, importantly, to be so distinguished in the rest of this essay — occurs when one sympathizes with the ridiculous animal-like breaker of rules because one sees the contradiction between it and the frame it cannot comply with. One may even think that the frame is wrong, which leads to criticism of a set of cultural and intertextual frames. In this sense humor is metasemiotic, casting in doubt other cultural codes. In Umberto Eco's terms, humor reminds us of the presence of a law that we no longer have reason to obey.

It is this sympathetic, supportive humor that we see in Woolf and that, I believe, derives from Victorian women's social status. From the distance of social class, she watches these unladylike — that is, animal-like — women who incongruously demand reform of the Law — Divorce Laws, taxation, Minimum Wage, maternity policy, Trades Board and Education Acts, and Adult Suffrage. She appreciates their frame-breaking, she even thinks that the paternalistic frame is wrong, yet they are humorous, she must admit, because their specific frame was not hers. "Something was always creeping in from a world that was not their world and making the picture false ... One sat in an armchair or read a book. One saw landscapes and seascapes, perhaps Greece or Italy, where Mrs. Giles or Mrs. Edwards must have seen slag heaps and rows upon rows of slate roofed houses ... the game [was] too much of a game (xxi)." "Therefore," Woolf concludes, "however much we had sympathised our sympathy was largely fictitious" (xxvi) and she passes on to describe the differences between ladies and working women, differences that lead to criticism of a set of cultural and intertextual frames, so that the outcome is that Woolf is empowered by watching working women break their own frames, codes, or sets of social premises.

Conversely, according to Woolf, the women of the Congress find humorous ladies' "mincing speech and little knowledge of what it pleases them to call 'reality'" (xxvi) — presumably because such speech would be inaudible and such reality absent in the lives of working women. Working women find humor in cross-class transgressions, as when their soi-disant superiors enter their world of necessity to make ludicrous trivial gestures or when they try to imagine themselves in middle-class situations. The midwife Mrs. Layton recalls an absurd image of a lady, a complete stranger, looming out of Victoria Park to assail her with bourgeois values when she was a child. The alien lady "asked my age and if I went to school and a lot of other questions. She said I was a bright, intelligent little girl, and asked if I could read a few verses out of a nice Testament she had in her hand ... and made me promise that I would never neglect to wash myself before leaving home ... and never miss an opportunity of improving myself if only I had more time" (*Life as We Have Known It* 5). Then, Mrs. Layton recalls, the lady vanishes. The Bohemian dancer Betty May was sold on the White slave market as a child and spent her adolescence in Apache Gangs in Paris. She wryly records the incongruity between herself and the parents of her gentle barrister fiancé in Cornwall when she attempted to assimilate herself at the rectory: "I was not regarded as the interesting person I had expected to be, as someone who had been through experiences they would never encounter, who had seen sides of life that they had only read of in novels ... But I tried: I even used to go to lectures on potatoes and that sort of thing" (May 86). As a child, Emma Smith had been abused regularly. Leaving the penitentiary, she is advised by a nun to marry and tries to imagine domesticity: "A wife and mother? Was it possible? Suddenly, in my mind's eyes, I saw a little home, furniture, curtins, a cradle — and I tried to imagine (only this was more difficult) a man in slippers" (Smith 151).

In none of the hundreds of working women's autobiographies I have read have I found jokes about sex or jokes at the expense of unfortunates: the sole source of humor is real or imaginary transgressions relating to social class. The form these humorous transgressions take is not disparagement or release, nor brief laughter, but rather a process of imaginative engagement. Woolf's confrontation with the Co-Operative Working Women is one of the most penetrating class confrontations in modern British discourse precisely because Woolf allows herself to imagine a full intertextuality or exchange of frames. As she muses on the working women challenging the laws of privilege, she writes, "This force of theirs ... is about to break through and melt us together so that life will be richer and books more complex and society will pool its possessions instead of segregating them — all this is going to happen" (xxviii). Most women of her class, however, simply believed that the rules were different for working women and for ladies, that ladies could break their own rules but that extrasystemic transgression was out of the question.

To the extent to which this "separate spheres" view prevailed, there was comparatively little humor in working women's autobiographies. For the rules that concerned working women — at least the majority of working women who had not begun to undergo embourgeoisement — were the rules of survival and necessity, not polite society, and writers seldom break or see others break the rules of survival without providing pathos rather than humor. Similarly, in order to protect their own status, upper-class women seldom let social inferiors see them breaking rules, so working-class women could seldom learn from the example of rebellious upper-class women. And working women were aware of their relative lack of humor. In *Jipping Street* (1928) Kathleen Woodward confesses that in her reading for self-improvement she was acutely conscious of losing much of the sense of middle-class authors, especially, she imagined, in her inability to detect when they were being humorous (130), that is, breaking middle-class rules or codes that remained largely mysterious for her.

On the other hand, the significantly greater number of rules to be broken, relative to the few — and iron — rules of a worker's life, makes middle-class woman's writing rather more humorous than that of working women. In memoirs of educated middle-class women, humor is very often exclusively directed toward one thing: the rules of the school, or the education that would make them ladies. Again, faced with codes that were incongruous with women's perceived powers, women launched sustained and anarchic attacks upon those codes.

In her *Life* (1894) Frances Power Cobbe describes the 100+ ladies' schools in Brighton with their hundreds of rows of identical girls in full evening dress, facing the wall for breaking the rules. After a curriculum of — in descending order of importance — music, dancing, deportment, drawing, Continental languages, English, and Religion ("fasting will be good for our souls *and* our figures"), the young Cobbe left school secure in a position that the older philanthropist, suffragette, and anti-vivisectionist could only record with considerable humor. Upon leaving school, Cobbe recalls, she thought: "I know as much as any girl in our school, and since it is the best school in England, I *must* know all that it can ever be necessary to know. I will not trouble my head ever again with learning anything; but read novels and amuse myself for the rest of my life" (vol. 1, 60-69). Cobbe's humor, of course, turns to disparagement of what she calls "feminine futility" by the second volume, as illustrated by the ludicrous description of a lady attempting for three pages to uncork a bottle (vol. II, 229-32). Ladies and labor — even such labor as opening champagne — were incongruous, but the humor for Cobbe consists in the disparity between this image of febrile femininity and what she knows of women's capabilities.

In *A Little Learning: or A Victorian Childhood*, the educationist Winifred Peck (née Winifred Knox) recalls the 250 rules that could not be broken daily at Miss Quill's Day School for Christian Ladies in the 1870s. Peck recalls the rule to "Assume your underwear as modestly as possible under the covering of your night gown" and grows riotous trying to envision some flagrant disregard of the rule (66). Peck also mocks her childhood education from standard texts like *Near Home and Far Off* for their ludicrous and incongruous formulae of national stereotypes (the mechanical encrusted upon the living) to be learned by rote by British schoolchildren, such as "The Irish are a merry people and fond of pigs," or "The Italians are a dark, revengeful race where [sic] the stiletto is in frequent use" (22). And she grows hilarious at the specious rules of English grammar after the Romans, as in "Castle: noun, accusative; third person, neuter gender, etc."

In Mary Vivian Hughes's *A London Family 1870-1900: A Trilogy* (1934-37), the educator Hughes also finds humor the only way to describe her own education. Her twenty-sixth edition of Brewer's *Guide to Science* (1869) presented itself in the form of a catechism: "Q. What is heat? A. That which produces the sensation of warmth. Q. What is light? A. The unknown cause of visibility. Q. What should a fearful person do to be secure in a storm? A. Draw his bedstead into the middle of his room, commit himself to the care of God, and go to bed" (43). Surrounded by strictly enforced rules at North London Collegiate in the 1880's, Hughes philosophically laughs at the impossibility of not breaking them: "We were forbidden to get wet on the way to school, ... to drop a pencil-box, leave a book at home, hang a boot-bag by only one loop ... One felt that if a girl were to knock over the blackboard by mistake there would be a rule against it the next day" 8165).

Perhaps the most eloquent humor at the expense of school rules for ladies appears in my last example of this kind, Antonia White's *Frost in May* (1933), which is only nominally fictive. In the Convent of the Five Wounds, Fernanda Grey (Antonia White) rebels against the master narratives of Roman Catholicism that frame every aspect of the girls' lives. Nothing can be seen "for its own sake" (169), for things are freighted with a density of religious signification that organizes and interprets the child's experience:

To Our Lady and the Holy Child and the saints [Nanda] spoke as naturally as to her friends. She learnt to smooth a place on her pillow for her Guardian Angel to sit during the night ... to jump out of bed at the first beat of the bell to help the Holy Souls in purgatory ... The donkey in the paddock reminded her that all donkeys have crosses on their backs since the day Our Lord rode into Jerusalem; the robin's breast was red because one of his ancestors had splashed his feathers with the precious Blood trying to peck away the crown of thorns. The clover and the shamrock were a symbol of the Blessed Trinity, the sunflower was a saint turning always towards God, the speedwell had been white till Our Lady's blue mantle brushed it as she walked in the fields of Nazareth. When Nanda heard a cock crow, it cried "Christus natus est"; the cows lowed "Ubi? Ubi?" and the lambs down at the community farm bleated "Be-e-thlehem." (46-47)

I now want to turn to a final Victorian example, perhaps the most bitter, of women's humor: Florence Nightingale's "Cassandra," which Nightingale was advised not to publish and which remained suppressed until the twentieth century. It was part of a work within a genre much attended to by women, the spiritual autobiography, and entitled *Suggestions for Thought to Searchers after Religious Truth.* In "Cassandra" the rules imaginatively broken, the boundaries imaginatively crossed, are the rules and boundaries of gender itself. It has long been known that the story of Nightingale cannot be contained by her two rigidly dichotomized popular images. Between the *Times*'s war correspondent's image of The Nurse (with her sweet approving smile, the ideal representation of ideal woman, the angel of mercy, the bedside madonna, the lady of the lamp) and Lytton Strachey's portrait of the "Eagle," the demonic slave-driver of Cabinet ministers, poets, and masters of Balliol, is Nightingale's own representation of herself as Cassandra, the prophet who knew the truth about the future but was doomed by Apollo never to have her prophecies believed.

In her commentary on the MLA panel from which this essay

derives, Nina Auerbach said that women turn their frustrations and hatred into humor and then turn their humor against themselves. Nightingale's text is the mad babble of Cassandra, representing "that perpetual day-dreaming [of women's emancipation], which is so dangerous" (397): Cassandra knows the possibilities for women in the future but due to the historical connotations of Victorian gender she is powerless to enact the changes that she knows will come. The text is of women babbling their transgressions by exchanging roles with *men*. On the restrictions on ladies' activities Nightingale writes, "But suppose we were to see a number of men in the morning sitting round a table in the drawing-room, looking at prints, doing worsted work, and reading little books, how we should laugh!" (400). Of the eternal waste of leisure-class women's time in morning calls, she asks, "If you offer a morning visit to a professional man, and say 'I will just stay an hour with you, if you will allow me, till so and so comes back to fetch me'; it costs him the earnings of an hour, and therefore he has a right to complain. But women have no right, because it is *'only* their time'" (402). In her most daring assault on the boundaries between the male and female spheres, Nightingale, a deeply religious woman, does a parodic and woman's reading of the Gospel, claiming that if Christ had been a woman, "He might have been nothing but a great complainer" (416) negligent of his duties to home and family. "For instance," she writes:

Christ was saying something to [the multitude] one day, which interested Him very much, and interested them very much; and Mary and His brothers came in the middle of it, and wanted to interrupt Him, and take Him home to dinner, very likely ... and He, instead of being angry with their interruption of Him in such an important work for some trifling thing, answers, "Who is my mother? and who are my brethren? Whosoever shall do the will of my Father which is in heaven, the same is my brother and sister and mother." But if *we* [women] were to say that, we should be accused of "destroying the family tie, of diminishing the obligation of the home duties." (417)

Such humor challenged the law that women like Nightingale no longer had reason to obey.

In sum we can say that in 19th- and early 20th-century self-representation, what women perceive as humorous is not Hobbes's "*sudden glory* arising from a *conception* of *eminency* in ourselves by *comparison* with the *infirmity* of *others*" but rather the very terms of their confinement.[7] Working women find humor in cross-class scenarios disrupting the social order, and upper-class women in disrupting the codes and regulations of their own class. This suggests that women's humor tends toward anarchy rather than the status quo, to prolonged disruption rather than, in Freudian theory, momentary release.

My second observation concerns status. In middle-class male public school memoirs — the social equivalents of the ladies' memoirs I've just cited, rules are figured in two ways: they are either accepted and played by, in which case the boy assumes his place in the social power structure, or they are despaired of, in which case the defeated boy retreats into isolation and obscurity.[8] Perhaps because women's status was lower, women did not perceive this tragic dichotomy. Facing the rules, they tended toward anarchy rather than insecurity. That is, women's lower status permitted them a lesser investment in the rules and more ease in undertaking their imaginative disruption through humor in the relative privacy of discourse among women. The corollary, of course, is that the greater the status, the more the rules are for one's benefit and the more one's relation to them is exposed to public view and may be defined as reverent, or potentially tragic.[9] It is within this frame that I have come to interpret some friendly advice to me from an academic administrator: that if I did not control my sense of humor I could never aspire to the administrative ranks.

Kate Clinton, the radical-lesbian-feminist-humorist has a wonderful sketch on *Debbie Does Dallas* that, like her hyphenated epithet, throws into relief multiple frames of difference in opposition to the law and thus provides my last example of anarchic humor. Not the ideal male spectator assumed by the producers of the film, Clinton muses upon Debbie and the other heterosexually-marked cheerleaders in the shower-room, washing their breasts. And washing, and washing their breasts, big circular motions. Clinton, who confesses that for her breasts are no big deal, neither here nor there, nonetheless sympathizes with Debbie and her cohort: "Well, we *do* know how dirty breasts *do* get. I, for example, sometimes change my bra three or four times a day." I will not analyze here the number of cultural frames being broken in this example or transgressions in play, but the dynamic is not unlike that between Woolf and the working women.

This frame-breaking, democratizing, and anarchic humor should by now recall the laugh of the Medusa. In her classic essay, Hélène

Cixous proposes that women write *for women*. What they should write should approach the Unconscious, that place where there are no rules and where boundaries break down, and where the oppressed have managed to survive.[10] Medusa's laughter, or "women's writing" in Cixous's sense, like Bergson's "living," opposes itself to undesirable ("mechanical") rules and laws.[11] "It will be conceived of only by subjects who are breakers of automatisms," writes Cixous reflecting Bergson's terminology, "by peripheral figures that no authority can ever subjugate. ... What woman hasn't felt, dreamt, performed the gesture that jams sociality? Who hasn't held up to ridicule the bar of separation? ... Who, by some act of transgression, hasn't overthrown successiveness, connection, the wall of circumfusion?" (Cixous 253-258). Here some would go on to employ an analysis after the work of Nancy Chodorow of women's fluid boundaries or after the work of Judith Kegan Gardiner of fluid characterization in women's writing; but I want only to insist upon the more limited arena of Medusa's *laughter* in stratified populations. For Medusa's anarchic laughter sheds some light on why — unlike those white men secure in their absolute signification who discern in isolation the hard core of humor — the black men in the study laughed at everything and the Victorian women never laughed alone.

Notes

1. For contemporary humor theory referred to here see Apte, Chapman and Foot, McGhee and Goldstein, and Raskin. These sources, especially Raskin and the two collections, provide compendious histories of previous work and full bibliographies of humor research. My essay is indebted to Jim English, who alerted me to much contemporary humor research and graciously commented on an earlier version of this paper; Regina Barreca, who organized the MLA panel on Women's Humor for which it was written; and to the Institute for Research on Women and Gender, Stanford University, which gave me another opportunity to present and discuss the material in its Jing Lyman Lecture Series, Spring 1987.
2. The technical formulation includes clauses of magnitude and degree:
   1. The more intense the negative disposition toward the disparaged agent or entity, the greater the magnitude of mirth.
   2. The more intense the positive disposition toward the disparaged agent or entity, the smaller the magnitude of mirth.
   3. The more intense the negative disposition toward the disparaging agent or entity, the smaller the magnitude of mirth.
   4. The more intense the positive disposition toward the disparaging agent or entity, the greater the magnitude of mirth. (Zillmann 91-2).
3. But see the weak explanation in Fine 171-2.

4. For critiques of such biological theories without reference to humor see Fausto-Sterling, especially 30-32, 44-53.
5. My major source of working-class autobiography is *The Autobiography of the Working Class: An Annotated, Critical Bibliography Vol. I: 1790-1900*, ed. John Burnett, David Vincent, David Mayall (Sussex: Harvester, 1984). For a broader analysis of some of these autobiographies see Gagnier "Social Atoms: Working-Class Autobiography, Subjectivity, and Gender" *Victorian Studies* (Spring 1987).
6. "Introductory Letter to Margaret Llewelyn Davies" by Virginia Woolf in *Life as We have Known It by Co-Operative Working Women* xvi. Further page references will be included in the text.
7. Strictly speaking, of course, there may be a little Hobbesian disparagement in women's mockery of rules that are generally followed or beliefs that are widely held, for with such mockery women implicitly elevate themselves and demonstrate at least a latent "conception of eminency." Yet although this may be the case theoretically, women get no purchase from the elevation: humor for women as I am describing it here is an imaginative process, whereas elevation or superiority is a fixed status. In Aristotelian terms the difference is between comedy and humor, or a laugh and reflective critical engagement.
8. Specifically, they typically retreated into aesthetics. See Gagnier, "'From Fag to Monitor; Or, Fighting to the front': Art and Power in Public School Memoirs" *Victorian Learning* ed. Robert Viscusi vol 15 (*Browning Institute Studies: An Annual of Victorian Literary and Cultural History*) forthcoming 1988.
9. For a compatible analysis of humor and status see Williams 1987, in which an anthropologist argues that humor intervenes in disputes in a rural Guyanese community in inverse proportion to the elevated status of the participants and formal litigation.
10. Cixous's term is "repressed" rather than "oppressed," but I want to emphasize the political point: women's humor in these texts allows for a continuous assault upon the social forms constraining women. See Cixous 250.
11. Bergson's seemingly narrow focus on the mechanical/living opposition in fact has a very wide range of application, his sense of the mechanical extending to "automatic" reliance on rules. For Bergson, humor's primary social function is that of offering a corrective to rigid, "automatic" behavior — a way of freeing the agent from undesirable social restraints. Thus Victorian women's humor points up the incongruity between rules (the mechanical) and women's real capabilities (the living, the *élan vital*). The question contested among Bergsonians of course is whether Bergson envisioned the kind of sustained critical process I claim for these women or the more conventional and conservative short-term releases that in the long run only serve to reinforce the status quo. Freudians debate the same question with respect to Freudian humor theory.

Works cited

Apte, Mahadev. *Humor and Laughter: An Anthropological Approach*. Ithaca: Cornell, 1985.
Aristotle. "Poetics" *Rhetoric*. New York: Random House, 1954.
Bergson, Henri 1899. "Laughter" *Comedy*. Ed. Wylie Sypher. New York: Doubleday, 1956.
Chapman, Antony J. "Humor and Laughter in Social Interaction and Some Implications for Humor Research" in McGhee and Goldstein Vol. 1.

Chapman, Antony J. and Hugh Foot, eds. *It's a Funny Thing, Humor.* New York: Pergamon, 1977.
Chodorow, Nancy. *The Reproduction of Mothering.* Berkeley: University of California Press, 1978.
Cixous, Hélène 1975. "The Laugh of the Medusa" *New French Feminisms: An Anthology* Ed. Elaine Marks and Isabelle de Courtivron. New York: Schocken, 1981.
Cobbe, Frances Power. *Life.* 2 vols. London: Richard Bentley, 1894.
Co-Operative Working Women. *Life as We Have Known It.* New York: Norton, 1975.
Eco, Umberto. "The Frames of Comic Freedom" 1-9. [I have been unable to locate the source of this article.]
Fausto-Sterling, Anne. *Myths of Gender: Biological Theories About Women and Men.* New York: Basic Books, 1985.
Fine, Gary Alan. "Sociological Approaches to the Study of Humor" in McGhee and Goldstein Vol. 1.
Freud, Sigmund 1905. *Jokes and Their Relation to the Unconscious.* New York: Penguin, 1976.
―――― 1928. "Humour." *International Journal of Psychoanalysis* vol. 9: 1-6.
Gardiner, Judith Kegan. "On Female Identity and Writing by Women" *Writing and Sexual Difference* Ed. Elizabeth Abel. Chicago: University of Chicago Press, 1982, 177-91.
Hegel, Georg W. F. 1835. *The Philosophy of Fine Art* Vol. IV. London: G. Bell, 1920.
Hobbes, Thomas 1650. *The English Works of Thomas Hobbes* Vol. IV. London: John Bohn, 1840.
Hughes, M. Vivian. *A London Family: 1870-1900: A Trilogy.* London: Oxford University Press, 1946.
Kant, Immanuel 1790. *Critique of Judgment.* New York: Hafner, 1951.
La France, Marianne. "Felt Versus Feigned Funniness: Issues in Coding Smiling and Laughing" in McGhee and Goldstein Vol. 1.
May, Betty. *Tiger-Woman: My Story.* London: Duckworth, 1929.
McGhee, Paul E. and Jeffrey H. Goldstein, eds. *Handbook of Humor Research* 2 vols. New York: Springer-Verlag, 1983.
Nightingale, Florence 1852. "Cassandra" in Ray Strachey *The Cause: A Short History of the Women's Movement in Great Britain* 1928; rpt: New York, Kennikat Press, 1969.
Peck, Winifred. *A Little Learning: or A Victorian Childhood.* London: Faber and Faber, 1952.
Plato. *Philebus.* Oxford: Clarendon, 1975.
Raskin, Victor. *Semantic Mechanisms of Humor.* Boston: Reidel, 1985.
Schopenhauer, Arthur 1819. *The World as Will and Idea,* Vol. I. London: Routledge and Kegan Paul, 1957.
Smith, Emma (pseud.). *A Cornish Waif's Story: An Autobiography.* London: Odhams Press, 1954.
Suls, Jerry M. "Cognitive Processes in Humor Appreciation," in McGhee and Goldstein Vol. 1.
White, Antonia 1933. *Frost in May.* New York: Dial press, 1980.
Williams, Brackette. "Humor, linguistic ambiguity, and disputing in a Guyanese community" *International Journal of the Sociology of Language* 65 (Amsterdam, 1987): 79-94.
Woodward, Kathleen. *Jipping Street: Childhood in a London Slum.* New York: Harper, 1928.
Zillmann, Dolf. "Disparagement Humor" in McGhee and Goldstein Vol. 1.

Slaying the angel and the patriarch: the grinning Woolf

DENISE MARSHALL

Heidelberg College, Tiffin, Ohio

"THE VILLAIN of my story was a woman ... the Angel in the House" ("Speech" xxix). By the time Woolf gave this speech to the London/National Society for Women's Service on January 21, 1931, her powers as an innovator and novelist were widely recognized. Her comedic power as a writer had increased her personal sense of detachment from but also her power within the "masculinist" culture. Her laughter in *Orlando* had connected her more intricately to an even wider audience than she had enjoyed before. Fittingly at this juncture she described her beginnings as a writer.

She wrote to get money in order to buy things. With her first check, "flown with glory — [she] bought ... a beautiful cat" and decided "What could be easier, simpler" than to write reviews and get checks in the mail, "But after all ... there is a villain" (xxix).

I now record the one act for which I take some credit — though the credit belongs rather to my income than to me — if one has five hundred a year there is no need to tell lies and it is much more amusing to tell the truth — I turned upon that Angel and caught her by the throat. I did my best to kill her. My excuse ... would be that I acted in self defense. If I had not killed her, she would have killed me — as a writer (xxxi).

Woolf's assault on the Angel in the House is closely connected with her perception of women in culture, especially their economic status; and demonstrates her ability to flex the comic muscles, to propose her vision of the world confidently, and to advocate her sense of the alternatives. She reveals her conscious struggle for that power. Her reasons appear straight-forward enough; these ideas, her freedom forces, led her to confront her society directly, and aggressively in public. She uses comedy of power, and she hints at its foundation in her acknowledgement that "if one has five hundred a year there is no need to tell lies and it is much more amusing to tell the truth."

Her speech was amusing. Vera Brittain was in the audience and reports the enthusiastic reception of Woolf's "Hilariously serious" vivisection of the Angel (qtd. in "Speech" xxxv). Brittain was careful to mention that "Mrs. Woolf attribute[s] ... success largely to the possession of a private income, which enabled ... [her] to flout the displeasure of authors and editors by writing honest reviews" (qtd. in "Speech" xxxv). So Woolf kills the Angel, or tries to. Woolf's perception of her career is bound up in her struggle to defeat this Victorian fixture, for when she was a girl, "Almost every respectable Victorian house had its angel" ("Speech" xxxi).

> It is the very stuff of the age's pet sentimental vapors, enshrined in notions such as 'the angel in the house', the 'good woman who rescues the fallen', and so on. It is the fabric of dreams. *But the dreams of an age are part of its life*, ... (Millett 150/emphasis added).

Such sentimental vapors are the mental fogs burned away by the fierce rejection of another age, another generation — or indeed by the realities these fogs conceal so desperately.

Woolf applies a stiff dose of the salts to these vapors. Angels abounded in her household — her mother Julia Jackson was the Pre-Raphaelite vision frozen in photographs and resurrected in Woolf's own Lady Bountiful, Mrs. Ramsay. The Angel, as Woolf describes her close to seventy years after her installation as cultural icon, was

> ... intensely sympathetic. She was immensely charming. She was utterly unselfish. She excelled in the difficult arts of family life. She soothed, conciliated, sacrificed herself[,] took the hash if there was only chicken enough for one, and in short was so constituted that she never had a wish or a mind of her own but preferred to sympathize with the wishes and minds of others. Above all — I hope I need not say it — she was pure. There were a great many things that one could not say without bringing a blush to her cheek. ("Speech" xxx).

And she was dangerous to Woolf's comedy. One of the creature's "most annoying characteristics" was that she "never had any real existence (xxx). She existed in the speaking silence of culture.

Woolf swoops onto this ideal of woman with murderous talons. Tennyson's "On tiptoes seemed to touch upon a sphere/Too gross to tread ..." (xxx) "is really disgusting ... and seems to me to imply a relationship between men and women that was both false and disagreeable" (xxx). More than that, the Angel attempted to dictate how a woman should write. And most fatal, according to Woolf, she advised: "Never disturb them [men] with the idea that you have a mind of your own. And above all be pure" (xxxi). Woolf was fully aware of the prison of these limitations. If she were prohibited any topic, she could not be legitimate as a writer. Nor could she be comedic. The Angel carried a silencer.

Woolf's own feminist and comedic phenomenology gave her criticism and fiction a fuller and different honesty. Her world vision compassed, not merely the formal styles and modes of criticism, but life alternatives born of an intelligence thoroughly humorous. So, Woolf does not merely analyze Carlyle's writing.

> Young and ignorant and unmarried as I was I did have to say ... that Mr. Carlyle ought to have had a child and that Mrs. Carlyle ought to have written a novel; I did have to say that there was a good deal more to be said for Fanny Brawne as a lover than for Keats; I did have to say that it did not matter a straw whether George Eliot were married to Mr. Lewes or not ... (xxxii).

Of course she needed to say none of these things. She also needn't have mentioned in one of her earliest reviews that their lives might have been happier and their writing more consistent if the Bronte sisters could have gotten away from Haworth, and away from their father. She needn't have nosed out Jane Austen's radicalism or fine-tuned the sound of the juvenilia and the novels so we could hear Austen's girlish giggling and womanly laughter. Had she been a traditional critic she would have neither mentioned, nor indeed even noticed these things. But, Woolf's radical comic vision connected to the universe in this feminist way. Her feminism and her comic vision were so ingrained that these radical perceptions pervaded all of her work. "In short I was forced to attack many of the most sacred objects in the house. ..." (xxxii).

Like Austen, Woolf's juvenilia, "A Society" (1921), "Friendship's Gallery" (1907), and "The Journal of Mistress Joan Martyn" (1906) are comic satire, burlesque, and fantasy shot through with hard-nosed reality. They deal with feminist ideas which are her most deeply felt topics, and to which she returns repeatedly; women's education, women's networks, the lives of the obscure, the fabric of the daily as it weaves into and out of the universal, power, influence, authority and honesty, madness and absurdity. Masked in her earlier works, these basic concerns became the major texts in her later sardonic grotesque comedy. Reviewing Austen's *Persuasion*, Woolf said of Austen what might have been said of herself.

> Was she not beginning, in her own gay and brilliant manner, to contemplate a ... voyage of discovery? There is an asperity in her comedy which suggests she has almost ceased to be amused by ... vanities or ... snobbery ... The satire is harsh ... (*Reader* 146-147).

Woolf's satiric comedy becomes harsh too as she is less amused. But as she notes of Austen's fiction, so in her own much "proves not merely the biological fact ..., but the aesthetic fact that she was no longer afraid to say so" (*Reader* 148). Austen died at forty-two. Woolf's assessment of "the six novels she did not write" was published when Woolf was forty-three and based on two earlier essays, "Jane Austen" (1913) and "Jane Austen at Sixty" (1923) (Steele 133). It precedes her own shift to even more innovative experiments — *To The Lighthouse, Orlando, The Waves, Three Guineas, Room of One's Own*.

Woolf's speculations on Austen foreshadow what was to happen in her own work. If she had lived, says Woolf, "she would have devised a method ... for conveying what [people] leave unsaid; ... what life is ... and seen [character] more as a group ... Her satire would have been more stringent and severe" (*Reader* 149). Woolf in her later works expands her earlier themes to espouse and refine these ideas assertively, in stringent satire. Having achieved her legitimacy and her credibility, she enters her most "experimental, and venturesome" writing, "wild, satirical, and profligate" (Love 189-191). Her comedy of power asserts her own politics and phenomenology. She is adept at a savagery which "confronts the idea of the universe with its imperfections" where the "harmoniousness of the universe is suspect" (White 5). This comedy is cuttingly double-edged and decisely anti-romantic. Tone and surface may be comic, but its text is essentially serious, full of semi-tragic anti-climaxes.

Woolf's *The Waves* (1931) is just such a novel. Its six characters are "anti: heroines/heroes locked in perpetual battle with an inscrutable monster," full of "cosmic disequilibrium" (White, 5). This monster is various and ambiguous — guising itself differently for each one. It is Louis's "great beast's foot [as it] stamps, and stamps," Bernard's "fin in a waste of water," it is "the gardeners sweep(ing) the lawn with giant brooms..." (*Waves* 180, 307, 186).

The Waves' obsessional characters mock themselves and their obsessions. One of the centers of their friendship is Percival who "goes to India, ... rides a flea-bitten mare, ... His horse stumbled..." (256-281). *The Waves* comedy is grotesquerie, "a riddle of misfortunes which must be accepted but before which one must not capitulate" (Durrenmatt in White, 1978, 9). Neville, who loved Percival, and who, when he hears of his lover's death says from "this moment I am solitary," perceives that "this farce is worth no more formal celebration" (280-281). He refuses to capitulate to his grief while yet he allows it to tear at him "for this moment, this one moment ... We are doomed, all of us ... Yet you shall not destroy me" (280-281). He recognizes that "there is a grinning, there is a subterfuge. There is something sneering behind our backs" (281).

In the structures of the later novels, the sardonic gruesomeness of life's absurdities is sometimes set inside a lyric quietness, a setting which emphasizes the grotesque even more. Increasing dissonance within the novels supports and maintains a tension of ambiguity which is not resolved. The "fantasy and humor" of such comedy is strangely mingled with ferocity and with compassion" (White 9).

In such comedies — as in many of Woolf's novels — "the underlying antagonist is death" in a "multiplicity of universes" (White 9-12). Death is an ironic, grotesque anti-climax to a glorious possible life, or a wry triumph, or the ultimate lover. As Stevie Smith put it: "and the thought of Death as a friend ... that Death must come when we call, although he is a god" sustained her, and underpins this comedic stance (Smith 110). Death in *Mrs. Dalloway* is summoned by Septimus Smith (and Rhoda in *The Waves*), embraced by Clarissa Dalloway, and heralded by Sir William Bradshaw. Death is a sneak thief in *To The Lighthouse*, an interval in a larger drama. Indeed Sir William Bradshaw, whose profession of psychiatry weaves him tightly into the metal fabric of the twentieth century, is Death's right hand man. Through him Death and its consciousness is the warp of the societal fabric. Thus, Death comes to Clarissa's party, Woolf's *Decameron*.

Another aspect of Woolf's savage comedy is the "grotesques who make their plight known through horrendous outbursts [and] combine morbid qualities with carnival spirit" (White 18). Old Bart Oliver in *Between the Acts*, and Mr. Ramsay in *To The Lighthouse* are good examples of the type. Bart frightens the daylights out of his grandson whom he is trying to make laugh with his facial contortions. Mr. Ramsay "grinning sarcastically ... combines the pleasure of disillusioning ... with casting ridicule ..." (10). Mr. Ramsay's outbursts come from his not having reached the letter R in his career. To Lily Briscoe, "Never was anybody at once so ridiculous and so alarming" (*Lighthouse*, 30-31). He made them all "vaguely uncomfortable" (32). This vague discomfort infects the world in *To The Lighthouse* which thinly overlays a traditional family novel on top of disarray in the cosmos. In earlier novels disarray exists underneath or beside the conventional without quite disturbing the texture of life. But in *To The Lighthouse*, "a psychological turning point" (Love 189), the texture is frayed, the disarray becomes cosmic.

"Cosmic disarray prompted new facets of dark disquiet in comedy" (White 11). For Woolf, this cosmic disarray transmuted her mother and father, their relationship to each other and to their family, perhaps not into understanding or acceptance, but certainly into a recognition of the complexities and the contradictions, without the necessity to provide explanation. This often "harsh, strident, subterranean comedy" runs beneath the rest of her work, girding some more obviously; with only glinting flashes of the underlying steel in others. "Let us inhabit the underworld" (*Waves* 189). In that underworld, "textures shred, plots become phantasmagoric, comic harmonies go dissonant, plot progressions feature scattered or overlapping fragments" (White 13). Woolf's comedies combine all these elements as she moves from the "outlandishly wild social fireworks" of *Orlando* to "the sardonic insight with the overall sardonic dynamism" of *Room of One's Own* and *Three Guineas* to the "surrealistic puzzles" of *The Waves, The Years*, and *Between the Acts* (White 5-7).

Power comedy, where one winces one moment and laughs out loud the next, derives from an extremely strong sense of definition, and sense of self — both personally and professionally. Woolf's first professional act out of that sense of self was killing the Angel; the second that she began to define self as woman. "And now when the

> Angel is dead, what remains? ... what remains is something quite simple and common enough — a young woman. ... she has now only to be herself. But what is 'herself'? I mean what is a woman? ... I discovered when I came to write that a woman — it sounds so simple, but I should be ashamed to tell you how long it took me to realize this for myself — is not a man. Her experience is not the same. Her traditions are different. Her values, both in art and in life are her own. ("Speech" xxxiii).

In Woolf's struggle to write what she wanted to write, her sense of humor was crucially important. I believe it is back of her admonition in *Room of One's Own* to keep anger out of writing. For *Room* is not an unangry book. On the sixth page of the essay, she curses the library at Oxbridge and "descends the steps in anger" (8). Nor does she defuse this anger, here or in any other book. She transmutes it; she reshapes it to a tool for clear expression. She transmogrifies the energy of anger into the energy of comedy. *Room of One's Own* itself is used in this fashion: to raise consciousness through anger by contrasting images with facts, and then to set about converting that energy into direction. In *Room* and in her other works after 1928, the anger is in the open. It is the informant of her scorn, her sardonic satire, her dark/light underworld of orts and fragments.

Outside of defining herself Woolf names and defines cultural things. *Orlando* begins this process. Woolf explores and exposes culture and cultural process as historical progression impinging on individuals and gender. She attacks the symbols of each age, its sacred icons, pretentious sillinesses, its revered characters, and cultural conventions. *Between the Acts* (1941) is a fulfillment of *Orlando* but at Woolf's most sardonic and savage comedic stretch. Both novels seek out and name the absent content of social structures; and, in the searchlight of the comically chaotic burn away foggy mental mists. But the lifting of the fog savagely reveals the real chaos underneath. In *Orlando* Woolf muses about what it would have been like to have been *really* witty in the eighteenth century. What might it have been like to have a Wit and his/her tribe to dinner? In "Dr. Burney's Evening Party" (1929), the great Dr. Johnson, summoned to meet Fulke Greville, casts a deadly pall over the party because he remains uncustomarily silent. Wits are unpredictable. Orlando finds that her/his life is likewise unpredictable.

Orlando falls prey to the delusions of the era; "'Addison, Dryden, Pope,' Orlando repeated as if the words were an incantation" (167). Once established in London after sorting her way through the legal complexities of charges that "(1) she was dead, and therefore could not hold any property whatsoever; (2) that she was a woman, which amounts to much the same thing; (3) that she was an English Duke ..." whose three sons were claiming the property of their father, Orlando discovers London from the gender of a woman, and an individual still fatally susceptible to writers and poets (168). "... for he had the wildest, most absurd, extravagant ideas about poets and poetry" (21).

Orlando, her self "in a highly ambiguous condition" is also deeply sensitive to cultural ambiguities. In London to search for "Life and a lover," Orlando discovers it difficult to "name a thing" (194). "At one and the same time therefore, society is everything and society is nothing. Society is the most powerful concoction in the world and society has no existence whatever" (194). Orlando had "inherited a drop too much of that black humour which ran in the veins of all her race," (195). Woolf herself had inherited that humor and tackles in *Orlando* what she has not directly addressed before — the tenuous economic security a woman 'enjoys', women's susceptibility to cultural fads bred from a training of ignorance disguised as innocence, and the empty but strongly significant conventions of a society erratic in its enthusiasms, doubled in its standards.

For Woolf wit shatters illusions and bowls "over the current conversation as a cannon ball lays low the violets and the daisies" exposing society's intricate hypocrisies (200). Now, George Meredith would have wit as a means to civilization, as the very essence of civilized behavior. But Woolf's use of wit is quite different, as is her idea of society.

Then the little gentleman said,
He said next,
He said finally,
Here, it cannot be denied, was true wit.
true wisdom, true profundity. *The company was thrown into complete dismay*, One such saying was bad enough; but three, one after another, on the same evening! *No society could survive it.* (202/emphasis added).

The little gentleman, like "little women" at all times in all places, is reprimanded for such reprehensible behavior. "'Mr. Pope,' said old Lady R., in a voice trembling with sarcastic fury, 'you are pleased to be witty'" (202). The poet flushed, the company stayed silent, and then slunk away, perhaps never to return. The withering of this society signals Woolf's actualization of the comic power to truth-tell with a vengeance. The only answer is silence, and silences increase in Woolf's novels as does her comedy. Pope was an Outsider, and he used the outsiders' weapons, and received the outsider's reward. Woolf advocates the Outsiders' Society (in *Three Guineas*,) giving advice on how to achieve it. The portrait of Pope, and Orlando, is that combination of ambivalent sardonicism which marks the later Woolf. "I'll be blasted ... if I ever write another word, or try to write another word to please ... Bad, good or indifferent, I'll write from this day forward, to please myself..." (*Orlando* 103). And please herself she did. Significantly she moved politically to — *Room of One's Own*, to her 1931 public testament, to her attempts to combine politics and prose.

Her phenomenology publicly attested, she takes on the world. "When a woman comes to write a novel, she will find that she is perpetually wishing to alter the established values — to make serious what appears insignificant to a man, and trivial what is to him important" (*Room* 81). The public Woolf directly addresses women's lives in their culture during the years (1927-1932) when she also makes statements about her personal and professional life. Women's lives — for Woolf — are a web of interconnecting issues.

Money is central as a means to freedom. Woolf's more difficult modes during this period engage in consciousness raising and cultural dissection. Anger backs her humor, fueling its energy, and her now public discourse. In *Room of One's Own* "women ... have other interests besides the perennial interests of domesticity. 'Chloe liked Olivia. They shared a laboratory together...'" (87).

Room of One's Own is revolutionary, in its pervading comedic stance, and in its discourse about the hypocrisies and deprivations of women spoken by a woman to women. Woolf subverts male Oxbridge and the correct method of academic research and Socratic dialogue, outside the academy. She undermines its exclusivity with its own tactics. Woolf counters the impoverishment of women's access by freeing a wealth of knowledge to be shared among the outsiders. "Literature is impoverished beyond our counting by the doors that have been shut upon women" (87).

She questions male authority, and advocates women's authority. While not as militant as she will be in *Three Guineas*, Woolf is assertive to the point of aggressiveness, especially as she indicts male images of women and the definitions of society as handed down by men. She does all this by comparing facts — the lyrical novelist is very much aware of the "unending stream of gold and silver ..., money ... poured liberally to set these stones on a deep foundation ..." (*Room* 9).

Woolf's assertion of the power of feminist vision and her confident willingness to support her facts against 'their facts', Oxbridge masculinist facts, describes her own perceptual shift. In her first sections of *Room*, a Manx cat, glimpsed in the replete afterglow of a sumptuous meal at Oxbridge "changed by some fluke ... the emotional light for me" (11). The truncated animal paused "in the middle of the lawn as if it too questioned the universe" (11). Woolf finds truncation in a culture which provides superbly for the 'ludicrous and disgusting' things the Tennysons wrote and thought of women and the women believed of themselves. Woolf "burst out laughing at ... what men hummed ... [and] ... women hummed ... under their breath ..." (12-13). Leaving her splendid luncheon party, "Gate after gate seemed to close with gentle finality behind me. Innumerable beadles were fitting innumerable keys into well-oiled locks, the treasure-house was being made secure for another night" (13). The woman, representing all women, admitted on sufferance by rare invitation was again on the outside.

Orlando's comic monologue was the true turning point; in it she abandons indirection to grapple directly with the universe in a variety of comedic forms. *Room* is an even more direct confrontation with socio-political issues of feminist professionalism. Mary Datchet works hard for her room in *Night and Day*, an exception as *femme sole*. But in *Room* and the late works, the single woman becomes a major character, one who is complex and human, whose perceptions validate the work she inhabits.

Women who like women break the cultural pattern. Comedy illuminates that break. Woolf's novels abound in comic moments when the women bond, totally confusing the men around them. Woolf encourages such breakage and confusion, by splitting images, by presenting images in a mirror cracked. Hers is a funhouse mirror which distorts to extravagant grotesqueness on one side and withers on the other. This doubling technique is maintained in high tension from *Orlando* throughout the rest of her work. The Oxbridge group feeds on "a confection which rose all sugar from the waves;" the Fernham women upon "Biscuits and cheese ..., and here the water-jug was liberally passed around, for it is the nature of biscuits to be dry, and these were biscuits to the core" (*Room* 11, 18). Food is political because it nourishes more than the body. Good food calls up "the more profound, subtle and subterranean glow, which is the rich yellow flame of rational discourse" (11).

Woolf's attention to food, and the gathering for meals is a rarity in books in the established canon.

> It is a curious fact that novelists have a way of making us believe that luncheon parties are invariably memorable for something very witty that was said, or for something very wise that was done. But they seldom spare a word for what was eaten. It is part of the novelist's convention not to mention soup and salmon duckling as if soup and salmon duckling were of no importance whatsoever, as if nobody ever smoked a cigar or drank a glass of wine. Here, however, I shall take liberty to defy that convention ... (*Room* 10).

Her celebration of food implies the possibility of festival, and communion as well as civilization. It can by degrees light up "halfway down the spine, which is the seat of the soul' that "rich yellow flame of rational discourse" so that "this grudge or that grievance" seems trivial (*Room* 11). But the "truncated animal" calls to mind other luncheon parties in other times, and with those memories many questions of cultural significance in the presentation and consummation of luncheons.

One of the cultural ironies Woolf uses in her books is the conventional refuser of festivity (Frye 152-153). This refuser is usually a male who needs to be coaxed into a good humor, who mutters and mumbles to himself, who denies that he has had a good time, or who spends the time throwing around as many monkey wrenches as he can lay his hands on. These males have a long history in Woolf's novels, but come more center stage in her later works. Mr. Ambrose (*Voyage Out*) is one, so is Mr. Hilbery (*Night and Day*). Mr. Ramsay is the first of the more vivid figures whose misanthropic/misogynist behavior is amply rounded out by Bart and Giles in *Between the Acts*.

Part of the excruciating irony of Woolf's work is that the males demand to be beguiled back into the society they rule. Reconciliation is accomplished at festive dinners and parties over which women preside. These are liminal occasions, outside the daily normalcy. Women declare these festivals — and conjure up a woman-powered society for a few hours at least, although still centered on men. Rarely do these occasions develop as the men expect, however. Role reversals empowering women to authoritatively organize the social structure are frequent in Woolf. Orlando's retreat is a feminist utopia much like Gilman's *Herland*. One's room becomes a small utopia — to be sweated for as a place of personal power, individual identity, and freedom.

Realms of power, phenomenal and social, clash continually in Woolf's fiction and essays. In this clash is the stuff of comedy. Woolf places value on the women; theirs are the human arts — democratic, sensitive, caring, nurturing, sane, and tolerant. Men don't do very well in this environment, or need time and help to adjust to behaving like humans. Often their sense of humor is wanting. Lily Briscoe writhes at Mrs. Ramsay's dinner party because she picks up her signal to help out Charles Tansley, a pretty poor human specimen. Woolf's women gradually, however, stop aiding the men, and start setting examples — without, however, nurturing men to understanding. As women grow freer in the novels, the clash of phenomenologies and human behavior becomes more severe and more strident and more savage.

It is a savage clash in *The Waves* (1931) but the clash manages to grind out some communication. In *Three Guineas*, *The Years*, and *Between the Acts*, the paradoxical becomes more pronounced as the levels of perceptual reality increase and are more incongruous. The world is less secure, but out of its fragmentation comes more community. And for women, Woolf turns the meaning of security on its head. As women are less and less secured by men and in domesticity, they become more and more secure in themselves. Their identities become more pronounced as the conventions break up. While women have more mobility, there are fewer escapes because less need to escape. But increasing freedom does not develop into an overall rosiness. On the contrary Woolf, the ironist, notes that women are free to be humans now — doubting, unhappy, searching, free to do with their own money without the cocoon of family. There may be fewer escapes from stifling patriarchal family, but there are also fewer escapes from a world shaped by generations of patriarchs. Woolf lets her women loose to discover the world their fathers made. It still is better to be out of the house with a room of one's own, and money of one's own. "There was another ten-shilling note in my purse; I noticed it because it is a fact that still takes my breath away — the power of my purse to breed ten-shilling notes automatically" (*Room* 37). It would have taken Jane Austen's breath away too.

Woolf's comedic detachment from money and her perception of it as magical is radically different from a man's. For men, money is given, the road to possession; for women it is a magical presence which sets them toward freedom and privacy. They can not only secure themselves from domestic slavery, but purchase things to enhance their room, a word which reverberates with meanings of privacy, time, space, identity, individuality, and comfort — necessities for creativity. "And, dearest Vita, we are having *two* water closets made, one paid for by *Mrs. Dalloway*, the other by *The Common Reader*: both dedicated to you" (#1621 *Letters*). Woolf valued such things for herself too because they aid women in achieving "the habit of freedom and the courage to write exactly what we think..." (*Room* 119). Water-closets and motorcars earned by her own money gave Virginia Woolf the habit of powerful comedy. But such comedy is a tricky business, because it energizes the strong passions and abjures the detachment associated with comedy of knowledge. It is the product of a habit of freedom, and the determined struggle "to write exactly what we think..." Woolf's anomalous fictions and her public speeches come at such a juncture in her life. Secure in her own knowledge, she divulges process, and finds her culture wanting, mean, and hostile to women.

In indicting patriarchal definitions, she is militant in her criticism. It would be surrealist Woolfian irony to be a militant pacifist. She risks more in her writing. Her work is more deliberately ambiguous, more aware of chaos. She smashes it against culture, to expose the fragmentary nature of both humans and culture. At the same time she begins to abandon the centrality of individual character in order to focus on the shape of events, and to re-define what a major event in human or cultural life is.

Within these works, the revolutionary wears the thinnest shred of a mask. A gossamer reality is disrupted by illusion, life-sustaining illusions are shattered by rude reality. The interplay and the uncertainty is surreal. In *The Years* Woolf throws another party at which a series of characters try to interpret their experiences at life and at the party. "But how can one speak when one is always interrupted?" (425).

The end of that party in *The Years*, a culmination of the book's years and also a threshold to more years, occurs at the juncture of night/day, more than night, less than dawn. The space of time is both a culmination and threshold. Comedy occupies similar space — it expresses the culmination of some knowledge or apprehension or experience or vision at the threshold of the difference made by its shared expression, smack dab in the center of ambiguities. It attempts to extend the moment of comprehension with awareness and communication, but that linearity plunges the ambiguity into the definitive. Completion is an act of violence in comedy.

At the party Eleanor wakes up from a doze "suffused with a feeling of happiness" (426). She tries to focus on a conversation made up of interruptions, but "She lost his words" (427). Like the man with the comic answer, "she was about to grasp something that just evaded her" (427). Woolf encapsulates the comedy of incompletion that is humanity and human communication. Always there is the sense of being just about to grasp or express an idea, if it would just sit still long enough. Eleanor "wanted to enclose the present moment; to make it stay ... It's useless, ..." (428). Eleanor finds no one listening when she tries to tell about her happiness. And the moment slithers away.

In the midst of this bittersweet irony, Woolf plants a grotesque. Children brought up to have some cake "stared at [the grown-ups] with a curious fixed stare as if they were fierce" (428). Martin commands them to "sing a song for sixpence!" (429). But the familiar nursery rhyme allusion does not lead to anything familiar. Of what the children sang, "Not a word was recognizable. The distorted sounds rose and sank as if they followed a tune" (429). The grown-ups are disconcerted; "did not know whether to laugh or cry" (430).

Thus at the donkey's tail-end of *The Years*, Woolf shatters the nostalgia for childhood. Martin's illusions about children and childhood are downed with the same savage glee the Marx Brothers tore apart the opera. The incomprehensibility of language, the interruptions, and the unaccountable children are signs of the fragmented present and the incomprehensible future. Woolf can't resist a typical Groucho comment in the face of the others' bewilderment. "'Cockney accent, I suppose,' said Patrick 'What they teach 'em at school, you know'" (430). Meanwhile the disruptive imps at the feast grinned the whole time and then "made a dash for the door" (430).

And then it is dawn. One character attempts a summing up but Nicholas interrupts: "There is going to be no peroration — no peroration! ... because there was no speech" (431). This chaos of the non-spoken and half spoken bowls down the patriarchy's power and paternalistic control. No speech means no one assuming the authoritative power to define experience. The grotesque of the children forbids the adults from an attempt to project possible definitions onto their future. In fact the most viable response is again laughter, what Christopher Fry calls "a narrow escape into faith" (15).

The comedy of *The Years* has this quality. "It believes in a universal cause for delight, even though knowledge of the cause is always twitched away from under us" leaving us only our own buoyancy (Fry 15). *Three Guineas* and *Between the Acts* are no longer so buoyant, and the narrow escape into faith is into a faith that human nature will remain cockeyed. But in *The Years* there is still the answer of laughter and the comic focus on the moment as a telescoping device. Eleanor's eternal moment is a comedic perception; for, "in comedy eternity is a moment," (Fry 15); and though that one glides away, she discovers others as she fingers her coppers and observes the young couple on their own threshold.

The party, a disjointed lolloping beast, disabuses readers of the cultural image of parties as warm unities. Woolf has varying degrees of disharmony in all her parties, but her best and most disharmonious are in *The Years* and *Between the Acts*. In *The Years* the party held in Delia's London home overwhelms several floors of the house converted to estate agent's offices and solicitor's rooms; and brings together a truly divergent set of people who are — in an odd but real sense — family.

Interruptions, disunities, bitternesses and burlesques add up to a vagueness represented by the word family. In *Between the Acts* they add up to the family human, "a confused but tumultuous clamor" (*Guineas* 129), "a mellay; a medley; an entrancing spectacle" but "skimble-skamble" (*Acts* 68-69). Woolf, a lover of the music hall, has converted the English panto, "a British tradition combining vaudeville, satire and music," into prose (Nemy). However, these families are no longer patriarchal or are patriarchies gone wrong. There is no shelter from the world to cloister in. In *The Years* the most travelled member in the family is a woman, Eleanor. Reversing the grand tour, Eleanor's travelling has happened, not in her youth, but in her age. Generations swirl, and bump against each other. This crazy-quilt party opposes the surreality of the party in *To The Lighthouse*. That dinner party is a grotesque, hot-house plant with boundaries and rules, fixed seating.

The Year's party is set in a rented place no longer a home through which the guests wander clumping here, breaking apart to re-clump. Instead of being a directed ritual, it is a haphazard participation and left-over form. Not any one person's creation, it is a weedy growth. No perorations, and no formal decorations, but a Dionysian-Marx Brothers concoction. Perhaps its skimble-skamble nature is why Maggie, when it is her turn to give a speech she knows will only be interrupted, laughs. Perhaps it is Woolf's and Maggie's feminist response to the absurdity of trying to 'wrap up' life and parties in neat packages of words. Pelt the crazy masculinist idea with laughter.

> Laughter took her and shook her. She laughed, throwing her head back as if she were possessed by some genial spirit outside herself that made her bend and rise, as a tree ... No idols, no idols, no idols, her laughter seemed to chime as if the tree were hung with innumerable bells, and he laughed too. (*Years* 425).

Woolf's playfulness with and irreverence for party conventions extends deeper and farther. In both *The Years* and *Three Guineas* her offense is a juxtaposition of satiric images of human behavior. Her tactics are bizarre paradox and scorn as a strategy of offensive and as a deliberate challenge to a patriarchal cosmos. *The Years* often disguises the "enormous amount of mischief going on in the text", but *Three Guineas* is direct and compressed, Woolf's flaring red cape (Lipking 142).

In *Three Guineas* innumerable beadles with their innumerable keys which fit into the well-oiled locks seal away treasures. Woolf's fierce chanting undertone exposes why the locks are kept so well-oiled, and announces what makes up the oil. The innumerable beadles, she points out, have invaded the tree, silencing and excluding the innumerable bells. It is time to pelt their tree with laughter, to shake the idols down, to discover what grows there, give it space to breathe and freedom to blossom. Naming the enemy, Woolf also provides the ammunition. "Laughter as an antidote to dominance is perhaps indicated" (*Guineas* 182). The laughter is scornful and the enemy is the patriarchy. At its highest aesthetic level, "scorn is succinct of form and irrefutable of content, an attitude utterly unanswerable by serious debate or clever retorts" (Schlack 147). Such comedy invokes laughter that "is often rather grim, gargoyle-faced, and many-clawed" (Schlack 147).[1] *The Years* uses scorn and its effects. In the 1880 section, the rain "slid down, till, reaching the mouths of those fantastic laughers, the many-clawed gargoyles, it splayed out in a thousand odd indentations" (47). Likewise in her novels Woolf's savage comedy splays out in a thousand odd indentations. She pours the rain of her scorn "with an impartiality which

> suggested that the god of rain, if there were a god, was thinking Let it not be restricted to the very wise, the very great, but let all breathing kind, the munchers and the chewers, the ignorant, the unhappy, those who toil in the furnace making innumerable copies of the same pot, those who bore red hot minds through contorted letters, and also Mrs. Jones in the alley, share my bounty. (48).

Here the scorn plumps to an end with anti-climax, but it warns that none will be spared Woolf's savage bounty.

Savage scornful comedy is Woolf's remedy for survival. And she doubles this beast back on itself. Scornfully she advises that women understand and honor the derision *they* suffer. Derision is one of "the four great teachers of the daughters of educated men;" for the law of England ensures that women "do not inherit great possessions," denies "the full stigma of nationality" (*Guineas* 79-82). Because of these laws and the pillars of state, tradition and culture,

> we can scarcely doubt that our brothers will provide us for many centuries to come, as they have done for many centuries past, with what is so essential for sanity, and so invaluable in preventing the great modern sins of vanity, egotism, and megalomania — that is to say ridicule, censure, and contempt (*Guineas* 82).

One need only think back to Woolf's earlier analysis of such conditioning to perceive her contempt, to Judith Shakespeare running mad under her restraints and killing herself. Meredith perceived comedy as *sanitas*, but as a tool for women to use on men. Woolf takes him up on that challenge. A position as participant/observer in culture helps maintain a high consciousness of the dichotomies and incongruities of that culture but not necessarily health *or* sanity — and feeds a strong dark satanic comic perspective, as culture feeds it endless streams of grist for the humor mill. "Mothers will laugh from their graves" (*Guineas* 83).

One of the most telling of these strategies of scorn, and also of the comedic beauties of *Three Guineas* is Woolf's naming process, defining or re-defining language and culture. Woolf is surprised that an educated man is asking the "ignorantsia," the daughters of educated men how to prevent war by protecting culture and intellectual liberty, "since when before has an educated man asked a woman ... her opinion" (87, 3). This, says Woolf, is a ridiculous question. Women have been contributing to culture and intellectual liberty for centuries. Haven't they been contributing to "Arthur's Education Fund?" (4). She redefines poverty as earning enough money "to be independent of any other human being and to buy that modicum ... needed for the full development of body and mind" (80). Chastity is refusing "to sell your brain for the sake of money" (80). She re-habilitates "derision — a bad word but once again the English language is much in need of new words —" (80).

Her rehabilitation attributes the deed to men even as she uses it against them; for the derision heaped on women which keeps them from "puffing up with pride" has also kept them from earning their own livings, having rooms and guineas of their own, and identities of their own. It is the almighty atmosphere at work again. But derision, a double edged blade, *can* be directed toward men, to cut down their vanity and reduce their mirrored magnification to real size.

Women can retain their sanity — by ridiculing, censuring, and scorning the vanity, egotism and megalomania of the male who as paterfamilias creates in the family a microcosm of state paternalism. And there are always such wars in Woolf's patriarchal families — and inequities. In *The Years* Delia, countering a fit of nostalgia on Martin's part, exclaims emphatically "It was Hell", and repeats it twice, "speaking quite simply" (417).

Woolf's scorn and ridicule moves this Hell outward from the family to the state and the culture, attacking three structures based on each other as intrinsically unethical. To point to inequities in state or culture is an acceptable form of critical activity, but to brand the family, most sacrosanct of cultural icons as unethical, and to exhibit its dissolution in fiction and advocate its abolition in a serious political statement is blasphemous. Ironically perhaps it would have been more acceptable if both were seriously done, but to do this humorously, with that black humor which runs in her veins, placed Woolf on the radical fringe — the lunatic fringe. "No society could survive it" (*Orlando* 202); if, that is, a society paid any attention to a *woman's* humor, or scorn, or ridicule.

In both *The Years* and *Three Guineas* the patriarch is dissected and minutely examined from all sides with all the strategies of laughter and scorn. She parodies the dominator's style, not only by restating her feminist themes in Aristotelian syllogisms which make a travesty of masculinist logic, mocking and destroying the patriarch's explanations of 'mankind'; but also by using the footnoted dissertationese which is supposed to overwhelm with unanswerable evidence, and is as biased in its choice of evidence as the logical propositions. Her evidence, however, convinces by bringing to light the unmentioned side of the human argument. She subjects her object to murderous verbal invective full of lethal alliteration and disdainful caricatures in titles such as "His Majesty's Royal Regiment of Ratcatchers" (*Guineas* 314).

Wordplay, redundancy, and aesthetic punning act as running commentaries on her text — to her readers, and on the gentleman to whom Woolf is writing. In the discussion she repeats "culture and intellectual liberty" *reductio ad absurdum*. Just when the daughters were beginning to think they might "filch not only a little of that same university education for themselves, but some of the trimming — travel, pleasure, liberty — here is [the] letter" which, because of what it asks, implies that the vast sum poured into Arthur's Education Fund "has been wasted or wrongly applied" (*Guineas* 86). Woolf's scornful humor against Establishment values makes a most telling use of understatement.

Woolf exposes a world wallowing in its own detritus. As an alternative to its traditions, she imagines no real structures, but disarray, constant interruption, language without meaning, humans who are certainly human but just as certainly ambiguous in the terms of the older standards. "Indeed, disorder *is* hope" especially in the comic cosmos (Lipking 144). In scathing language — which seems less so because so seemingly logical — she denounces church, family, and state, reserving her most sarcastic analysis for St. Paul as a representative of the patriarchal elite which invokes "the familiar but always suspect trinity of accomplices, Angels, nature and law, to support ... personal opinion" (*Guineas* 167). Even as she damns his obscure language and his scrambled logic, comparing his thinking to Nazi mentality, her use of the capital A for Angels alludes to the colluders with

Paul, the Tennysons and Patmores who worshipped that lovely secular projection of their own "infantile fixation" (*Guineas* 127-135). The Angel, Arthur's Education Funds, Oxfords, Cambridges and the words Miss and Mrs. have certain odors attached, "or shall we call it 'atmosphere'?" (*Guineas* 52) and combine in a surreal chaos where all juxtapositions are paradoxical and laughable.

"Atmosphere is plainly a very might power;" for it can cause shapes and sizes to shift and it affects solid bodies which might have been thought impervious to atmospheric influences (52). This "larger metaphysical, almost apocalyptic, scorn breaks through" in *The Years* in the characters' mockery of each other and in the "contemptuous pessimism" of their thoughts (Schlack 147), and in *Three Guineas* in Woolf's own voice. Woolf's mockery identifies "atmosphere [as] one of the most powerful, partly because it is one of the most impalpable, of the enemies with which the daughters of educated men have to fight" (*Guineas* 52). Her comedy makes the invisible visible, and human unity a series of ruptures. Woolf decries the impalpable but binding content of culture which is absent from conscious perception, and connects it with the visible structures of culture — things as they are. "... the public and the private worlds are inseparably connected; ... the tyrannies and servilities of the one are the tyrannies and servilities of the other" (*Guineas* 142).

Woolf's comedy in these two companionate volumes is feminist guerilla warfare, lobbing jokes and puns, heaping scorn and derision, claiming in Ciceronian humility that as a daughter of an educated man, she must speak only tentatively to these issues. Like Cicero, she then blasts away with the power of and in the metaphysical style of the gods themselves. Such a stance "should dispel any lingering notion that a lyric, 'delicate' sensibility like Woolf's was incapable of more substantial and defiant modes" (Schlack 147). Her phenomonology makes her anger

> an ethical anger, an impersonal issue like injustice ... which prompts the justifiable dissatisfactions of ... scorn ... [she] mocks and defies. It is a strategy of courage and integrity ... which sustains personal dignity confers intellectual honor ... if the gods themselves cannot defeat it, mere mortal chauvinists and a hypocrite society cannot stifle scorn ... either (Schlack 150).

Pelting anything — even with laughter — is not one of the more delicate arts; nor is comedy. Woolf's gift is that she combines aesthetic scorn with some extremely funny, laugh out loud comedy. When for instance she suggests that women ought to take to wearing tufts of hair on their shoulders to represent each birth they have given, the image is hilarious. It is also contemporary — the tufts of hair could easily be different colored stones set into the currently popular mother's ring, an object Woolf's sense of whimsy surely could not have ignored.

Between the Acts returns to the topics of *The Years* in another comic register and angle. Here the scorn is interlaced inextricably with affectionate mockery and a wry almost exasperated amusement. Her humor has asperity and her comedy more violent images. But the structure of *Between the Acts* is a multi-tiered parodic burlesque of just about everything. It gathers up all the strands of the last few works and puts them to use in the iconic "timeless" English setting, the English country house. This is also the standard setting of Restoration comedies of manners. Patriarchs have defined what acts of life are "worthy" — for history and novels and women; but Woolf takes issue with that. Life is not those acts. Woolf's history book, as she pointed out more than once, would be a lives of the obscure. Real life occurs between the acts, in the intervals.

Between the Acts conjures up a festive interval in the history of the village which centers around Pointz Hall. Woolf presents this history and her characters in half-notes, interruptions, and awkward party behavior in which salient depths are conveyed by a comedy of clanging silences and miscommunications. Mrs. Swithin asks her brother Bart Oliver to explain the origin of the phrase 'touch wood', a request which sets him off on all sorts of musings about her in which he accuses her of what Woolf shows him doing. "She would have been a very clever woman, had she fixed her gaze. But this led to that; that led to the other ... And all were circled" (21). But he had circled her winter plans, her religion, the minister, her concept of god, until Lucy recalls him to the point.

The village play is an interruption in the life of the area, a distraction from "real life". Within the distraction, the village reveals itself when the not-very-well-acted play interrupts itself. In the dance of these intervals, interruptions, and interstices, Woolf presents her parody of the history cycle, with fatal mockery. "Imagine?" said Mrs. Swithin. "How right! Acts show us too much" (100). Juggling the characters' illusions about their interval with the actualities, Woolf's dialectic of the interplay of reality and illusion is the meta-comic nature of being human. What Woolf shows us is also a multi-tiered dialectic of comedy and tragedy, with comic absurdity finally dominant. The village play is a make-shift affair; the players are all known to each other and to the audience. Paying attention to the stage alternates with audience comments on the players. "Here came Millie Loder (shop assistant at Messrs. Hunt and Dicksons, drapery emporium), in sprigged satin, representing Flavinda" (96). Another tier is Miss LaTrobe's trials and tribulations as she watches her hopefully wrought production run afoul of itself.

> Illusion had failed ... Then suddenly, as the illusion petered out, the cows took up the burden. One had lost her calf. On the very nick of time she lifted her great moon-eyed head and bellowed ... From cow after cow came the same yearning bellow ... The cows annihilated the gap; bridged the distance; filled the emptiness and continued the emotion. Miss LaTrobe waved her hand ecstatically at the cows. (99).

The absurd construct is played out in words and in silences, in half-sentences and in — intervals. "Armed in his seedy weaponry of words, man confronts the universe" (Fussell 266), "not shaping pellets of information or handing ideas from one to another, but rolling words, like sweets on their tongues," sweets which dissolve (*Acts* 11). This universe is a grotesque; words fail. Fittingly words in the play are always being "lost", drowned in "laughter, loud laughter," swallowed by their speakers, blown away by the wind, or scratched to insensibility by a creaky gramophone.

The "well-made" play also disintegrates. In bravely attempting its conventions, the play is more vividly revealed as a joke. There is no definitive ending to any act, except the one when the audience goes to feed. The eternal human comedy shreds the masculinist attempt to contain humans in the bounds of civilization. Woolf places the obscure center stage — and by doing so ridicules the concept of the famous, the infamous, the significant.

Between the Acts is Woolf's comic vision, her comedic phenomenology. Swirling her orts and fragments and shattered mirrors into congruous incongruity, she finds the primeval past lurking in the progressive present, and shows it to us. Iguanodons roam the Strand side by side with worry about the weather for the pageant. "There's a sense in which we all, I admit, are savage still ... It was the night before roads were made, or houses. It was the night that dwellers in caves had watched from some high place among the rocks" (139, 152).

Mirrors no longer reflect anyone at twice their normal size; indeed mirrors are fragments, orts and scraps.

"To snap us as we are ... Here a nose, ... There a skirt ... Then trousers only ... now perhaps a face ... Ourselves? ... before we've had time to assume ... and only, too in parts ... That's what's so distorting and upsetting and utterly unfair ... People in the back rows stood up to see the fun ... and the barriers ... were dissolved ... the back rows were tittering ... What simplified absurdity ..." (128-132).

The disunity dissolves identity barriers; the chaos creates a likeness out of fragments. The comic craziness reveals no pattern.

As in all her works, Woolf is feminist — fully aware of the savagery ingrained in the structures of culture. "Is the old savage who has killed a bison asking the other old savage to admire his prowess? Is the tired professional man demanding sympathy and resenting competition?" (129). Giles and Isa end *Between the Acts* in this implicit mood, "in the heart of darkness, in the fields of night ..." (152).

Woolf parodies, puns, burlesques and mimes it all. In Woolf's neat hands comedy is quick, flashing, various. Virginia Woolf wields comedy, the "loudest expression of ... little civilization, ... short of slaughter" with consummate skill, in all its grinning and grimacing (Meredith 5). "Further she cannot go in rendering absurdity incarnate" (Fussell 263). But she does not — in the name of a culture she finds surreal and dishonest — stop short of slaughter.

EPILOGUE: MUNCHERS AND CHEWERS AND RED HOT MINDS — FLATTENING THE WAVE

Virginia Woolf's comedy has been generally ignored, except during her lifetime, and most recently in criticism of the early 1970s. Since comedy underpins so much of her work and that double-edged vision is so important to understand the complex of meanings in Woolf's writing, why has the comedy been missed?

Woolf implicitly criticized the male establishment in all of her work, and explicitly during the latter half of her career. The conspiracy of silence on her humor is bound up with her critique of the "masculinist" and their culture. Criticisms women make of males and their society tend to be suppressed and made invisible. This conspiracy of silence removes the immediate threat women pose to male power. Certainly women's comedy has received this silent treatment more completely than other women's writing, and feminist comedy has been quashed most of all.

Thus, until one starts digging for it, one *could* easily believe that feminists do not create humor. But they do, and Woolf was one of the best. Kate Clinton says it well, "I call myself a feminist and a humorist — a fumerist. I fume and make light: Light enough to see where we are going in these dark times, and light enough to move through these issues. This is a women's movement" (1982).

Woolf's dark times needed the light of humor too. She "roasted ... the habits, expectations, demands and beliefs which are borne of presumptions of male dominance, male privilege, male power, and a male version of humanity" (Rosenberg 6). What Tillie Olsen calls "the invisible worm" and Dale Spender calls the problem of "invisibility" has muted Woolf's skewering of society. Students read Swift's "Modest Proposal", but not Woolf's "A Society"; they see the illustrations in male texts, but not in *Three Guineas*. One could argue that reproducing photographs is an expensive proposition were it not that photographs accompany all of Woolf's biographical texts. The photographs in *Orlando* have been faithfully reproduced. *Three Guineas* contains fewer illustrations than any; yet, these have been curiously omitted from the edition currently available. All these editions are from the same publisher. Why the curious omission of the *Three Guineas* illustrations? Spender claims it is to cut women off from their history, and render women as invisible as possible in the culture.

Woolf was a major figure in her lifetime, but forty years after her death she has, in a fairly recent assessment, been called "a remarkable, though not major figure;" although late in the same chapter of the same book extolled for "the determined pursuit of control and authenticity which invigorates even the slightest of her work," and called "solid with integrity and rich with inventiveness" (Lee 14-24). Critical praise has been defused by being diffused over ten pages. This is one of the strategies for making women disappear.

Another is to assess the woman as "eccentric" or "an isolated instance" or "neurotic" (Spender). All of these epithets have been leveled at Woolf as well as at those most meta-comical of her works.

Both detractors and admirers tend to mistake the degree of Woolf's satiric and ironic tone. She is still critically patronized and extolled not as a comic writer but as a novelist of sensibility or, even worse, of female sensibility — a Sensitive Plant drooping in a Bloomsbury hothouse. (Fussell 264).

Fussell goes on to note that Wayne Booth, in revealing James Joyce's satire, failed to notice Virginia Woolf's, and in fact attacks her for her retreat to a private world. Fussell states the obvious (well, the facts). One (and only one) of her satiric arenas "*is* the Bloomsbury hothouse and the drawing room" (Fussell 264).

Dale Spender discloses the ability and willingness of those who control the presses to partially eliminate a writer if it will serve to stop the "arousing awareness" that patriarchy is a problem in itself (Olsen 34). In this strategy the offending portion is removed by being "inconsistent" or "inaccurate" or "muddled logic" or "unartistic" (Spender).

Since Woolf used comedy to such devastating effect, this part of her work has suffered the most. Her critical and political assessments have suffered secondarily. They are less easy to hide since at least two of them appear in book form; but, which of them is more often read, more widely known, and more frequently quoted — although also very selectively? *Room of One's Own*. It has been judged "less" political, although an honest and keen political sensibility could not fail to notice that she is advocating a radical restructuring of history, rehabilitating cultural knowledge, and calling for a revolutionary redistribution of wealth (cf. Professor Jane Marcus's many essays).

Three Guineas, "did not fit their definitions of politics and in typical patriarchal style determined that she was not political" (Spender 673). They in this case is Leonard Woolf and Quentin Bell, the two men who have "almost exclusively" filtered the accepted versions of Virginia Woolf (Spender 673). Readers know all about Woolf's madness, her frigidity, her delicacy, her lack of stamina, her melancholy and her general fragility. Nigel Nicolson, however, presents his boyhood impressions of her which set this portrait askew. "She was Virginia. Virginia who was fun, Virginia who was easy, ... and who floated in and out of our lives like a godmother" (Nicolson 216). The easy Virginia has disappeared inside the 'difficult' artist.

Three Guineas, a very funny book, and Woolf's "most outspoken denunciation of patriarchy, *had* virtually disappeared" as well (Spender

673). With *Three Guineas* there is the unique opportunity to hear the well of silence that has blanketed this book since the early 1940's; for, readers can follow the progress of its reception through Woolf's diary. American readers should find it no surprise that they had difficulty in getting hold of the book until recently since "... 3 Gs a dead failure in USA, but enough" (Diary 269). It was not so in England.

Woolf wrote after she had finished *Three Guineas* that "The pack may howl, but it shall never catch me. And even if the pack — reviewers, friends, enemies — pays me no attention or sneers, still I'm free" (141). The pack did pay attention. Lady Rhondda was "profoundly excited and moved ..., Theo Bosanquet ... thinks it may have a great effect" (141). This Woolf thought a good omen, because "certain people will be stirred; will think; will discuss it; it won't altogether be frittered away" (142).

An ecstatic letter from Philippa Strachey preceded "the coming out day" of June 3, 1938. "the Lit Sup has 2 columns & a leader; and the Referee a great black Bar Woman declares sex war" (147). The headline actually read "WOMAN STARTS NEW SEX WAR/Says Men's Clothes are 'Barbarous'" (qtd. in *Diary* 148). The process of filtering by redirecting attention and trivializing had already begun in this popular headline; even though "the Listener says I am scrupulously fair, & puritanically deny myself flights" (148). In the "2 columns" in the *Times Literary Supplement*, Woolf read perhaps the most gratifying critique of all. "the Lit Sup says I'm the most brilliant pamphleteer in England. Also that this book may mark an epoch *if taken seriously*" (148/ emphasis added).

But soon reviewers were howling. G.M. Young called it "the endeavor of belated sex-egotism" (qtd. in *Diary* 155). On September 1st of that year, "A violent attack on 3Gs in Scrutiny by Q. Leavis ... A symbol though of what wiggings are to come" (165). Leavis castigated the book for "dangerous assumptions, some preposterous claims, and some nasty attitudes" (qtd. in *Diary* 165). In November Woolf reflects "on my position as a writer" (188).

exalted to a very high position, say about ten years ago: then was decapitated by W. Lewis & Miss Stein; not I think ... out of date; not a patch, with the young, ...; yet wrote *The Waves*; yet am unlikely to write anything good again; am a secondrate, & likely, I think, to be discarded altogether. I think that's my public reputation at the moment. ... 3Gs has queered the pitch ... my own friends have sent me to Coventry over it. *So my position is ambiguous*. (188-189/emphasis added).

It is a bit eerie to read such a sensitive writer preside over the process of her own disappearance. Luckily she did not totally disappear. But the professors of culture and intellectual liberty were still angry. "How explain the anger of the Professors? ... it was anger disguised and complex, not anger simple and open" (*Room* 32). This patriarch "was protecting rather hot-headedly and with too much emphasis, because it was a jewel to him of the rarest price ... his own superiority" (*Room* 35). Men, as Virginia Woolf laughingly pointed out any number of times, "hate to be told that any cause to which they have given their affection has after all a tinge of absurdity" (Martin 8). And she carefully pointed too that the tinge was a deep coloration.

Woolf's humor, her comedic range, her scorn, her sardonic funny satire, her anger became invisible because she pinned the patriarchy to the wall. Her feminist humor and her feminist theory threatened the order of things. The uproar that *Three Guineas* might have caused was halted by the approved and authoritative silence of culture and intellectual liberty. Because the political phenomenology of *Room of One's Own* and *Three Guineas* pervaded her comedy, the comedy had to get lost. Woolf became the serious, delicate, hothouse Bloomsbury lunatic. It is well to remember that Lear's fool spoke home truths; and lunatics are defined by the patriarchy.

The final irony of Woolf's comedy is that as she was assessing herself as "secondrate", she was completing one of her most thorough-going comic masterpieces, *Between The Acts*. She would have appreciated that twist to her fate. There is another she might have enjoyed. The image of Woolf as smiling and never laughing is perpetuated in many books. The photographs in the *Letters* show an amused but not laughing woman, yet she apparently laughed a great deal. "Laughter shook her." "Elizabeth Bowen recalls her 'whoops of laughter,' while Clive Bell affirms that 'she was about the gayest human being I have known' ... and all who knew her remark that fun and gaiety [was] her most identifying characteristic" (Fussell 265).

My favorite photograph of Woolf is in Ottoline Morrell's album of Garsington guests. She is surrounded by people, all laughing, as she is herself. She is dressed in the most vivid dress, and her head is thrown back in a full laugh. The book is out of print, and the copy I saw secured in a rare books room.

Note

1. My discussion of Woolf's scorn is based on Beverly Schlack's analysis in her "Virginia Woolf's Strategy of Scorn in *The Years* and *Three Guineas.*"

Works Cited

Clinton, Kate. Jacket notes. *Making Light.* Whyscrack Records. Cazenovia, N.Y.: Making Light Productions, 1982.
Friedman, Ralph, ed. *Virginia Woolf: Revaluation and Continuity.* Berkeley: Univ. of California P., 1980.
Fry, Christopher. "Comedy." *Comedy: Meaning and Form.* Ed. Robert W. Corrigan. San Francisco: Chandler, 1951. 15-7.
Frye, Northrop. *Anatomy of Criticism.* Princeton: Princeton Univ. P., 1957.
Fussell, B.H. "Woolf's Peculiar Comic World: *Between the Acts.*" in Friedman. 262-283.
Lee, Hermoine. *The Novels of Virginia Woolf.* New York: Holmes and Meier, 1977.
Lipking, Joanna. "Looking at the Monuments: Woolf's Satiric Eye." *Bulletin of the New York Public Library* 80: (1977): 141-5.
Love, Jean O. "*Orlando* and Its Genesis: Venturing and Experimenting in Art, Love, and Sex." in Friedman. 189-218.
Marcus, Jane. "Enchanted Organs, Magic Bells: *Night and Day* as Comic Opera." in Friedman. 97-122.
Martin, Robert Bernard. *The Triumph of Wit: A Study of Victorian Comic Theory.* Oxford: Clarendon, 1974.
Meredith, George. "An Essay on Comedy." *Comedy.* Ed. Wylie Sypher. Garden City: Doubleday Anchor, 1956. 3-57.
Millett, Kate. *Sexual Politics.* New York: Avon, 1971.
Nemy, Enid. "A 'panto' called 'Poppy' to open in November." *New York Times* 19 April 1985: C2.
Nicolson, Nigel. *Portrait of a Marriage.* New York: Bantam, 1974.
Olsen, Tillie. *Silences.* New York: Delacorte/Seymour Lawrence, 1978.
Rosenberg, Avis Lang, curator. *Pork Roast: 250 Feminist Cartoons.* Vancouver: Pink Primate Projects, 1981.
Schlack, Beverly Ann. "Virginia Woolf's Strategy of Scorn in *The Years* and *Three Guineas.*" *Bulletin of the New York Public Library* 80: (1977): 146-50.
Smith, Stevie. *Me Again: Uncollected Writings of Stevie Smith.* Ed. Jack Barbera and William McBrien. New York: Vintage, 1983.
Spender, Dale. *Women of Ideas; and What Men Have Done to Them, From Aphra Behn to Adrienne Rich.* London: Ark, 1983.
Steele, Elizabeth. *Virginia Woolf's Literary Sources and Allusions: A Guide to the Essays.* New York: Garland, 1983.
White, Kenneth S., ed. *Savage Comedy: Structures of Humor.* Amsterdam: Rodopi, 1978.
Woolf, Virginia. *Between The Acts.* 1941. Harmondsworth: Penguin, 1953.
———. *The Common Reader.* 1925. New York: Harvest/HBJ, 1953.
———. *The Diary of Virginia Woolf.* Ed. Anne Olivier Bell and Andre McNeillie. 5 vols. New York: Harvest/HBJ, 1984. Vol. 5:1936-1941.
———. *Jacob's Room and The Waves, Two Complete Novels.* New York: Harvest/HBJ, 1923, 1931.
———. *The Letters of Virginia Woolf.* Ed. Nigel Nicolson and Joanne Trautmann. 6

vols. New York: Harvest/HBJ, 1977. Vol. 3: 1923-1928.
———. *Mrs. Dalloway.* New York: Harvest/HBJ, 1925.
———. *Orlando.* New York: Harvest/HBJ, 1928.
———. *A Room of One's Own.* New York: Harvest/HBJ, 1929.
———. "Speech Before the London/National Society for Women's Service. January 21, 1931." Repr. in *The Pargiters.* Ed. Mitchell Leaska. New York: Harvest/HBJ, 1977.
———. *To The Lighthouse.* New York: Harvest/HBJ, 1927.
———. *Three Guineas.* 1938. New York: Harvest/HBJ, 1966.
———. *The Years.* New York: Harvest/HBJ, 1937.

(En)gendering laughter: Woolf's *Orlando* as contraband in the age of Joyce

JUDY LITTLE

Southern Illinois University, Carbondale

THE VERSATILE ORLANDO, still awkwardly learning the code of the Victorian woman, does a little ham-acting as she tests the new role. Realizing that she must obtain a wedding ring and learn to depend on a man, she kneels on the window sill and histrionically asks whom she can lean upon. Her biographer seems to interpret these words as involuntary: "It was not Orlando who spoke, but the spirit of the age. But which ever it was ..." (246). The assured rhetoric of the first sentence is destroyed by the "but" and the "whichever" of the next one. The first sentence says which it was: the spirit of the age, the code of an era, the way womanhood was being "written" at the time. Then the "whichever" undercuts the rhetoric of assertion and suggests that Orlando herself might have used the language of coy feminine passivity — as indeed she did. Orlando is not outside the text, even though she doesn't like the text very much, and her mocking imitation of it demonstrates her distrust of it.

Both Orlando and the narrator-biographer here say something about the way comedy (and gender) are engendered or written. Orlando's gestures and remark are gendered. That is, they are "feminine" according to the style of an era, and for the moment they are part of the "content" of the passage. Yet Orlando's femininity is engendered or written by the spirit of the age. Although among critics the spirit of *our* age is self-consciously textual and more likely to focus on the linguistic engendering, or "production," of sexual difference than on the difference of gender considered as content or data, yet comedy often emerges from the sloppy, unstable connection between verbal play and the phantom "subjects" which the verbal play produces, subjects such as sex identity, the mores of an era, or a feminine stereotype. Orlando, in the passage just described, is both creating herself and being herself — temporarily. Here as elsewhere during her varied history, she or he (or the narrator) engenders a gender and then lets it go.

The comedy in *Orlando* arises as the linguistic movement collides with, and "deconstructs," what it tries to say. The "what" is important, however. In comic literature, if the jest hinges on foibles or eccentricity, the comedy is not as radical as it is when the subject is myth, gender, or a long accepted cultural code. Linguistically oriented critics emphasize that such codes and myths are mere productions, just verbal contrivances. In his *Mythologies*, Roland Barthes asserts that "myth is depoliticized speech" (143). But for this very reason myth, and cultural codes concerning human nature and gender, are extremely political and important. The disguised, or depoliticized, myth is powerful and needs to be named.

Sandra Gilbert, for instance, discusses "costumes of the mind" in *Orlando* and other works by women; she compares the woman author's more flexible view on gender with the generally rigid "truth of gender" as perceived by Joyce, Lawrence, Yeats, and Eliot (391-417). Such a study of the "content" of literature is valuable evidence of how depoliticized, how very hidden, mere speech can become. For the male authors surveyed by Gilbert, the speech, the linguistically produced concept of gender-distinction, was so depoliticized that it was assumed, by them, to be real. For the major male modernists, Gilbert concludes, "the hierarchical order of society is and should be a pattern based upon gender distinctions, since the ultimate reality is in their view the truth of gender, a truth embodied or clothed in cultural paradigms which all these writers see as both absolute and Platonically ideal..." (393).

Gilbert is careful to say "in their view" (i.e., in the way these authors "write" their world), yet Mary Jacobus finds Gilbert's premises too close to the "fixities" that Woolf's writing is trying to dislodge; Jacobus, prefacing her remarks about *Orlando*, sets forth the textual-deconstructive approach: "If there is no literal referent to start with, no identity or essence, the production of sexual difference can be viewed as textual, like the production of meaning" (4, 7). Jacobus says one must look at the linguistic process, while Gilbert focusses primarily on the *results* of the process, that is, on the cultural paradigms which are the result of all the continuing verbal play. Each of these critical approaches offers a distinctive challenge to the reader (and to the text, culture, and feminist criticism), and both are necessary.

Certainly both approaches are necessary when we are considering comedy. An understanding of comedy requires some acknowledgement of both the code or paradigms, and the linguistic production of meaning. The collapse of a phantom "truth of gender" into and through the raveling net of language is the center ring of comedy; that collapse or collision is where the comedy happens. The produced truth, or "content," is a necessary focus of critical attention, because this linguistically devised content is one measure of the radicalness of the comedy, one measure of the political risk the narrator (and perhaps the implied author) is willing to take. I have elsewhere argued that some women authors do indeed direct their comedy at just those (unstable, non-existent) truths of gender and nature that are affirmed as ultimate by writers such as Joyce and Lawrence (Little 1-21). In the present essay, I want especially to examine the comic collision course between such values and Woolf's language, especially the language of the narrator-biographer of *Orlando*. To do this, I will need occasionally to use a discourse that allows me to talk about "content"; I will also want to look at the textual strategies. I need to do both because comedy itself exists between the distinction of textual and essentialist approaches. Many of Virginia Woolf's comic sentences in *Orlando* pretend to be "true" — in order to be false. And sometimes the truths that they pretend to are royal and noble ones, exactly those (assumed) realities of gender and nature that less subversive writers of comedy have allowed to stand as norms. When the "spirit of the age" is assumed to be Joyce, the contraband comedy in *Orlando* is radical indeed.

In *Orlando*, a fiction that teases century by century, and sentence by sentence, the ambivalence of gender (as well as the ambivalence of fame, status, and literary glory), the narrator's discourse often slides easily from the rhetoric of affirmation into comic doubt. The narrator is eager to understand Orlando, to describe and "read" him or her, and often has to qualify and adjust a misreading, though the narrator survives these lapses with full energy and then enthusiastically resumes the biographer's task of describing, qualifying, offering explanations.

Woolf's narrator in *Orlando* is virtually a parody of a reader responding. Very appropriately Wolfgang Iser, in his discussion of the reader, cites Woolf's remarks about Jane Austen's style; Woolf writes that Austen "stimulates us to supply what is not there" (CE I: 148). Iser calls special attention to this statement, as he develops his argument that the gaps in the text spur the reader into interpretive activity (163-70). The reader-narrator of *Orlando* is thrilled by such gaps, and describes the kind of reader for which he, or she, writes:

> For though these are not matters on which a biographer can profitably enlarge it is plain enough to *those who have done a reader's part in making up from bare hints* dropped here and there the whole boundary and circumference of a living person; can hear in what we only whisper a living voice; *can see, often when we say nothing about it, exactly what he looked like,* and *know without a word* to guide them precisely what he thought and felt and *it is for readers such as these alone that we write* — it is plain then to such a reader that Orlando was strangely compound of many humors.... (73 my emphasis)

In describing the ideal reader here the narrator indicates by the inclusive "we" that the narrator also belongs to this sophisticated community of nearly clairvoyant readers (who "know without a word"). The narrator is a comic exaggeration of the reader that Woolf's remarks about Austen apparently describe.

Orlando's biographer invites us into rash affirmations; we can know "exactly" what a person looked like, even when the narrator has said "nothing about it." Understandably, such a reader-narrator must continually revise a statement, often in the midst of the statement itself. We too, the reader-audience, having been well trained by the narrator's style and by the comments on readers, follow right along, enjoying the comedy of our own errors, as we revise and re-read. The narrator's adroit production of "content" insures the reader's amused skepticism about the content, about those large presumptious ultimates like "nature" or "gender." These ultimates are exposed, rhetorically, as being devised by the spirit of the age (or even the spirit of the narrator).

The very first sentence asserts Orlando's gender, and then betrays the assertion all in one breath: "He — for there could be no doubt of his sex, though the fashion of the time did something to disguise it — was in the act of slicing at the head of a Moor which swang from the rafters" (13). The first word announces a masculine subject. Yet before Orlando's action can be described, the long and complex clause between the dashes protests too much. If there is no doubt, then why such an elaborate assurance that there is indeed no doubt? And why is the biography interrupted after only the first word in order to accommodate a fussy explanation of the narrator's presumed assurance? What the narrator deploys as content, as the distinctly male subject of the biography, is immediately and comically dismantled by the interruptive qualifications. And such dismantlings continue as Orlando changes clothes and as the "fashion of the time" varies. The first sentence is what every sentence in the book is about and what every sentence continues to produce and unproduce in rhetorical play.

When the narrator is not employing the syntactic guise of description, but presuming to explain instead, the explanations pile up ambiguously in the form of questions, or clauses that begin with "perhaps." From minor comments about the Queen's rigid posture ("perhaps in pain from sciatica" — 22) to Orlando's response to the change of sex, the questions and the doubtful "perhaps" clauses are privileged. The narrator, being his (her) own favorite kind of reader, cannot resist filling in the gaps, even when, as the narrator often says, almost nothing is known about the matter. No one knows why Orlando slept for a week after the flood and Sasha's deception: "there is no explaining it" (65). Yet the narrator offers to explain, giving us seven consecutive and climactic questions that pose as answers (67-68). The series of self-questioning hypotheses range from the psychological (a severe trauma) through the metaphysical or medical (taking death in small doses), to the simultaneously miraculous and scientific: Orlando may have died and come to life again. "And if so, of what nature is death and of what nature life?" (68) The narrator forces the question to its limits, to a consideration of ultimate reality, the "nature" of life and death. Musing about Orlando's strange sleep, the narrator demolishes the question by answering it — by answering it with questions.

The explanations are always ready, but they always get in the way. And they are most outrageously and radically a comic nuisance when the posed subject is one of those large, traditionally important ones like the nature of life and death, or human nature, or the nature of gender. When Orlando, now a woman and sailing home to England, is experiencing the trammels of a dress for the first time, the narrator considers the "strange fact" that Orlando up to this point "had scarcely given her sex a thought. Perhaps the Turkish trousers, which she had hitherto worn had done something to distract her thoughts; and the gipsy women, except in one or two important particulars, differ very little from the gipsy men" (153). Orlando had hardly given the sex change a thought, but the narrator as usual is willing to give it a thought, indeed to offer many thoughts about it, beginning with an explanation of why Orlando has *not* thought about it.

The narrator's tentative "perhaps" introduces the Turkish trousers which might have "done something to distract her thoughts." The force of "distract" is — distracting. The narrator has invited the reader to consider why Orlando's potentially available, and expected, thoughts about gender have been so strangely becalmed (a "strange fact"). But the "perhaps" explanation indicates that the trousers (covering the legs of both male and female gypsies) are intensely interesting, so interesting as to be distracting. The supposedly neutralizing or androgynous garment has bemused Orlando so much that her thoughts, which would ordinarily have been tending toward a consideration of her sex (the narrator believes), have instead been fascinated by the trousers. By calling attention to the neutralizing of sex distinction, the trousers recall that very distinction. The sentence produces its own comic distraction (and deconstruction). Orlando's thoughts about sex difference were distracted, the narrator theorizes, from thoughts about sex difference *by means of* thoughts *about* sex difference. The entire question of gender virtually self-destructs in this clause, with the result that the pseudo-scientific footnote which follows (where "very little" erases the urgency of "important particulars"), is a mere epitaph marking the site of the rhetorical damage.

The characters themselves, necessarily caught up in the narrator's discourse and dependent on it, collude with the narrator in sentencing themselves to ambiguity — or to freedom, since the demolition of one illusion leaves them free to invent another. The Queen, for instance, fails to read Orlando accurately, though the narrator affirms that "she read him like a page," named him Treasurer and Steward, and awarded to him the order of the Garter (25). The narrator as usual is ready with explanations: "For the old woman loved him. And the

Queen, who knew a man when she saw one, though not, it is said, in the usual way, plotted for him a splendid ambitious career" (26). The word "knew," placed in a proverbial cliché, credits the queen with the simple acknowledgement of Orlando's gender and virility. But by the time we get to the word "usual," we are in a hallway of warped mirrors, and the signification of "knew" has been marvelously skewed. The "though" and the "not," and the narrator's crafty delegation of responsibility at "it is said," have cluttered the (usual) twofold implication of the word "usual." One needs an indication of what is usual in order to learn what is unusual ("not ... in the usual way"). The occurrence of the word "usual" in the narrator's sentence emphasizes in retrospect a highly sexual connotation for the earlier word "knew." But is this erotic emphasis the "usual" one (and was it so when "knew" first appeared in the sentence)? Or is the erotic implication, since it is only emphasized and stressed late in the sentence, one that can't really be considered a highlight of the earlier idiom of cliché (she knew a man when she saw one)? And if the *usual* way of knowing is not defined clearly, then how can the reader measure the implications of the *unusual* way?

The possibilities vacillate in many directions at once. The Queen doesn't know *how* she knows and loves Orlando; she cannot count the ways, and neither can the narrator and the reader. Because of the complexity which the narrator and Queen share in their effort to produce a reading of Orlando, the reader is scarcely surprised to learn that the Queen has failed to understand Orlando; she is vigorously upset when she believes Orlando has betrayed her affection and patronage by kissing a girl (26).

Orlando also, caught up in the same creatively ambiguous rhetoric as the other characters, learns that absolute statements corrupt themselves absolutely. Moving through an open-ended history of open-ended sentences that vary with the style of the age (and which themselves style or write the age), Orlando must continually revise perceptions about everything from his early passion for Sasha, to the style of his or her poem "The Oak Tree." Even such pervasive cultural codes as fame, human nature, and gender, which a given spirit of an age will see as absolute, Orlando learns to see as illusion, as something unspoken. ("It was not Orlando who spoke, but the spirit of the age. But whichever it was. ...") Whichever it was, it was a rhetorical illusion.

The youthful Orlando, for instance, glimpsing the attractive skater on the ice, several times must adjust his reading of the gender of the person, though he is certain of the person's "extraordinary seductiveness" (37). Yet the narrator (with the reader following along) surveys the "images, metaphors of the most extreme and extravagant" which clutter Orlando's mind (37), as these indeed flourished in the age itself; so maybe even Sasha's extraordinary seductiveness is partially a product of Orlando's extraordinary readiness to be seduced — which is itself a product of the contemporary poet's rhetoric.

The narrator's own rhetoric dashes off a portrait of the vivid Elizabethan temper in mind, heart, society, and even climate: intense sunsets, vehement rain, poets advising lovers to seize the day, and lovers doing as advised (26-28). The amusing thing is that the narrator, just after taking pains to show that love was largely a matter of rhetoric, then calls it "nature." Orlando, falling in love suddenly, "did but as nature bade him" (28). No — he did as the spirit of the age bade him. The narrator's use of "bade" shows the spoken, or rhetorical, nature of nature. The narrator had almost "depoliticized" the Elizabethan myth about the lover's nature. That is, the narrator had almost concealed the fact that "nature" is a rhetorical contrivance. Yet the rhetorical contrivance itself speaks — in the word "bade."

Although Orlando's love for Sasha becomes his central preoccupation for some time, his manner of falling in love with her was sudden and unconsidered. Like everyone in his era, he was willing to be seduced; the spirit of the age ("nature") decreed it to be so. Orlando's love for Sasha is one of those illusions which his own psychological style, itself styled by the age, may have produced, and from which he (and Orlando later as "she") continues to suffer from and to recover from. Buoyantly, however, Orlando accepts the challenge of recovering from her own illusions, even when these illusions are virtually codes that the spirit of the age often takes quite seriously and perceives as ultimate values or as ultimate, natural, differences between people.

One of these depoliticized illusions or myths is the difference of gender. From the first sentence onward, however, this particular myth is comically *re-politicized*. That is, its political quality of being the spirit and rhetoric of an era, is exposed by the narrator's language and by the record of Orlando's transitions from several different kinds of men to several different kinds of women. The very "nature" of Orlando as a young man must "bend" to the nineteenth century (when she is a woman), because of "the indomitable nature of the spirit of the age" (244). The spirit of that age also has, like human beings, a (rhetorical) nature. The narrator does not say that Orlando had some transcendent nature that allowed her to protest the age even while bending to it. Instead the narrator, offering a theory as usual (and this time a quite post-structuralist one), links the self to history and to rhetoric: "For it is probably that the human spirit has its place in time assigned to it; some are born of this age, some of that" (244). Orlando is thirty or so: "the lines of her character were fixed, and to bend them the wrong way was intolerable" (244). The narrator does not say that Orlando cannot change anymore, but she resists bending "the wrong way." She is simply not "assigned to" the Victorian age. That is, she is not signed to or marked down for it; she has after all been partly "written" by an earlier age, even though she will have to respond to the Victorian spirit. By virtue of her relative maturity, she maintains a certain flexible resistance to the nineteenth-century code of womanhood; yet her character, or nature (or gender), is still a matter of "lines" (written? drawn?), as is her poem along with the spirit of the age.

Like the narrator, Orlando waxes reflective about these issues. Some time after the change of gender, she considers, while pacing through her enormous house, some other large myths that can, like gender-codes, assume the status of truth. She considers the faults in her own writing style (173), her earlier fierce ambition to be a poet (175), and she recalls how the gypsy Rustum had recently provoked some abatement of the pride she had felt about her family and ancestors; their long line of several hundred years was nothing compared to that of the gypsies who claimed descent from the ancient Egyptians (147, 174). Orlando realizes that she is "losing some illusions ... perhaps to acquire others" (174-75). Fame, status, gender are illusions, and not absolute truths. They are assigned to an age; they are written or spoken; once they become myths, they have been effectively depoliticized.

Orlando, since being a poet is part of her "assigned" character, supplies a metaphor as she considers these illusions: "habits that had seemed durable as stone went down like shadows at the touch of another's mind" (176). And for "mind" here we can understand "words" or "speech"; Orlando has been considering Rustum's mind — his words about fame; she is also remembering the "affair with Greene" (175) — Nicholas Greene who had such harsh words about Orlando's early poetry. One's character, the age, the nature of fame and of gender difference, are largely a matter of (verbal) line. They are a manner of speaking. These presumed truths are illusions which the discourse of the narrator, and the musings of Orlando comically unravel as the biography proceeds.

Appropriately the biography ends with a cliché and a date. Orlando's ecstatic meeting with her husband is deflated by Orlando's exclamation, "It is the goose!" The single wild bird over Shelmerdine's head is "the wild goose ..." (329). The ambiguity of "it" (the bird, Shelmerdine, the centuries-long adventure?) is an effective reminder that the entire text has been spoken, assigned; it has been a wild goose chase, in which "truth" was written by the reader-narrator and by Orlando's reading of an age.

Then the narrator announces the date of the present moment and stops. The text ends with the present. All texts continually end with the continuing arrival of the present. Although Orlando's biographer has always been zealous to offer interpretations of what has already happened, this biographer makes no assumption about the text of the future. It is yet to be written. The radical implication of *Orlando* is that the future is open, that the spirit of one age will not necessarily speak the text of the one to follow. Values, nature, and gender roles are not universal in definition, but await the poets like Orlando, politicians like the Queen, and literary critics such as Nicholas Greene.

This openness, this refusal to pose as a universal, comic statement about the "human condition," gives *Orlando* its contraband character. Like Orlando herself, who suspected she had contraband thoughts in the nineteenth century (265), Woolf's biographical/historical comedy bends with, yet resists the spirit of the age. *Orlando* plays with the concept of the "nature" of things, or the nature of human beings or the nature of gender. All of these presumed realities undergo major transformations as the spirits of different ages re-write the cultural text and as the dedicated narrator inscribes, and frequently scrambles, an explanatory gloss upon a new code. The comedy engendered by *Orlando* resists — indeed mocks — the temptation to "gender" human beings into absolute roles.

In this respect *Orlando* is comedy of a more radical character than is

Joyce's *Ulysses*. (In this respect, this one respect; like the interruptive narrator of *Orlando*, I want to admonish my reader to re-read that last sentence.) The laughter engendered by *Orlando* re-politicizes certain myths — especially those myths that presume to define gender in universal terms. In an age whose major male writers found in traditional western myths some "form" that could hold twentieth-century literature together, *Orlando* mocks, and plays with, that very idea.

The comic epic *Ulysses*, for instance, leaves substantially unquestioned the gender roles that have been assigned to the sexes for millennia. Although there are critics who see a kind of flexibility of gender in Molly and in Bloom, the counter arguments are very strong. Molly makes fun of men's philosophical arguments, but, as Elaine Unkeless demonstrates, Molly's anti-intellectual remarks arise from her lack of ability to understand such arguments. Nor is she "androgynous" when she muses about being a man in order to "get up on a lovely woman" (*Ulysses* 770). Molly is merely thinking of her own body here in a narcissistic way (Unkeless 156-64). Similarly Bloom's Nighttown sex-change is not an image of wholeness, maturity, or androgyny; he is, as Gilbert and others have argued, simply a disgraced male victim in this sado-masochistic episode.[1] Even Bloom's parental sharing of cocoa with Stephen is an image of paternity (not maternity), as the western hero and patriarch, Ulysses-Bloom, at last gains a son and heir. One cup of cocoa doth not an androgyne make — though it perhaps shows a proud father. Thus it celebrates a great western quest; it is a quest that implies a theological one, the father's search for the son, and the son's search for, and union with, the father.

God is not mocked, not really in Joyce's work. That is, the value, or the presumed ultimate importance, of certain western scripts, is not mocked. These scripts include the myth of the "universality" and value of the male's quest, and the myth of the ultimate nature of gender distinctions. *Orlando*, by contrast, mocks these gender-gods and other such presumptious symbol systems. Introducing her book on *Ulysses*, Suzette Henke observes in highly reverent language that Joyce gives us ultimate symbols; quoting *Ulysses* (581), she writes: "throughout the cannon of his work, he utters the 'word known to all men' — the Logos that defines being, engenders sympathy, and identifies the symbol-system of the race" (3). Henke accurately interprets the implied author of *Ulysses* (and of *Finnegans Wake* as well). Through all the wonderful and comic permutations of language in Joyce's fiction there are certain assumptions that are put forth as ultimates, as the groundwork of the human comedy. These assumptions include the maleness of the hero, whether Stephen or Bloom or Ulysses or Here Comes Everybody (everybody? women and men?), and the presumed value and truth of the oedipus myth. But the contraband premise of *Orlando* is that there is no "symbol-system of the race." There are only symbol-systems that are spoken by, or assigned, or bidden (or forbidden) by the spirit of an age.

Joyce implies that there is a spirit *behind* the spirits of an age. For him there is a grand pattern, a symbol-system of the race, great universal texts (among them the Christian one)[2] that hold modern life together as well as the modernist "chaosmos" (118.21) of *Finnegans Wake*. Joyce does attempt to show that the grand pattern includes a strong female voice, such as the one heard when the Prankquean speaks, or the fascinating ALP, and the foot-noting Issy. Yet, even though Issy is preoccupied with "gramma's grammar" (268.17), it is really grandpa's grammar that dominates the wordplay of *Finnegans Wake*. The erudition of Joyce's puns relies on the white male European philosophical and literary culture (with some use of the oriental and the Celtic) that this very learned novelist had absorbed.

It is grandpa's grammar and grandpa's myth that *Finnegans Wake* elaborates and celebrates. The oedipal drama is assumed to be *the text* of the human race. A violent, abusive oedipal scenario is portrayed as the human condition, while the *felix culpa* leitmotif stammers its ambivalent blessing over cycle after cycle of the *status quo*. It may be that the central myth of the Wake is not the oedipus myth itself, but *the importance of* the oedipus myth. *Finnegans Wake*, like *Ulysses*, affirms the myth that there *is* a myth of the race.

The radically contraband comedy of *Orlando*, by contrast, challenges the assumption that such a myth or symbol-system exists. The supposedly central and ultimate codes have changed as the spirits of different ages have spoken them. They may change again, Orlando well knows, as she realizes that she progresses not from rhetorical illusion to transcendent truth, but from one rhetorical illusion to another. And the things that she identifies as illusions are not simply the manners and dress of an age, but those large cultural codes which a less radical comedy would identify as truth and norm. Orlando perceives the rhetorically constructed "nature" of love, and the verbal politics that (en)gender the "nature" of the sexes.

Notes

1. Gilbert (394-96). The debate about Bloom's androgyny recurs frequently in criticism. Over a decade ago Carolyn Heilbrun made the strongest argument for Bloom as having the "feminine characteristics" of sympathy and passive kindness (95). Bonnie Scott reviews the debate and sees Bloom's supposed androgyny as doubtful (50).
2. Among those who have emphasized the Christian, indeed Trinitarian, paradigm of *Ulysses* are Noon (123-43), and Schlossman (3-66). Bernard Benstock, looking chiefly at *Finnegans Wake*, argues emphatically that Joyce did not believe, and that critics who underline the Christian themes in any of his fiction are in error; yet Benstock concedes that Joyce describes "modern Christian society" (86-87, 68-103).

Works Cited

Barthes, Roland. *Mythologies*. Trans. Annette Lavers. New York: Hill and Wang, 1972.
Benstock, Bernard. *Joyce-Again's Wake*. Seattle: University of Washington Press, 1965.
Gilbert, Sandra. "Costumes of the Mind: Transvestism as Metaphor in Modern Literature." *Critical Inquiry* 7 (Winter 1980): 391-417.
Heilburn, Carolyn. *Toward a Recognition of Androgyny*. New York: Alfred A. Knopf, 1973.
Henke, Suzette. *Joyce's Miraculous Sindbook*. Columbus: Ohio State University Press, 1978.
Iser, Wolfgang. *The Act of Reading: A Theory of Aesthetic Response*. Baltimore: Johns Hopkins University Press, 1978.
Jacobus, Mary. *Reading Woman: Essays in Feminist Criticism*. New York: Columbia University Press, 1986.
Joyce, James. *Finnegans Wake*. New York: Viking, 1969.
———. *Ulysses*. New York: Random House-Modern Library, 1961.
Little, Judy. *Comedy and the Woman Writer: Woolf, Spark and Feminism*. Lincoln: University of Nebraska Press, 1983.
Noon, William T., S.J. *Joyce and Aquinas*. New Haven: Yale University Press, 1957.
Schlossman, Beryl. *Joyce's Catholic Comedy of Language*. Madison: University of Wisconsin Press, 1985.
Scott, Bonnie Kime. *Joyce and Feminism*. Bloomington: Indiana University Press, 1984.
Unkeless, Elaine. "The Conventional Molly Bloom." *Women in Joyce*. Ed. Suzette Henke and Elaine Unkeless. Urbana: University of Illinois Press, 1982. 150-68.
Woolf, Virginia. "Jane Austen." *Collected Essays*. 4 vols. London: Hogarth, 1966-69. vol. 1: 144-54.
———. *Orlando*. New York: Harcourt Brace Jovanovich-Harvest Book, 1956.

Truth-telling: the self and the fictions of humor

MARY ANN RORISON CAWS

Graduate School, City University of New York

Say you will remember it. That it wasn't all lost, and that you'll forgive me for this outburst, and always be my friend ...[1]

SOME FICTIONS of the self, perhaps by their very nature, by their own deep seriousness, have their own most secret humor. Seen from a step back, our most intimate passions can be turned against us, all the more efficaciously by ourselves. That House of Mirth we all live in, in our unfunny ways, in habit — as if by a peculiarly fitting choice — is no less lethal than that of Lily Bart; we are all, no less terribly than James' telegraph operator. In the Cage. And beyond the societal, personal, and professional imprisonments imposed and necessarily accepted, there seems often to stretch out an unending lifelong avenue of other houses, cages, and oh most solitary confinements. As for this collective personal pronoun I adopt here, it may be taken to include both sexes, or no, depending on the reader's stance. It may include no one, in fact, beyond the writing self and its lonelier projections — how am I to know? (This is, in some sense, a fiction, written by a female: is it a female fiction?) I write of writing as speaking out, about a situation entailing, after its pity and its terror, its own brand of wry humor. My own fiction of humor assumes the humorous stance to be, in the very face of tragedy, both its refusal and — at the same time and for odd and human reasons — a complicitous smile.

It may well be that, as well-taught types, we are accustomed to telling the truth only about the unimportant or at least — and they often coincide — the unembarrassing. Those things we hide may indeed compose our truest passion, and what we tell, our truest trivia. It may well be that we need something to hide, and to hide something.

There is, on the other hand, the virtue of openness, less diplomatic, probably less intelligent, but with its own high value. One solution many of us may adopt is that of fiction. Of emotional fictions, as fables for the grownups we presume we, at least partially, are. Aren't the fictions we tell really our forms of telling the truth, just less committing in their supposed distance? Fictions do not violate, for they do not come sufficiently close. They leave intact that truth we most care about: they leave us where we were — having said our truth in its humor or the humors of its tragedy, but having kept what we sometimes think important to us — our private self. Yet, still now, there is another solution, involving a greater or lesser measure of fiction, and a corresponding compromise of that privacy. It entails a certain openness of the self, thus risking a certain ruin, of the self and its previous compromises, including the needful ones. It is this other outspoken solution that I wish to examine, however privately or collectively, that of the literary and personal speaking out, in one's own name and from one's own plight.

Lord, when shall we be done growing? ... Lord, when shall we be done changing?
Melville to Hawthorne,
Nov. 7, 1851

This letter from the younger Melville to the older Hawthorne, whom he adored, says, probably, too much that is true. Melville speaks here of what he had previously called "incorporation": "your heart beat in my ribs and mine in yours." and then pours out his soul — unspeakably, unbearably, and wonderfully.

The language of truth is, in this case, truly unspeakable, and would shake the most stubbornly impassive of readers, as he continues: "Whence came you, Hawthorne? By what right do you drink from my flagon of life? And when I put it to my lips — Lo, they are yours and not mine ... I shall leave the world, I feel, with more satisfaction for having come to know you. Knowing you persuades me more than the Bible of our immortality."

I would write you on an endless scroll of foolscap, says the loving Melville in an unrestrained postscript: I would write you a "thousand — million — billion thoughts ..." But then, the writing of sudden withdrawal, for the truth was indeed too much. He adds a post-postscript to cancel out the preceding, as if it could be so simply done, and to beg at the same time: the document is as bothersome as it is moving. "P.P.S. Don't think that by writing me a letter, you shall always be bored with an immediate reply to it — and so keep both of us delving over a writing-desk eternally. No such thing! I sh'n't always answer your letters, and you may do just as you please."

For the reader, the truth is clear. The truth of the love first declared openly, then folding back in on itself in a terrified awareness of its too-muchness. Never done growing, never done changing, the lover speaking and subsequently trying to unspeak the truth teaches, himself and us, a terrible lesson. That growing, or extending ourselves, requires learning to speak what we see as truth, the kind of truth which in all probability there is no backing off from. And that it then requires that we figure out what, in our different worlds and cases, to do about it, once it is spoken. But that is another issue: the point here is the speaking itself, and when it is most difficult to do so.

Growing, it is my at least temporary contention, relates to just such speaking out, at the cost of a bitter humor against the self, in a thoroughly frightened consciousness. What are the dangers of speaking out, and what limits are to be placed on it, and its results? What options have we, once we have spoken? To these questions we each bring our peculiar training, as partial answer. From the classics we learned, early too, that the essential cause of much tragedy is just this obsessive declaration of ourselves; that our guilt, about loving or anything else, properly inappropriate as it might be, that the social and classical sin *par excellence*, is speaking out. Phaedra was doomed not just for loving Hippolytus, who could not love her (in the Greek, for Greek reasons: wrong gender; and in the French Racinian tragedy, for French reasons: the dull and "timid Aricie," his fiancée; surely, however, the reasons for non-reciprocity matter little.) She was doomed, not because she was a prey to passion, but because she *told* him, and us. Melville had it a little better, for turning back, and in on himself, it was as if he had done speaking. Even if that meant, essentially, he had done living in that intense mode, declaring his colors.

The great doomed passionate speaking types haunt us as we think and write and speak our own truths. Haunt us here in Cambridge,[2] as they might well do elsewhere, those great speakers-out of truth. Two unforgettable women in particular, both associated with Bloomsbury. The first many of us share as mentor, and our Virginia Woolf was so frank in her hilarious attack on the underprivileges of the women's college in her time: on the Girton up the hill a piece, and — by extension, on the Newnham I cycle by each day (telescoped into her "Fernham") — that the latter place takes on a strange aura for me, on my grateful way to a study of my own in Clare Hall. I feel somehow, and magnificently, escorted. To speak the truth about loving Virginia — as she did about loving Vita, in her letters, her journal, and, fictionally (the greatest way of truth-telling, if not the safest), in *Orlando* — is not of the same order as Alice B. Toklas speaking about loving Gertrude Stein, her reason for living. Loving Virginia is quite like loving everyone else's football hero. No more compromising. But in a sense couple love, of whatever mix, should not be embarrassing in its declaration — if it works, fine, for however long; if not, not. There are more compromising truths, those that try the soul, both in their silence and in their speaking. For they place us at risk, these difficult loves, these inappropriate passions.

And the other figure who haunts me is more problematic still than Virginia Woolf, and her love, of a different sort, more difficult too than Virginia's for Vita. Not the sort that works, and so, it seems to me, of a more difficult declaration, and of a humor more bitter, in her letters and journal, called by her: *D.C.: HER BOOK*, as indeed it was. Editing these texts, David Garnett declared his own colors (are others' colors ever our own?) that she, Dora Carrington, who so unembarrassedly and wholeheartedly and hopelessly loved Lytton Strachey who could not love her or her gender, was endlessly tormented by being a woman, mortified by being a woman, unhappy because she was a woman. Reflecting on her eventual suicide after Lytton died, he regrets that she couldn't just pull up her socks and get on with her work. But then, we should and do indeed remember, she was a woman. Foolish in her love. About her own despair, she wrote to Virginia that she would best understand. She probably did. "Will you come to us", Virginia had asked on the day before Carrington pulled the trigger on herself; to which Carrington replied, truthfully, "yes, I will come, or not." Carrington had already, being told Lytton was soon to die, tried poisoning herself by carbon monoxide fumes, but was pulled from the garage because it was thought that Lytton was dying at that moment. "It is ironical," she wrote in Her Book, "that Lytton by that early attack at 6'ock (sic) saved my life, when I gave my life for his, he should give it back." (H, 1065) Of her clumsiness at the moment of firing, she said, heartbreakingly, that she had bungled her death, as she had her life.

Carrington's most vivid way of truth-telling was the quite extraordinary portrait she painted of Lytton, which she then most desperately didn't want to show to others, as if the sight of it would profane the sanctity of her love and its expression. Nor did she want to complete it: she wanted to paint it continually, with no exposure. The portrait could only have been done by someone very much in love, in love with his long fingers, his draped-out body, his remarkable self-absorption in his reading; her own absorption in and by the painting seems the utter limit of truth-telling in its panicked state, relating to what has been most loved. When she tells her journal of her unwillingness to share its sight, her eagerness to dwell in it daily and all alone, she nevertheless addresses Lytton in the entry, even as he is shut out from the passage to sight: I don't want even you to see it. That the address should not reach its object is the utter bitterness of that humor fate exposes us to, telling it or not as we see, and choose to see and tell it. The utter complication of such revealing non-revelation, both visual and verbal, elevates the panic of truth-telling to its summit: how do you, why should you, expose and place on exhibit your truest self? Is this one more fiction, and how is it to be used?

The irony of an artist not wishing to expose the art of love is not of a different order from the art of a writer (Virginia Woolf or another) writing of love. That awful and wonderful act of declaration — to a world that may or may not care — of an emotion felt to be private, at once consecrates and violates. The irony implicit in an artist's creation of an object that exhibits the very desire of non-exposition parallels an art of love whose presentation involves both truth as well as concealment, gift and withholding, whether it be announced or kept secret. I would write you a thousand million billion words, endlessly on an endless scroll, in a first declaration Melvillian in kind; and then I would not, for the world, show or answer, for fear of my own too-muchness.

It is not that Melville's self-underselling has its lessons for us, necessarily. Not, either, that the declarations and ambivalences of Carrington's or Virginia's truth-tellings, have private lessons to teach us, about humor or tragedy, or their intertwining. The drastic ends of the two female truth-tellers were other, we hope, from ours. It is rather the problems that they pose us that are of ultimate value: how can we make our discretions, as well as our declarations, match our talent? How can we make our creations, as they are outwardly available, match our innermost dedication? If the truth of our truths is learned, or exposed, by ourselves or others, let it at least not be just for exposition's sake. If we mask — with our highest intelligence — our truths with fictions or fabulations, let us at least not make haste to do our own unmasking. Those fictions have their nobility: *Orlando* is far more fun to read than Vita's own novels, Carrington's portrait of Lytton reveals the soul of the man as much as his own works, and Melville's *Pierre*, as well as his "Mosses from the Old Manse," is vastly more textured than some of Hawthorne's more obvious prose. Our journals and letters and fiction bear their own, perhaps no less fictional, truths. Our loves, rendered verbal, are already elsewhere from their emotional essence, are already grown and changed from being words. Should we not celebrate, insofar as we can, those words and that art — even if in the guise of artlessness — right along with whatever truth they necessarily mask? We know, from Rousseau's *Confessions*, how telling enfables; we know, from our own letters, how declaring befuddles. And we know, from our own lives, most of us, what fictions we live. No matter how much we would wish it otherwise.

I've been thinking over a parable painted on a friend's wall here in Cambridge, sensing its relevance to the problematics of truth-telling and reading, of humor and its tragic interweaving. Columbine, loves, or thinks she does, Pierrot, that tragic figure. She passes him, or thinks she does, a note about meeting, which is intercepted by Harlequin in a Pierrot mask. But at the rendez-vous, as he doffs his mask, she continues to love the usurper instead of the true Pierrot. Pierrot mourns, and we — I would suppose it of all of us — along with him. The unmasking of the false makes its own truth, not necessarily a joyous one. For the parable is wry about the final reading. The one who knows how to get, receive, read, and smile, perhaps, at the letter, no matter to whom it thinks itself addressed, makes the truth of the reading. Reception theory and truth-telling meet on the uneven ground of fiction. Contemporary truth entails how we are read and who bothers to get what we send, quite as much as the ways we tell or send the truth. Masks can be lifted, and truths have many sides. But it is reading that takes our entire and multiple intelligence, and it is the humor as the wry understanding within such intelligence we most hope for.

My growing story, in its fictions as in its truth, has been about how truth is read and not just about how it is told. Intelligent reading presupposes that the growing process has as many participants as there are readers for our tales, of ourselves as of others. Melville, even feeling one with his beloved receiver of his letter, didn't want to crowd him. Many of our truths find themselves laden with postscripts of fear, tag-ends of tag-ends. When did growing ever require that we see and speak the truth whole and all at once? Those scary truths are not, I believe, there in the neat middle of our lives and letters and essays — those truths past or present about hurting and being hurt, about having been in states of love and loss, about loving inappropriateness of all sorts, may come at any moment. Even after we think we are through speaking, as a ps. to a ps. If telling the truth means speaking it out to the end of creation, then reading the truth is surely about knowing how to face it to the end.

This includes, finally, being brave enough, and maybe, funny enough, to assume and live out those truths we've told in our fictions — for they may well be what is, is almost unbearably — most real. We may, after all, have done something about telling and creating and teaching, but we haven't, thankfully, any of us reading or writing, this or anything, done growing.

Note

1. Carrington, letter to Lytton Strachey, quoted in Michael Holroyd, *Lytton Strachey: a Biography* (Penguin: Harmondsworth, 1971), p. 819 (sic).
2. (And now, still here in the New York of 1988.)

Sylvia

NICOLE HOLLANDER

Ironic autobiography: from *The Waterfall* to *The Handmaid's Tale*

NANCY WALKER

Stephens College, Columbia, MO

I

TOWARD THE END of her novel *Heartburn*, Nora Ephron has her narrator, Rachel Samstat, explain why she has told her story:

> Because if I tell the story, I control the version.
> Because if I tell the story, I can make you laugh, and I would rather have you laugh at me than feel sorry for me. (176-77)

Near the beginning of Margaret Atwood's *The Handmaid's Tale*, the narrator, Offred, makes a similar comment about her role as storyteller:

> I would like to believe this is a story I'm telling. I need to believe it. I must believe it. Those who can believe that such stories are only stories have a better chance.
> If it's a story I'm telling, then I have control over the ending. Then there will be an ending, to the story, and real life will come after it. I can pick up where I left off.
> It isn't a story I'm telling.
> It's also a story I'm telling, in my head, as I go along. (39)

Despite dramatic differences between these two novels — Ephron's comic account of her divorce from *Washington Post* reporter Carl Bernstein and Atwood's grim futuristic description of the repressive Republic of Gilead — they share an autobiographical method, a focus on the woman *telling her own story*. Both Rachel Samstat and Offred wish, in the telling, to control the accounts of their own lives, and both narrators reveal a consciousness of the ironic difference between reality and their "stories," a consciousness that separates the narrator into two "selves" — one that endures the anguish of her own reality and a second self that stands apart and comments, often quite humorously, on the plight of the first.

Margaret Drabble, in *The Waterfall*, employs an even more overt method to create these two "selves." By alternating third-person and first-person narratives, Drabble provides a continual double perspective on her character's life: the story of Jane that is told in the third-person narrative is an edited version of reality created by Jane herself at a later date. The first-person ironic narrator announces her role as "author" of her own story at the beginning of the fifth chapter:

It won't, of course, do: as an account, I mean, of what took place. I tried, I tried for so long to reconcile, to find a style that would express it, to find a system that would excuse me, to construct a new meaning. ... And yet I haven't lied. I've merely omitted: merely, professionally, edited. (47)

Having admitted that the story of Jane — of herself *as* Jane, rather than as "I" — is a partial one, this narrator resolves somewhat later to "go back to that other story, to that other woman, who lived a life too pure, too lovely to be mine" (70). Drabble's narrator thus tells her own story, a story she acknowledges to be a fiction, edited so that she can, to use Ephron's words, "control the version." In a similar blending of past and present, third- and first-person narratives, Fay Weldon's narrator Chloe, in *Female Friends*, recounts the histories of herself and her friends Grace and Marjorie, shifting constantly from present to past tense, from "I" to "Chloe," attempting in the telling to discover some pattern or reality. At the end of the novel, Chloe speaks to the reader about this attempt:

Marjorie, Grace and me. What can we tell you to help you, we three sisters, walking wounded that we are? What can we tell you of living and dying, beginning and ending, patching and throwing away; of the patterns that our lives make, which seem to have some kind of order, if only we could perceive it. (309)

As the ironically detached narrator, Chloe presents the stories of these three women as having the kind of logic and inevitability that can be imposed only by the author of fiction.

These four novels by women, published between 1969 (*The Water-*

fall) and 1986 (*The Handmaid's Tale*), represent a significant development in the consciousness and method of the female fiction writer in Britain and America. The consciousness of the social "self" as somehow fictive, created in large part by cultural rules and expectations, leads the author to use an ironic method in which the central character or narrator is presented as a creation of her own imagination. The voice of the ironic self comments with exasperation or amusement on the thoughts and actions of her "created" self, while viewing her sympathetically, as one hopelessly enmeshed in the absurdities of women's lives. The resultant comedy demystifies women's existence in the late twentieth century; the mutability of self points up the arbitrary nature of the restrictions that the women's movement has fought so vigorously during these years.

From the late 1960s to the present, novels by women have increasingly been biographical or autobiographical in method, if not usually in fact, depicting the progress of individual women toward greater autonomy and fulfillment during a period of social upheaval. Judith Rossner's *Nine Months in the Life of an Old Maid* (1969), Gail Godwin's *The Odd Woman* (1974), Marilyn French's *The Women's Room* (1977), Marge Piercy's *Fly Away Home* (1984), and many others have even reflected in their titles a thematic concern with change, space, and status — a quest for self-definition rather than definition by the culture. Nor is this recounting of a woman's struggle for control over her own life an entirely new phenomenon in English and American fiction by women. Fanny Fern's 1855 novel *Ruth Hall*, Kate Chopin's *The Awakening*, Edith Wharton's *The House of Mirth*, and Virginia Woolf's *Mrs Dalloway*, among others, are precursors of the contemporary women's novel in their investigation of a female character's more or less successful attempt to define the terms of her own life. What distinguishes the recent works by Drabble, Weldon, Ephron, and Atwood is their ultimate refusal to take seriously the cultural prescriptions that seek to define their central characters — a refusal that is reflected in the use of an ironic mode.

Traditionally, the women's novel — certainly the *popular* novel — has affirmed rather than questioned the values of the culture. As Lynne Agress points out in *The Feminine Irony*, it was not until Fanny Burney's *Evelina*, in 1778, that women began to write about women, and in the early nineteenth century, women's novels that featured female main characters tended to reinforce the submissiveness and subordination that were touted as ideal feminine traits:

> Their works were mainly didactic: as writers they would guide women in performing their proper roles as subordinate creatures, as helpmates to men. In attempting to be messiahs to women, they often ended up as the devil's disciples.
>
> So long as women were willing to subscribe to the subordinate role created by society and endorsed by most women writers, their lives could not really change. (172-73)

The term "irony" in the title of Agress' book, in fact, points to the very lack of this quality in the consciousness of the early female novelist. That is, without skepticism about the culturally-sanctioned subordination of women, the novelist could achieve no distance from it, and therefore accepted — and promoted — it as part of an immutable social fabric.

The contemporary novel by women has unquestionably challenged the established social fabric, though not as overtly as has the distinctly ironic novel. By presenting female characters who break away from traditional roles and bonds (marriage, motherhood, etc.), as do writers such as French, Piercy, and Rossner, the author implicitly indicts the system that has made such escape necessary for a woman's self-fulfillment. The double vision of the ironic novel, in contrast, makes explicit the flaws or the plain evils of the culture by exposing them to the narrator's clear-eyed vision and thus demonstrating their absurdity. That is, this critique is explicit *if* the reader is able to "read" the irony. Wayne Booth, in *A Rhetoric of Irony*, maintains that the reading of ironies requires four steps, which are usually accomplished almost simultaneously. First, the reader must "reject the literal meaning" of the author's words because of an incongruity "among the words or between the words and something else that he knows."[1] Secondly, the reader casts about for alternate meanings. Third, the reader makes a decision "about the author's knowledge or beliefs." "It is," Booth notes, "this decision about the author's own beliefs that entwines the interpretation of stable ironies so inescapably in intentions." Fourth, and finally, the reader must reconstruct a meaning that he believes is the author's actual intended statement. "Unlike the original proposition, the reconstructed meanings will necessary be in harmony with the unspoken beliefs that the reader has decided to attribute to [the author]" (10-12).

Thus in Atwood's *The Handmaid's Tale*, when the Aunts, who

instruct the Handmaids on their duties, change the wording of the Bible verses the Handmaids are required to memorize, or attribute to the Bible statements from other sources, they depend upon the Handmaids' inability to "read" ironies. Atwood, on the other hand, depends upon her reader to read them quite clearly. For example, as Offred describes the occasion of one of the Handmaids giving birth, she remembers one of the Aunts' brainwashing refrains:

> *From each*, says the slogan, *according to her ability; to each according to his needs*. We recited that, three times, after dessert. It was from the Bible, or so they said. St. Paul again, in Acts. (117)[2]

Even if the reader does not initially notice the substitution of the feminine pronoun "her" in this statement from Marxist doctrine — a substitution that accords with the Gileadean use of women for the needs of men — he or she will recognize that the statement is not from the Bible, as the Aunts claim. Furthermore, Offred is herself close to seeing the incongruity, as revealed in the phrase "or so they said." The ironic juxtaposition of the religious and the secular/political (or, rather, the incorporation of the latter into the former) indicates the extent to which the rulers of Gilead bend reality to their own purposes.

The continual cross-referencing of past and present in these ironic novels allows for clear examples of the second kind of ironic statement that Booth mentions, in which the incongruity exists between "the words and something else that [the reader] knows." Such ironic statements are frequent in Weldon's *Female Friends*. Early in the novel, for example, Chloe begins a description of a scene involving her friend Grace as follows:

> Envisage now another scene, one summer Sunday some twelve years later, when Grace is in the middle of her dream marriage to Christie. (Grace has a dream marriage the way other women have — or don't have — dream kitchens.) (61).

Not only is the statement made inherently ironic by the concept of the "dream" and the undercutting of the negative phrase "or don't have" — both of which expose by inversion the reality of Grace's marriage — but it is also incongruous alongside Chloe's earlier description of Christie as "arch-villain of a decade" (16). Therefore, it comes as no surprise to the reader that Grace's "dream" is shattered on that "summer Sunday."

These four novels by Atwood, Weldon, Drabble, and Ephron, despite their differences in setting and style, share several important characteristics, all of them linked to the use of irony — both verbal and situational — that reveals a particular relationship between women and social reality, women and the concept of "self." Each has a narrator who self-consciously and deliberately tells her story, addressing the reader directly as she detaches herself from the everyday realities that her undetached "self" experiences. In his monograph *Irony*, D. C. Muecke identifies several "basic features" of irony, one of which may be identified by a number of different terms: "detachment, distance, disengagement, freedom, serenity, objectivity, dispassion, 'lightness,' 'play,' urbanity" (35). Muecke continues by explaining the relationship between this "detachment" and the stance of the ironist:

> This lightness may be but is not necessarily an inability to feel the terrible seriousness of life; it may be a refusal to be overwhelmed by it, an assertion of the spiritual power of man over existence. (36)

The narrators in these novels clearly feel the "terrible seriousness of life," but their strength is their refusal to be "overwhelmed" by it.

In addition, each author employs a plot structure that continually juxtaposes past and present in order to demonstrate the influence of past upon present in the formation of identity and behaviour — in particular, to examine changes, both positive and negative, in women's lives during the past twenty years. Finally each novel displays a feminist consciousness that is capable, by means of ironic distance, of viewing the subordination of women as an absurdity rather than a necessity. The resulting effect is comic — wildly so in *Heartburn*, grimly so in *The Handmaid's Tale* — in the sense that the reader is forced to see as ludicrous some fundamental assumptions about woman's nature and role in society.

II

Although none of these four novels is, properly speaking, an autobiography (*Heartburn* comes closest, but Ephron intended it to be read as fiction), all share some of the classic elements of autobiography: the first-person narration, and especially the emphasis on detailing the development of a *self*.³ For women writers, autobiographical writing has been problematic because the concept of selfhood has itself been problematic. Women have traditionally been defined in relation to others — as daughter, sister, wife, mother — rather than as autonomous entities, and this fact has affected the nature of women's autobiographical writing. Mary G. Mason has pointed out that in the earliest autobiographical writings by women in English, from the fifteenth through the seventeenth centuries, there is a dual consciousness:

> The self-discovery of female identity seems to acknowledge the real presence and recognition of another consciousness, and the disclosure of female self is linked to the identification of some "other." This recognition of another consciousness — and I emphasize recognition rather than deference — this grounding of identity through relation to the chosen other, seems ... to enable women to write openly about themselves. (210)

The most common "others" have been God and husbands or fathers, depending on whether the autobiography is spiritual (Anne Bradstreet's "To My Dear Children") or secular (Margaret Cavendish's *True Relation*) in nature.

In the contemporary ironic novel, in contrast, not only is there a "self" that exists without necessary relation to an "other," but this self is capable of self-scrutiny by a separate part of her consciousness, in the form of the alternate narrator. This splitting of the self is directly related to cultural realities, as women have increasingly adopted nontraditional roles. Thus, in the late 1960s, the narrator in Drabble's *The Waterfall* feels "split":

> I felt split between the anxious intelligent woman and the healthy and efficient mother — or perhaps less split than divided. I felt that I lived on two levels, simultaneously, and that there was no contact, no interaction between them: on one level I could operate well, even triumphantly, but on the other I could only condemn myself, endlessly, for my inadequacy and my faults. (108-109)⁴

It is this split between the intellectual and the familial roles that makes appropriate Drabble's dual narrative in *The Waterfall*. The third-person narrative tells the story of Jane's affair with her cousin's husband, James, while the first-person narrative with which it alternates comments on the various ironies in Jane's (her) situation.

The overarching irony in *The Waterfall* is the fact that Jane is not punished for her sin in the way the heroines of earlier novels have been. Reflecting on her fictional predecessors, the narrator remarks on the distance that separates them:

> Perhaps I'll go mad with guilt, like Sue Bridehead, or drown myself in an effort to reclaim lost renunciations, like Maggie Tulliver. Those fictitious heroines, how they haunt me. ... Maggie Tulliver never slept with her man: she did all the damage there was to be done, to Lucy, to herself, to the two men who loved her, and then, like a woman of another age, she refrained. In this age, what is to be done? We drown in the first chapter. (161-62)

Maggie Tulliver drowns despite her virtue in "refraining"; Jane, by contrast, "drowns" metaphorically in the first chapter of *The Waterfall* by succumbing to her desire for James. Yet a suitable punishment for her "sin" eludes her. Even the automobile accident that Jane and James have later in the novel does not suffice, because both of them survive it, a fact that does not fit with Jane's sense of inherited guilt:

> We should have died, I suppose, James and I. It isn't artistic to linger on like this. It isn't moral either. One can't have art without morality, anyway, as I've always maintained. ... In fact, I am rather ashamed of the amount of amusement that my present life affords me, and of how much I seem to have gained by it. One shouldn't get away with such things. (249)[5]

The irony in this passage is obvious, especially in the statement that "one can't have art without morality"; the narrator, "author" of her own story, and hence an artist, has proclaimed the immorality of that story, a fact which negates her own statement.

The only punishment Jane receives for her sin is itself ironic when compared to the fates of earlier heroines: a blood clot that results from her use of birth-control pills. On the last page of the novel, the narrator remarks on this particular twist:

> No, I can't leave it without a postscript, without formulating that final, indelicate irony. ... I think I mentioned that on the eve of our departure to Norway I lay awake imagining a pain in my leg: well, it was a real pain, it was a swelling, a thrombic clot. The price that modern woman must pay for love. In the past, in old novels, the price of love was death, a price which virtuous women paid in childbirth. ... Nowadays it is paid in thrombosis or neurosis: one can take one's pick. (256)

Freedom of choice — the ability to "take one's pick" — is here reduced to the choice between physical and mental illness. Women still suffer for love, but modern science has made it possible to avoid pregnancy and develop blood clots instead.

Like the other three novels considered here, *The Waterfall* collapses past and present, not only the past of the "fictional heroines" to whom the narrator compares herself, but also the two narratives of which the novel is composed. The first-person narrative threads through the third-person narrative, holding up bits of the latter for scrutiny: amending, confessing half-truths, seeking a pattern. In order to "comprehend" the life of Jane, the first-person narrator vows to "reconstitute it in a form that I can accept, a fictitious form" (53). The conscious creation of a reality that one can accept — essentially, of a *self* that one can accept — distances the character from her own life; life itself becomes a fiction to be molded by its creator, particularly when the actuality of life is too painful. Yet the neatness of a perfect fiction finally eludes the narrator: "I was hoping that in the end I would manage to find some kind of unity. I seem to be no nearer to it" (220).

This desire for unity or pattern also motivates Chloe, the narrator of Weldon's *Female Friends*, for whom her own life and those of Marjorie and Grace "seem to have some kind of order, if only we could perceive it more clearly" (309). Chloe's tone is more consistently ironic than that of Drabble's narrator; as she intersperses the account of one day in her own life with the accounts of the individual histories of the three main characters, Weldon shifts quickly back and forth between third- and first-person narratives to juxtapose the fragmented lives of Chloe, Marjorie, and Grace to Chloe's detached, often cynical commentary. Brought together by the relocation of children from London to the countryside during World War II, the three girls grow up almost as sisters, though they are from radically different backgrounds. Marjorie is the daughter of a Jewish father and his beautiful, constantly unfaithful Gentile wife; Grace, to whose home outside London the other two are (mistakenly, it turns out) sent, is the daughter of local gentry; and Chloe's widowed mother finds work as a barmaid in the local pub. It is Chloe's position as outsider in terms of social class that makes her the ideal ironic narrator; she is the one who perceives that things are not what they seem.

That is, Chloe *as narrator* is the objective observer. As Chloe, in the third-person portions of the narrative, she is the victim of a brutish husband who openly sleeps with their French maid and regularly bullies his wife into tears. But the Chloe who addresses the reader directly is stoic and philosophical:

When we [Marjorie, Grace, Chloe] walk alone in the night planning murder, suicide, adultery, revenge — and go home to bed and rise red-eyed in the morning, to continue as before.

And either the worst happens, or it doesn't. Or one is mistreated, or one is not, the answer is never made clear. Life continues. (143)

Like Drabble's narrator Jane, Chloe believes in fate, not God. "The Fata Morgana are tricky ladies, and obstinate too. ... Conceive of defeat, and it is already upon you — yet to avoid it, it must be conceived of" (201-202). With such ironic statements, the narrator advises the reader. Women in particular must be advised, warned, prone as they are to miscarriages, and unfaithful husbands, and injuries to children:

Oh my friends, my female friends, how wise you are to have no children or to throw them off. Better abort them, sterilise yourselves, or have your womb cut out. Give birth, and you give others the power to destroy you, to multiply your hurts a thousand times, to make you suffer with them. (204)

That this hyperbolic advice is meant ironically is made clear a few lines later, when the narrator advises, "And never have parents, either. ... Blessed are the orphans, and the barren of body and mind" (204-205). Yet the three women in the novel — Chloe, Marjorie, and Grace — continue to suffer the indignities peculiar to women, and only the voice of the narrator provides the perspective that makes these indignities absurd rather than tragic.

The use of — and finally the distrust of — language itself is another of the ironies that *Female Friends* shares with the other three novels. The narrator in *The Waterfall*, attempting to make a satisfactory fiction of her own life, finds words seductive and misleading: "Lies, lies, it's all lies. A pack of lies. I've even told lies of fact, which I had not meant to do" (89). Lying permeates *Female Friends*: characters lie to themselves and to each other; language itself is suspect. Chloe's mother, Gwyneth, secretly in love with her pub-owner employer for twenty years, does not speak to him of her love because she — mistakenly — believes in the power of words:

Gwyneth believes she has only to speak the words and Mr. Leacock will be hers; and forever procrastinates, and never quite speaks them. Thus, lonely women do live, making the best of what they cannot help: reading significance into casual words: seeing love in calculated lust: seeing lust in innocent words; hoping where there is no hope. (108)

Gwyneth's belief in the power of words includes the aphorisms she gives as truths to her daughter Chloe. Like the teachings of the Aunts in *The Handmaid's Tale*, these are presented in such a way that they contradict each other ("Marriages are made in heaven." "Marry in haste, repent in leisure."), contradict other evidence in the novel ("The Lord helps those who help themselves."), or are simply illogical ("Red flannel is warmer than white.") (45).

Chloe's final victory over Oliver, her self-centered, sexist husband, is accomplished finally when she is able to adopt in the third-person narrative the objective, ironic voice of her first-person narrative self. Following an argument in which Oliver is particularly abusive, Chloe's two selves essentially come together when Oliver makes the typically sexist comment that he has no control over his sexual responses:

CHLOE[:] It must be dreadful to be a man, and be so helpless in the face of one's own nature.
Is she laughing at him? Yes, she is. Her victory is complete.
She does not much enjoy her victory. Mirth cuts at the roots of her life. (266-67)

Humor is thus a two-edged sword: it frees her from emotional bondage to Oliver, but the freedom is itself frightening.

The use of humor as a freeing mechanism is the basis of Nora Ephron's novel *Heartburn*. By telling the story of her dissolving marriage in a comic fashion, Ephron's narrator, Rachel, maintains her dignity even while enduring the agony of loss.[6] The novel begins just after Rachel has discovered that her husband, Mark, is having an affair with Thelma Rice, and proceeds by a series of flashbacks to chronicle Rachel's life to this point. Rachel is a hopeless romantic who has learned to adopt the ironic stance as a means of survival, a fact that she announces on the first page of the novel:

The first day I did not think [the separation from Mark] was funny. I didn't think it was funny the third day either, but I managed to make a little joke about it. "The most unfair thing about this whole business," I said, "is that I can't even date." (3)

Rachel, seven months pregnant at the time of the separation, is staying at her father's apartment in New York, crying, she tells us, most of the time, but the voice with which she tells the story has a buoyant flippancy that allows her to achieve distance on her circumstance.

Like Atwood's *The Handmaid's Tale*, *Heartburn* is entirely a first-person narrative. Ephron conveys the sense of two "selves" in the novel in two ways. One is the difference between the anguish Rachel tells us she feels and the humorous way in which she tells about it. In her father's apartment, for example, Rachel considers her next step:

> I considered staying in bed all day. I considered getting out of bed and into the bathtub and staying *there* all day. I wondered if even considering these two alternatives constituted a nervous breakdown. (Probably not, I decided.) I contemplated suicide. Every so often I contemplate suicide merely to remind myself of my complete lack of interest in it as a solution to anything at all. (46)

In fact, just as Jane, in *The Waterfall*, has difficulty with the life and fate of the romantic heroine, Rachel has rejected this role altogether:

> There was a time ... when I longed to be the sort of girl who knew the names of wildflowers and fed baby birds with eyedroppers and rescued bugs from swimming pools and wanted from time to time to end it all. ... I have come to accept the fact that there is not a neurasthenic drop of blood in my body, and I have become very impatient with it in others. (46)

The distance between Rachel's emotions and her tone is the distance between the self that suffers and the self that stands apart to comment. Although admitting that she cries easily, Rachel also notes that "crying is a highly overrated activity: women do entirely too much of it, and the last thing we ought to want is for it to become a universal excess" (88). Like the narrators in *The Waterfall* and *Female Friends*, Rachel needs to control her own story. When she tells her therapy group about Mark's infidelity, one of the members asks why she has to make everything into a joke. "'I don't have to make everything into a joke,' I said. 'I have to make everything into a story. Remember?'" (54).

Instead of alternating between first- and third-person narration, Ephron alternates between scene and narrative, on the one hand, and Rachel's direct address to the reader. Because Rachel is a cookbook writer, some of these addresses take the form of recipes, and at one point she interrupts the story for a brief essay titled "Potatoes and Love: Some Reflections." At other times she reminds the reader that she knew better than to marry Mark, thus maintaining her distance from her own anguish. After a lengthy passage about the impossibility of making any marriage work — "it seems to me that it's just about impossible to live with someone else" (84) — Rachel says to the reader:

> I started out telling you all this because I wanted you to understand why I resisted getting married again. It seemed to me that the desire to get married — which, I regret to say, I believe is fundamental and primal in women — is followed almost immediately by an equally fundamental and primal urge, which is to be single again. (84)

The irony is that, despite all of these beliefs, Rachel falls in love with Mark, and is in part seduced by words: "Forever and ever, he said. Forever and ever and ever, he said. *I'll be loving you always*" (84). Toward the end of *Heartburn*, Rachel recites a litany of contradictory truisms that recall the aphorisms Gwyneth gives to Chloe in *Female Friends*:

> Sometimes I believe that love dies but hope springs eternal. Sometimes I believe that hope dies but love springs eternal. Sometimes I believe that sex plus guilt equals love, and sometimes I believe that sex plus guilt equals good sex. Sometimes I believe that love is as natural as the tides, and sometimes I believe that love is an act of will. Sometimes I believe that some people are better at love than others, and sometimes I believe that everyone is faking it. (164)

By such juxtapositions, language loses its meaning, and all truth becomes partial and relative. Unlike Gwyneth, Rachel manipulates language rather than being manipulated by it.

The distrust of language is basic to Atwood's *The Handmaid's Tale*. On the one hand, Offred's only salvation is to believe — and behave according to — what she is told by the Aunts about her proper behavior as a Handmaid. Not to do so would lead to exile as an "Unwoman." Yet Offred's psychic survival, and her role as the ironic narrator, depend upon her suspicion of the official rhetoric of the Republic of Gilead. Although the brainwashing and repression she endures makes her distrust of such rhetoric somewhat tentative — "It was from the Bible, or so they said" (117) — she clearly distrusts the ability of her own language to convey the reality of her circumstances:

> This is a reconstruction [she says of her narrative]. All of it is a reconstruction. ... When I get out of here, if I'm ever able to set this down, in any form, even in the form of one voice to another, it will be a reconstruction then too, at yet another remove. It's impossible to say a thing exactly the way it was, because what you say can never be exact, you always have to leave something out, there are too many parts, sides, crosscurrents, nuances; too many gestures, which could mean this or that. ... (134)

In a more fundamental way than the other three novels, *The Handmaid's Tale* is an ironic text, in which every statement is suspect and subject to reconstruction. Even in this passage, which strikes the reader as essentially "true" in the sense that words on a page are always inadequate to convey actual experience, there is a basic ironic incongruity: Offred speaks in the present tense, as though she is writing these thoughts at the moment of thinking them, yet this sense is contradicted by the phrase "if I'm ever able to get this down, in any form," which moves the recording to some future, hypothetical time. Furthermore, as we learn from the "Historical Notes" at the end of the novel, the manuscript that is Offred's story is itself a reconstruction made 200 years later from the cassette tapes on which Offred recorded her narrative after her escape from Gilead. In fact, the "Historical Notes" consist largely of Professor Pieixoto's talk, "Problems of Authentication in Reference to *The Handmaid's Tale*"; Pieixoto refers to it as a "soi-disant manuscript," and says he "hesitate[s] to use the word *document*" (300-301).

Such doubts about the authenticity of Offred's "manuscript" stand in ironic contrast to the matter-of-fact realism of her narrative. From the first pages of the novel, in which Offred describes the converted gymnasium in which the Handmaids sleep during the time of their training to be breeders of babies for the Commanders of Gilead, Atwood creates a grim reality that takes on an air of inevitability as the novel proceeds. The totalitarian repressions of Gilead (the United States at the end of the twentieth century) are logical outgrowths of cultural trends apparent at the time of the novel's publication: the backlash against feminism, surrogate parentage, the growth of fundamentalist religion. Although Offred hopes that this is only a "story" she is telling, so that "there will be an ending, to the story, and real life will come after it" (39), she meanwhile lives the prescribed, highly routinized life of a Handmaid: shopping, having ritual intercourse with her Commander, and dreaming of a past she only dimly remembers.

As in *The Waterfall, Female Friends,* and *Heartburn,* past and present are continually juxtaposed. Despite the efforts of the Gileadean regime to eradicate the past, it lingers in memory as well as in converted artifacts, such as the gymnasium. As the novel begins, Offred's narrative blends past, present, and future:

I thought I could smell, faintly like an afterimage, the pungent scent of sweat, shot through with the sweet taint of chewing gum and perfume from the watching girls, felt-skirted as I knew from pictures, later in miniskirts, then pants, then in one earring, spiky green-streaked hair. Dances would have been held there; the music lingered, a palimpsest of unheard sound, style upon style. . . . We yearned for the future. (3)

The future that teenaged girls have "yearned for," however, has arrived in a form that none of them could have predicted. The changes in the lives of women depicted in the other three novels — birth-control pills, careers, consciousness-raising groups, and other movements toward freedom and autonomy — have been negated in the Republic of Gilead. As Aunt Lydia says to the Handmaids, "There is more than one kind of freedom. . . . In the days of anarchy, it was freedom to. Now you are being given freedom from. Don't underrate it" (24).

In the earlier novels, language is shown to be untrustworthy; in *The Handmaid's Tale* it is all but forbidden. The Handmaids exchange ritualistic utterances rather than conversation; reading is prohibited; Scrabble is a game to play in secret. "What you don't know won't tempt you," says Aunt Lydia, once more bending an aphorism to her own purposes (195). Words are knowledge, and knowledge is power. Yet Offred is fascinated by words, frequently engaging in word play, as when she remembers having held a job:

Job. It's a funny word. It's a job for a man. Do a jobbie, they'd say to children when they were being toilet-trained. Or of dogs: he did a job on the carpet. You were supposed to hit them with rolled-up newspapers, my mother said. I can remember when there were newspapers. (173)

Everything leads back to the Word, and words are manipulated in Gilead, a society governed ostensibly by the Word of God.

Yet despite the multiple repressions of her life, Offred retains a certain power through the very use of words. On the most obvious level, she does tell her own story, however partial or "unauthenticated" it may be. And by playing with language, she maintains an ironic distance from her life, as do the other three narrators. Offred's version of the Lord's Prayer, for example, is filled with language that mocks the official rhetoric of Gilead:

I wish I knew what You were up to. . . . I don't believe for an instant that what's going on out there is what You meant. . . . Then there's Kingdom, power, and glory. It takes a lot to believe in those right now. ... If I were You I'd be fed up. I'd really be sick of it. ... Oh God. It's no joke. (194-95)

The final despairing statement here indicates that joking is ultimately no remedy for Offred's statement, but the ironic tone in which she speaks to God is typical of Offred's voice throughout the novel. In one of her many direct addresses to the reader, she apologizes for the grimness of her tale:

I wish this story were different. I wish it were more civilized. ... I'm sorry there is so much pain in this story. ... I've tried to put some of the good things in, as well. Flowers, for instance, because where would we be without them? (267)

The introduction of "flowers" as a palliative for the horrors of life in the Republic of Gilead seems initially to be ludicrous, but the following question — "where would we be without them?" — is sufficiently ironic to remind us that Offred is being playful. In a society without love, or trust, or freedom, what remains as the "good thing" is not flowers at all, but Offred's ability to offer them to us.

The role that Offred, Rachel, Chloe, and Jane play in these works is central to the concept of "ironic literature" as Muecke defines it:

Ironic literature ... is literature in which there is a constant dialectic interplay of objectivity and subjectivity, freedom and necessity, the appearance of life and the reality of art, the author immanent in every part of his work as its creative vivifying principle and transcending his work as its objective "presenter." (78)

The first-person narrators represent "objectivity" and "freedom" from the lives they simultaneously describe as their own, and thus rise above — at least intellectually — the conditions that would subjugate them as women. That this "freedom" is itself a fiction is less important than the fact that the ironic method renders absurd the realm of "subjectivity" and "necessity." The figure of the *eiron* (originally meaning "dissembler" and the source of the word "irony") pretends not to know the truth even while presenting it.

These four novels form a continuum in their approach to women's lives during the past twenty years. In the earliest, Drabble's *The Waterfall*, the narrator struggles to free herself from the past, especially the fictional past of the romantic heroine. Jane's ironic first-person narrative shows her wrestling with a sense of guilt and sin that she has inherited from earlier times. Atwood's *The Handmaid's Tale* inverts

Jane's story in several ways. Not only is it a projection into the future, but the "sin" of adultery that Jane commits is a required activity for Offred; rather than trying to free herself from the dictates of female biology, as does Jane, Offred must conceive a child or be doomed as an "Unwoman."[7] In the middle of the continuum are the novels of Weldon and Ephron, in which the narrators are relatively free of historical precedents for their behavior or its consequences, but must still balance emotion with reason in their attempts to achieve independence from male dominance. All four novels deliver strong feminist statements. As ironists, their central characters are able to present as absurd and arbitrary the forces that seek to subjugate women, and that which is absurd loses its authority.

Notes

1. Bertrice Bartlett, in "Reading Negation and Ironies," suggests that "the first step in comprehending irony is not so much to cancel a meaning as it is to recognize a contrast and that it is contrast rather than cancellation which invites evaluative inference." This is a useful amendment of Booth's statement, because it places the ironic statement, like the negative one, in what Bartlett calls "the social logic of communication," requiring the reader to make an inference on the basis of an understanding of social context.
2. The May, 1987, issue of *Harper's* magazine reports that 45% of Americans believe that "from each according to his ability; to each according to his need" is found in the U.S. Constitution ("Harper's Index," p. 13).
3. Contemporary literary theory disputes the validity and even the existence of the author of a text, a dispute that has particular implications for the autobiography. See Michael Sprinker, "Fictions of the Self: The End of Autobiography," in *Autobiography: Essays Theoretical and Critical*, ed. James Olney, Princeton: Princeton Univ. Press, 1980, pp. 321-42.
4. This last statement makes explicit what is implicit in women's humorous writing of the period between World War II and about 1970. By writing comically of their failure to achieve perfection as wives and mothers, writers such as Jean Kerr, Shirley Jackson, and Phyllis McGinley subtly protested the relegation of women to tasks that required so little of their intellect. See Nancy Walker, "Humor and Gender Roles: The 'Funny' Feminism of the Post-World War II Suburbs," *American Quarterly* 37:1 (Spring 1985): 98-113.
5. In contrast, Martha Sinnot, in Mary McCarthy's *A Charmed Life* (1950), *does* die in an automobile accident. See Thelma J. Shinn, *Radiant Daughters*, pp. 94-96.
6. One of the weaknesses of the film version of *Heartburn*, produced in 1986, was that the narrator's tough, witty perspective was not maintained, so that Meryl Streep, who played Rachel Samstat, appeared as a weepy rather than ironic character.
7. Another interesting comparison is that between *The Handmaid's Tale* and Hawthorne's *The Scarlet Letter*. Both novels are set in Boston, both feature the color red as the mark of the main character, and both describe societies ruled by strict religious principles but filled with hypocrisies. Atwood also inverts

Hawthorne's story by making the adultery that is Hester Prynne's sin in *The Scarlet Letter* a necessity of Offred's existence in Gilead.

Works Cited

Agress, Lynne. *The Feminine Irony: Women on Women in Early-Nineteenth-Century English Literature.* Cranbury, NJ: Associated University Presses, 1978.

Atwood, Margaret. *The Handmaid's Tale.* Boston: Houghton Mifflin, 1986.

Bartlett, Bertrice. "Reading Negation and Ironies." Paper delivered at the Northeast Modern Language Association meeting, Rutgers University, April 1985.

Booth, Wayne C. *A Rhetoric of Irony.* Chicago: Univ. of Chicago Press, 1974.

Drabble, Margaret. *The Waterfall.* 1969; rpt. New York: Fawcett, 1977.

Ephron, Nora. *Heartburn.* New York: Knopf, 1983.

Mason, Mary G. "The Other Voice: Autobiographies of Women Writers,' in *Autobiography: Essays Theoretical and Critical,* ed. James Olney. Princeton: Princeton Univ. Press, 1980, pp. 207-35.

Muecke, D. C. *Irony.* The Critical Idiom Series, #13. 1970; rpt. London: Methuen, 1978.

Shinn, Thelma J. *Radiant Daughters: Fictional American Women.* New York: Greenwood Press, 1986.

Sprinker, Michael. "Fictions of the Self: The End of Autobiography," In *Autobiography: Essays Theoretical and Critical,* ed. James Olney. Princeton: Princeton Univ. Press, 1980, pp. 321-42.

Muriel Spark's *unknowing* fiction

JOHN GLAVIN

Georgetown University, Washington, D.C.

MURIEL SPARK rewrote Robert Browning's poem "The Pied Piper" when she was nine years old. Her first *work*. She began her revision with the poem's conclusion. "I gave it a happy ending. The Mayor and the Corporation give the Piper his money. '*Five thousand guilders. I have won,' he cried!* Everyone rejoices. I didn't hesitate to improve on Browning" (Arezzo).[1] In just such 'improvements' her mature fiction has continued to locate — with complexly enriched hesitation — both its primary source of authorization and its cardinal trope.

The child-reviser felt impelled to revise the poem because "I didn't want all the children disappearing into the mountain" (Arezzo). But in Browning's poem, the children do not, in fact, disappear forever. Her improvement actually overlaps a suggestion embedded in Browning's text. At the end of the poem, his narrator remembers that he 'must not omit to say/ That in Transylvania there's a tribe/ Of alien people" who descend from "fathers and mothers having risen/ Out of some subterraneous prison/ Into which they were trepanned/ Long time ago in mighty band/ Out of Hamelin town" (lines 289-299). To annul the poem's stated catastrophe, her revision, appropriating the children's ultimate but repressed, and therefore unknowable resurrection, predates their release, thereby cancelling their, and the poem's closure. At the same time, the child-writer rescues "fathers and mothers" from becoming in history adults who constitute an "alien people," "outlandish," cut off irrevocably from an accurate knowledge of their own origin and identity. "But how or

---

Women's Studies, 1988
Vol. 15, pp. 221-241
Reprints available directly from the publishers
Photocopying permitted by license only

© 1988 Gordon and Breach
Science Publishers, Inc.
Printed in Great Britain

why," the Transylvanian tribe came to be itself, the text claims, "they don't understand." Revision thus saves the children from death, and the adults from deracination. She accomplishes this change by overwhelming patriarchy, by having "fathers" behave like "mothers". The town fathers, this time, cede power, preferring feeling and fidelity to contracts to which they have sworn. In such a *feminized* world, "Everyone rejoices." By a single "improvement," the emergent author has prevented a Fall and cancelled a fallen history.

Here, departure both denies and depends on the norm it modifies. Supplement becomes transfigured into substance, distancing itself from a source to which it remains, significantly, connected. The dynamic within this description — aimed at rescue, working toward discovery — seems absolutely foundational to the working of Muriel Spark's imagination. (Indeed, a "norm to depart from" is her preferred way of describing Roman Catholicism to which she was converted in 1957 (Arezzo).) In one way or another, as we shall see, her dark and elegant fictions have been reaching out, through similar modifications, to reclaim her fellows from analogous trepan ever since her first revisionary swerve.

A Selective Survey of Muriel Spark's Fiction: The prize-winning "The Seraph and the Zambesi" (1951), her first short story, rewrites Baudelaire's *La Fanfarlo*. Her first novel, *The Comforters* (1957), similarly revises *The Book of Job*. *Robinson* (1958) transforms, as its title proclaims, Defoe's *Robinson Crusoe*. *The Hothouse by the East River* (1973), the plot of which turns on the rejection of a dreadful revisionist production of *Peter Pan* cast with sexagenarians, itself rewrites Barrie's Never-Never Land as the New York of the late 'sixties, a city filled with ghosts who refuse to grow old: "Manhattan, the mental clinic ... where we analyse and dope the savageries of existence" (*Hothouse*, 89). *The Abbess of Crewe* (1974), taking history as its text, refigures Watergate, the revision of the infamous tapes transumed into a revisionary conspiracy in a cloistered convent of nuns. *The Takeover* (1976) rewrites *The Golden Bough*. *Territorial Rights* (1979) revises both the *Aspern Papers* and *The Ambassadors* of Henry James. In the brilliant *Loitering With Intent* (1981) the entire genre of autobiography, headed by Newman and Cellini, comes under revision. And, finally, in her most recent novel, *The Only Problem* (1984), Muriel Spark returns to

Job, revising not only the founding biblical text, but also her own first novel.

The powerful revisionary ratio that engenders these and other Spark fictions is significantly at odds with the paradigm of influence so brilliantly adumbrated over the last decade by Harold Bloom. Her assured, joyful, and generous rescripting shares little of the desperate, agonic processes described in studies like his *The Anxiety of Influence*. For Muriel Spark, the goal of revision is not rejection and replacement, as it is for Bloom's "strong" poets, but reconnection. She finds reality whole, and seamless. No meaningful distinction separates in her mind text from act, nor text as production from text as consumption. All books, those one reads equally with those one writes, are, for her, simply "part of our experience of life" (Arezzo). The predecessor is thus not one's antagonist for literary eminence, as he is for Bloom. His text and one's own both stem from the same and single creativity.

Just as she admits no distinction between the experience gained from books and other kinds of experience, Muriel Spark also sees no line separating the supernatural from the natural. For her, they are neither contradictory, nor even merely analogous. Instead, she insists, "they are implicit in each other" (Arezzo). Their separation by empirical thought into unreconcilable, and even at times hostile, antinomies distorts her experience of actual life; it is a trap, like the trepan into which the people of Hamelin are mistakenly lured. Revision, synthesizing dry and separate facts into continuity and relationship, thus emerges for Spark as a way of being-toward-the-world, an *improving* task of literally vital necessity. Through its complex dynamic, she is able to recover for herself and for her readers an original, still immanent oneness in the world, a "divinite" obscured beneath and beyond the factitious divisions of false and current knowing.

Counterpoised to that knowing, the misleading dichotomies of phallogocentrism, she has set, in a series of luminous and witty conceits, *unknowing*, the *unknowing* celebrated by the anonymous, fourteenth-century author of *Denis Hid Divinite* and *The Cloud of Unknowing*, texts by which she has been deeply and constantly impressed (Arezzo).[2] Working itself out in fiction, this *unknowing* requires not the affirmations of apologetic fictions ("Is Muriel Spark, really, a *real* Catholic Writer?"), but the deconstruction of both affirming and denying, the unhappy mechanisms of closure, including the affirmations and denials of those gifted with and/or burdened by the 'Faith'. With the author of *The Cloud,* Spark's fiction inhabits a world which mirrors a creator whom "we may neither set nor do away, nor in any understandable manner affirm him, nor deny him" (*Denis,* 18). In such a world, since divinity's "not-understandable overpassing is understandably above all affirming and denying," any attempt to circumscribe and categorize the world must fall short of its true complexity, its polyvalent mystery. *Unknowing* thus pries false knowledge from its tyranny over experience. Transcending — rather than destroying — a logic based on contradiction, *unknowing* transfigures the commonplace back into its original, *unknowable* and available self.

Guided by these tracts of and toward *unknowing,* we come to see how influence opens toward, not the oppression and rebelliousness suffered by Bloom's Gnostic *ephebes,* but the fulfillment of Spark's and her heroines' constant goal: to be thoughtfully in charge of her own mind, not any sort of victim (paraphrased from *The Only Problem,* 126). While Gnostic revision only fitfully relieves an ultimately inexhaustible anguish, *unknowing,* by paradox, produces even in Muriel Spark's darkest texts, comedy, the recovery of continuity, a fundamental reconnection to all our lost but still abundant sources of meaning and joy. Her old friend Derek Stanford has said that "Truth, for Muriel Spark, implies rejection" (Stanford,45). But it seems to come closer to the truth to say that Truth, for Muriel Spark, demands, and delights in, revision.

At the end of her first, and already masterful short story, "The Seraph and the Zambesi," Muriel Spark strands both characters and readers in her characteristic terrain, the landscape which all her subsequent fiction writes to revise, the mere ground of *knowing.*

We came to the cliff's edge, where opposite us and from the same level the full weight of the river came blasting into the gorge between. There was no sign of the Seraph. Was he far below in the heaving pit, or where?
    Then I noticed that along the whole mile of the waterfall's crest the spray was rising higher than usual. This I took to be steam from the Seraph's heat. I was right, for presently, by the mute flashes of summer lightening we watched him ride the Zambesi away from us, among the rocks that look like crocodiles and the crocodiles that look like rocks. (*Stories,* 121).

MURIEL SPARK'S *UNKNOWING* FICTION 225

On first reading, the two paragraphs may seem to enclose the happy ending to be expected of a Christmas story, especially a prize-winning Christmas story, an exemplary pericope of hermenuetic loss and recovery. In a landscape which seems to obliterate signification — "There was no sign of the Seraph" — the narrator successfully tracks the clue — "I noticed ... the spray" — and thereby recovers the absent signified: "I was right ... for presently we watched him." But this passage must in fact be much more darkly read.

As the first paragraph makes clear, the landscape — gorge created by a fall — does obliterate signification: "the full weight of the river" "opposite us" *blasts* sequence into chaos, "the heaving pit." And that phrase even suggests that this blasting is somehow demonic: a world, not so much of fallen angels (Cramer as the First Seraph) but much worse, one which can compel even angels to fall: "Was he far below ... or where?" Opposed to man, and the human effort to make sense and find meaning, is an equal power, natural or perhaps unnatural, "opposite us and from the same level," that renders nugatory not only any human but also any superhuman (Seraphic) attempt at epistemology.

The situation is reversed, apparently, in the second paragraph by the time-tried methods of observation and inference. Memory and comparison coalesce to create hypothesis: "This I took to be steam." And the sought-after result is "presently" discovered. Human reason, scientific and objective, thereby converts demonic, obliterating absence into eneffable presence: "I was right, for presently ... we watched." But what is watched is absence enacting itself: "ride the Zambesi away from us." The final result signals not a hermeneutic triumph, but a final plunge into hermaneutic impasse: "among the rocks that look like crocodiles and the crocodiles that look like rocks." At the same time, time alters, from the narrative past to the present shared alike by narrator and reader. Narrator, story, reader conclude enmeshed in a landscape in which danger lurks everywhere, undetectable. Spark thus begins her career in fiction denying her readers the consolations of both transcendent epiphany and rational analysis.

In this world, the hermeneutic struggle is continually lost because the *knowing* self insists it be what Bloom would call the "strong poet" of its own mythogony. Like the narrator of "The Seraph," the Gnostic ephebe knows the world is not user-friendly. Rejecting the mimesis of a hostile reality, he wraps himself instead in the text of a powerful predecessor, emptying its sublimity to make room for his own counter-sublime lie-against-time. Of course, this is exactly what Samuel Cramer attempts, wrapping himself in the First Seraph's "toga" to declaim his own Nativity Masque. But Muriel Spark cannot imagine successful Gnostic revision. In her fiction, the self is always inadequate when it mistakes itself as source rather than as agent. Her strong late-comers, when they do not simply fail, can only destroy, can only play variations on her key counter-Gnostic fiction: *The Prime of Miss Jean Brodie.*

Miss Brodie reads for us the space that gapes between Bloom's myth of revision and Spark's, a limen, as it were, that outlines without opening the inner mythology of *unknowing.* In this inimitable fiction of origins and originality — recovering closely Spark's early history and later conversion — influence and revision figure, as they do throughout her work, the central dynamic of the text. Yet here influence is merely bane. The prize pupil, Sandy Stranger, betrays her mentor, Jean Brodie, because she is neither powerful enough to empty out the original, nor loving enough to reconnect herself back within her source. Her attempts at revision, inevitably, only debase the latecomer, and destroy the progenitor. Thus, despite its profound connection to her own origins, the novel models not the 'matter' of Muriel Spark but its penumbra: what Muriel Sarah Camberg might have become, had she remained in Edinburgh and not revised herself into Muriel Spark.

At the beginning of the novel, Sandy starts off as a potentially strong reviser. She takes up and continues her teacher's love story, enriching it almost as fully as Miss Brodie does herself (28). In these childish romances, like the young Muriel Spark, she intervenes to prevent separation and loss, to reconnect Hugh and his love, Miss Brodie, to prevent catastrophe and evade trepan. But her revisions change as she grows older. She begins to usurp for herself the heroine's role in the stories she subsumes. She does not revise Charlotte Bronte; she becomes Jane Eyre (86). And ultimately, of course, she attempts to become Jean Brodie, by taking that place in Teddy Lloyd's embrace Miss Brodie has plotted for Rose Stanley as her own surrogate. But Sandy is not powerful enough to rewrite Jean Brodie's fiction. The progenitor's plot, instead, subsumes the ephebe. "'His portraits still resemble me?' said Miss Brodie ... 'Then all is well, ... and after all, Sandy,' she said, 'you are destined to be the great lover, although I would not have thought it. Truth is stranger than fiction'" (181).

Sandy Stranger can devise no fiction so powerful as the "truth" of that all-enclosing predecessor text. This failure roots, ironically, in the ground of Gnostic success. Bloom's revisers *know* that supply — of whatever it is they need: inspiration, identity, recognition — will never meet demand. Their world is not only Freud's, it is Malthus's. (Is there, finally, any difference between the two, bridged as they are by Darwin?) The world's inadequacy before the ego's demands, what the Gnostics mean by its "fallen" nature, compels them to turn their backs on any form of imitation. They usurp, instead, and then protect their own counter-text. Their inadequate world is also Sandy's, the hungry and homeless Depression of the 'Thirties, where the frightened girl recognizes, and flees from her "brothers" on the Dole. Sandy is neither bold enough nor, paradoxically, generous enough, to usurp.

She steals what she lacks. Her "odd psycholohgical treatise on the nature of moral perception called 'The Transfiguration of the Commonplace'" (3): what else can it contain but the method and morality of Miss Brodie's inimitable, magical teaching? Plagiarizer rather than usurper, Sandy can neither effect the Gnostic's crime, nor enter their reward: "When you have the Gnosis ... then you are in the place of rest, you are in your own internalized pleroma" (*Agon*, 69). Despite her apparently Gnostic flight from the world, as Sister Helena of the Transfiguration, her cloister harbors neither fullness nor respite. The world continually breaks in on Sister Helena as she clutches "the bars of the grille ... as if she wanted to escape from the dim parlour beyond" (52). Fretting her narrow cell — cloister become closure — Sandy expiates her failed revision in endless narrowness and storied deprivation.

Prizing the source, *unknowing* privileges fidelity. As a child, Sandy "loved Miss Brodie" (48). But she does not keep faith with that love. As we shall see in *The Hothouse by the East River*, for Spark that faith means revising with wit and self-protection the loving relation, despite any harm the loved one may, and inevitably does, do. Such a love is, obviously, larger than the ego can supply. It can be effected only through connection with an abundance Sandy's sour jealousy cannot even acknowledge. Such an abundance refigures influence as — not catastrophe — but, what I would term, antistrophe. *Antistrophos*: "turned so as to face one another: correlative, coordinate or counterpart ... to a thing" (*Liddell and Scott*, 81).

In a luminous and paradigmatic scene, we can see antistrophe break into and momentarily transfigure Spark's most recent novel, *The Only Problem*. Its hero, Harvey Gotham, becomes obsessed in the Museum at Epinal with a "serious, simple and tender" painting by Georges de la Tour, *Job Comforted By His Wife*. The painting has revised powerfully the Book of Job, the Biblical text that absorbs Harvey's own life. "The scene here seemed to Harvey so altogether different from that suggested by the text of *Job*, and yet so deliberately and intelligently contemplated that it was impossible not to wonder what the artist actually meant" (77). And that wonder leads to discovery. For de la Tour, "Job and his wife are deeply in love."

Instead of "studying a subject, preparing an essay, a thesis" (17), as Harvey had been doing, de la Tour has recovered in the parent text a human situation, a hitherto unexplored possibility for human feeling and human relationship. Responding to that uncovering Harvey responds to the liberating possibilities of being "altogether different" — the unclosure that comes through generous revision. "Of course, the painter was idealizing some notion of his own" (78), but that notion enriches, rather than diminishes, the possibilities of Job.

Antistrophe thus images influence operating toward initiation, and as gift. "It is necessary that we first be lifted up toward it, the source of good, by our prayers," writes the Areopagite, "and then, by drawing near it, that we be initiated into the all-good gifts of what is founded around it" (*The Divine Names*, 129). Catastrophe sets texts against their precursors; antistrophe aligns them. Catastrophe works toward substitution; antistrophe ends in continuity. Catastrophe is covert; antistrophe openly adverts to the "gifts" to which it is drawn. Thus, in *The Only Problem*'s manifold antistrophe — Job, de la Tour, Harvey: each facing toward the other held by the common myth — Harvey achieves an access in feeling and comprehension completely alien to the vexation of his sterile and solitary scholarship.

But he can not finally or fully risk de la Tour's "dream." That dream might cost him the critic's control: control over others, over himself, over *Job*, as a text to appropriate, to understand, but not ever to assimilate. "'Quiet!' bawled Harvey. 'Either you listen to me in silence or you all go'" (108). Rather than continue to locate in himself the emotional possibilities the painting suggests, a *Job* beyond reproach and recrimination, Harvey chooses to offer a "seminar." Instead of revising *Job*, he reenacts it (106). In the painting Job is comforted by his wife. In the novel, Harvey is tormented by his wife, whom he has surrendered to violence and meaningless crime. They could be the same wife. "Job's wife's face, . . . Right from the first he had been struck by her resemblance to Effie . . . Oh, Effie, Effie, Effie" (78). What he, like the biblical Job, insists he "must" *know* costs Harvey the illumination and connectedness of antistrophe, stationing him permanently in a bogus happiness he can never properly enter, and never really leave: "his back door was his front door" (15). Where the painter images nuptial compassion, the commentator can only identify a sundered corpse. "You must know that this is your wife." "Yes, it's my wife, Effie" (177).

What Harvey Gotham fails to accomplish within *The Only Problem*, his creator, Muriel Spark, achieves through it. She embeds her narrative of revisionary evanescence in a text that simultaneously enacts and records a brilliant antistrophic success. It is finally Spark, rather than Harvey, who corresponds to de la Tour and continues the fruitful chain of influence emanating from the original myth of Job. Her revision of the biblical text plays the content of her fiction against its form, and from that play the novel derives the wit and tone that turn it back from failure toward comedy, a comedy of failure. What her characters cannot or will not achieve, her writing does. This antithesis, already in embryo in her revision of "The Pied Piper," shapes much of Muriel Spark's career, even from its beginning in the apparently uncomic "Seraph."

In "The Seraph and the Zambesi" Spark powerfully revitalizes the time-worn genre of the Christmas tale. Emptying out Dickens, she encounters in Baudelaire, in his marvelous story *La Fanfarlo*, the ground of a witty fable of failed revelation and refused repentence. No revenant, not even a seraphic one, can word a message powerful enough to move her recreant Scrooge to good will toward men: a Carol appropriate to post-war, post-Imperial, post-Christian Britain. The narrator of "the Seraph" openly exploits her connection to the source-text. In the first paragraph, proclaiming its antistrophe, we learn that her protagonist, Samuel Cramer, in Africa in 1946, "was the same man" who had been "going strong in Paris in the nineteenth century." And when the narrator first speaks to Cramer, she asks, "Are you the man Baudelaire wrote about?" "'Yes,' he replied, 'What made you think of it?'" (*Stories*, 115). But Cramer is now "modified. For instance, in those days, more than a hundred years ago, Cramer had persisted for several decades, and without affectation, in being about twenty-five years old. But when I knew him he was clearly undergoing his forty-two-year-old phase" (112). The crucial term here is "modified."

Spark modifies her source by centering her story on Baudelaire's hypothetical supplement, postromantic failure, "the forty-two-year-old phase" (112). She takes *La Fanfarlo*'s crucial image of Cramer in ecstacy, "*seul dans son paradis*" (*Oeuvres*, 398), and realizes it as a literally present Seraph. At the same time, the vaguely outlined future Baudelaire imagines for his lovers, "*peut-etre... sera*" (401), she literalizes as a frowzy, failed present. Antistrophe, benign but active, thus writes itself into the continuous potential that is the parent text. Cramer, insistent on his own script, sees in the Seraph only catastrophe, an otherness illuminating his own impoverishment, (His make-up melts in the Seraph's unbearable heat.) But Spark, transcending the limitations of *knowing*, locates in Baudelaire an available envelope into which she can insert her own invention, an unused, available pocket she can open out and fill with inscription. Despite any short fall of recovery in the plot, antistrophe's rediscovery of usable plenitude issues inevitably, joyously, in comedy.

For roughly the first decade of her career as a novelist such revisionary success continues to depend on the novelist herself rather than her characters. It is only with the transfiguration of the heroine in the monumental *The Mandelbaum Gate* that Spark significantly shares her skills with her heroine. From that novel on, revisionary power begins to be found within rather than only beneath her fiction. It is as though, after ten years of growing acclaim, Spark could begin to sense in herself the kind of authorial power she had earlier located in figures like Baudelaire, power which now permitted her to become the antistrophic source of her own inventions. This transformation reaches its fulfillment in the mordant, baleful, ceaselessly funny *The Hothouse by the East River*. There for the first time we find in Elsa Hazlett a heroine the equal of her creator. With the process of its comedy the counterpart of its plot, *The Hothouse* emerges as Spark's masterfiction. It is also, one should point out, one of the master comicpieces of High

Modernism, *Finnegan's Wake* miniaturized, inverted, and feminized.

Actuality in this novel is like the view behind the east window of the Hazlett's apartment, "which looks out on the dark daylight full of snow, a swirling grey spotted-muslin veil, beyond which, only by faith and experience can you know, stands the sky over the East River" (46). Refusing both "faith and experience," that is — like Cramer and Sandy Stranger — refusing antistrophe, the three principal men in the novel: Major Tylden, Garven Bey, Paul Hazlett, attempt to victimize and profit from Elsa Hazlett, by the manipulation of a kind of imaginary and male *knowing* which privileges each of them at her expense. Those phallogocentric manipulations the novel undercuts through Elsa's ultimate, heroic and loving, refusal of the anxieties of influence.

For Major Tylden, the Intelligence Officer, knowledge comes down, literally, to power. Interrogation after interrogation, he discovers nothing. He can only, but very successfully, intimidate those whom he questions. Garven Bey, the Guidance Director, whose last name suggests the hegemony he seeks to consolidate, treats knowledge as the means to profit and self-aggrandizement. Like Tylden, he too wields "a policeman's authority" (10). But Tylden has submerged himself in the impersonality of the army unit and the war he serves. Garven snoops on Elsa from self interest. (The effete, noxious male snoop recurs throughout Spark's fiction as a particularly unpleasant form of the male-will-to-know. Her female blackmailers are generally much more powerful, and more evil.) The Major's slavish absorption in facts by themselves precludes him from the synthesis that might reveal meaning. Garven's single-minded focus on "his thesis and his career" (7) blinds him to complexity of any kind, "unable to gather all at once the many things he has probably heard"(12).

The Intelligence Officer and the Guidance Director represent supporting figures to the central flawed *knowing* in the novel, the husband's all-consuming jealousy. Paul Hazlett's "intellect has a hundred eyes," his mother boasts (60): the hundred eyes of Argos, employed by Juno to watch without rest the victim of her jealousy, Io. "Angrily in love with" Elsa (12), Paul wishes to know the answer to only one all-pressing question: 'Am I real?' Its naked self-exposure too risky to be put that openly, he must offer it in deflected form to others: "are you real?" (165). And so, in a demonic parody of Cartesian ontology, he summons his wife back from the dead to mirror a narcissism even death cannot still: 'You are, therefore I *know* I am.' But in the all-pervasive structures of male desire familiar to readers of Rene Girard's *Desire, Deceit and the Novel*, Paul cannot recollect his wife without recollecting his rivals for her affection: his "imagination running away with itself" (151). For him "imagination is suspicion" (16): "with your terrible and jealous dreams [you] set the whole edifice soaring" (113).

Elsa counters *knowing's* jealous dream with *unknowing* re/vision: with seeing again, and by an uncompromising insistence on fidelity to what is, and has been, seen. She begins by insisting to her husband that she has again seen, clerking in a shoe store, their former campmate, Kiel, the protomartyr of Paul's jealousy. She will not allow Paul to persuade her out of that unlikely revision, not will she permit him to evade the consequent resighting of their past as it invades his fictive present. This reconnection to source parallels the novelist's own antistrophic commitment to a progenitor text, in this case, to Barrie's *Peter Pan*, her ground for this cautionary fable against the "vivesection of the mind" in the Never-Never Land of escapist Manhattan. The two revisionary commitments — the writer's to prior text and the subject's to prior experience — merge at Pierre's production of Barrie's play. Here Elsa rejects a Gnostic revision in which male *knowing* — the very "in" production at the Very Much Club — has usurped the parent text, and returns the theatre, by her counter- and connective thrust back to the "author". Indeed, she can boast, as she is led from the theatre, "I'm the mother of the author" (111). At the same time, in the same gesture, with her "squelchy tomatoes," Elsa is also, of course, rejecting Paul's insistence that she play Wendy to his superannuated Peter.

The success of Elsa's gesture depends on Paul's reading. Her silent action, which, like Spark's own text, points but does not close, does not impose meaning on itself. To keep possibility open and individuality alive, *unknowing* cannot force. Combining fidelity and invention, it conserves the otherness of the other — that is, it is loving — and thereby creates comedy. "Still Elsa's shadow dances with Paul's" until "He backs away. laughing, and lets her dance by herself" (161). That lovely and loving moment, the climax of the novel's extraordinary final *totentanz*, also serves to epitomize the novel's, and the novelist's, movement as a whole. Here for the first time in Muriel Spark's fiction, with character and creator so much at one, *unknowing* is explicitly named: "he following her, watching as she moves how she trails her faithful and lithe cloud of unknowing across the pavement" (168). The sentence names both a plot and a career: the female *unknowing* shadow, fantastic and mysterious, trailed in and over male patterns of *knowing* until fantasy is willingly surrendered and priority reseen.

In the novel's resistance to that revision Spark uncovers the most powerful form of evil in the world of her fiction. Garven, unable to cope with Elsa's energy and wit, opens "his mouth wide, then [says] in a high-pitched top note, 'Sick!'" (103). Striving to sound the "top note" marks speech as male, throughout this novel, and, indeed, throughout all of Muriel Spark's fiction. The analyst's megalomania, the policeman's sadism, the husband's jealousy: each manifests that deployment of binary opposition fundamental to *knowing*. Garven's manipulation of sick/well echoes in the interrogator's various deployments of closed (true)/open (false), and in Paul's desperate attempt to associate himself with the privileged side of real versus imaginary: "Her delusion, her figment, her nothing-there" (18). These artificial, power-seeking oppositions Deconstruction labels phallogocentric. Muriel Spark prefers to see them as manifestations of *necromancy*, that ancient, black and essentially male magic which is for her the prime mover in the power politics of *knowing* (Arezzo).

Spark takes the term from Chapter Fifty-Five of *The Cloud of Unknowing*, which she finds "from the psychological point of view" almost "stands out as a treatise by itself"[3] She places this strong emphasis on the chapter and its analysis because, I think, necromancy completes for her the mytholect of revision. It names antistrophe's counter. The necromantic operations described in *The Cloud* work their poison in the world whenever someone, claiming to "be stirred thereto by the fire of charity" (*Cloud*, 70), applies his knowledge to the interpretation, judgement and, inevitably, to the control of another: the "cure" of another's soul.

The necromancer achieves his end by turning his subject away from both the complexity of the world and the privacy of the self, "to see in ... to his [the necromancer's] brain." "And if he might make a man look in thereto," and substitute the necromancer's knowledge for his own experience, the necromancer "wants no better. For at that looking [his subject] should lose his wits forever" (71). Described in this way, necromancy clearly includes not only the psychiatry of Garven Bay, the policing of Major Tylden, and certainly, the husbandry of Paul Hazlett, it extends out to cover all the operations of *knowing*, wherever men "shoot out their curious conceits, and without any advisement they will take upon them to blame other men's faults over soon." The necromancer's "brain," *The Cloud* insists "is noght else but the fires of hell" (71).

Muriel Spark does not fear Gnosticism. In her fiction, figures like Cramer will always fail. The self is too weak to serve as any kind of source. It is in necromancy that she spots the real villainy, because the necromancer, vampire-like, draws his strength, not from his hero, but from his victim. On the smaller scale, then, from Georgina Hogarth in *The Comforters* on, her lesser villains are the blackmailers, side-show, black magicians who purloin knowledge for power. On the larger scale, necromancers proper, figure men like Paul Hazlett and Sir Quentin Oliver in *The Only Problem*, narcissists who batten on and destroy others, simply to prove, not that they are right but that they are.

These necromancers demonstrate why someone like Jean Brodie is not, for Muriel Spark, a villain, though she certainly may seem to flirt with necromancy, as she attempts to manipulate others to her own purposes and control. Jean Brodie's "brain" contains not only her own plot but also the Primavera and Giotto. And her way leads her sheltered, suburban girls to encounter for the first time the blunt realities of hunger and homelessness: "other people's nineteen-thirties" (50). Miss Brodie's fault is not *knowing*; rather, she is *knowing*'s dupe: "In Italy the Unemployment problem has been solved" (59). The Black Shirts have worked their black magic on her also. It is Sandy, her betrayer, who comes much closer to necromancy, to that *knowing* which takes upon itself the "cure" of another's soul. Against entrapment within such *knowing*, and the leveled sameness toward which it leads, all of Spark's fiction, in one way or another, struggles to revise.

But Spark herself may seem compromised by precisely the kind of *knowing* she attempts to marginate. In a way, she is the most *knowing* of novelists, constantly interrupting narrative chronology with prolepses of future events, creating comedy out of a wit the characters can rarely share. This sense of self-incrimination we can find shaping quite explicitly her first novel, *The Comforters*, which functions as a kind of manifesto from the emerging novelist of what fiction should and should not be. It seems almost to be an anti-novel, a commination of the harm fiction enacts, and the threat it offers to those who practice its tyrannizing, omniscient form.

At her lowest ebb, Caroline Rose, the heroine of the novel, terrifies herself that the blackmailing Georgina is "somehow in league with her invisible persecutor," the ghost-novelist who has invaded Caroline's consciousness and seems to be shaping her life (112). The novelist *knows* not only what Caroline is thinking but what she will do (102). And despite her desperate attempts "not to be involved in any man's story" (116), she is apparently forced against her will to undergo the plot that has been assigned her. If Georgina is the Satan of this *Job*, then the unseen and unknowable, ghostly novelist must be its Divinity, a malevolent Deity who at least consents to, if he does not demand, the heroine's demonic ordeal. *The Comforters* seems here to align the writer's design with the Intelligence Officer's sadism. We are left to infer that fictive art, "the know-all assumption of the words" (224), must tend toward necromancy — "those voices, it was Hell!" (56), just like the necromancer's brain.

But connecting Georgina and the novelist, Caroline realizes even as she thinks it, is "her deepest madness, a fear void of evidence, a suspicion altogether to be distrusted" (112). The accident that hospitalizes Caroline is not accidental. Its causes root in the character's choices, not in the novelist's demands. The writer — both Spark and her ghost — clearly does, in an important sense, know, but she does not "know-all". Her prolepses do not predestine.

The second half of *The Comforters* makes this point with wonderfully playful irony. When Caroline, "supernormal, clairaudient" (181), rather than trying simply to "spoil" the novel (115), chooses instead to "savour her private wakefulness," she becomes capable of "exerting an undue, unreckoned, influence on the narrative," even though "she is supposed to be absent for a time" from it (150). So the ghost-writer must against her own design dwell for a space on Mrs. Hogg's large bosom, because Caroline cannot get its monstrous proportions out of her own mind. And as she becomes increasingly speculative (198) about her situation, Caroline is able "to interfere with the book" even more effectively. "Private wakefulness" seems the key here. Muriel Spark is constantly "wakeful" to the "privacy" of her characters. And the more those characters awaken to their own privacy, to the uniqueness of their own experience, the more their creator protects that privacy.

Unlike the necromancer for whom knowledge is, finally, power, Muriel Spark does not impose her knowing on her invention. Her interruptions of narrative chronology actually undercut the conventional novelist's hegemony over time and interpretation. And her wit attends to but does not circumscribe her characters. She can claim with her heroine Fleur Talbot: "I don't go in for motives, I never have" (*Loitering*, 83). Rather than forcing us to look into her brain she looks out into the world, noting for herself and for us, the continuously surprising mysteries she sees there, inviting but not enforcing us to revise our vision of reality, to see again clearly. When Willi Stock attempts to get Caroline Rose to believe that Mervyn Hogarth practices black magic, he appears "to her more and more in the nature of a demanding creditor." In contrast, she tells him; "for my own experiences, ..., I don't demand anyone's belief. You may call them delusions for all I care. I have merely registered my findings" (198). Registering her findings, that is the task, and art, of the novelist of *unknowing*.

The difference that separates demanding belief from registering findings — that separates the male from the female sense of an ending — registers with admirable panache in the twinned conclusions to *The Comforters*. Laurence, snooping in Caroline's flat, writes a letter indicting her failings as both character and novelist, denying her accuracy in representing men, affirming his own centrality as both lover and interpreter (223). "But actually you yourself understand nobody, for instance the Baron, my father, myself, we are martyred by your misunderstanding." His letter, time-framed, hierarchic, self-glamorizing, roots in antithesis and closure. It aims at knowing and command, and ultimately — inevitably, in the fiction of Muriel Spark — it fails to satisfy. Even Laurence realizes that the letter does not satisfactorily "express his objections" (224). He tears it into small pieces — the ultimate gesture of power over and through language — and scatters the bits over Hampstead Heath. At which point the female novelist intervenes, in a sudden and surprising revisionary swerve.

She revises the Parable of the Sower, and with that revision concludes the novel. "He saw the bits of paper come to rest, some on the scrubby ground, some among the deep marsh weeds, and one piece on a thorn-bush: and he did not then foresee his later wonder, with a curious rejoicing, how the letter had got into the book" (224). Ceding the phallogocentric criteria of control: accuracy and credibility, the female-Sower, with a bold and kindly swerve, seeds together Laurence's language and her own in a landscape where spirit bests the limitations of the letter, a landscape antithetical to the barren *knowing* at the brink of the Zambesi. She thereby and confidently reconstitutes the document that damned her, embedding it within her own text. In Spark's revision of the gospel parable, point by point Hampstead Heath corresponds to the gospel proffer — except that within the novel's boundaries there is no "good soil". No one aspect of reading can privilege itself against any other. Like Elsa Hazlett's tomatoes, words can take only their fair chance at coming "to rest" wherever "the wind bore them away". Only in that evenness do the anxieties of affirmation and denial recede before the delights of a "later wonder" and a "curious rejoicing."

Unknowing, like female speech, has been historically silenced by the *knowing* of the phallogos, the affirmations and denials of dogmatic theology marginating what it easily mutes as mysticism. Now, however, the contemporary critical search for an authentic female discourse and Muriel Spark's recovery of *unknowing* seem not only to be parallel but to coincide. One could, for example, without distortion easily replace Julia Kristeva's name with Spark's in Roland Barthes's characterization of Kristeva's work. She "changes the place of things, ... she subverts authority, the authority of monologic science" (Moi, 150). But one could not also apply to Spark the passage erased by ellipsis: "she always destroys the latest preconception, the one we thought we could be comforted by." For Kristeva, subversion and dissidence demand struggle: destruction. For Spark, struggling to destroy traps one, offsides inside the male arena, in the *agonia* that follows inevitably from the phallic identification of truth with power. *Unknowing*, female or male, her fictions insist, must make its way not by aggression but by confident antistrophe.

The way of such antistrophe Pseudo-Dionysius, the architect of *unknowing*, images as a great chain or ladder: "as if a brilliantly lit cord, suspended from the highest heaven and brought down to us, is always grasped so that we ascend upwards to it by putting one hand over the other. It would seen as if we were bringing it down whereas, in fact, we do not bring it down ... but we ourselves are raised up" (*The Divine Names*, 129). So, for Fleur Talbot, Spark's most successful reviser, "images and phrases that I absolutely need for the book simply appeared as if from nowhere into my range of perception. I was a magnet for experiences that I needed" (*Loitering*, 17). In this world of antistrophic improvement, "everything happens to an artist; time is always redeemed, nothing is lost and wonders never cease" (116). The primal scene of such antistrophe, a scene for which Pseudo-Dionysius seems almost to have prepared a gloss, takes place midway through *Loitering with Intent*.

Fleur has discovered that the manuscript of *Warrender Chase*, is missing from her room, stolen to be used as blackmail by the archnecromancer, Sir Quentin Oliver, that "psychological Jack the Ripper" (60). Horrified, she searches the room, in vain. Finally, to take her mind off her troubles, she begins to page through *The Autobiography of Benvenuto Cellini*, one of her, and Spark's own, favorite books.

> I was reflecting that one could take endless enchanting poems out of this book simply by flicking over the pages, back and forth, and extracting for oneself a page here, a paragraph there, and while I was playing with this idea it came to me with all apparent irrelevance that Dottie, who knew very well how my possessions were disposed in my room, had certainly taken my package that night the houseboy had let her in to wait for me. (126)

Fleur's own, purloined text becomes available to her again, as she plays with the only apparently "irrelevant" ideas suggested by rereading Cellini. "Nothing came" earlier of her own "frantic thinking" (122). To solve her difficulty, she has had to enter into an *unknowing*, beyond the search for knowledge she impells herself to perform. But this *unknowing* is not simply a passive reading of the prior text. Fleur is literally "loitering with intent" — that strange crime against, surely, all the laws of *knowing*. Apparently absent-minded, she is in fact actively cooperating with Cellini, "extracting for oneself a page here, a paragraph there." And as she, in effect, inducts herself into the earlier text, she is enabled to grasp the truth she cannot arrive at on her own. "I always preferred what I saw out of the corner of my eyes" (37).

Here Spark finds joy, not only in her female reviser but, significantly, in her male source, Cellini, as later she will find it in de la Tour. This joy, the artist's characteristic feeling of delight, delight-in-work as well as delight-in-the-world art resees, releases Fleur from the anxious paranoia that has blinded her to the true disposition of her manuscript. Her final rejoicing thus both enters into and also extends Cellini's own. Her book and his end with the same line: "by God's grace, I am now going on my way rejoicing" (125). No line, not even a fine one, can here separate cause into effect.

And this joy continues productive beyond the immediate experience the scene describes. It is literally the font of writing in the remainder of the novel, and beyond. Her discovery sets Fleur off on the successful search for her manuscript which becomes the plot of the second half of the novel. And the final recovery of the manuscript not only ensures the publication of *Warrender Chase*, and all the other novels Fleur will write in her career, it also brings about the destruction of the necromancer and the liberation of his deluded followers. In effect, as source-text in joyous antistrophe, the Cellini opens to its cooperating reader/reviser entrance to a kind of textual *pleroma*, from which radiate infinitely renewable lines of reinscription. "Every page I turned was, to me, as it still is, sheer magic" (123).

All of Bloom's *ephebes* are male. His theories derive exclusively from male theories of discourse and male models of development. In her improving fictions, Muriel Spark seems to be countering such phallogocentric criticism with a radically alternative model of influence and revision, a model that works itself out, not exclusively, but primarily through women. And at the same time she seems to be offering to feminism a model of discourse that moves out of, and into, joy. This aesthetic of proffer, of generosity and illumination, turns the self away from its fears of inadequacy and toward the mysterious, inexhaustible richness of the world.

That inexhaustibly abundant world Muriel Spark not only describes, but inhabits. Her novels, she says, begin from a title, a phrase that strikes her fancy, one for which she feels drawn to devise an ensuing tale. And as she writes, she refuses to permit her own anticipation for the growing text to close off its own continuing possibilities for development. Nor does she revise in the sense of rewriting successive drafts of her fiction. She follows the story through until she is herself suddenly surprised to learn that the work is now complete, there, that she has nothing else left to do in its pages. Then she stops writing (Arezzo). And "from there by the Grace of God," she goes on her way "rejoicing."

And so a joyful pericope to conclude, and to counter *knowing* by the Zambesi: While writing *The Only Problem*, travelling in France she learned from a guidebook of a Job painting at nearby Epinal. Intrigued by the coincidence of her subject and the painting's, she went to the Musee and was so struck by the de la Tour — just as Harvey Gotham is in her novel — that she immediately worked *Job Consoled By His Wife* into her book, already one-third written (Arezzo). Yet the painting is perfectly fitted to the fiction. It seems to have been there always, fulcrum to the plot, waiting for its pivotal moment of discovery by the hero. And, indeed, all *unknowing*, for Muriel Spark it was there, waiting. No wonder, or rather all wonder that she has always felt, as she says, so comfortable living in other peoples' houses (Arezzo). At once bestower and bestowed upon, for and from Muriel Spark all is, and everywhere has been, gift.

Notes

1. Muriel Spark graciously agreed to speak with me about her work on May 10, 1987, in Arezzo near her home in Italy. Information from that conversation appears in the text as (Arezzo). I am extremely grateful to Mrs. Spark for her warmth and kind interest on that and subsequent occasions. This essay, obviously, would not have been possible were it not for her generosity. I wish also to thank Muriel Spark's friend and companion, the sculptor Penelope Jardine, for her friendly assistance and interest in the development of this project.
2. *Denis His Divinite* and *The Cloud of Unknowing* are the most important works of an anonymous, fourteenth-century English mystic, about whom almost nothing else is known. The *Hid Divinite* is a free version of the *Mystical Theology* of Pseudo-Dionysius (Dionysius the Areopagite), a fifth-century Syrian monk, whose persona claims to be the Athenian converted by St. Paul on the Areopagus. The Areopagite is the dominant figure in the entire development of both western and eastern, Christian mystical or negative theology. And the *Cloud* author is the most original and influential writer in the particularly English treatment of negative theology that derives from pseudo-Denis. Mrs Spark reads *Denis* and *The Cloud* in the edition of Dom Justin McCann which is also used in this paper. It is cited as (*Cloud*) or (*Denis*) when quoting from the medieval text and as (*McCann*) when quoting from the introduction. I wish to thank here Professor John D. Jones of Marquette University, an eminent scholar in the study of the Areopagite, for his extremely generous response to my inquiries concerning the work of Pseudo-Denis.
3. Quoted from a letter to John Glavin from Muriel Spark, 26 June, 1987.

Works Cited

By Muriel Spark:
'———. The Seraph and the Zambesi." *Collected Stories: I.* New York: Knopf, 1968. 112-121.

———. *The Comforters*. Philadelphia: Lippincott, 1957.
———. *The Prime of Miss Jean Brodie*. New York: New American Library, 1961.
———. *The Hothouse by the East River*. London: Macmillan, 1973.
———. *Loitering With Intent*. New York: Coward, McCann & Geoghegan, 1981.
——— *The Only Problem*. New York: Putnam's, 1984.

Other:
Baudelaire, Charles. *La Fanfarlo. Oeuvres Completes*. Vol. 2. Paris: Lemerre, 1949. 363-402.
Bloom, Harold. *Agon*. New York: Oxford U P, 1982.
The Cloud of Unknowing And Other Treatises. Ed. Dom Justin McCann. 5th Ed. London: Burns Oates and Washbourne, 1947.
Moi, Toril M. *Sexual/Textual Politics*. London: Methuen, 1985.
Pseudo-Dionysius Areopagite. *The Divine Names and Mystical Theology*. Ed. John D. Jones. Milwaukee, Marquette U P, 1980.
Stanford, Derek. *Muriel Spark*. Fontwell: Centaur, 1963.

Metaphor-into-narrative: being very careful with words

REGINA BARRECA

Department of English, University of Connecticut.

I WANT TO SUGGEST that there is a pattern woven into women's writing, particularly women's comedic writing, which I can most easily call metaphor-into-narrative. The basis of the strategy relies on re-literalizing what has become merely symbolic. Rather than creating a word/object/action that accrues meaning through repeated appearances in a text, metaphor-into-narrative illustrates the stripping away of symbolic or over-determined meaning in order that the "original" significance of the word/object/action should dominate. It involves a linguistic strategy that takes a metaphor, simile, perhaps a cliche, and plays it out into the plot of the text. We do not expect, in reading *The Comforters*, that Muriel Spark will present us with Georgiana Hogg, a character described as "not all there" (169). Georgina gradually disappears — she doesn't metaphorically disappear, she "really" vanishes from the back seat of the car where she is napping. Fay Weldon writes of a certain character that "presently he will get into the habit of saying he's going to die of boredom, and presently indeed he will" (*Down Among the Women* 30).

Metaphor-into-narrative works something like an optical illusion, like the patterns used in psychology classes to illustrate false perception and with a view towards the same end; perspective is all and all in our definitions of reality. Conflicting contexts, weighted equally, disturb our prepared interpretative strategies. We might misread a phrase because our perceptions code the metaphor as a "category mistake" when it is in fact an accurate statement. People can't die of boredom, we say, and so we read the phrase wrongly until this radical narrative strategy initiates us into a new code that revives the "dead" metaphor. This is nothing new to the idea of comedy; Bergson *et al.* have discussed the concept of the comic mis-reading of words.[1] Freud, in *Jokes and their Relationship to the Unconscious*, seems to argue that comedy is made during the process whereby we attach meaning to the meaningless, only to delight in discovering our mistake.[2]

There is however a significant difference in the metaphor-into-narrative strategy: by attaching a buried, literal meaning to what is intended to be inert and meaningless, women writers subvert the paradigmatic gesture of relief that is seen to characterize comedy. A joke usually depends on the equation between initial error (taking something literally) and final pleasure (discovering that it is only meant figuratively). Here the process is reversed; the joke depends on the error of believing language to be used figuratively when it is used literally. There is little relief in this comedy; it is more apocalyptic than reassuring.

Metaphor-into-narrative links language with magic, and not only in its ability to bring the 'dead' back to life. This strategy illuminates the manner in which discourse has the power to shape the way things happen, not just the way things are seen or the way they are described. Language has a formative, not merely an evaluative, function. As Fay Weldon states in *The Fat Woman's Joke*:

> One must be careful with words. Words turn probabilities into facts and by sheer force of definition translate tendencies into habits (24)

Words are alchemy, transforming one order into another, and they are a fundamental link to the supernatural. That something is said, as well as the manner in which it is said, becomes crucial. In many works by women writers, particular words are volatile, infused with power: "Acknowledgment is dangerous; it gives body to the insubstantial" ("Watching Me, Watching You" 75). Reality is encoded in language; language shapes rather than reflects an otherly substantial, otherly authorised universe.

Metaphor-into-narrative is Atwood's *Edible Woman*, it is the basis for Lessing's story "How I Finally Lost My Heart," it is the fact that Fay Weldon's novel *Life and Loves of a She-Devil* plays out quite literally the changes Ruth must go through in order to "look up to men." It is what May Sinclair does in *The Three Sisters* when the vicar, bothered by his daughter's renditions of Beethoven and Chopin, forces Alice to literally change her tune. In its lowest key, it is Marianne's fall when she sees Willoughby; it is at the heart of many of Flannery O'Conner's stories and some of George Eliot's most salient remarks. Metaphor-into-narrative is a ritual, linguistic, and I believe, feminine transsubstantiation that makes a word the thing itself as well as the representation of the thing. When someone in these stories says 'over my dead body' it usually means just that. The disenfranchised language of the dead-metaphor or cliche provides a narrative structure for the stories themselves.

To focus on metaphor and the woman writer is not new. Margaret Homans has brilliantly discussed in a number of texts the psychoanalytic aspects of the feminine literalization of metaphor. In "Dreaming of Children: Literalization in Jane Eyre and Wuthering Heights," for example, Homans introduces her argument by pointing out that "the literal is traditionally classified as feminine," in drawing on Nietzsche's identification of 'truth' as woman (Female Gothic 257). Gilbert and Gubar write in *The Madwoman in the Attic* that "women seem forced to live more intimately with the metaphors they have created" (87). Domna Stanton's important discussion of metaphor, "Difference on Trial," included in *The Poetics of Gender*, asks whether "metaphor itself must be interrogated to see whether it provides the best means for exploring the many aspects of the female unknown..." (159). Stanton mentions Cixous' remark that metaphor is "desirable and efficacious" for women writers because it "presupposes faith in its capacity to transform existing meanings," and quotes from Irigaray's statement that "analogy, in contrast to the rigor/rigidity of male geometricity, 'entails a reworking of meaning'" (161). Perhaps Mary Jacobus' argument in "The Question of Language" concerning George Eliot's use of maxims provides the most provocative discussion of women, "dead" metaphors and cliches wisdom. Jacobus argues that "impropriety and metaphor belong together on the same side as a fall from absolute truth on unitary schemes of knowledge" (48). She states, picking up from Maggie's remarks in *The Mill on the Floss*, that "if words may mean several things, general rules or maxims may prove less universal than they claim to be and lose their authority" (44). This is applicable to the question of metaphor-into-narrative, I think, because Jacobus argues that it is the "special cases or particular contexts" that "determine or render indeterminate not only judgement but meaning, too" (44). As Maggie can revive the "dead language of Latin" through her decision to "skip the rules in syntax" because the examples became so absorbing, so do the women writers of metaphor-into-narrative revive so called "dead metaphors" by breaking the code that killed them. Jacobus argues that Eliot's use of metaphor can undermine "the realist illusion of her fictional work, revealing it to be no more than a blank page inscribed with a succession of metaphoric substitutions . . ." (47). It is this transformation of "the familiar into the exotic and strange" (45) that is at work in the comedy of metaphor-into-narrative in writers such as Muriel Spark.

Muriel Spark's works often turn on the axis of this strategy. Her literalization of metaphor has been noticed although not explored by a number of critics who, as one reviewer mentioned in a rather throwaway remark, see that Spark "contrives to work a metaphor, a conceit into a narrative . . . Spark is the John Donne of English fiction, a few centuries behind her time, but nonetheless interesting for it."[3]

One of Spark's short stories, "Portobello Road" is a linguistic tour-de-force, making a most obvious and deliberate use of metaphor-into-narrative. It is a translation of metaphor from image to structure. Spark makes literal what has come to be disregarded as simply conventional, reconnecting the signifier and the signified in order to explode meaning. "Portobello Road" seems to be a working out of metaphor-into-narrative, if the term can be permitted to embrace the wider concepts of simile, cliche and even an occasional broader rhetorical device such as maxim. The narrator of Spark's story, for example, is nick-named Needle because

One day in my young youth at high summer, lolling with my lovely companions upon a haystack, I found a needle (7).

This, she says, confirms her idea that she was "set apart from the common run." Immediately we are given a shock both to our powers of belief and disbelief: finding a needle in a haystack is a stock phrase used to describe the impossible, but this is both the opening and the 'legend' for mapping the rest of the story. We must take this literally to be able to proceed with the story at all. Needle, by the way, is a ghost. She was murdered in, as might be expected, a haystack. She was missing several days before her body was discovered; the newspaper headlines read "'Needle' found in haystack" (7).

There is more. The reader is unaware that Needle is a ghost, and is only informed of this fact several paragraphs into the story. When she greets a friend who is surprised to see her, the reader cannot yet fully comprehend the extent of this friend's surprise, and Needle's comment

> I suppose ... that from poor George's point of view it was like seeing a ghost when he saw me standing by the fruit barrow ... (11).

seems to be simple cliche. Only after the reader is initiated fully into the ghostly significance of such apparently casual remarks does the playful and deadly meaning become evident.

Needle often says that she saw George "just before my death five years ago" (29). George, in fact, is the one who kills Needle, his childhood friend, and the phrase "just before my death" also takes on renewed meaning. What we believe we can read over lightly suddenly begins to tug at us, forcing us to read more slowly and recognize the implications of almost every word. There is nothing too ordinary to be important, Spark indicates, and readers cannot consume her sentences all at once, but must weigh and consider each phrase.

Needle describes her living life (to borrow from her phrase "young youth") with phrases like "I was not conscious that I, Needle, was taking up any space at all. I might have been a ghost" (14). Once again, such usage of a conventional term, always regarded metaphorically, begins to make us question, consciously, the very premise of conventional language. Commonplace phrases and metaphors are no longer inert. They have meaning in terms not only of imagery, but of narrative; they are no longer mere rhetorical devices, but the very "stuff" of the stories themselves.

Spark tends to make use of the metaphor-into-narrative device in such a way that there is less and less time for the reader to go over or go back to earlier portions of the text in order to derive full meaning. The phenomena is synthesized most elegantly at the climax of the story when Needle says, in one short sentence,

> He looked as if he would murder me, and he did (29).

The wild power and meaning behind the conventional "he looked as if he would murder me" is restored. There is implication that the world of "as if" and the world of "as is" are not, in fact, separated by anything except perception and acknowledgement.

In Fay Weldon's *Remember Me*, Jarvis, Madeleine's ex-husband, spurred on by too much drink and his second wife's conversation concerning Madeline, offers the following toast to his guests: "Death and damnation to all ex-wives. Down with ... the succubi ..." (90). Jarvis speaks at ten to one in the early morning. At nine minutes to one Madeline's car "veers off through the dividing rail, hits a post, carries on, crumbling as it goes ..." (93). The clocks in Jarvis's house stop at the moment of Madeleine's death, the very moment that Jarvis is wishing her dead. Second-wife Lily, feeling vicious on the morning after all this, states

'She must have died about the time you were wishing her dead,' says Lily unforgivably, 'so I think you're being very hypocritical ... what's more, the clock stopped at the time she died.' She says it in triumph, as if this last fact somehow proved her value and his worthlessness (123).

Jarvis responds by warning Lily that if they are to get through the experience she can "start by not implying that it was I who killed Madeleine" (123). But even Lily, so out of touch with anyone's emotions but her own, realizes that by stating "Madeleine, die," Jarvis' words have in some way affected reality.

Jarvis continues to name events that he calls "the farago of superstitious nonsense" which are, in fact, a fairly accurate summation of the previous night's events:

'It was Madeleine's ghost swept through the house last night, opening the windows, sticking a cosmic pin into Margot Bailey's leg, another into Jonathan and another into Hilary ...' (123).

What Jarvis sees as hyperbole and hysteria, what he states, certain that his statement is rhetorical, is really a description of the narrative. It is precisely what Weldon has encouraged the reader to believe. That words do not simply describe but instead actually define a world is a central focus for the writings of these authors.

It must be noted that pattern discussed here in terms of women writers is in keeping with, for example, E.M. Forster's thought that a remark may be untrue but may nevertheless be the kind which "if stated often enough, may become true," or Proust's claim that "... sometimes the future is latent in us without our knowledge, and our words, which we suppose to be false, forecast an imminent reality." As women writers explore the links between the symbolic and literal uses of language, they do so in a way that reflects their 'engendered' position as speakers of the necessarily patriarchal discourse. Feminist critics, as we have seen, suggest that women somehow live more deeply with the metaphors they create; I would like to take this a step further, and suggest that women live more deeply, or even live out, the metaphors that control the systematic constructs labeled as the natural world. They live out the metaphors they inherit, but they live them with — quite literally — a vengeance. Discussing the displaced daughter in *Words of Advice,* Fay Weldon tells us that Wendy takes her father's words literally. In doing so, she dislodges them from their intended context and therefore subverts his meaning. Paradoxically, she invests his trite comment with a power that then enables her to transform his off-hand dismissal into a catalyctic dictum:

> "Yes, run along," says Victor, as he used to say ... run along, from the very first day she rose from crawling position to sway on her tiny feet. Eventually she became good at running, and made a very fine wing at hockey, and even later, occasionally captained the school team ... (54).

Wendy both does and does not do what her father intends. She takes his language and literally runs away with it.

In *The Girls of Slender Means,* Spark gives us a group of women living in the May of Teck Club for young ladies in London at the very end of the second world war. Spark describes them as follows: "[a]s they realized themselves in varying degrees, few people alive at the time were more delightful, more ingenious, more movingly lovely, and, as it might happen, more savage, than the girls of slender means" (6). The prettiest and most popular girls live on the top floor and compare waist and hip measurements as if their lives depended on them.

Which, as it turns out, they do. There is a fire in the Victorian house, and only those slender enough to pass through the bathroom window survive.

In *The Life and Loves of a She-Devil,* Weldon offers us Ruth who laughs her grating, uncomfortable laugh and explains that she wants only "to look up to men ... Little women can look up to men. But women of six feet two have trouble doing so" (22). Initially, we find it merely amusing to learn that Ruth's problem is literal: she is an enormous woman, altogether bigger than her husband Bobbo. But Weldon plays out the looking-up-to-men cliche to the point where Ruth has major surgery to reduce her overwhelming stature: she has inches of bone removed from her legs in an operation. We follow Ruth's picaresque journey across continents in creation of a more publically acceptable self, one who need no longer look down on men. Looking up to men is neither an extended metaphor or a leitmotif: it is the central structure for the plot and the catalyst to action. You can't use these phrases and not expect us to take them seriously, Ruth's actions imply. When Bobbo calls her a "she-devil" for the first time (for having done nothing but weep at his infidelity and drop the chicken vol-au-vents), there is "a change in the texture of the silence" (42) that comes from Ruth's closed door. Ruth wonders whether "it was possible by mere words, to influence the course of events" (23) while Weldon illustrates with savage precision exactly how possible it is for Ruth — and the rest of us — to do this.

By defining a situation, by limiting it and categorizing it through language, the words themselves are clearly both maniputative and powerful. It is a return to an almost primitive and superstitious belief in the magical powers associated with language. Every word has a formative purpose. These writers forge a complex narrative structure that both appeases our desire for verisimilitude while simultaneously forcing us to question the very nature of truth. By encoding a system of language shifts that continually displace us from the fixed, naturalized meanings of commonplace phrases, our 'naturalized' mythology is called into question. If we wish to call their style or tone ironic, we must see that irony here means a justaposition between an initial truth and a final truth: the concept of a unified reality is constructed word by word.

There is no going back because once words are said they stick, they become opaque, a presence. When being left by her accountant husband, Ruth cries out "What about me?" which will join, Weldon tells us, "myriad other women, abandoned that very day by their husbands. Women in Korea and Buenos Aires and Stockholm and Detroit and Dubai and Tashkent, but seldom in China where it is a punishable offence. Sound waves do not die out. They travel forever and forever. All our sentences are immortal. Our useless bleatings circle the universe for all eternity" (46).

The acknowledgment of the central role of language is linked, by these authors, to the acknowledgment of the validity of female experience. Actions themselves do not offer definitions: the words describing the actions become the central factor in the text. The manner in which language frames a situation determines that situation. During times of war, for example, women like the protagonist Stella from Bowen's *The Heat of the Day*, are engaged in the work of the world from which they had traditionally been barred. Seeing clearly, and often for the first time, the uncertain and tautological nature of the structures on which political and social reality is in fact based, these women must begin to redefine their vision and their roles. One thing is sure: words matter. This is a rejection of traditional concepts of wartime experience which tend to privilege only violent action. Faced with the assertion that what someone says (as opposed to "does") can hardly be of much importance, a Bowen character argues that: "conversations are the leading thing in this war! Even I know that. Everything you and I do is the result of something that's been said" (67). In *The Heat of the Day*, a young woman named Louie is in a state of dislocation for much of the war because she is unable to find the words to describe herself and her situation:

Look at the trouble there is when I have to only say what I *can* say, and so cannot ever say what it is really. Inside me it's like being crowded to death — more and more of it all getting into me. I could bear it if only I could say ... I would more understand if I was able to make myself understood ... (275).

Words — cliches and trite phrases — offered by the press eventually construct Louie's view of herself and the world around her. Louie embraces newspaper stories about the war because they make "people like her important." Perhaps it can be argued that women embrace comedy for the same reason. Louie takes at face value what she reads in the paper and so creates an acceptable character by piecing together bits of typeface in much the same way as Ruth takes at face value the dictum that shapes her life and so creates a desirable creature out of herself.

Bowen states explicitly the relationship between language and reality: "One can live in the shadow of an idea without grasping it. Nothing is really unthinkable; really you do know that. But the more one thinks, the less there's any outside reality — at least, that's so with a woman" (214). The sense that language is self-referential and that the apparently immovable structures of reality can be undermined and shaken apart: these are the lasting effects of metaphor-into-narrative.

In Spark's "The House of the Famous Poet" there is a focus on the metaphoric versus the literal use of words. For example, the narrator is concerned with the current adoption of the word "siren" for the purposes of war: "... I was thinking of the word 'siren'. The sound [of the warning siren] became comical, for I imagined some maniac sea nymph from centuries past belching into the year 1944" (196). Perhaps the narrator's concern also arises from the gender implications of the word, as well as from the obvious but unstated change in role: "warning siren" seems to be an oxymoron. The Sirens lured people to their deaths, their feminine voices seducing sailors away from reason; the sirens set up during war were meant to drive people from danger, an almost maternal "voice" calling all to safety. Certainly the meanings overlie and reflect back on one another; is the safety offered by sirens, in fact, safe? "Actually," admits the narrator, "the sirens frightened me" (*The Stories of Muriel Spark* 196).

The unnamed narrator agrees to accompany a young women to the house where she works as a caretaker. The narrator explains her action: "It had the element of experience — perhaps, even of truth — and I believed, in those days, that truth is stranger than fiction" (193). At one distinct point, however, the story pivots and swerves on its axis: it is more than a blurring of distinctions. It becomes a deliberate "tangling" of language: it becomes a challenge. Through this narrator, Spark addresses the reader directly: "You will complain that I am withholding evidence. Indeed, you may wonder if there is any evidence at all ... You will insinuate that what I have just told you is pure fiction. Hear me to the end" (197). After a fairly conventional story about a young woman describing how she suddenly finds herself in the house of a famous writer, and who is thrilled and appalled that she did not realise this sooner, Spark introduces a surreal element. A soldier, who has appeared briefly in the first few parapgraphs, tracks the narrator down in order to get some money. He doesn't want to borrow it, he tells her; rather, he has something to sell:

"It's an abstract funeral," he explained, opening the parcel ... I handed over eight shillings and sixpence. There was a great deal of this abstract funeral. Hastily, I packed some of it into the hold-all. Some I stuffed into my pockets, and there was still some left over ... (197).

This passage illustrates the way in which Spark cleaves the absurd and the surreal onto apparent realism. The "hold-all" is now really holding all, since it holds this abstract notion. The abstract funeral, sold to the narrator's companion and to the famous poet is responsible for their deaths; only because the narrator throws her notion out of a train window, wanting instead "a real funeral ... one of my own," (199) does she survive. Getting rid of certain notions does make the difference. The story resembles Lessing's "How I Lost My Heart" in its refusal to back down from manipulating the "real" into the "surreal" without apology.

It might be thought that this strategy is particular to twentieth-century novelists who have read Freud, Bergson or Nietzsche on the use of metaphor in comedy and elsewhere. I would like to suggest that while metaphor-into-narrative can be read in light of, as well as being reflective of, the work on metaphor done by Searle, Ricoeur and so many other linguistic theorists, it should also be seen as a structure employed particularly by women writers, and particularly by women writers of comedy, because of their engendered relationship to language. A general discussion of the use of metaphor does not consider the very aspects most in need of exploration, those concerning gender.

Women's use of metaphor, as well as their use of comedy, is disruptive in its refusal to accept the conventions which propagate the language of the father. This is emblematic of the fact that women are not offered the possibility for full initiation into the symbolic order, but still maintain a level of power to affect the cultural codes because of their boundary position. "Societies do not succeed in offering everyone the same way of fitting into the symbolic order," explains Clement, "those who are, if one may say so, between symbolic systems, in the interstices, offside, are the ones who are afflicted with a dangerous symbolic mobility" (7).

The phrase "dangerous symbolic mobility" is significant for a study of comedy by women. It echoes the earlier phrase "all laughter is allied with the monstrous" and reflects Kristeva's assertion that woman as "semiotic" space is allied with pre-Oedipal discourse that does not accept the absolute of language but rather plays with language, using non-sense and puns, as part of its refusal to embrace initiation into the symbolic order. Metaphor-into-narrative can be seen as an effect/indication of this relationship between women and language.

At the risk of repeating what is already established, women and words form a problematic alliance within the symbolic order. This is important to keep in mind in any discussion of women and comedy, but particularly for the discussion on metaphor and comedy. Women are not meant to give utterance: when they do, they "step out of their function as sign". When they create comedy, they are stepping out of their "destined communication" and are deviating from it in order to transform their position. They are also risking the maintainance of the system of exchange because they are shifting the ground on which the system rests. Should women remove themselves or "de-value" themselves in terms of exogamy, the system is in danger of collapse:

> ... Ultimately one might even think, as we know, that the woman must remain in childhood, in the original primitive state, to rescue human exchange from an imminent catastrophe owing to the progressive and inescapable entropy of language. Words have been able to circulate too much, to lose their information, to strip themselves of their sense. At least let women stay as they were in the beginning, talking little but causing men's talk — stay as guardians, because of their mystery, of all language. Levi-Strauss calls what they are thus able to retain "affective wealth," "fervor," "mystery," "which at the origin doubtlessly permeated the whole world of human communications" (Cixous and Clement 28).

Women writers are able to make use of the shiftings of the system. The symbolic dimension, as Juliete Mitchell describes it, enables the subject/child to disentangle words "from the snares and fascinations" of the imaginary (392). The child's accession to language coincides with the advent of the Oedipus complex, according to Lacan, and through this process women can be defined "as excluded by the nature of things which is the nature of words".[4] The symbolic order — the "highest" order — is linked to the masculine and to language. To play with language, then, seems to be to play with the authority of the symbolic/masculine view. There is a renewed exploration of the comedic in the exploration of play with language, of the use of non-sense and pun and, finally, of metaphor-into-narrative, to undermine the authority of language itself.

The symbolic order is what allows for unification of perspectives through an apprehension of the so-called authority of language, that attaches one meaning eradicably to one word; the problem in this equation arises when the instability of language is brought to the forefront. This links logocentrism with phallocentrism, according to a number of writers: looking for the one, unchallenged, "correct" point is common to both.

Metaphor-into-narrative, then, becomes emblematic of women's refusal to accept this inherited, codified understanding. Like George Eliot's Maggie Tulliver in *The Mill on the Floss*, they play with the syntax and focus on the particular. We will take the instruction to "run along" quite literally. In the haystacks created by these writers we *will* indeed find needles; big women are indeed prohibited from looking up to men. We read wrongly if we read with an eye towards automatic correction. This should be stressed. There is no "mistake" in these metaphors; they are accurate namings insofar as any naming can be accurate. It is we who initially mis-name by looking for the single correctly symbolic reading, unable to see the play with meaning that paradoxically offers a subversively "literal" reading in place of the traditional, symbolic ones.

Notes

I would like to thank my friends and colleagues, particularly Margaret Higonnet, Mary Ann Caws, Jean Marsden, Sian Mile and Lee Jacobus for their comments and suggestions.

1. See Henri Bergson's "Laughter. An Essay on the Meaning of the Comic," trans. C. Brereton and F. Rothwell. (London 1911.) For a good recent discussion of comedy, see Scott Cutler Shershow *Laughing Matters* University of Massachusetts Press Amherst 1986.
2. For example, Freud writes that "Words are a plastic material with which one can do all kinds of things. There are words which, when used in certain connections, have lost their original full meanings, but which regain it in other connections" (34) Jokes and their Relation to the Unconscious.
3. Sharon Thompson. "The Canonization of Muriel Spark." Review. *Village Voice Literary Supplement.* October 1985.
4. Quoted in Gilbert and Gubar, *Sexual Linguistics: Gender, Language, Sexuality.* New Literary History, Volume XVI #3 Spring 1985. Baltimore: The John Hopkins Press.

Works Cited

Atwood, Margaret. *The Edible Woman.* New York: Warner Books, 1983.
Bowen, Elizabeth. *The Heat of the Day.* New York: Alfred Knopf, 1949.
Cixous, Hélène and Catherine Clement. *The Newly Born Woman.* Trans. Betsy Wing. Minneapolis: University of Minnesota Press, 1986.

Eliot George. *The Mill on the Floss.* New York: Penguin Books, 1982.
Gilbert, Sandra and Gubar, Susan. *The Madwoman in the Attic.* New Haven and London: Yale University Press, 1979
Homans, Margaret. "Dreaming of Children: Literalization in Jane Eyre and Wuthering Heights". *The Female Gothic.* ed. Juliann E. Fleenor. Montreal: Eden Press, 1983.
Jacobus, Mary. "The Question of Language: Men of Maxims and The Mill on the Floss." *Writing and Sexual Difference.* ed. Elizabeth Abel. Chicago: University of Chicago Press, 1980.
Jardin, Alice. "Opaque texts and Transparent Contexts: The Political Difference of Julia Kristeva." *The Poetics of Gender* ed. Nancy K. Miller. New York: Columbia University Press, 1986.
Kristeva, Julia. "Approaching Abjection." *Oxford Literary Review* Volume 5. Number 1 & 2. Nottingham: The Russell Press Ltd. 1982.
Lessing, Doris. "How I Finally Lost my Heart." *Stories.* New York: Random House, 1980.
Mitchell, Juliet. *Psychoanalysis and Feminism.* New York: Vintage Books, 1974.
Sinclair, May. *The Three Sisters.* London: Macmillan, 1914.
Spark, Muriel. *The Comforters.* New York: Putnam, 1957.
———. *The Girls of Slender Means.* New York: Alfred Knopf, 1963.
———. *The Stories of Muriel Spark.* New York: E.P. Dutton, 1985.
Stanton, Domna C. "Difference on Trial: A Critique of the Maternal Metaphor in Cixous, Irigaray and Kristeva." *The Poetics of Gender.* Nancy K. Miller ed. New York: Columbia University Press, 1986.
Weldon, Fay. *Down among the Women.* Academy Chicago Publishers, 1984.
———. *Remember Me.* New York: Random House, 1976.
———. *The Fat Woman's Joke.* London: Coronet, 1982.
———. *The Life and Loves of a She-Devil.* New York: Pantheon Books, 1984.
———. *Words of Advice.* New York: Random House, 1977.

Uncommon woman: an interview with Wendy Wasserstein

ESTHER COHEN

New York

CHALLENGED BY my esteemed editor to write a printable article on women writers and humor in theatre (try to imagine a scene from *The Front Page*, only in an Indian restaurant — "Esther, get me that article, and pass the poori!"), I decided that I had nothing to say that one such writer couldn't say for herself. Thus, with the lure of a bottle of Diet Coke and the promise of being quoted in an academic journal, Wendy Wasserstein agreed to be interviewed for this article. I met Wendy, the noted playwright, author of "Uncommon Women and Others", "Isn't it Romantic?" and "Miami", and a contributing editor to "New York Woman", while working as a stage manager on "Isn't It Romantic?", and I knew her to be a witty, straightforward and eminently quotable woman. Eager to hear her views on humor, in both her work and her life, I met with Wendy on a sweltering afternoon in August, 1987.

Esther: I guess my first question is, when did you decide you liked to write? When did writing become something that you liked to do?
Wendy: I remember as a child thinking that my family was very funny. I think this was because my mother was somewhat eccentric. And I do remember watching shows like "Make Room for Daddy" and thinking that those kids were pretty boring. And I actually thought, like Rusty Hammer and Angela Cartwright, they are such good kids, and I thought "no one's family is really like this." And actually I thought our family was far more entertaining than that. So I

think partially from that, though I didn't really write those things.

I wrote in high school. I went to school in New York City at Calhoun, and I figured out that one of the ways I could get out of gym was if I wrote something called the Mother-Daughter Fashion Show. I know very little about fashion, but they used to have this Mother-Daughter Fashion Show once a year at the Plaza Hotel, and you got to leave school to go to the fashion show. But if you wrote it you didn't have to go to gym for like two or three weeks, it was fantastic. So, I started writing those.

E: So you were always an observer of people — watching your family, watching your friends.

W: Yeah, I think so. I think that's true.

E: What did you write in these fashion shows?

W: I don't know. I remember writing some song to "King of the Road" about "Miss Misunderstood." I don't know *what* I wrote.

E: So did you write in college?

W: Uh huh. I went to Holyoke and one of my best friends told me — I was taking a course to go become a Congressional intern, and I used to read the Congressional Digest at the Holyoke library and fall asleep, I just couldn't do it — and then she said to me "Well why don't you come to Smith and take playwriting with me, and then we could shop." So she said the magic word and the duck came down, and I said "Yes, I'll go shop." So we went up to Smith and I had a wonderful teacher. I started writing plays for him, really. And that's how that all happened. But I grew up going to the theatre and I used to dance, I used to go to dancing school at the June Taylor School of the Dance. It was never somewhat intellectual theatre, never had that sort of bent.

E: But was it always funny, was it always comedy?

W: Yeah, it always was sort of comic. It's kind of interesting. I think what happened to me, the real bend in the road for me, was that after my senior year in college I went to California with some friends of mine to Long Beach State to a summer dance program, which is really crazy of me to have done, and we had odd jobs. I mean one of my friends worked at a Union 76 station, and I had some job in some sweet shop. It was crazy. But I had thought that I would maybe stay in California and try to write television. And instead, I hated California so much — I think it was because I couldn't drive; I just loathed it — that I came home back to New York and applied to drama school.

And I think I'd be a very different writer, very different person, if I had stayed in California.

E: Do you think living in New York itself has affected the kind of writing you do?

W: Yes I think so. Because when I dream or think, I think in terms of the rhythm of theatrical comedy. It's not — I mean it's certain kinds of theatrical comedy because it's what you're around. I mean as a kid I used to go to those Neil Simon plays. By the time I got to drama school, those Albert Innaurato/Chris Durang plays. So it depends, what comes into your brain.

E: Do you find, as you're writing, that your humor comes more out of the situation that you're writing about, or are the characters themselves funny?

W: Sometimes the characters are funny. I mean, sometimes I like to do bright colors, and then they can be quite funny. Sometimes, you know — I haven't learned to use a computer, so I still type, and it's such a pain in the neck — sometimes I just retype scenes and start putting in things. I couldn't believe it — I'm writing a play right now about twenty years of peoples' lives, and this girl is telling this boy how unhappy she is, and for some reason I started writing Yasser Arafat jokes. For no reason. Because it's so boring retyping this stupid thing. But, you know sometimes it's funny to see. I think for myself, I'm slightly shy actually, and sometimes it's fun for me to write some character that's larger than life. That would say things I would never say but I know they're funny. And I like to do that a lot. And I also think, to get further into humor and women, that a lot of comedy is a deflection. If you look at "Isn't It Romantic?", Janie Blumberg is *always* funny, so as not to say what she feels. And so, I think you use it — you use it to get a laugh, but you use it deliberately too. I mean, the best is when you use it deliberately.

E: Do you think that your women characters are more prone to doing it that way — using their humor as a deflection?

W: Sometimes, yes, the women use it more as a defense, I think.

E: Do you think that — among your friends, people you know — do women use their humor in different ways than the men do?

W: Yes, I think they do. I think sometimes, men sometimes top each other. Women don't do that. Women know how to lay back and have a good time, you know, and the gossip is great. Great!

E: The best. The best.

W: The best! Exactly! I mean, that's delightful. Nothing could be better. And I love it when it's people you absolutely don't know, whom I don't know a thing about. I mean, people call here and tell me about John Updike's personal life. I don't know him!
E: But you know more about him than he does.
W: I'm sure I know more about him than he would ever know about me! But I think that that — so that's kind of different too. And I don't mean it in a bitchy way, it's just different. It's kind of like sitting around.
E: I think that — certainly in my relationships with my women friends — life is just funny between us, and we share those sort of humorous moments. We're not always telling each other jokes.
W: No, and I don't even know how to tell a joke. But, you know, if you come home from a bad date, or something's happened, you know, and you've been fired — you know, you've just lost your job to some 21 year old girl who's blond and can't do anything, but the boss ... You know that if you go home and tell your story to somebody, you will make it funny. And it will release the pain from you of whatever it is. Because you can't take that nonsense seriously.
E: Do you try to incorporate that way of reacting to people in your plays? In "Uncommon Women" I thought the characters really reacted naturally to each other, and in "Isn't It Romantic?" they had real relationships, and that humor sort of showed.
W: It's a little different than the one I'm doing now, but I think that's part of them, it's part of the relationship. People who are funny — I mean, one of my very best friends ever is Chris Durang, and there's nothing like a conversation with Christopher, because he's so funny! He's just wonderful. And when he's funny, he's hilarious. Just hilarious. And that's a wonderful thing. I mean, that's like a riff, almost. It's a great comfort. So, it's hard. But there are different kinds of humors, too. I don't like mean humor very much. I find nastiness is difficult for me, a little bit.
E: In the plays that you've written, do you think of them as being "women's" plays or written from a "women's" perspective? Or are they more written from *your* perspective?
W: I guess it's from my perspective, although sometimes I do think those stories have to be told. And if they're not, if I don't tell them, I mean someone else will tell them, that's for sure. But sometimes I look at these girls and I think I want to put them on the stage. I used to

have great pleasure when I would see the audiences come to "Isn't It Romantic?" sometimes. Like you'd see five women together going out, and I thought that's great. There should be something for them. There really should be. And I think the thing is the women I write about are kind of middle class, upper middle class people, who have good jobs and they're good looking, and there's no problem. I mean, they're not Philip Barry people, but they're not sort of working class. So they're not the people one would tend to dramatize. Because there's nothing tragic there. And there's nothing romantic there. So I think that's why they're interesting to write about.
E: Because you can relate to them.
W: Because you can relate to them. It's like someone you knew in college. And I think that to make those people theatrical is interesting. I hope.
E: How do you choose what to write about?
W: It depends. I think that writing a play is such a long and arduous task that it has to be something you care about pretty much, that's going to interest you longer than twenty pages. They're long, plays, they're like 90 pages, and it's a lot of typing!
E: And you have to live with them while they're running, too, for two years or ...
W: Yeah, you do, so I think it's got to be something that interests you enough. There are different things that interest you in different times. The play I'm writing right now is very personal. I have an idea for a musical after this that's based on a 19th century American play, just because I'd like to lose myself in something that's foreign to me.
E: It depends on where you're at at that particular moment. You haven't just written plays. You've written articles and TV screenplays. Is it different writing for the different media?
W: Very different. Sure it is. It's like one time I adapted a Cheever story for television that was called *The Sorrows of Gin,* and the climax was the child realized the adult world was tattered like a piece of burlap. Well, you can't, like in a play, have the kid pick up the burlap and say "Gee Dad, tattered like the adult world." I mean, what you do is bring the camera in on the kid. Just like in a play you can't have people drive along — you know, you can't do it. Television is a closeup medium. You go in for the face, and they don't have to talk. I just wrote a TV movie that's going to be done in the fall about Teri Garr learning to drive, because I just learned to drive.

E: And you always pictured yourself as being Teri Garr.
W: Exactly, exactly. We're very similar. But anyway, at the end — she's this terrible driver, terrible terrible driver, and she finally passes her test by dressing up as Catherine Bach in "The Dukes of Hazzard." When she passes her test, she's like the millionth person in her town to pass the test. There's this high school band that comes out and starts playing *The Little Old Lady from Pasadena*, because she passed, I mean it's crazy. But see, you could never do that on the stage. I mean, there's no way you could go to Playwrights Horizons and say "And now I'd like a high school band."
E: On an Equity salary.
W: What's nice about plays is they're about words, and they can get long, and they can be your feelings, and I think that's wonderful. It's very joyous.
E: How about writing for a nonperformance medium? Like articles. Do you have a different emotional reaction to writing those than to writing something that's being performed?
W: I've been writing some for a magazine called "New York Woman" recently. And it's fun. It's different though. You know what it is? I remember as a kid someone once told me that I had to learn to postpone gratification. And the thing about magazine things is it gets published pretty quickly. I mean, a play you can write and two years from then maybe you'll work it out. And I think magazine, because it's a shorter form, you can get — like I just wrote an article about manicures. I'd never write a play, a two hour play about manicures unless, you could do it quite artistically I guess with dancing fingers and stuff.
E: And Tommy Tune ...
W: And Tommy Tune, right, right. So that was fun to do for the magazine. I mean, I like that, I find it a release. You know why? Because I think of myself as a playwright, so I hold that very important to me. And when something's that important to you, you get scared of it. Whereas magazine writing doesn't scare me that much, because what's the worst they'll say? Wendy, you're not a magazine writer. And I'll say, that's right. But actually, I've enjoyed this magazine writing.
E: Does your humor translate the same way in each of these different media?
W: It depends. I mean, the magazine I wrote for sent me off to meet

Philipe de Montebello at the Met. It was pretty funny. But in these magazine things I always use "I", first person, and there's a persona that I elect to use. You know, there's an "I" that's always talking about how I wish I wore leather miniskirts and I hate pantyhose and things like that. I don't do that so much in the plays. I mean, what's fun about plays is you can divide yourself into a lot of characters and hide yourself in different places.

E: But you really consider yourself a playwright. That's really what you enjoy.

W: I think so. Yeah, I mean I hope so.

E: Even though you're not on the stage, do you enjoy that audience feedback?

W: I do. I mean, when it works, it's great. When a production goes wrong, it is hell. It's really hell, it's so painful. That's the other thing. I mean, so you write an article and people don't like it. Or you write an article and they never call you again and they don't publish it. It's not the same pain, it's really not. From the word go, from the no actors are available to the director doesn't show up, to the show doesn't work and no one's laughing, to you pick up some terrible review — I mean, all of that is devastating. It's just terrible. It's enough to give you a sense of humor. I mean, it's really awful! I'm writing this play here and I can't even think about all that stuff. It's just too awful.

E: Well, it's such a process.

W: It's a real process. And you don't know what's going to happen. You just don't know.

E: It's true, it's not just your imput that will make it in the end. There are so many other factors and people involved.

W: Exactly.

E: Is that intimidating, that there are so many other people who influence?

W: When it works, like with Gerry Gutierrez [director of] "Isn't It Romantic?", it's fantastic. Because, there you were giving birth to something alone in your room and then you've got a partner. And when that happens, it's great, because they ... I mean, I'm not a director, I have no sense of visuals, nothing! I'll do anything to tell a joke. There's this story about "Isn't It Romantic?". There was something about, there was some joke about three hundred running Hasidic Jews, or something, that Gerry Gutierrez kept telling me to cut because I should stay on the through line of the play. And I cut things like someone's mother being the last white woman to shop at Klein's — jokes like that. And I kept cutting them. But the running Hasidic Jews I really didn't want to cut. And so finally, I lit a cigarette and I turned to Gerry and I said "do you know, Gerry, it's not just the joke. It's the zeitgeist of the play. When the hubris of the character ..." I don't know what the hell I was talking about. All I wanted to do was keep my joke. So I thought if I can talk to this man in the most high-faluting terms I can possibly pull out ... I was talking about anecnorisises of the audience, I didn't know what I was saying. But I just wanted to keep my joke. But I think that, when you have someone with you who's on the same line as you are, and can take you further, that's a thrill. If you're an artist, you want someone to challenge you, and extend you. But you can also simultaneously have somebody who cripples you. And that's hard, it's so painful. It's just terrible.

E: Is it the same in film?

W: I think film is different, because film — I think the pain is up front. Just cutting the deal is painful. And then you know it's a director's medium. And it belongs to the producer. Unless you're going to direct your film or produce it, it's not the same thing. It's not your baby, it's their's. You're like a hired hand. You know, they can hire six different writers to do one of these things.

E: Do you consider yourself funny?

W: I can't tell a joke. And I am shy. I mean I can go to a meal and not say anything. I have that unique capability of, if I'm scared of someone, I won't say anything. But sometimes I can be funny. I can be funny with a girlfriend. I can be very sarcastic. So yes, I have that ability to make people laugh, I always have. I know how to make friends and get on with people because I could be funny. Not funny in like stick my tongue out with food on it, but sort of funny in a nonthreatening, likable way.

E: Were you always funny? Were you funny as a child, do you think?

W: I think I was, yeah. Or pleasing, in a way. There's a line about Janie in "Isn't It Romantic?". I think Harriet says "That's the thing about Janie, she's not threatening to anybody. That's her gift." I think that's somewhat similar with me.

E: You said your family was funny. How were they funny?

W: Well, my mother's very eccentric. She's like the woman in "Isn't It Romantic?". Her name is Lola, she goes to dancing classes six hours a day, she's — I won't say her age — but she's a very eccentric woman. She's very lively, very colorful. She's quite amusing, actually.

E: Did you have to compete with that as a child?

W: She's kind of an Auntie Mame figure. I think as a child you think it's very colorful. Then when you get sort of shy, you know, when you get to sixth grade and everyone's mother is showing up in a suit, and they've got a station wagon, and your mother pulls in with a Carmen Miranda hat, you've got to think, "Oh God." I think that's a little difficult.

E: You've said before that you have humor with your friends and that a friend like Chris Durang is very funny. Do you think Chris is the funniest person you know? Who do you think is?

W: He's a pretty funny guy. Yeah. Actually, he might be the funniest person I know. Although you can meet Chris, you know you can have dinner with Chris and he can decide not to talk, too. So you know, you can have a lovely meal with both of us and we could both not talk. But actually I do think he's very funny. You know who's terrible funny too? Paul Rudnick. He wrote a novel called *Social Disease*. He's a dear friend of mine, and he is hilarious. The other day I was chatting up a friend and she was telling us about some man who was reading Boswell's Life of Johnson, and Paul Rudnick said "Of Don Johnson?" Which I thought was so funny. Terribly funny. He's quite witty. I mean, Christopher is so brilliant and imaginative that he just gets, you know, large, it's just wonderful. Yes, I would say they were the funniest people I knew.

E: I know Chris and he is brilliant and imaginative. But he's also sly.

W: Yes, he's very sly. He's witty. I mean, I don't like sort of locker room jockey humor. I've absolutely no interest in it. And I don't like sort of sex jokes either. Actually, because I don't get them.

E: Would you say humor is important in your relationship with people?

W: Yeah, very. Very. I think it's sort of how I get by. I giggle a little too much. But yes I think so, because one it makes one entertaining, two it deflects, and also it's a way of commenting on things. So yeah, I think it's very important to me.

E: It's a point of view on life.

W: It is a point of view. It really is. And it sort of pricks a hole in things, too, keeps things in line. And then also it helps you deal with things which are overwhelmingly tragic, which are undealable with. I mean the bad things are just horrendous. They're not funny at all, so you might as well make fun of everything else.

E: When you're writing, whether you're writing a screenplay or a play or an article, do you think about the audience that it's aimed for?

W: I don't think about the audience. You do think of the rhythm of the things and people laughing. You don't think about the audience per se. I mean, sometimes you think about, you don't want to — I don't like to be offensive, really. I know some people don't mind that at all.

E: In fact, aim for it.

W: Aim for it, right. But it depends. No, I don't mind offending peoples', you know, moral grounds. Fuck 'em. But you wouldn't want to write a character as offensive that you didn't want to be offensive. That's what I meant. But do I think about the audience that it's for? Not really. Not really. Sometimes.

E: Does it sometimes surprise you who ends up being the audience for your play? Or the reader?

W: Yes. I just saw "Isn't It Romantic?" in Tokyo. You know, that's a play that I can't get done in London, no one has wanted to do it. But for some reason that show really worked in Japan. So, yes, that's a shocker.

E: Why do you think that was? Did they relate to the family-ness of it?

W: I think they related to the family-ness of it, and also, in Japan a woman who's over 25 who isn't married is known as a wedding cake after Christmas. Actually it was very interesting because this play worked almost as a political play. So that was quite interesting. But in terms of, one is always shocked who likes their plays and who doesn't. The person that you think will most like your play doesn't like it, and then someone else will like it. It's usually some maniac, some mass murderer; David Berkowitz will say "oh you're my favourite playwright."

E: Have you gotten reactions from your plays that surprised you? Interpretations that blew you over?

W: Sometimes, or you see a bad production that doesn't make any sense.

E: Do you have a specific emotional reaction to your plays? I mean, do you feel differently about "Uncommon Women" say, than "Isn't It Romantic?"

W: Yes you do. Well, yeah you do. Because you're so close to them that you do. I . . . It's funny, I have a real love I think for "Uncommon Women." I really, I find it very dear. I think because whoever wrote it really cared a lot. There's a lot of raw emotion there. That monologue of Holly's is very raw, and dear. I admire "Isn't It Romantic?" because it's better crafted. It's very clean, that play. Sometimes I thought that people didn't take that play as seriously as I would have liked them to. Because I thought there were very serious things being slyly discussed there. That's what was interesting about Japan. The director told me that he did my play because he was a revolutionary. That's like saying you did "Barefoot in the Park" because you're a revolutionary. But I found that very moving. I wrote this musical "Miami" that's not finished that I have to finish. And because it went through a difficult workshop production, I have a difficult relationship with it. So it all depends. What's nice about writing a new play is we don't know each other that well yet. So you do have different feelings about things.

E: This is a question I wanted to ask you. Do you think the 1980's are funny?

W: No. I was just writing about them. I really don't like the 1980's very much. I don't. It's all sort of retro-'50 or retro-'60. You know what it is? It's commenting. Or as Gerry Gutierrez would say, indicating. I do think they're funny. I mean Ronald Reagan and "I can't remember" is hilarious. I mean, someone must do something with that. What, you can't remember? I mean things like that are outrageous. So, a man can't become president because he slept with a model, but you can start your own CIA and become a hero? That's nuts!

E: But maybe not inherently amusing.

W: But not amusing. No, I don't find it funny. Do you find it funny?

E: Well, I asked this only because a friend of mine and I were discussing political humor the other day. And saying how it seemed the 1980's were ripe for political humor, except that it was all so awful that the humor is sort of different. It's not like '60's humor.

W: It's true. You know what's sort of funny? When I was in London, all these people said to me, "How come you people don't write anything about the government? I mean, about Ronald Reagan. Why are there no plays about this? I mean, look at him." And in some ways, Mrs. Thatcher is funnier. Because she's so fucking dour and has no sense of humor that you want to lance her right away. I mean you just look at her and you want her to put her panty hose on her head. I mean she's just, she's horrible. Ronald Reagan is slightly different.

E: Well, George Carlin once said "If a stupid person goes senile, how can you tell the difference?" Your plays are not topical humor plays, but some of your pieces obviously in newspapers must treat topical matters. How do you approach that differently than in a play?

W: Well it's different with a play because the newspaper thing gets published right away so you can reflect off of the topicallity of it. In a play I try to go more through the character of it. If I'm writing now about Reagan it would be as filtered through the characters who lived through that period. "Uncommon Women" is in a way about feminism. It's just as filtered through the people who were participating in it at that time.

E: Do you find that women have a different reaction to your writing than men?

W: Sometimes. It can go either way. They can either take me more seriously and see what's there, and have connection to it, or — you know, everybody has an opinion, and you know the opinion of "well, we know all of this already, and we've moved beyond this." So you get a little bit of that too. You know, one time I was at a bar in Westport, Connecticut, waiting for the train, which was late, and some little girl with brown curly hair and glasses, and looked sort of sad, came up to me and recognized me, and said she loved my play, and I thought "she is the saddest girl in the room. Of course she loves my plays! Anywhere you go, you look for the saddest girl with the brown curly hair and they're the ones who like my play!" I thought, "I bet Beth Henley gets like good looking blonde girls, nice and thin, coming up to her and saying they liked her play. They don't have those sad eyes."

E: Do you think that men always get it when they see your pieces?

W: I think sometimes they do. I think sometimes they don't. I mean, sometimes they might think they're trivial, I think. But no, I don't think that much, really. I don't think so. I hope not.

E: Do you think that, when you say trivial, do you think that smaller things are more important to women?

W: No, but I also don't think that women write plays like "Fuck you, fuck me, fuck you, fuck you, fuck the duck, fuck the dog, fuck a this, fuck a that. Goodbye." I mean you don't, that's not how you hear it. And if that's what's good and taut, well then, I don't write good or taut. You know, I think there's room for everything. Because there are women who can write like that, too. I don't, but there are people who do, and do it well, and do it brilliantly. I mean, Caryl Churchill's new play is wonderful. It's a tough piece of work, you know. But it's, it's good.

E: Do you find it's a small community of women writers? Or is it just a small community of *known* women writers?

W: I think maybe known. It's funny, I was on the NEA [National Endowment for the Arts] panel the other year, playwriting panel, and we gave grants. I think the grants went to 60% women writers. I think there are more and more women writers. Definitely more and more. And wonderful writers, too. And when you think about Marsha Norman and Beth Henley, all those people, they're terrific.

E: Do you think it's hard for women to get started? To get funding, to get . . .

W: You know what's hard? It's hard to keep one's confidence. It's hard to keep yourself in the middle, not to be a nice girl and not to be a tough girl, you know, but somehow to be yourself. That's hard. And as soon as you start playacting in your writing or in your life, there's trouble, a little bit. Especially in your writing. Because what works is going to be whatever's honest to you. So I think in that way, yes, there's somewhat of a problem. But, I mean, I think the most important thing is that decent women write and get those plays out. I think that's very important.

E: But you see more women now, I mean, nobody goes into shock when a Marsha Norman play is done.

W: No. I don't think any play does not get done because [it's by] a woman. I mean, I'm a product of the O'Neill and Playwrights Horizons, Yale Drama School; these aren't specifically women's institutions. When you write plays and you're a woman writer, you get these questions like, are you a feminist? She's a dear writer. She's a tough writer. You don't get this stuff when you're a man.

E: He's just a writer.

W: He's a writer, right, it's not he's tough, he's dear, he's a feminist, she's a sweetie. I mean, what is this? You know? She's got balls? The men, they all have balls. They don't have this problem! So, I mean, that's sort of, that's hard.

E: Is it hard to take emotionally?

W: Yeah, I think that is hard, a little bit. Yeah, I do.

E: You say you're not a joke teller, but do you have a favorite joke?

W: I don't. I can't tell a joke. I can't, I don't know any jokes. I forget them. People tell me them and I can't remember. I can't remember topical jokes like Chernobyl jokes about Chicken Kiev, I can't remember them. I just don't. I don't know how to write one, or tell one. There was even a joke character, I mean a comedian in "Miami" and I had a hard time telling his jokes. Because the comedy for me comes out of character. If I had to write, not somebody who's a comedian but someone, if it came out of their character, I could do that. But that's different jokes. And I always think whoever makes up those jokes that get spread around so quickly must be terribly bright.
E: What makes you laugh?
W: I don't know. Rubber chickens. It depends, there's a variety of things. I think when Ricky Ricardo shows up and Lucy has a baby and he's dressed in his voodoo outfit for the Club Tropicana — I think that is so funny. I have a bit of a whimsical sense of humor. I like puncturing things, though. I think that that's quite funny. And verbal play, too, I think is very funny. I don't like slapstick very much. But I think other people do, I just don't care for it very much. Although some things I think are very funny. I know there's a Woody Allen movie, is it *Take The Money and Run* where his parents are both wearing Groucho glasses? That's *very* funny. Very funny. You know why? Sometimes funny things are almost like the fantasy, and then it comes real.
E: It's sort of like trying to find the fine line between the completely absurd and the everyday.
W: That's right, that's right. Or seeing it. Seeing the completely absurd *in* the everyday.
E: It's sort of the description of my life.
W: Yes, it's true. Mine too. So, Esther...?
E: So darling. Well thank you, darling, very much.
W: Oh, darling, a pleasure.

Feminist humor: rebellious and self-affirming

LISA MERRILL

Hofstra University, Hempstead, N.Y.

GEORGE MEREDITH, in *The Idea of Comedy* called on women to recognize that the comic muse is one of their best friends. Meredith claimed that women are blind to their own interests when they gravitate towards sentimentalism, rather than comedy; because comedy is indicative of the (potential) social equality of the sexes.

They will see that where they have no social freedom, comedy is absent; where they are household drudges, the form of comedy is primitive; where they are tolerably independent but uncultivated, exciting melodrama takes its place and a sentimental version of them ... But where women are on the road to an equal footing with men, in attainments and liberty ... there, and only waiting to be transplanted from life to the stage, or the novel or the poem pure comedy flourishes, and is, as it would help them to be, the sweetest of diversions, the wisest of delightful companions (118-119).

Meredith wrote those words in 1877. In the intervening century women have come further along the 'road to an equal footing with men' than Meredith ever dreamed. If we accept his premise that sexual equality affects the nature of comedy, then comedy should have changed significantly in the ensuing hundred years, particularly in its depiction of women. But Meredith, despite his egalitarianism for his era, still spoke of 'Comedy' and of 'Woman' as diversions and companions for men, not even considering the most dramatic change of all, a comedy written by women for women.

Yet, perhaps the special relationship between female experience and the comedic voice has more ancient resonances than Meredith ever considered. It is generally assumed that comedy, in fact, all grew out of ritual improvisations and professional celebrations. vast majority of theatre historians who attempt to trace comedy to tes of the Greek god, Dionysius, attach to this development a particularly male cast. For example, Walter Sorell claims that comedy was "born in the name of the phallic symbol" (19), since Dionysian rituals were associated with phallic dances.

However, current feminist historians "consider comedy itself a female form — ancient, tribal, used to celebrate family bondings like marriage ... always moving dramatically towards relational conclusions in which people are united and conflict is dissipated" (Jenkins 11). In fact, Linda Walsh Jenkins suggests the presence of a psychological association between the angst of the estranged tragic hero and male separation from the domestic sphere. She notes that "tragedies again and again enact the tension between values of the oikos (home unit) and values of the polis" (11). Thus, if tragic form is associated with a specifically male psychological experience, might comedy be an affirmation of female experience? And, as women have grown increasingly more autonomous, how might we identify a feminist sensibility in current expressions of women's humor?

In order to explore these questions we must first examine some of the conventions of the comedic form. As Freud has established, comedy is an assertive genre. Because humor depends upon a perception of events or behaviour as unexpected or incongruous, the individual who publicly points up such inconsistancies risks making a statement about the status quo. Consequently, satire, irony and comedy pointedly directed can wield enormous social and political power. However, women have been discouraged from embracing this form at even its most basic level; the telling of a joke.

Rose Laub Coser, in a study of joke-telling among colleagues in a psychiatric institution, noted that the three variables in joke-telling, the maker of a witticism, its target, and who laughs at it, were organized along hierarchical lines. Physicians could tell jokes in which subordinates were ridiculed in the presence of those subordinates, but the reverse was not done. The most powerful persons told the vast majority of the jokes; and the 'target' of a witty remark was never higher in the hierarchy than the person making the joke (81-95). As Nancy Henley has observed, if humor is a releasing of tension, then in traditional comedy "Tension is released downwards, against the vulnerable" (71).

Hence, those few women writers and performers who have achieved mainstream acclaim in this traditionally 'unfeminine' genre are those who are so self-deprecating as to 'make fun of' other women, or themselves; thereby reinforcing the status quo. Illustrative of this comedic style is the work of comediennes Joan Rivers and Phyllis Diller. In 1958 Phyllis Diller, who usually appeared in an intentionally unattractive 'fright wig', reinforced some of the stereotypes about male-female social roles in a routine that began, "Supposing you are a housewife and you have goofed. Well, let's put it this way — it's 4:30 and you're still in bed. And you know, that's gettin' pretty close to overtime. And when the beast comes home, the beauty better be ready ... (Beatts and Stillman 28). Now, almost thirty years later, Joan Rivers' current routines still ridicule herself and other women for their lack of attractiveness while reinforcing the need to please men. For example, actress Elizabeth Taylor has been subject to Rivers' scathing abuse for being 'too fat'. Rivers supports the sexual double standard, as well, by her frequent barbs at the sexual behaviour of her 'friend' Heidi Abramowitz. Clearly, both Diller and Rivers are aggressively employing the tools of their genre. But as long as their 'barbs' (note the violent imagery) are directed against women, or themselves, they have traditionally been considered 'funny.'

Most women who foray into the comedic forms of expression have not been so favorably regarded. In fact, a claim made frequently about women writers and performers who challenge male authority is that they do not have a sense of humor, or that they "just can't take a joke." For example, poet Theodore Roethke, in his essay on the poetry of Louise Bogan, asserted that "Two of the charges most frequently leveled against poetry by women are lack of range ... and lack of a sense of humor." Roethke justified both charges (133-134).

But perhaps women's so-called 'lack of humor' is, in fact, a refusal to comply with the *premise* of a joke. Henry Bergson said that "our laughter is always the laughter of a group." A group of like-thinking people is required because a sense of shared norms or values are necessary to perceive something as humorous. When women no longer identify with the ways in which we traditionally have been defined, humor which ridicules our departure from those expectations no longer amuses us. But that which women do find funny is frequently misunderstood or devalued, as well, thereby giving more fuel to the charge that women are humorless.

Anne Beatts, in an article published more than ten years ago, attempted to analyse the male assumption that women just are not funny. In trying to understand the largely male comedy writing establishment's reaction to women humorists, Beatts wrote:

> Humor is aggression ... Indiscriminate niceness is not conducive to humor. Humor implies discrimination, a choice between two alternatives, taking a stance — as economic dependents of a male-dominated society [women] have seldom had very much ground of their own on which to stand (184).

Because of conventional sex roles, women have had to be practical; pragmatists rather than idealists. The mundane day-to-day business of life has been women's domain. As Jenkins noted, "The world of the mundane is named by the keepers of the domestic sphere. Mundane once meant the world; now it means ordinary, in a demeaning fashion" (12). Hence, the catchwords of day-to-day experience; product names, grocery lists, etc., function as icons for the ways in which we have been socialized. Women's comedy is infused with these realistic associations. Beatts said, "If a sense of humor has to do with a perception of the world askew ... then women's humor may be subtler than men's. All it takes is a half-twist on reality to make us laugh." (184). Perhaps this is one more reason why men may not understand and find women's humor 'funny', and why women often find male jokes too broad and exaggerated.

Traditionally, women have been expected to identify with comedy which insults us, so as to 'belong,' to be seen as having a sense of humor and the shared values this sensibility implies. The psychological dangers of identifying against one's fundamental interests were explored most poignantly in Roberta Sklar and Sondra Segal's play *Feast or Famine* (1985). In the second act of the play, Segal portrays a nightclub stand-up comic who finds herself compulsively delivering ever-increasingly demeaning jokes about women.

As I wrote in a review of the production:

> Now we see the aggression, the misogyny behind self-deprecating jokes about women. Like the ethnic jokes with which they are interspersed, humor which is leveled at woman as target, as 'butt' of the joke is just not funny. Segal's laughter freezes into a grotesque mask as she delivers jokes like 'What's the difference between garbage and a woman? ... They both stink ... when you dump garbage, it doesn't call you on the phone and beg you to take it back.' The audience sees Segal's pain in telling these 'jokes' and hearing them we become aware of our own discomfort. To laugh is to

reinforce the negative view of women depicted in the joke. Suddenly, the audience becomes aware of our own complicity in our self denigration (Merrill 19).

However, the point-of-view represented in feminist comedy is one that affirms women's experience, rather than denigrating it. According to psychologist Naomi Weisstein, a feminist comic sensibility would be one in which the details of women's lives were presented in such a manner as to allow the female audience to mock our traditional roles, to "question their sanctity their quality of inevitability" (88). Oppressive contexts and restrictive values would be ridiculed, rather than the characters who are struggling against such restrictions.

I first became interested in the subject of women's perceptions of humor over ten years ago when I observed various stand-up comedians at *Improvisation*, a New York City night club showcasing new comedic and musical talent. I laughed, along with the men in the audience, at the male comedians. Then one woman performed her comedy routine. The audience was receptive — but it was undoubtedly the women in the audience who laughed loudest and nodded in recognition. Recognition of our shared socialization and shared concerns. Elayne Boosler's routine dealt with such things as warding off frightening men in the subway (She dribbled and chortled in an attempt to disgust the would-be attacker, only to have him dribble and chortle back), having to pay the phone company for an unlisted number (and extending the parallel to paying a supermarket for the groceries she didn't want to purchase), and joking about her anatomy (instead of eating a chocolate bar she should just apply it directly to her thighs, since that's where it ends up anyway.)

Boosler's on-stage persona was a wise-cracking, street-smart, middle class, white, heterosexual woman. Although she did not challenge the status quo in terms of the assumed values she embodied, or her chosen method of presentation (joke telling, stand-up comic) she nonetheless, demonstrated by her parrying with the audience as well as through her routine, that women could be aggressive, brash and funny; survivors rather than victims.

In the early 1970's women like Elayne Boosler and Bette Midler were presenting, in performance, the social disparities which other women humorists were exploring in print. In 1976, Anne Beatts and Deanne Stillman edited *Titters*, a collection of humor by women.

Titters contains parodies of advertisements for women such as, schools for nurses' aides so they can meet and marry a doctor, Magna Vibe earrings that ring when 'Mr. Right' comes along, as well as multitudes of take offs on beauty suggestions. Using the typographical format of contemporary women's magazines from *Mademoiselle* to *Ms.*, books from the *Fear of Flying* to *My Secret Garden* (a book of female sexual fantasies), poetry, *T.V. Guide, True Confessions*, war comics, and the Girl Scouts, nothing about the experience of growing up female in this culture is beyond the humorous investigations of the women in *Titters*.

One of the most interesting aspects of *Titters* is that the editors clearly assumed a female readership. Besides the women-identified subject matter, even the typefaces they employed are those that many female readers would recognize from popular advertisements and magazines directed toward women. The implied address is from woman author to woman reader.

According to reader-response theory, every text is written to an assumed reader with a particular set of values and experiences. Similarly, every performance is directed to an assumed spectator. This is most pointedly obvious with comedy since humor always implies shared values.

Comedy depends on perspective. A certain aesthetic distancing or tension between empathy and judgement is needed for one to view the irrational or incongruous as comic. Is there, then, an overriding method of presentation unique to a feminist comic perspective?

Susan Silver, (T.V. writer for *The Mary Tyler Moore Show, Maude*, and others) believes so. Silver said:

Until the *Mary Tyler Moore Show* there was a different kind of comedy — a set up and then a punch line. I went into the MTM offices with six stories from my life and they thought they were fantastic. They weren't really. They were women's stories that any woman could tell you, but that business had been so male oriented that men weren't even thinking along those lines. (Rainer 86).

What Silver says of women and television can certainly be applied to the recent one-woman shows of comediens Whoopi Goldberg, Lily Tomlin and Danitra Vance. Each presents us with an arsenal of characters in all their human contradictions and their naivete. If there is a judgement to be made, we must make it for ourselves; the writer/ actress/performer exercises no obvious editorial statements. Goldberg,

Tomlin and Vance have each portrayed characters of both genders, all ages and various ethnicities.

For more than fifteen years Lily Tomlin (along with her partner and writer, Jane Wagner) has been one of the leading architects of what I have referred to elsewhere as a celebratory women's humor (97). In Tomlin's most recent one-woman show, *The Search for Intelligent Life in the Universe* (1986), with no props or costume changes, Tomlin 'becomes' twelve different characters, from prostitutes Brandy and Kate to middle-class, suburban divorcée, Lynn. Each character is presented empathically and allowed to tell her or his own story. Within the same dramatic frame Tomlin presents, lesbians and heterosexuals, socialites and homeless 'bag ladies,' a large cross-section of female experience.

Tomlin's characters display insight and integrity which allows them to be self-critical without being self deprecating. For example, Lynn, the self-proclaimed "radical on Sabbatical" describes her early relationships with Janet, a "Don Juanita" whose vibrator used to interfere with neighboring T.V. reception, and Bob, who she married because he was the only man she'd ever known 'who "Knew where he was when Sylvia Plath died."

Tomlin, like Goldberg and Vance, portrays each of her characters by assuming their speech patterns, stance, gestures, facial expressions and world view. In 1975 Amy Gross wrote of Tomlin's characters:

> ... one of the great charms of Lily's characters is: none of them recognizes any authority outside themselves ... She's operating more and more from a comic perspective she discovered, and from there things are not so much funny ha-ha as funny amazing. Watching her being one of her characters, you would not double over in hysteria, but you might well shake your head, marveling, and smiling a smile of recognition: ain't that the truth. And the Tomlin truth is that we humans are totally absurd but endearingly so. (Gross 141)

This posture allows the character to appear to initiate a dialogue with the assumed spectator thereby introducing the spectator to the lifestyle and value system the character embodies, without the performer exercising an obvious editorial statement. The more unexpected an actual dialogue may be between the two assumed personas (those of the character and the spectator), the more potentially radical is the statement made when the spectator is enabled to see the humor and share the world view of the character; to laugh *with* her, rather than at her.

In *The Search* Tomlin speaks of the resulting feeling of community which humor provided as "sharing for the sharing-impaired." As Kate Davy has asserted "The fact that Tomlin and Wagner unabashedly present lesbian characters and material from a feminist perspective in a Broadway context has subversive undertones just by virtue of the way it plays, the theatre it plays in, and the spectators it plays to." (46).

In the case of Goldberg and Vance, assumptions about racial identification, as well as sexual and socio-economic identifications are confronted. One of Goldberg's characters is a little Black girl who fantasizes having "luxurious long blond hair." Vance portrays an adopted preppie teenager in Bloomingdale's who only discovered that she was Black when a little white girl pointed to her, and said, "Look Mommy, a baby maid!" In another characterization, as a Black dance therapist, Vance points up the absurdity of a racist value structure, by exaggerating a racial stereotype (ie: Blacks have rhythm) from a Black vantage point, as her character ponders the question, "Are colorless (white) people really rhythmically retarded?" In these performances we see more than an individual, idiosyncratic character portrayed and 'made fun of,' rather we are presented with a representation of racist and sexist value systems and an individual's unwitting reaction to them.

Vance also addresses issues of gender identification. As she frequently mentions at the beginning of her performances, "I think of myself as *Every* Woman — and some men." The ease with which she switches from portrayals of female and male, lesbian and heterosexual characters is itself a political statement. The presentation of gender as a social construction, or a role which can be put on or taken off as a performer chooses, humorously points out the inflexibility of the way we generally organize the values in our lives; and the truly arbitrary nature of that organization.

Comedy is both an aggressive and intellectual response to human nature and experience. A cognizance of women's right to be both aggressive and intellectual is a relatively new historical phenomenon. What is even more recent, and radical though, about feminist humor is that it addresses itself to women and to the multiplicity of experiences and values women may embody. This may be evidenced in a shorthand of words and references related to women's experience, or in a style of performance which does not reinforce a male power perspective as universal and normal.'

The female audience member at a feminist comedy performance, (like the woman reader of a feminist text written with her in mind), is a party in the dialogue between performer and spectator; she is not an eavesdropper or a voyeur. She does not have to devalue her own experience to identify with a male persona against her interests, as women do in traditional, masculinist humor. For example, when a male comic says, "Take my wife, please" the female auditor is thrown into a quandry. If she wishes to participate, to find the joke 'funny', she must identify with the male speaker who feels saddled with his wife. But simultaneously, the female audience member may (potentially) *be* the wife in question, or at least be aware of being so regarded by her own partner. So her identification with the joke teller, and the joke is somewhat schizophrenic. To be amused she must discount and devalue her own experience.

Feminist humor, on the other hand, posits a female spectator. This is true of literature as well as performance. As Catherine Clinton said in her review of Deanne Stillman and Anne Beatts anthology, *Titters*:

> ... the majority of the humorists in this book address themselves to women. In this, the work transcends the feminine and becomes feminist. *Titters*, not in spite of, but *because* of its ability to reflect male culture (as a wall to bounce off, as a cage to break out of) presents a predominantly feminist posture. Women have been defined by their sex. Rather than a strident rejection of this, most contributors use this basic bias as a concept worthy of ridicule and as a trampoline to humor (30).

Humor addressed to women; comedy that recognizes the value of female experience may be an important step in developing a culture that allows women to self-critically question the sterotypes that have governed our lives. A strong, rebellious humor empowers women to examine how we have been objectified and fetishized and to what extent we have been led to perpetuate this objectification.

In feminist comedy, we are no longer cast as an omniscient audience laughing at a character 'unknowingly betraying' herself, rather, the context and the character interact in such a way as to stir our empathy as much as our amusement. It is the situation which is ridiculed, rather than the characters struggling to negotiate their circumstances. Questioning one's circumstances is a rebellious posture. To refuse to see the 'humor' in one's own victimization as the 'butt' of the joke or the 'object' of ridicule, while seizing and redefining the apparatus of comic perspective so that it is inclusive of women's experience is a necessary and powerful gesture of self-definition.

As Weisstein said:

> ... Women have not had a tradition of fighting and rebellious humor because the humor of the oppressed is based on a knowledge of shared oppression, and this has been hidden from us. ... We must ... throw off the shackles of self ridicule, self abnegation; we must tap ... that knowledge of our shared oppression. We must construct a women's culture with its own character, its fighting humor, its defiant celebration of our own worth. (90)

Works Cited

Beatts, Anne. "Can A Woman Get a Laugh and a Man, Too?" *Mademoiselle* Nov. 1975: 184.

Beatts, Anne, and Deanne Stillman, eds. *Titters*. New York: MacMillan, 1976.

Clinton, Catherine. Rev. of *Titters*. *Cultural Correspondence: Sex Roles and Humor*. 9 (Spring 1979): 30.

Coser, Rose Laub. "Laughter Among Colleagues." *Psychiatry*. 13 (1960): 81-95.

Davy, Kate. "Constructing the Spectator: Reception, Context and Address in Lesbian Performance." *Performing Arts Journal* 29 (1986): 43-53.

Gross, Amy. "Lily Tomlin on Lily Tomlin." *Mademoiselle* Nov. 1975: 141-186.

Henley, Nancy. *Body Politics*. Englewood Cliffs: Prentice, 1977.

Jenkins, Linda. "Locating the Language of Gender Experience." *Women and Performance: A Journal of Feminist Theory* 2 (1984): 5-20.

Meredith, George. *An Essay on Comedy*. 1897. Port Washington, N.Y.: Kennikat, 1972.

Merrill, Lisa. Rev. of *Feast or Famine* by Sondra Segal and Roberta Sklar. *Womannews* June 1985: 19.

Merrill, Lisa. Rev. of *The Search for Signs of Intelligent Life in the Universe*. by Jane Wagner. *Woman and Performance* 5 (1986): 97-99.

Rainer, Peter. "Five Women Comedy Writers Talk About Being Funny for Money." *Mademoiselle* Nov. 1975: 86.

Roethke, Theodore. *On The Poet and His Craft: Selected Prose of Theodore Roethke*. Ed. Ralph J. Mills. Seattle: U of Washington, 1965.

Sorell, Walter. *Facets of Comedy*. New York: Grosset and Dunlap, 1972.

Weisstein, Naomi. "Why We Aren't Laughing Anymore." *Ms*. Nov. 1973.

Daughters of anger/ material girls: con/textualizing feminist criticism

JANE MARCUS

CUNY Graduate Center and the City College of New York

> Her unemployment was about to run out. She had no car. She bicycled everywhere and claimed she would not work again until her anger was twenty-one.
> I'm dedicating my life to her, whatever the trends of the times. No more anger-sitters. No more camps or schools. No more lollipops. She's going to get all the advantages my expanse of years can provide, every opportunity to become what she wants to become, even if she just wants to get married and have lots of little angers.
> June Arnold, *Sister Gin*
> (Plainfield, Vermont: Daughters, Inc., 1975, 200)

"MATERIAL GIRLS"

A GESTURE OF connection between feminist critical theory and popular culture may be an appropriate beginning for this inquiry into the construction of the subject of feminist criticism. It asserts that there is a connection between the teens who cruise the malls and the feminists who cruise the halls (of academe). Madonna's popular song and rock video unsettles female commodity fetishism by buying into it and by asserting (especially to a Catholic working-class subculture in the U.S.) that women are the agents of their own desire and actors in history, not simply spiritual virgins who represent culture to men. Precedents for such a gesture are to be found in Elaine Showalter's "Critical Cross-Dressing" which reviews Jonathan Culler's work along with the film "Tootsie", the essays of Julia Lesage in *Jump-Cut* and Lillian Robinson in *Sex, Class and Culture*, which have consistently connected theory and canonical "literature" with film and non-canonical forms. "I'm just a material girl living in a material world."

It may seem obvious to some readers and outrageous to others that the process of the con-textualizing of feminist criticism, which I undertake here, should place our professional reading and writing practices in the context of the cultural production of a popular song. But it is becoming clear that the production of feminist literary theory is a result of our reading and writing practices as women in this culture. We read the texts of our fellow critics as we read women writers' texts, and this process is related to that of young women of a different class who "read" videos and listen to popular songs. That is, I am in the same relation to Gilbert and Gubar as my students are to Madonna. The construction of the female subject *in her body*, with her own history, is the project of *The Madwoman in the Attic, A Literature of Their Own* and Madonna's "Material Girl." As a reader of critical texts by feminists I experience a specific political pleasure in a material reading practice which goes beyond my "work". What is the relationship of one's problematic pleasure in the commodification of feminist criticism to our pleasure in reading the Virago Modern Classics? Should one resist these forms of the capitalization of feminism?

In the last ten years feminism as a movement has made it possible for "middlebrow" readers to consume texts with pleasure in the Barthean sense. We may now buy reprints of women's fiction stunningly packaged in paperback with jackets reproducing paintings of and often by women painters in either the early black Virago/Dial imprint or the new green Penguins. They are easily available in chain bookstores so that one is not obliged to seek out a specialist bookseller, and one may indulge and buy several at a time, in the same way that consumers of romance novels do. Intellectual women have their very own brand of commodity fetishism. We do not know the plots of these novels in advance as romance readers do, but we expect as they do, enormous pleasure in the reading process itself. We read feminist criticism with pleasure edged with danger. We are threatened and validated at the same time. Thus our personal and professional reading practices as women merge at the site of reading pleasure. We underline the fiction. We underline the criticism.

It should come as no surprise then that our writing practice as critics should change in relation to this experience, that hermeneutic decoding leading to mastery of the text should give way to a display of narrative pleasure. The intertextuality of ourselves with women writers' texts, in which we participate in shared experience as well as inscribing our own difference, allows us to write critically about the text without needing to master it, but rather to continue it. The pleasure in reading our fellow critics is not so pure. Male critics, if they feel these same tensions and joys, do not write about them. Professional/personal pulls, and the process of analyzing our work as we do it seems to be a result of our political feminism. The proliferation of new books of feminist criticism allows us to cross work and play, common experience and difference, as consumers and readers, and this is the most surprising example of pleasure in reading practice, that for the feminist critic it extends to the reading of other feminist critics. But it is also the site of extreme displeasure, arousing feelings of competition, neurotic involvement and envy. Our intertextuality with women's critical texts is as "dangerous" as the "fluid boundaries" we study among women writers and readers or mothers and daughters.

For the plot of my conceptualization of feminist criticism in this essay, I want to name Elaine Showalter and Susan Gubar and Sandra Gilbert the "Material Girls" of the discipline, in giving women's writing a body and a history, to claim their early work as "historical" in comparison with other modes of discourse within the field. The naming, like my plot, is clearly a fiction, for there are many ways in which this pioneering work is only minimally historical except in comparison with the voices of Lacanian or French psychoanalytical "feminisms". Their practices will then represent here a particular pragmatic "American" practice of textualizing the work of women writers as well as the explicit political activism of "institution-building", the formation of Women's Studies programs and the battle to establish a permanent place in universities for feminism, which seems to be the chief effect of the difference between "French" and "American" feminisms. The "Material Girls" do not share what British sociologist, Michèle Barrett, calls, in her paper for the 1986 Alabama Symposium, "psychic essentialism," nor the recently popular critical discourse of deconstruction in a social vacuum. They also represent, along with Annette Kolodny, to our male colleagues and to those outside the field, what feminist criticism is, although this perspective is always changing.

This places the American critics who use French theory in an odd position. Barbara Johnson, Elaine Marks, Jane Gallop, Peggy Kamuf — seem to differ from the "Material Girls" in that the primary commitment is to theory, while for Gilbert and Gubar and Showalter, the text is primary and theory often evolves from the study of the text. This may be an over-simplification, but it is, to my mind, the crucial distinction in the forms of critical practice among feminist critics. Despite their differences with other feminists, Gilbert and Gubar, as authors of *The Madwoman in the Attic* and editors of the *Norton Anthology of Literature by Women* are seen as leaders and path-breakers, their senior positions reflecting a very material presence in the academy, while younger feminists find them too angry or untheoretical.

My narrativization and contextualization of a version of the history of feminist criticism derives from contradictory tensions felt in negotiating my own position while teaching a seminar in Feminist Criticism and Theory at the University of Texas in 1985 and 1986. Since reviewers and students accepted Toril Moi's version of our history, it seemed necessary to correct her wholly inaccurate narrative, and to try to understand the ways in which I share the generational position of the "Material Girls" and their commitment both to establishing a history of women writers and restoring lost texts to the canon, and the building of Women's Studies as a field. But the differences are also clear — in my Marxist or socialist literary critical position and my interest in the "pre-history" of feminist criticism especially in the work of Virginia Woolf as a critic. While I admire the work of a Marxist-feminist critic like Gayatri Spivak, for example, I am troubled by her position on Women's Studies as a field. Here I want to address the problems of the disciplining of both feminist criticism and Women's Studies and their replication of male academic "gate-keeping." The peculiar pleasures and displeasures of reading narratives of the history of feminist criticism generated this re-writing and suggested an attempt at discussing the particular problem feminist critics have with the acknowledgment of predecessors, especially Virginia Woolf. This historical blind spot, the need to see themselves as "first feminists" I have dramatized in this paper using Woolf's story of "killing the angel in the house" in "Professions for Women."

The stimultaneous radicalism and conservatism of the "Material

Girls" may be attributed to the peculiar time-warps affecting feminist critical practice within the profession. Discussions at the Feminist Theory Symposium at Alabama, ("The Differences Within: Feminism and Critical Theory", organized by Elizabeth Meese and Alice Parker) and the SCMLA in New Orleans in Fall 1986, where a version of the present essay was delivered, served to sharpen one's perception of the time-warp. Many older scholars complained of finally having moved from their traditional work on the male canon to some form of Showalter's "gynocritics" only to find their work dismissed as unsophisticated by younger theorists. Younger theorists complained that established feminists felt threatened by their work and often refused professional help and support on the grounds that they had struggled alone against men in their departments or fields and were too wounded and exhausted from the struggle to help, as well as being jealous of the ease with which the younger women seem to build their careers. In addition, some perceived a problem with "ghettoized" conferences and journals where only the like-minded speak to each other. There is also a "horizontal hysteria" of competition among feminist critics which a sisterly ethos derived from the critics' experience as political feminists doesn't like to think about, much less analyze. I have argued that we read each other's work with pleasure in the same way that we read women's fiction. Our deep anxieties about these texts have yet to be examined. But because we read the critical texts of other feminists *as women*, we have more interest in and more to lose as readers if the plots of the critical texts differ from our own. If we are involved as women readers of women's fiction as co-makers of the text, in women's criticism we expect the same reading patterns to obtain, and are disturbed if they don't. In my experience, feminist critics are more disappointed if their readers misunderstand them than others, and feminist readers often feel as if they have *written* the book they are reading. As Anne Thackeray Ritchie said, it is sometimes hard to tell where the book ends and the reader begins. How does one get from identification to the "affinity" defined by Patsy Schweikart as the mark of a truly feminist reading practice?

The theoretical trajectories of individual critics are difficult to map. One may trace Gayatri Spivak's moves in *In Other Worlds* from Lacanian readings of Romantic poets to deconstruction to Marxism to feminism to a concern for Third World women. Nancy K. Miller traces her own moves from structuralism and narratology to a political concern with Women's Studies, while Mary Jacobus in *Reading Woman* seems to have moved from materialist culture-criticism to a French psychoanalytical position. But even these are not linear progressions and "isms" overlap or are used as strategies in different contexts. Because of the different rates at which talks are given and books and articles are published, read and absorbed by the community of feminist readers, the author has herself often moved in another direction by the time her theories are being discussed. Once we have read Kristeva's "Stabat Mater," how do we use and re-evaluate her previous work? All of this is, of course, healthy and invigorating for the field, if rather confusing for the reader.

The politics of inclusion, exclusion and allusion (in that strong sign of ideology, the footnote) in the new histories and anthologies of feminist criticism (which I shall discuss here) makes reputations and alliances, stakes out territory and marks boundaries. It is our responsibility to analyze and critique this process in ourselves and our new discipline as conscientiously and disrespectfully as formerly we attacked the male establishment. The other voice behind this essay ventriloquizes Virginia Woolf's in *A Room of One's Own*, where, in order to make a plot of a history of "cramped and thwarted" women writers she has had to create an angry Charlotte Bronte as a modern Judith Shakespeare and precursor to her own angry position. Readers and feminist critics have complained bitterly about what they see as Woolf's snobby dismissal of Bronte as "coarse" and angry, but they have ignored the internal logic of the historical movement of the text as it invents "mothers" to think back through, and her need to establish Bronte as "angry" and frustrated. From the perspective of awareness of the intersection of women writers and readers, it is obvious that Woolf knowingly reads Bronte as an enraged interrupter of her own discourse and names that practice as feminist because Bronte does it, and then does it herself as a reader and rewriter of Bronte. I have needed to highlight the anger in the political stance and in the definition of women writers in the work of Gilbert and Gubar and Showalter to make them into the Judith Shakespeare and Charlotte Brontes of feminist criticism, fictional outrageous and angry "Material Girls", a position which in their own time-frames they may have left far behind. In fact there are several ironies here. As they have become the establishment, the anger and the study of anger in women writers have diminished. They are no longer martyred like Judith Shakespeare. They live; they write; in fact, they flourish. It is the Marxist-feminists who are the movement's real martyrs.

THE DE-FANGING OF FEMINIST CRITICISM

The particular conjunction of anger with gender and reading marks the feminism of the seventies, with Kate Millett's powerful *Sexual Politics* setting the tone. The sublimation of that anger and the formation of feminist discursive communities of women readers and writers has produced a distinctive style of feminist discourse in the eighties. I would argue that the distinguished and unique style of feminist criticism, the wily wit, self-conscious word play and outrageous punning characteristic of the recent writing of Catharine Stimpson, Nancy K. Miller, Carolyn Heilbrun, Elaine Showalter in "Critical Cross-Dressing," Mary Ann Caws in "Ladies Shot and Painted" in *The Female Body in Western Culture* and the editorials of Shari Benstock in *Tulsa Studies in Women's Literature*, are at least in part, a dramatization of anger transformed into verbal skill.[1] While the work of Foucault, Derrida, Kristeva and Cixous may also be a model for *jouissance* in criticism itself, the strategy of writing criticism to please the reader, to share pleasure rather than rage, laughter rather than scoring points against the patriarchy, heralds a new self-assurance on the part of feminist critics, implying an already convinced audience of women readers. If the critic can situate herself within a circle of sympathetic readers, the necessity for lifting a lance against "the enemy" becomes less acute. Like the heroine of June Arnold's *Sister Gin*, the offspring of that angry generation may have gotten married and produced "lots of little angers." The little angers have reproduced themselves in great numbers in the graduate schools. The big angers have a space in which to make jokes. When we laughed together we had become a community.

In my own case the shift in tone may be strictly economic, indicating a job and tenure in the academy, including but just barely, as the joke has it, tenure before menopause, a real problem in women's career patterns. I was not born a theorist, but was made into one, at least temporarily, by teaching a theory seminar. I have learned a great deal I would have preferred to ignore by burying myself in the library. "Still Practice"[2] was the result of trying to define a female aesthetic in terms of repetition, dailiness and process, as well as to distinguish socialist feminist criticism from other modes. Here I would like to survey the current scene and look at the future. Perspective makes all the difference. I wrote the first version of this essay in Paris after having spent a semester learning from my students the variety and quality of French Feminisms in the newly translated volumes of Irigaray, Sarah Kofman and the work of Kristeva. I have been dazzled by Jane Gallop reading Lacan and wish that her school had the respect for American material historicism that many of us are trying to give to French linguistic psychoanalysis.[3]

This experience of reading theory has reinforced my commitment to the historical, for I believe that every new argument I have admired would have been strengthened by contextualization as well as by serious textual scholarship. I worry that theory isolated from scholarship may become a cynical game students may play with any text, without that experience of reading easily and deeply within all aspects of culture which makes Barthes' "play" so rich a critique. But then it is equally true that practical criticism without theory is often dull and uninspiring. If the two work together in a particular essay and its language is accessible to the reader in a practice which disavows mastery of the text, something of permanent value will have been accomplished. One difference between French and American feminisms is the difference in their habits of asking questions. If I have learned nothing else from Sarah Kofman's recuperation of Freud in *The Enigma of Woman*, the boldness of her question, What would have happened if Freud had studied women criminals instead of hysterics? resonates in the mind.[4] This seems to me a particularly French question, linking women with criminals as outsiders. It has a particular poignance now that fate has linked Simone de Beauvoir with Jean Genet in their deaths, and their photographs and books sit together in the window of Left Bank book shops. This cultural difference, it occurs to me, might make an interesting slant on the reading of lesbian novels. *La Batarde*, for example, written against the French homosexual novel, defines lesbianism in relation to the criminal with Genet's work as a defining predecessor. American coming-out novels dramatize a family romance plot within a different cultural script.

However much writers from other schools may criticize Elaine Showalter, Sandra Gilbert and Susan Gubar, they have completed a great historical task, by insisting on the separate study of women writers and by collecting, naming and criticizing those writers. This reaching out to the mass of readers, however much one may quibble over the choice of texts, is characteristic of the political nature of American feminism and its struggle to change institutions, unlike the French intellectual engagement with individual male thinkers, like Freud or Lacan. The writing of the American critics is aimed democratically at a very large audience of "common readers," not a small academic coterie, in a political gesture to change hearts and minds. They have played the role Virginia Woolf ascribed to the political feminism of Ethel Smyth, as the "amoured tanks" who make it possible for foot soldiers to cross the narrow bridge of art. They have withstood the enemy's fire. One wishes to defend them from the distortions of Toril Moi, but can we remain silent about the homophobia and racism which mark some of this writing? The paradigm of the "battle of the sexes" is too narrow to explore all the varieties of women's writing.

What is this sudden rush to write histories of feminist criticism, the publication of several different anthologies claiming to cover the field? Is feminist criticism dead, that everyone is writing its epitaph and lining up the gravestones in order? Actually, I think it is a case of "she who writes history makes history." That is, feminist criticism has become respectable enough as a discipline for the gatekeepers to come out of the closet to certify the practitioners and license their continued work. The hierarchy is being established, and female genres, schools of writing and reading, pervasive themes and the ranking of literary and critical texts as first or second rate marks the containment of an undisciplined discipline which vowed never to be contained. The vital anger in the language of insubordination in, say, the work of Jane Gallop, Nina Auerbach, Nina Baym, Lillian Robinson, is being defanged by "objective" historical naming and ordering of their voices, herding their essays into schools major and minor, choosing "leaders" major and minor.

I am not opposed to literary history and there is a great deal to be said for writing the biography before the author is dead. But the first historians of any subject assume a tremendous authority. It is very difficult for the next generation to deny or oppose their categories and judgments. Women writers have been written out of literary history by this very process, a lesson feminist critics know very well. But recognition of a mistake doesn't keep one from making it. There is a story I tell my students about the power of the historian. When I went to England as a graduate student to study the Women's Suffrage movement, I had read Sylvia Pankhurst's history, which stresses the role of working class women. As a socialist feminist I identified both with her and her political values. In addition she had written a "big" book, a "serious" history, and the memoirs of her mother and sister were slight or ghost-written, lacking in "authority." It was very painful to me as a young scholar with my mind made up, having swallowed Sylvia Pankhurst's version of events, to be forced by arguments with Jill Craigie, to read the primary documents, newspapers, letters and speeches, and to recognize Sylvia Pankhurst's self-serving analysis as one-sided. The power of that first history is such that we still do not have a reliable history of Women's Suffrage in England, one which can overcome the authority of the initial text. Jill Craigie argues that Mrs. Pankhurst and her daughter Christabel were so confident that many survivors of the campaign for the vote would write the "true" history that they did not make strong objections. The problem with all the new histories of feminist criticsm is that they have nothing in common. The territory being staked out is nothing less than the *construction of the subject* of feminist criticism. We cannot allow this process to continue unmediated by consciousness of ideologies at play and at work here. Have feminists themselves reproduced patriarchal "gatekeeping" in our journals, and our roles within institutions?

The self-defined "firstness" of Showalter's *Feminist Criticism and Theory* is one of its dangers. Aside from ignoring her contemporary predecessors, she ignores the past, and defines a mainstream feminism from personal practice, thereby relegating all "different" feminisms to the margins once again. Each of the new histories has a gap or gaps, leaving out work which is crucial to others. Each privileges a particular methodology, theory or theorist. Each has virtues but not all the virtues. You cannot order one text for your class. My students felt that Elaine Showalter's anthology, *Feminist Criticism and Theory*, was obsolete on publication, a gesture backwards toward history rather than providing them with current models for their own work.[5] (This canonization of particular feminist essays has its own problems.) They point out that even as a collection of important American work, it leaves out essays by Catharine Stimpson, Myra Jehlen and Gayatri Spivak, which were equally important in the early development of the field.

Most of the new feminist anthologies reprint or discuss Bonnie Zimmerman's well-known essay on lesbian criticism as well as including a section on Black feminist criticism. The editors might have more challengingly reprinted Monique Wittig's "The Straight Mind" (from *Feminist Issues*) as well. Few of the writers integrate the insights of these works into their own concerns and these fundamental issues of race, class and sexual identity remain isolated from mainstream discussions. Yet Black feminist criticism is the most exciting work being done.

This does, of course, reflect the problem on the pragmatic front of integrating women into the university curriculum as well. For often we can only succeed in adding courses relating to women rather than changing the basic structures of the disciplines. Then one is preaching to the converted. Each of the new volumes, K.K. Ruthven's *Feminist Literary Studies*, Gayle Green and Coppelia Kahn's *Making a Difference: Feminist Literary Criticism* and Toril Moi's *Sexual/Textual Politics: Feminist Literary Theory*, like Elaine Showalter's book, claims to present a history and overview of the subject.[6] Several other volumes with other contributors are announced or in press. *Each "history" then is an act of erasure as well as an act of preservation. Each historian commits murder as well as resurrecting the dead.*

Each of the accounts of the rise of feminist criticism presents a different, though thoroughly presentist, a-historical account of the origins of feminist criticism. Toril Moi castigates Kate Millett for not acknowledging Mary Ellman as predecessor, but she does not cite Germaine Greer, Juliet Mitchell or Sheila Rowbotham, whose thinking helped to form the basis of early American feminist criticism. Including the "French" Americans would destroy her case, so she leaves out Johnson, Gallop, Kamuf, etc. Only K.K. Ruthven seems to take Mary Daly seriously. Why do most American feminists ignore Daly's work, especially when our students find it so invigorating? The strong American group studying mothers and daughters using Object Relations theory and Nancy Chodorow's work is completely ignored by Toril Moi and K.K. Ruthven, and given a cursory nod by Showalter, though it is meticulously explicated as methodology in *Making a Difference* by Judith Kegan Gardiner, whose rigor as a scholar and bibliographer might have been taken as an example by other careless editors and contributors. Ruthven gives French feminism short shrift. Toril Moi's chapters on Lacan, Cixous, Kristeva and

Irigaray are so clear, well-argued and exemplary, that one is amazed at the complete ignorance, prejudice and bias in her chapters on Woolf and the feminist critics and on specific American feminist critics.

Mary Ellmann, Kate Millett and Ellen Moers all consciously used *A Room of One's Own* as a model for their own work. Susan Friedman often points out the way that Simone de Beauvoir's concept of woman as other is absorbed by feminists and not acknowledged. What does it mean for the history of feminist criticism that Showalter and the other editors categorically define the origins of the discipline in the 1970's? Why do they reject their own precursors? Why do Elaine Showalter and Sandra Gilbert attack Virginia Woolf? That two such prominent feminist critics consistently make a point of attacking their feminist precursor (who is not acknowledged as a *critic*) makes one wonder if Harold Bloom's theory of the 'anxiety of influence" applies to the history of criticism as well as to poets. Since the Oedipal struggle seems to apply only to men, perhaps we will need to analyse this critical act on the part of feminist critics as a form of "killing the angel in the house." Woolf's drama of the woman writer murdering the female voice of caution may explain their need to repudiate or deny her. Those of us who struggled in the last decade with the Woolf literary estate and their devaluation and distortion of her work have often felt that it was a losing battle, if Showalter called *A Room of One's Own* "a tomb," and Gilbert claimed that war was the pacifist's muse. Perhaps they need to see Woolf as crippled in the same way that she neeed to see Charlotte Bronte as cramped and thwarted. Woolf would have been shocked at this turn of events. Some form of literary irony is being enacted when Showalter and Gilbert label Woolf a spiritual angel or inhibiting force in feminist progress. They have thrown their inkpots (or word processors) at her head. Rejecting Woolf as a literary mother they have named themselves as mothers of feminist criticism. Matricide is as limited a model for literary history as patricide. D.W. Winnicott deconstructs the good mother/bad mother dichotomy with the "good enough mother." Feminists might profit from discarding their good sister/bad sister judgmental categories for the "good enough sister." It may be mischievous of me to see them as Judith Shakespeares in the history of feminist criticism when their denial of the critical power of Virginia Woolf is so strong. My motives are neither pure nor objective. Assumption of maternal authority and denial of their own "mothers," merely mimics the patriarchal paradigm. Aside from being historically inaccurate, it invites the fury and rebellion of the next generation of "daughters of anger" to name them as "bad mothers." Along with Susan Lanser, who is working on a history of women critics, I would argue that there has always been a feminist criticism. We just need to find it and to name it and to claim it as our own.

One could quickly put together a volume of Victorian feminist criticism, and the suffragettes produced many fine examples of the genre in their journals and papers. Rebecca West poured forth a stream of brilliant and provocative feminist reviews and essays for over seventy years. I think fondly of her annual attacks on *War and Peace* as a patriarchal travesty. I'm sure that there are French and American examples of such at the very least proto- feminist critics. Why this myopia? What are the political reasons, and surely the reasons are political, for ignoring the fact that we write in a tradition with radical predecessors? We may safely suppose that Sappho was surrounded by feminist critics, that Germaine de Stael and George Sand could be said to have contributed to the field. We would do well to take the vertical long view as well as the broad multi-cultural view. If we complain about the lost or muffled voices of women in history, how can anyone write the history of feminist criticism in America without recalling its oral splendors, the era of speeches and eloquent addresses, the angry and inspiring voices of Adrienne Rich, Florence Howe, Carolyn Heilbrun and Tillie Olsen, stuttering out our own inarticulateness, the editorial voices of Catharine Stimpson and Domna Stanton at SIGNS, the collective at Feminist Studies, the lesbian and black presses, Kitchen Table and Daughters, Inc.? The theories came out of political practice, out of meetings and debates. History is not merely what was printed in books. In addition, the feminist critical manifestoes of the poets, Rich's "When We Dead Awaken," Tillie Olsen's *Silences*, Alicia Ostriker's essays — have served as models for the tasks we have in common. The literary historian might well ask whether other kinds of criticism were stirred around in the pots of poetry and politics, the pragmatics, for example, of Annette Kolodny's tenure case and the national support of women scholars for her cause, the polemics and fact gathering of the Women's Caucus of the MLA and the Commission on the Status of Women. It seems to me essential when studying the differences between French,

American and British feminist criticism and theory, to set them in relation to institutions, to the academy and the presses. The political events of May, 1968 in France as well as Irigaray's struggle with the Lacanian school are important here. Gisela Ecker's *Feminist Aesthetics*, for example, gives Anglo-American feminists a sense of how different the German questions are, working in a different national context of the philosophy of aesthetics.[7]

As an example of cross-cultural misunderstanding we may look at Toril Moi's misreading of the treatment of Woolf by American feminists. As a Norwegian student of Terry Eagleton writing in England, she defines herself as semi-marginal to the discourse she discusses. Because Elaine Showalter is an acknowledged leader in the field, Moi assumes that her book was accepted uncritically in the U.S., which was certainly not the case, and that the hostile last chapter of *A Literature of Their Own* is indicative of American feminist wholesale rejection of Woolf. This is not only ridiculous and inaccurate, it denies the real issue, which is the rejection of Woolf by British feminists working in a field dominated by Leavis-trained intellectuals who valorized Lawrence because of his correct class credentials and rejected Woolf as an elitist. As a "lupine critic" my bias and concern for the collective nature of our enterprise in *New Feminist Essays on Virginia Woolf* and *Virginia Woolf: A Feminist Slant*, is evident. A full bibliography of American feminist Woolf criticism is provided in "Storming the Toolshed." Since Moi lists the *SIGNS* collection in which this essay appeared in her bibliography, one may assume it was not ignorance but politics which allowed her to dismiss a decade and a half of American feminist interpretation of Woolf. Moi disclaims "lupine" biographical and textual studies of Woolf. In particular she mocks the "assertions" in "Thinking Back Through Our Mothers," failing to recognize the strategy of counter-assertion about Woolf in an essay written in the middle 70's to oppose Quentin Bell's assertions in his biography. Her other objection is to my proposition that Woolf be read as a "thinker" with Walter Benjamin. Such elementary spade work may be boring in comparison to flashy intellectual theorizing, but if we are going to theorize over our mother-writers' graves, we had better know who is buried there and whether the stones are marked correctly.

Obviously, Toril Moi does not know that Elaine Showalter's Woolf chapter has been discreetly avoided by American feminists.[8] I have been troubled by British feminist rejection of Woolf, particularly on the left, since my first year working in English libraries in 1969. Michèle Barrett recently told me that she was forced to remove the word "theory" from her discussion of *A Room of One's Own* by Woolf's publishers because they insisted that Woolf was a writer, not a thinker. My own analysis is that Showalter's negative view of Woolf may have been a gesture toward the Leavisite legacy of the '70's, although others feel that her attack on Woolf was meant to distinguish her work from that of feminist Woolf scholars, or, alternately to reject the notion of "androgyny" and its identification with Woolf which surfaced in feminist criticism at the time. The dismissal of Woolf was a mark of one's Left credentials in British circles, an ideological identification mark which appears to have gone unread by those whose allegiance was sought. Consequently, Toril Moi's attack is all the more ironic.

Leavis' legacy still lives, for similar views are expressed in Cora Kaplan's essay in *Making a Difference*. While Moi rejects the work of feminist Woolf scholars on the grounds that it was written without benefit of post-structuralist theory, which is indeed the case, she then asserts as her own the main points of the arguments, claiming to be the first critic to see the importance of the politics of *A Room of One's Own* and *Three Guineas* and the deconstructive nature of the presentation of gender in Woolf's novels. Though I have a personal stake in this evaluation, Moi's mistakes seem to me to be a classic representation of the problem of valuing the theoretical over the practical.

Gilbert and Gubar are at least given the courtesy of a summary of their argument before being dismissed by Moi as weak on post-structuralist theory. Anyone claiming to write a history of feminist criticism cannot ignore the major part played by Gilbert and Gubar in creating and defining the field. In addition one must protest that Kristevan and other French theory which Moi valorizes, lacks the great contextualizing force of Gilbert and Gubar's book. Trained in close reading and intellectual history in the American tradition, they excel at the practice which French psychoanalytical feminism ignores, of reading texts in history. This is not an excuse; it is a fact. Working against mainstream practice, in their own universities and isolated from the few places where European theory was read, they yet produced a solid body of work. They are "good enough mothers" of all our subsequent work. Students will doubtless take their work further, combining history with new theoretical questions. But *The Madwoman in the Attic* remains a monumental accomplishment, in some senses, because it provides students of women's writing with one version of that history, open immediately to revision and rewriting. The virtue of the work of the new generation, the "daughters of anger," is that they move comfortably back and forth between material and theoretical practice, as in the work of Christine Froula, Elizabeth Abel or Celeste Schenck.[9] While it remains to be seen in practice which theories will survive, the great work of recuperation of women's texts in English has been begun by Showalter and Gilbert and Gubar. Much remains to be done, especially in the recuperation of Black and other minority writers, in which the groundwork has been done by critics like Barbara Christian, Nellie McKay, Hortense Spillers, Mary Helen Washington, Deborah McDowell, Barbara Johnson, Trudier Harris, Hazel Carby and Susan Willis.

We must continue our feminist political work within the institutions of our cultures, produce histories of women and their writing in mainstream and minority cultures, read and teach the writing of women from other cultures than our own, and read, write and re-write theory to account for global perspectives on race and class as well as gender. We also need to discuss openly the false divisions and taxonomic tyranny of separating feminist theoriests from Women's Studies scholars. One of our most serious problems is that our age produces more "theory" than we can comfortably assimilate, and very little of our work actually builds on the work of others. It remains to be seen in the work of the next generation of critics what the integration of these points of view will produce. Judging from the work of my own students I predict some very interesting readings based on the combination of materialist, psychological and linguistic analysis. My own recent work on Djuna Barnes, while grounded in the American tradition of recuperation of a "a lost" text of female modernism, seeking to place it in the context and anti-fascist politics, benefits greatly from Bakhtin's analysis of the language of carnival and Kristeva's concept of abjection in *Powers of Horror*. In both cases, however the theories have had to be extended to cover the female example.[10]

What exactly is at issue in this absolutely false battle between European theory and American practice? It seems to my suspicious and historical mind that the idea of death of the author, the lack of authority in unstable texts and the exclusion of women from language itself, have arrived on the intellectual scene at a very convenient historical moment for the patriarchy. Like Nancy K. Miller and Elizabeth Fox-Genovese, I find it necessary to reject this philosophical stance. *Their* authors may be dead, but ours, to use Woolf's description of Judith Shakespeare, have hardly put on their bodies. We need some historical space and time, to praise, dispraise and appraise their writing before we bury them. While a "hermeneutics of suspicion" may not seem appropriate for reading literature, it does seem appropriate for reading the new histories of feminist criticism, to understand their political inclusions and exclusions. Why, I wonder, when we have just begun to write women's biographies and tried to reconstruct their lives, as well as the lives of other oppressed peoples, is the whole enterprise deemed a waste of time? Male critics are understandably bored with their canon and its authority, but their problems are very different. We are still in the process of recuperation of lost women writers and there are those who are concerned that Gilbert and Gubar's alternate "canon" with its paradigm of anger, excludes other women's texts which do not fit. Counter-canons can be as limiting as canons.

Must the feminist condense a century's worth of reading practice into one essay in order first to revive the writer and work, then deconstruct the whole edifice to show her skill? The feminist critic is expected to be like the working wife and mother, superwoman who can do three jobs at once. I am also suspicious of the language question for it arrives at precisely the moment when women are speaking in unprecedented numbers and reviving the words of those who spoke before them. I endorse Catharine Stimpson's "transparent, but adhesive, allegiance to placing women and language in a kinetic history that we can nevertheless map." I agree with her confession that "So erring, feminist critics (I among them) have used literature as proof simple of patriarchal squalors," but that this was a necessary stage in our growth.[11] In *Making A Difference*, two psychoanalytic Shakespeare critics survey the field with bibliographical essays covering the major work in each particular branch. The Gardiner essay is as thorough and exemplary as the introduction and the chapters by Nelly Furman and Ann Rosalind Jones. Susan Willis' essay argues that "black women problematize the notion of community" and resist the tendency in bourgeois fiction to isolate the individual, that journey is an extended metaphor for the process of self-definition. Like Nina Auerbach in the theory issue of *Tulsa Studies in Women's Literature*, Adrienne Munich takes a deconstructive stance against Showalter's "gynocritics," arguing that feminist critics should analyze male texts. She reads Nel and Sula in Toni Morrison's novel as "two kinds of female critics," arguing that simply reviling the male text "participates in the dialectic." "Nurturant criticism," Munich cautions, "is particularly dangerous for feminist critics of canonical texts; 'milkwarm commiseration' turns sour because it infantalizes. One way out of the dilemma is benign disrespect." Can we read feminist criticism with the same "benign disrespect"?

GRACE POOLE'S LAUGH

Unlike most of the other contributors to *Making a Difference*, whose project was to produce thorough bibliographies for specific subdivisions of the discipline, Cora Kaplan provides a minimum of notes, thus it appears that there is a very short list of socialist feminist critics. In the unfortunately titled "Pandora's Box", which makes no reference to the ironies of using the myth most well-documented as a reversal of a story of women's power, Kaplan joins Showalter and Gilbert in denying Woolf's power as a feminist predecessor in critical theory, but her denial is different; Woolf is rejected on the grounds of her attitude toward class. Despite the citation of Gareth Stedman Jones' *The Languages of Class*, which argues against one essential anterior reference point of class in a text, Kaplan reads Woolf's response to *Jane Eyre* in the essentialist style she disavows, in relation to what she reads as "contempt" for her servants in Woolf's diaries, and a class bias on the part of Woolf to the revolutionary vision of Jane Eyre on the top floor of Thornfield, linking millions of men "in silent revolt against their lot" with women. It is strange that Kaplan ignores the socialism which is inseparable from Woolf's feminism.

The romantic socialist vision of the charwoman informs all of Woolf's fiction and remains in constant dialectic with her real experience with servants in daily life. As the socialist daughter of a privileged family, Woolf was in revolt against her background and lived an austere life by comparison. We may note as well that the post-war reduction of the servant class left masters and servants alike confused as witnessed by interminable BBC debates on the topic. Woolf's portraits of servants and charwomen in her fiction are extremely resonant with all the contradictions, including the conservative views of old servants, like Crosby in *The Years*, still subservient when the system itself had dispersed. To castigate Woolf for being disturbed by the personal problems created by having responsibilities to old family servants when the ideology which upheld the tradition was in its last stages of disintegration, is myopic. Unlike Kaplan, I happen to agree with Woolf that Charlotte Bronte never did get "her genius expressed whole and entire." Our efforts to read class as well as gender in Woolf's text have failed if so many readers ignore or misread its class issues or its lesbian connections in favor of reading it as a bourgeois feminist text. The passage which Virginia Woolf leaves out of her long quote from *Jane Eyre* is not only not evidence of class bias but the most interesting passage from the point of view of the importance of the trope of absence as a key to *A Room of One's Own*. The hermeneutics of absence problematizes *A Room of One's Own* in its use of ellipses as an organizing principle to mirror the absence of women from patriarchal history, of women's writing from the canon. What is absent from the quotation from Jane Eyre — "*to open my inward ear to a tale that was never ended — a tale my imagination created and narrated continuously; quickened with all of incident, life, fire, feeling, that I desired and had not in my actual existence.*" (emphasis added) (page 110, 1976 Oxford edition) — is Jane Eyre's narrativization of herself as the heroine of Woolf's text, Judith Shakespeare. The woman listening to herself speaking, the dialogue between Jane Eyre's "inward ear" and the continuous tale, is exactly what Woolf means by "thinking back through our mothers" in *A Room of One's Own*. Woolf's ellipses mark a feminist reading practice in punctuation. The gaps, signifying what has been struck out or suppressed, are privileged as the feminist "political unconscious" of the text, awakening the attentive reader to the holes in the historical narrative. Charlotte Bronte qualifies for a place in this process by her anger and suffering. If Bronte had overcome the obstacles to women writing, Woolf's whole argument would fall apart. Woolf's text needs another victim/heroine here, a 19th century Shakespeare's sister, to complete her historical pattern. She is not "indicting" Charlotte Bronte (surely the praise which begins in Woolf's very first published essay and continued to the end of her life belies this) as Kaplan claims. Woolf's "How could she help but die young, cramped and thwarted?" is a melodramatic question dictated by the necessity of her narrative, to bring the ghost of Judith Shakespeare up to the present. Charlotte Bronte is young as a writer but old to be pregnant, which links her to the pregnant Judith Shakespeare and gives a physical dimension to the words "cramped and thwarted," relating writing to giving birth. The elided passage is privileged in its revelation of the clue to Bronte's place in ths history of woman's thwarted genius, her place in "the tale that was never ended." The tale really doesn't end. Isa's "abortive" poems in *Between the Acts* are unfinished lyrics of flight from the patriarchal family. She is Woolf's last Judith Shakespeare. Woolf not only did not reject Bronte's or Jane Eyre's aesthetic, as Kaplan argues, she incorporated it into her own. In addition, the radical statement which is quoted from *Jane Eyre*, which links the class revolt with feminism, is explicitly restated in *A Room of One's Own* in aesthetic terms, moving Jane's argument from the realm of history to the realm of art in Woolf's socialist argument that "masterpieces are not single and solitary births." It is my belief that to deny to the English reading public the individual genius of Shakespeare, a belief which no amount of Marxist or feminist criticism has yet been able to shake, is a very radical statement, and it is puzzling that a socialist critic should miss this.

Woolf's version of what she calls the "jerk," "the awkward break" in Bronte's style, the mention of "Grace Poole's laugh" after the passionate passage on the confinement of women, is the use of similar "jerks" and "breaks," the deliberate use of ellipses (especially to signify the censored subject of lesbianism as well as the subjectivity of censorship particularly in relationship to *The Well of Loneliness*) to mark her own text with its unsaid lesbian obsession as part of the history of cramped and thwarted unexpressed female genius. *Jane Eyre* is valorized by Woolf's imitation of the "jerks" and "breaks" as the signs of women's writing practice and Woolf thematizes interruption (in the story of Jane Austen) as well as rhetorically structuring the whole book as a series of narrative interruptions. What Kaplan does not experience as a reader is the nature of Woolf's inside/outside class position, problematized by the multiple narrative voice in *A Room of One's Own* of at least four "Marys." Woolf is not narrating with authority, but placing the very text we are reading in the tradition of "deformed and twisted" writing by women. *A Room of One's Own* is indeed a "deformed" and "twisted" text in the female tradition, which includes *Jane Eyre*, but not because of its class analysis. Rather, it argues a lesbian separatist case for feminism and then backs off.

I would argue as well that as a reader Woolf was disturbed by Jane Eyre's mention of hearing "Grace Poole's laugh." Later Jane learns that the laugh belongs to Bertha Mason, the madwoman in the attic. The sliding of nurse into patient, the Kristevan "semiotic" sound of libidinal voices, I suspect, reminded Virginia Woolf of her own experience of madness, the hearing and uttering of that laughter, the forbidden sounds of sexuality and aggression (King Edward shouting obscenities and the birds speaking Greek). She knew first hand what it was to be locked up and guarded by a nurse. I think of Rachel's vision of the sinister nurse in *The Voyage Out*. Suppose that Woolf read *Jane Eyre* as Jean Rhys did in *Wide Sargasso Sea* and this "jerk" or "break" shifted her reading from identification with Jane to identification with Bertha Mason? What I am arguing then is that Woolf marks Bronte's jerks and breaks as signifiers of a woman's writing practice thus valorizing the trope of interruption in her own text, her dashes and ellipses, the violent breaks in her own narrative. Bronte is then the producer of the mother text to which *A Room of One's Own* is daughter.

Woolf's reading experience of "rage" in the text of *Jane Eyre* might mark another "class" difference between Kaplan's reading and Woolf's and Rhys', where Bertha's absent semiotic screams are heard in "Grace Poole's laugh." If Jane Eyre is the 19th century Judith Shakespeare, the thwarted woman artist; Grace Poole's laugh indicates the voices of the other oppressed female figures excluded from art, the servant, the madwoman, the racial "other." We know Woolf as the other writing the other Other in Susan Squier's reading of *Flush*; and I have argued that Woolf writes the voice of the charwoman in every novel, making a socialist subtext articulating the political unconscious of working women in her fiction. In addition, as an ex-madwoman, Woolf was always aware of the suspicious eyes and ears of servants, family and friends in her own life, waiting to hear in Virginia Woolf's laugh the voice of the "Bertha Mason" she had been and could well become again. The laugh of the servant/nurse might also have been read by Woolf as the mark of the servant's power over a mad mistress, in which roles were reversed, a reminder of the ambivalent social and sexual position of the nurse/nanny in Victorian families. Freud's obsession with this figure is brilliantly analyzed by

Jane Gallop in *The Daughter's Seduction*. In Woolf's family the resident servants, as well as the nurses in private clinics, knew the secrets of a family with many "mad" members. The possession of these secrets gave them the power of emotional blackmail and gave a double edge to the guilt a socialist woman would have felt about the murky border between exploitation and responsibility, which gave a peculiar form of power to the powerless, similar to the "power" of subservient women in patriarchy.

Woolf's attribution of rage to Charlotte Bronte was a compliment, a ticket into the select company of Shakespeare's sisters. My own anger in this essay will indicate to future readers my precise historical place in American feminist criticism; the jerks and breaks in this critical discourse will be heard by a new generation of Virginia Woolfs as Grace Poole's laugh, and perhaps be traced to its origins in Bertha Mason's semiotic screams. Also I am convinced by Jean Wyatt in "A Patriarch of One's Own" that Jane Eyre and Bertha Mason collaborate in a fantasy to satisfy the reader's rage against the patriarchy, where Jane's speech and Bertha's laugh combine "to appeal to the reader's unconscious fantasies of revenge while analyzing the oppression that cause them." (207) And I take heart from Mary Ann Caws' recent argument that eventually feminist critics will find "an integration of ourselves" in the larger interpretive community, that meanwhile we have the right to spell out the difference within difference in the circulation of gifts of reading and rereading, the energy to "grit our teeth," "arm our wits and tongues," using our anger and refusing silence.[12]

READING LIKE A WOMAN

Someone complained that I always stopped while I was driving to read the sign posts even when I knew the road and all I could explain was that I am fond of reading, well I am, I like people and politics and painting but I am really fond of reading, there that's all.

(Gertrude Stein, letter to Edmund Wilson)

The question I have tried to answer in discussing Kaplan's critique of Woolf, the failure to try to understand Woolf's reading of Bronte, in her own terms as a feminist critic, raises the issue of why feminist reader response criticism is not included in any of the new anthologies. What Gertrude Stein is talking about is the material pleasure in reading-for-itself, a fondness for the sign in spite of its relation to the signified, a reading practice which I see as marked by gender. Women readers stop to read the sign posts even when they know the road. The members of my seminar shared my pleasure in Patsy Schweickart's "Reading Ourselves: Toward a Feminist Theory of Reading."[13] Schweickart explicates the process of reading like a woman, and she argues her case with a firm material base in historical reality. She points out that feminist literary criticism is an act of reading and that the site of our political quest to change the world is at the intersection of reader and text. Schweickart writes:

> The relative tranquility of the tone of these theories testifies to the privileged position of the theorists (Booth and Culler). Perhaps, someday, when privileges have withered away or at least become more equitably distributed, one or other of these theories will ring true. Surely we ought to be able to talk about theory without worrying about injustice....

Like Patsy Schweickart and Catharine Stimpson, I consider it absolutely necessary to worry about injustice, to remember that feminism is a politics and that the practice of feminist criticism need not suppress its anger to mimic the tranquility of tone of privileged critics. In *A Room of One's Own* Woolf called the woman reader's anger "simple and open" as compared to the "disguised and complex" anger of the male professors. This "disguised and complex" anger at feminism is a strong subtext in K.K. Ruthven's *Feminist Literary Studies*. It also marks the power moves of Culler and Eagleton in situating themselves above feminist theory as producers of knowledge about it. Taxonomy, once the province of pedantry, is now the hallmark of hegemony. When Adam names the game, he depoliticizes and de-materializes feminist theory as just another strategy for reading texts.

Schweickart cites Adrienne Rich's essay on Emily Dickinson, "Vesuvius at Home," as an exemplary feminist reading strategy, non-resisting, arguing by metaphor, and personal in a way which presents the reader as witness in defense of the writer and proposes a "conversational" relationship between the woman writer and reader. How can this model take the place of the pleasure/displeasure case outlined at the beginning of this essay? Is such a sisterly reading only possible for a poet reading another poet? Is competitiveness necessary in culture criticism? The intersubjectivity of text and author, Schweickart explains, is kept from being dominated by the reader since the author and text cannot talk back) by the reader's awareness of the historical context of writer and work, and assertion of affinity with the writer, not identification. Further, Schweickart argues that Rich's model reading of Dickinson is validated by the offering of her reading to a community of feminist readers and writers. Critical reading and writing is more of a problem. We are all victims and perpetrators of the politics of inclusion, exclusion, and allusion.

The "benign disrespect" advocated by Adrienne Munich in "Notorious Signs" toward canonical male texts may be seen as one of the postures of "daughters of anger." It seems a useful strategy for the discussion of K.K. Ruthven's *Feminist Literary Studies* as well. Shrewdly, Munich argues "Critical discourse has tended to be more misogynist than the texts it examines," so it should come as no surprise that a male critic summarizing and categorizing forms of feminist discourse should exhibit impatience, exaggeration and the "disguised" and "complex" anger Woolf attributed to academics of his gender. But it is not his gender alone which distorts Ruthven's text. All of the new histories are flawed by haste in the race to become gatekeepers to the new discipline, sole distributors of legitimacy and licenses to practice. Linnaean classifications are often useful but they are not as scientifically objective as they pretend to be. Mr. Ruthven is betrayed by his tone. His distance, irony and skepticism are meant to form an alliance with a reading audience assumed to be equally skeptical, but willing to spend an hour on this slim volume to assimilate a few names and concepts to show the students who show an interest in his critical theory course that he has mastered the field. Indeed, I suspect that this has already happened, since so few older academic men have read any women writers at all, and even fewer feminist critics. Ruthven argues the opposite of my position in this essay (that the practice is more interesting than the theory) by stating at the beginning that "the theory is more impressive than some of the practices."

I believe that the more abstract the discourse of criticism becomes, the less it can change the lives of readers and the oppressive practices of institutions. He resents the "accusatory" style of feminist criticism which is "unrelentingly intimidatory": "Feminist terrorism is a mirror image of machismo." Recognizing the chip on Mr. Ruthven's brawny shoulder as knocked off the same block as my own early angry gestures toward an exclusive male discipline, I am inclined to be tolerant. He wants in. (Actually, the line forms behind Jonathan Culler, Wayne Booth, Terry Eagleton, etc.) But, Mr. Ruthven, "feminist terrorism"? In literary criticism? Our Australian colleagues are pretty tough-minded but terrorism means the indiscriminate murder of civilians, and the "battle of the sexes," vicious as it may be verbally within institutions still does not have enough women to constitute a fair fight, let alone to hijack English Department chairpeople or even infiltrate the editorial board of the *New York Review of Books*. Ruthven doesn't comprehend the basic ideology of feminism as politics if he can entertain such a contradiction. Ruthven's imaginary feminist terrorist is a case of political pornography. Most women critics, however well they write and speak, are still struggling out of centuries of silence, aware of how brief has been their tenure in academe, how unaccustomed the meeting rooms are to the sound of women's voices.

Last spring I had dinner with a Korean mathematics professor in Paris. When she went home to lecture in the country of her birth, there was no word in the language to accommodate a woman Ph.D. They didn't know how to address her. Her colleagues and students had only words to name her as her husband's wife or as "Eugene's mother." English is a little farther along than that, but only a little. If it is "terrorist" for feminist literary critics to ignore Ruthven's plea, what does one call centuries of misogyny and the refusal to educate women, genocide or gender-cide? Lest my "disrespect" go over the border of Adrienne Munich's 'benign" toward "malignant," I will say that Ruthven does contextualize the recent surge of feminist criticism with both Marxism and post-modernism, and he connects it to New Left politics. He wants men to pay attention to its premises and join in its practice: "The feminist intervention strikes me as being incontestably the most important challenge faced by English studies" in the last twenty years. He likes it because it is "oppositional" and "disruptive," and he wants to be on the side of the revolution. Alas, that whole English public schoolboy notion of teams with sides, so nicely deconstructed by Virginia Woolf in *A Room of One's Own* no longer structures institutions or disciplines. Otherwise we could subscribe together to send Mr. Ruthven a Virginia Woolf T-shirt and be done with it. He could dream of scoring a goal for feminism in the

Critical Theory World Cup.

Meanwhile, it is in the multiplicity of its practices that feminist criticism will grow, critiquing the canon, reviving women's texts, rewriting history, endlessly interesting projects to revitalize the profession and change our lives. Like June Arnold's heroine, I have nurtured and protected my feminist anger like a cherished daughter. It is time for her to strike out on her own. One cannot argue too strongly for a "permanent revolution" in feminist criticism. If that drama takes the form in criticism of a narrative of "killing the angel in the house," the denial of the mothers of our own work or reading them as conservative and inhibitive, the reading of this narrative must be part of our practice as well. We are, indisputably, material girls, working in a material world. A nurturant sisterliness which denies difference among feminist critical practices infantalizes us all. Our gendered reading practice will engender new histories of feminist criticisms, more historically vertical and sickly horizontal than we can now imagine, if, like Gertrude Stein, we stop to read the signposts even though we think we know the road.

Notes

This essay has benefited from critical readings by Catharine R. Stimpson, Elizabeth Meese, Celeste Schenck, Tom Foster and Nancy K. Miller.

1. Showalter's "Critical Cross-Dressing" is in Raritan 3.2, Fall, 1983, 130-149. See also the essays by Stimpson, Miller and Caws in *The Female Body in Western Culture*: ed. Susan Suleiman (Cambridge: Harvard University Press, 1986), and my review in *The Women's Review of Books*, December, 1986; for a particularly telling example of *jouissance* in feminist criticism, see Lillian Robinson's "Is There Class in This Text?", a review of the *Norton Anthology of Women's Literature* in *Tulsa Studies in Women's Literature*, Fall, 1986.
2. "Feminist Issues in Literary Scholarship", *Tulsa Studies in Women's Literature*, Volume 3, Numbers 1/2, Spring/Fall, 1984, in book form from Indiana University Press, 1987.
3. All these works have been translated and published in 1985-6 by Cornell University Press. Kristeva's *Revolution in Poetic Language* and *Powers of Horror* are published by Columbia University Press.
4. Kofman's *Enigma of Woman* is also published by Cornell.
5. N.Y.: Pantheon, 1985.
6. K.K. Ruthven, *Feminist Literary Studies: An Introduction* (Cambridge: Cambridge University Press, 1984); *Making a Difference: Feminist Literary Criticism*, ed. Gayle Greene and Coppelia Kahn (London: Methuen, 1985); Toril Moi, *Sexual/Textual Politics: Feminist Literary History* (London: Methuen, 1985). See also Nancy K. Miller, ed. *The Poetics of Gender* (New York: Columbia University Press, 1986) and Mary Jacobus, *Reading Woman* (Ithaca: Cornell University Press, 1986) and

Teresa De Lauretis, ed. *Feminist Studies, Critical Studies* (Bloomington: Indiana University Press, 1986).
7. Beacon Press, 1986. Elaine Showalter's famous critique of Virginia Woolf is in the last chapter of *A Literature of Their Own* and Gilbert's critique is in "Soldier's Heart: Literary Men, Literary Women and the Great War," SIGNS, 1983, vol. 8, no. 3, 422-450.
8. *A Literature of Their Own* (Princeton: Princeton University Press, 1977).
9. See Elizabeth Abel, "Cam the Wicked," in *Virginia Woolf and Bloomsbury: A Centenary Celebration* Indiana Univ. Press, 1987; and Celeste Schenck, "Feminism and Deconstruction: Re-Constructing the Elegy" in *Tulsa Studies in Women's Literature*, Spring, 1986, and Christine Froula's "The Daughter's Seduction: Sexual Violence and Literary History," SIGNS, Summer, 1986.
10. "Laughing at Leviticus: Djuna Barnes' *Nightwood* as Woman's Circus Epic" forthcoming in M.L. Broe, *Silence and Power: Djuna Barnes, A Revaluation* (Carbondale: University of Southern Illinois Press, 1986).
11. See also Catharine R. Stimpson, "Feminism and Feminist Criticism," Massachusetts Review, XXIV, 2 (Summer, 1983) 272-288.
12. In "Ladies Shot and Painted," in *The Female Body in Western Culture*, ed. Susan Suleiman.
13. Patsy Schweickart, *Readers, Texts, Contexts: Essays on Gender and Reading*, co-edited by Schweikart and Elizabeth Flynn, John Hopkins University Press, 1986.

Works Cited

Arnold, June. *Sister Gin* (Plainfield, Vermont: Daughters, Inc, 1975).
Auerbach, Nina. *Romantic Imprisonment* (New York: Columbia Univ. Press, 1985).
Barrett, Michèle. Paper delivered at Alabama conference, "The Differences Within: Feminist Criticism and Theory," October, 1986.
Benstock, Shari, ed. *Feminist Issues in Literary Scholarship* (Bloomington: Indiana University Press, 1987).
Benstock, Shari. Paper delivered at SCMLA, October, 1986.
Benstock, Shari. Editorials in *Tulsa Studies in Women's Literature* 1981-85.
Broe, Mary Lynn. *Silence and Power: Djuna Barnes, A Revaluation* (Carbondale: Univ. of Southern Illinois Press, 1987).
Bronte, Charlotte. *Jane Eyre* (1847) (New York: Norton Critical Edition, 1971).
Caws, Mary Ann. "Ladies Shot and Painted," in Suleiman.
Gallop, Jane. *Reading Lacan* (Ithaca: Cornell Univ. Press, 1985).
Gallop, Jane. *The Daughter's Seduction* (Ithaca: Cornell Univ. Press, 1983).
Gallop, Jane. Paper delivered at SCMLA, October, 1986.
Gilbert, Sandra, and Gubar, Susan. *The Madwoman in the Attic* (New Haven: Yale Univ. Press, 1979).
Gilbert, Sandra and Gubar, Susan, eds, *The Norton Anthology of Women's Literature* (New York: W.W. Norton, 1985).
Greene, Gayle and Kahn, Coppelia, eds. *Making a Difference: Feminist Literary Criticism* (London: Methuen, 1985).
Jacobus, Mary. *Reading Woman* (Ithaca: Cornell Univ. Press, 1986).
Kofman, Sarah. *Enigma of Woman* (Ithaca: Cornell Univ. Press, 1986).
Kristeva, Julia. *Revolution in Poetic Language* (New York: Columbia University Press, 1986).

Kristeva, Julia. *Powers of Horror* (New York: Columbia University Press, 1986).
Lanser, Susan. Work in progress on history of women critics.
Leduc, Violette. *La Batarde* (New York: Farrar Straus Giroux, 1965).
Lesage, Julia. *Jump-Cut.*
Madonna. "Material Girls," popular song.
Marcus, Jane. "Laughing at Leviticus: Djuna Barnes' *Nightwood* as Woman's Circus Epic," In Mary Lynn Broe, *Silence and Power*.
Marcus, Jane. *Virginia Woolf and the Languages of Patriarchy* (Bloomington: Indiana University Press, 1987).
Marcus, Jane. "Still Practice, A/Wrested Alphabet: Toward a Feminist Aesthetic," *Tulsa Studies in Women's Literature*, vol. 3, #1/2. Spring/Fall, 1984.
Miller, Nancy K., ed., *The Poetics of Gender* (New York: Columbia Univ. Press, 1986).
Miller, Nancy K. "Changing the Subject," in *Feminist Studies/Critical Studies*, ed., Teresa de Lauretis (Bloomington: Indiana University Press, 1986).
Meese, Elizabeth. "Ex" Tensions, forthcoming.
Meese, Elizabeth and Alice Parker. *The Differences Within: Feminism and Critical Theory* (proceedings of the 1986 Alabama Conference) forthcoming 1988.
Moi, Toril. *Sexual/Textual Politics: Feminist Literary Theory* (London: Methuen 1985).
Pankhurst, Sylvia. *The Suffragette Movement* (London: Lovat Dickson and Thompson, 1931).
Robinson, Lillian. *Sex, Class and Culture* (rpt New York: Methuen, 1987).
Robinson, Lillian. "Treason Our Text," in Showalter, *Feminist Criticism*.
Robinson, Lillian. "Is There Class in This Text?" review of the *Norton Anthology of Women's Literature, Tulsa Studies in Women's Literature*, vol 5, #2, Fall 1986.
Ruthven, K.K. *Feminist Literary Studies: An Introduction* (Cambridge: Cambridge University Press, 1984).
Schenck, Celeste. "Feminism and Deconstruction: Re-Constructing the Elegy." *Tulsa Studies in Women's Literature*, vol. 5, #1, Spring 1986.
Schweikart, Patsy. *Readers, Texts, Contexts: Essays on Gender and Reading* (Baltimore: Johns Hopkins Univ. Press, 1986).
Showalter, Elaine. *A Literature of Their Own* (Princeton: Princeton Univ. Press, 1977).
Showalter, Elaine. *Feminist Literary Criticism* (New York: Pantheon, 1985).
Showalter, Elaine. "Critical Cross-Dressing," *Raritan*, vol. 3, #2, Fall, 1983.
Spivak, Gayatri. *In Other Worlds* (New York: Methuen, 1987).
Stein, Gertrude. *The Letters of Gertrude Stein and Carl Van Vechten*, ed. Edward Burns, 2 vols., (New York: Columbia Univ. Press, 1986).
Stimpson, Catharine. "Feminism and Feminist Criticism," *Massachusetts Review*, XXIV, 2, Summer 1983.
Suleiman, Susan, ed., *The Female Body in Western Culture* (Cambridge: Harvard University Press, 1986).
Woolf, Virginia. *A Room of One's Own*, 1928 (New York: Harcourt Brace Jovanovich)
Wyatt, Jean. "A Patriarch of One's Own: *Jane Eyre* and Romantic Love," *Tulsa Studies in Women's Literature*, vol 4, #2, Fall 1985.

Towards a humorous view of the universe

FAY WELDON

London

LET ME TELL YOU a joke. It was told to me over the phone, by my agent, whom I like and admire.

'Tell me,' said my agent, when we'd got a contractual matter or so out of the way, 'how is the Zeebrugge ferry like a used condom?'

Now this was at the time when they were raising the unfortunate craft from the bottom of the sea, less than fifty miles from where we spoke. Many bodies had already been removed from this new type of roll-on, roll-off, quick-turn-around ferry, which we the car-drivers of Britain so badly need if we're to get to the rest of Europe, and had assumed to be not just efficient but safe. (The ferry was, moreover, called the Spirit of Free Enterprise, which is what our government keeps recommending as the way ahead) but there were still bodies, thought to be mostly lorry drivers and crew, trapped beneath vehicles and mountains of Duty Free goods, waiting for extrication.

'I don't know,' I said. 'Tell me. How is the Zeebrugge Ferry like a used condom?'

'Because it's roll-on, roll-off, and full of dead sea-men.'

A pause.

'Semen. Geddit?'

I laughed. So did my agent. My agent, for your information, is a woman. She's a nice gel, as we call them over here. I'm a nice gel, too. I reckon we were both in a state of shock. Not just we two. All of us. I heard the joke quite a few times in the following few days, and from the most surprising people; delicately nurtured folks some of them, men and women, who'd never say boo to a goose or write the word ... in an article. There were variations, too — roll-on, roll-off, roll-over, and so forth. One of our steadiest, most capitalist, most unlikely politicians even stood up and made a Zeebrugge joke in Parliament. Shock, horror; but not for long. Everyone understood.

Five years ago (was it five?) before the days of 'safe sex' — is it called that in the States? the condom culture? — I sat in a taxi with your editor Gina and some fiercely feminist friends and we laughed ourselves to tears over:

How many radical feminists does it take to change a lightbulb?
Answer: That's not funny!

What a relief! But how we've moved on since then, down dreadful, dreadful paths! Our TV screens lately, over here, have been awash with giant papier mache penises (penes as the highly educated call them) while stars of stage and screen demonstrate the rolling on and off of condoms. (My mother, at 80, says 'Well, I never thought to see the day. I'm glad I have!') And then bubble-bubble, gurgle-gurgle, down goes the roll-on, roll-off ferry, the Spirit of Free Enterprise, to the bottom of the sea. Is someone, somewhere, trying to tell us something? Get a message through from the other side? That roll on and roll off as we may, it's all USELESS?

Did you, by the way, notice my use of the phrase 'unfortunate craft' in the third paragraph of this piece? Did it offend you? Stick out like a sore thumb? It was meant to. There is a certain kind of verbal humor — and I am, you will notice, seeing humour very much as an escape from pain — which is dismissive of that pain, diminishing of those who grieve and which I find unacceptable and try not to use. It has a class base — it is certainly old-fashioned. I reckon those who lost relatives and friends in the ferry disaster could better endure 'roll-on, roll-off and full of dead seamen' than they could the standing back, nothing to do with me, ha-ha-iness of 'unfortunate craft'. Do you see what I mean? Will someone write a paper on it? I haven't time. I'm being serious. To describe a sunk ferry, full of dead bodies, as an 'unfortunate craft' uses words alone, not substance, in order to be funny, and no longer works. Why?

Feminists get accused of not being able to make jokes. I don't think it's an accusation, either. I think it's a compliment. I use humour because I'm weak minded and always in a hurry. Go back to the phrase two paragraphs before: 'What a relief!' That's kind of funny, I suppose; but more a form of punctuation, separating what went before from what comes next. But also, for me, more importantly, it's shorthand. It saves me writing a long paragraph about how feminists get accused of not being able to make jokes, and a few of us certainly can't, which makes a few others of us uneasy, which is why it's a joke in the first place, and we all laughed so much in the taxi, and yet not being funny is not an accusation but a compliment, because rape, poverty, exploitation and so forth are *not* funny. All that I got in 'What a relief!' It's funny (if it *is*. It may not be the best example in the world) because I the writer understand all that and so do you the reader, and what a relief, we don't have to go through it all again.

Roll-on, roll-off, and full of dead seamen. Ha-ha. Just.

Look. Lately we've had some pretty severe shocks to our corporate souls, to our group determination that the world is a pleasant place and getting better, that the people in it are well-intentioned and that the universe is fundamentally benign. That all we need do, as women (if we're that kind of woman) is love our children (if we have them) and our friends (if we're that kind) and everything will be just fine. That there are dreadful unfairnesses about (sexism, racism, nuclearism, adultism) but we're working on them. But it just isn't like that any more.

AIDS has been the worst shock: a sexually transmitted disease in adults invariably fatal in mothers and babies, seems to me to spell the end, inevitably, of the human race (like the dinosaurs, given an aeon or so or less, if I understand this matter of exponential growth, which I barely do). That's it, for the human race! So what, if we're never to perfect ourselves, we must ask, is the bloody *point*? In a world deprived of its dignity: condoms all over the screen, the glug-glug of free enterprise, Irangate and so forth, not to mention the ozone layer flying off, and our pleasures increasingly limited as our knowledge of what keeps us healthy, well and alive improves — there's just not much fun left, and I reckon mirth, which is free, safe and shared, is just about all we have for our consolation.

About the Contributors

REGINA BARRECA is author of *Punch Lines: Comedy and Subversion in Women's Writing* (Wayne State University Press, 1989). She is editor of *Coming and Going: Sex and Death in Victorian Literature* and Coordinating Editor of the critical journal *LIT*. She is an Assistant Professor of English at the University of Connecticut, Storrs.

RACHEL M. BROWNSTEIN teaches at Brooklyn College and the Graduate School, CUNY. She is author of *Becoming a Heroine: Readings About Women in Novels* (Viking Penguin, 1982/4).

MARY ANN RORISON CAWS, Distinguished Professor of Comparative Literature, French and English at the Graduate School of City University of New York. Past President of the Modern Language Association, and President-Elect of the American Comparative Literature Association. She has been on the faculty of the School of Criticism and Theory and held N.E.H., Fulbright, and Guggenheim fellowships. Among her many books on poetics and contemporary writing are *The Eye in the Text Essays on Perception, Mannerist to Modern*, *Reading Frames in Modern Fiction*, and, most recently, *The Art of Interference: Stressed Reading in Visual and Verbal Texts*.

ESTHER COHEN is currently marketing director for New York Theater Workshop. As a stage manager, she worked on The New York productions of *Sister Mary Ignatius Explains It All For You, Baby With the Bathwater, Isn't It Romantic?* and *Tintypes*. Ms. Cohen is a graduate of Dartmouth College, and is an MFA candidate at Columbia University.

REGENIA GAGNIER author of *Idylls of the Marketplace: Oscar Wilde and the Victorian Public* (Stanford, 1986), is completing a study of subjectivity, value, and the uses of literacy in the lifewriting of Victorian working-class, public- and boarding school, and canonical literary subjects. She is Assistant Professor of English at Stanford University and a member of the Feminist Studies Program Committee, the Policy Board of the Institute for Research on Women and Gender, and the Cultural Studies Group.

CATHERINE GALLAGHER'S *The Industrial Reformation of English Fiction* was published in 1985 by University of Chicago Press. She is Associate Professor of English at the University of California, Berkeley. Her current research focuses on the connection between economic and sexual ideologies in women's fiction.

JOHN GLAVIN is an Associate Professor of English at Georgetown University in Washington, D.C. He has published on Milton, Hopkins, Trollope, Dickens and Wilde. He is also a playwright whose plays, *God's Boys* and *Winter Cup*, have been performed by the Philadelphia Company. He is currently working on a study of the frivolous in nineteenth-century culture and an adaptation for the stage of Freud's *Interpretation of Dreams*.

NICOLE HOLLANDER is creator of the cartoon character "Sylvia." She is author of twelve collections of Sylvia cartoons, including her latest work *Never Take Your Cat to a Salad Bar*. She is co-author of a comedy with music called *Sylvia's Real Good Advice*. She lives quietly in Chicago with her cats and a flock of Shetland ponies.

JUDY LITTLE teaches courses in modern literature and women's studies at Southern Illinois University Carbondale. Her book, *Comedy and the Woman Writer: Woolf, Spark and Feminism*, was published by the University of Nebraska Press in 1983.

CAROL HANBERY MACKAY, Associate Professor of English at the University of Texas, is author of *Soliloquy in Nineteenth-Century Fiction* and editor of *Dramatic Dickens*. She has written several articles on Ann Thackeray Ritchie as well as the critical introduction to *The Two Thackerays*. Her major work in progress is a study of Victorian novelists as thwarted dramatists.

JANE MARCUS, Professor of English at the City University of New York Graduate Center and the City College of New York, is the author of *Art and Anger* (1988), *Virginia Woolf and the Languages of Patriarchy* (1987) and editor of *Suffrage and the Pankhursts* (1987) and *Virginia Woolf and Bloomsbury* (1987).

ABOUT THE CONTRIBUTORS

DENISE MARSHALL is currently Assistant Professor of English at Heidelberg College, Tiffin, Ohio. Her continued work on the comedy of power and knowledge has extended into popular culture. She is working on a book about the cultural status of women, and comedy, and the space society allots them both.

LISA MERRILL is a Professor of Speech Communication Arts at Hofstra University. She is co-author of *The Power to Communicate: Gender Differences as Barriers* (Waveland Press, 1985), a member of the editorial board of *Women and Performance: A Journal of Feminist Theory*, and theatre critic for *The Villager*.

LINDA A. MORRIS is on the faculty at University of California, Davis. Her work *Women Venacular Humorists in Nineteenth-Century America: Ann Stephens, Frances Whitcher and Marietta Holley* is being published in 1988 by Garland Press. She is currently preparing a full-length work on Frances Whitcher.

KAY ROGERS, a Professor at the City University of New York, is currently Visiting Professor at George Mason University. Her most recent books are *Feminism in Eighteenth-Century England* (1982) and the *Meridan Anthology of Early Women Writers* (co-edited with William McCarthy, 1987). She is now working on a full-length study of Francis Burney.

PATRICIA MEYER SPACKS is author of several books of scholarship and criticism. Prominant among these are *Gossip*, *The Adolescent Idea* and *The Female Imagination*. She is Professor of English at Yale University.

JANET TODD is Director of Studies in English at Sidney Sussex, Cambridge University. She is author of *Women's Friendships in Literature* and editor of *British Women Writers*.

NANCY WALKER is the author of *A Very Serious Thing: Women's Humor and American Culture*, and the co-author of an anthology of American women's humor, *Redressing the Balance: American Women's Humor from the Colonies to the 1980's*, both to be published in 1988. She has contributed articles to *American Quarterly, Denver Quarterly Studies in*

American Humor, and *Tulsa Studies in Women's Literature*, among others. She chairs the Department of Languages and Literature at Stephens College.

FAY WELDON has published a number of highly successful novels, among them *The Leader of the Band, The Hearts and Lives of Men, Life and Loves of a She-Devil, Praxis, Female Friends* and *The Heart of the Country*. She has written on Rebecca West and Jane Austen and has adapted novels by Austen and Brontë for the stage and screen. She lives in London and Somerset.

Index

Abel, Elizabeth, 296
Addison, Thomas, 156
Adorno, Theodor, 6, 18, 20
Agress, Lynne, 205, 206
Allen, Woody, 270
Amis, Kingsley, 12
Apollo, 143
Apte, Mahadev, 137, 138
Aristotle, 136, 139, 167
Arnold, June, 281, 287, 306
Arnot, John, 104
Atwood, Margaret, 203, 205, 206, 207, 208, 214, 215-218, 219, 244
Auerbach, Nina, 137, 144, 289, 298
Austen, Jane, 4, 6, 7, 11, 12, 13, 55-70, 71-85, 101, 124, 126, 127, 138, 151, 152, 161, 182, 300

Bakhtin, Mikhail, 6, 296
Barber, John, 44
Barnes, Djuna, 296
Barreca, Regina, 310
Barrett, Michele, 283, 295
Barrie, J.M., 222, 232
Barry, Philip, 261
Barthes, Roland, 180, 237, 282, 288
Bartlett, Beatrice, 219
Baudelaire, Charles, 222, 229, 230
Baym, Nina, 289
Beatts, Anne, 273, 274, 275, 279
Beauvoir, Simone de, 288, 292
Behn, Aphra, 23-42, 45, 46
Bell, Clive, 175
Bell, Currer, 58
Bell, Quentin, 173, 294
Benjamin, Walter, 294
Benstock, Shari, 287
Bergson, Henri, 135, 146, 244, 253, 255, 273
Berkowitz, David, 266
Bernstein, Carl, 203
Bloom, Harold, 12, 62, 223-227, 239, 292
Blyth, Reginald, 3
Bogan, Louise, 273

Boosler, Elayne, 275
Booth, Wayne, 62, 173, 206, 207, 219, 303, 305
Boswell, James, 265
Bowen, Elizabeth, 175, 251
Bradsteet, Anne, 209
Brittain, Vera, 150
Brontë sisters, 151
Brontë, Charlotte, 226, 286, 292, 299, 302
Browning, Robert, 221
Brownstein, Rachel, 127
Brunton, Mary, 63
Buhle, M.J., 99
Burney, Fanny, 63, 87-96, 124, 205
Butler, Samuel, 119

Carby, Hazel, 296
Carey, Lady Elizabeth, 27, 28
Carlin, George, 268
Carlyle, Thomas, 151
Carrington, Dora, 196-198
Cartwright, Angela, 257
Cavendish, Margaret, 209
Caws, Mary Ann, 9, 287, 302
Cellini, 222, 238, 239
Chapman, Anthony, 137
Charles I, 44
Charles II, 44, 46
Cheever, John, 261
Chodorow, Nancy, 62, 146, 291
Cholmondeley, Mary, 129
Chopin, Kate, 205
Christian, Barbara, 296
Churchill, Caryl, 269
Cicero, 168
Cixous, Hélène, 12, 14-18, 146, 245, 254, 287, 291
Clemens, Samuel, 104
Clement, Catharine, 14, 16, 18, 253-254
Cleveland, Duchess of, 46
Clinton, Catherine, 279
Clinton, Kate, 145, 172
Cobbe, Frances Power, 141-142
Congreve, William, 3, 5

INDEX

Coser, Rose Laub, 272
Cott, Nancy F., 115
Craigie, Jill, 290
Cross, Whitney, 102
Culler, Jonathan, 281, 303-305

Daddy, Make Room For, 257
Daly, Mary, 15, 20, 291
Darwin, Charles, 227
Davies, Margaret Llewelyn, 138
Davy, Kate, 278
Debbie Does Dallas, 145
Defoe, Daniel, 45, 48, 222
Derrida, Jacques, 287
Descartes, René, 231
Dickens, Charles, 229
Dickinson, Emily, 15, 126, 129, 130, 303-304
Diller, Phyllis, 273
Dionysius, 164, 237, 238, 272
Donne, John, 246
Douglas, Mary, 15
Drabble, Margaret, 204-212, 218
Dryden, John, 30, 47, 156
Du Pleiss, Rachel, 8
Dukes of Hazzard, 262
Durang, Christopher, 259, 260, 265
Durrenmatt, 153

Eagleton, Terry, 294, 303, 305
Ecker, Giselda, 294
Eco, Umberto, 139
Egerton, Sarah Fyge, 46
Eliot, George, 3, 11-15, 58, 62, 101, 126, 151, 245-246, 255
Eliot, T.S., 180
Ellmann, Mary, 6, 15, 17, 58, 67, 291-292
Ephron, Nora, 203, 205, 208, 213-215, 219

Feibleman, James, 13, 14, 18
Fern, Fanny, 58, 104, 205
Fetterley, Judith, 115
Fine, Gary, 138
Finney, Charles Grandison, 102
Foot, Hugh, 137
Forster, E.M., 248
Foucault, Michel, 287
Fox, Elizabeth Genovese, 297
French, Marilyn, 205, 206
Freud, Sigmund, 12, 80, 136, 145, 227, 244, 253, 272, 288, 301

Friedman, Susan, 292
Froula, Christine, 296
Fry, Christopher, 163
Frye, Northrop, 159
Furman, Nelly, 297
Fussell, B.H., 170, 171, 173, 175

Gagnier, Regenia, 5
Gallop, Jane, 284, 288-289, 291, 302
Gardiner, Judith Kegan, 146, 291, 297
Garnett, David, 196
Garr, Teri, 261-262
Gaskell, Elizabeth, 4
Genet, Jean, 288
Gilbert, Sandra, 9, 10, 13, 17, 180, 189, 245, 255, 282-284, 288, 292, 295-298
Gildon, Charles, 31
Gilligan, Carol, 128
Gilman, Charlotte Perkins, 160
Giotto, 234
Girard, Rene, 232
Godey, Louis, 106, 111, 113
Godwin, Gail, 205
Goldberg, Whoopi, 276, 277, 278
Goreau, Angeline, 27
Gould, Robert, 27, 43
Green, Gayle, 291
Greer, Germaine, 291
Gross, Amy, 277
Gubar, Susan, 9, 10, 13, 17, 245, 255, 282-284, 288, 295-298
Gutierrez, Gerry, 263, 267

Halperin, John, 71, 83, 84
Hammer, Rusty, 257
Harding, D.W., 7
Harris, George Washington, 104
Harris, Trudier, 296
Hathaway, Anne, 119
Hawthorne, Nathaniel, 194, 198, 219-220
Hegel, Georg, 136
Heilbrun, Carolyn, 287, 293
Henke, Suzette, 189
Henley, Beth, 269
Henley, Nancy, 272
Herbert, George, 62
Hobbes, Thomas, 29, 80, 82, 136, 144
Holley, Marietta, 104, 115
Homans, Margaret, 245
Howe, Florence, 293

Hughes, Mary Vivian, 142

Inchbald, Elizabeth, 95
Innaurato, Albert, 259
Irigaray, Luce, 245, 288, 292, 294
Iser, Wolfgang, 182

Jackson, Andrew, 104
Jackson, Julia, 150
Jacobus, Mary, 180, 181, 245, 246, 286
James, Henry, 193, 222
Jardine, Penelope, 240
Jehlen, Myra, 290
Jenkins, Linda Walsh, 272, 274
Job, 222-223, 228-229, 240
Johnson, Barbara, 284, 291, 296
Johnson, Don, 265
Johnson, Paul, 102
Johnson, Samuel, 64, 155
Jones, Ann Rosalind, 297
Joyce, James, 8, 173, 179, 180-181, 189-190
Juvenal, 47

Kahn, Coppelia, 291
Kamuf, Peggy, 284, 291
Kant, Immanuel, 135
Kaplan, Cora, 295, 298-302
Keats, John, 151
Kerr, Jean, 219
Koestler, Arthur, 127
Kofman, Sarah, 288
Kolodny, Annette, 12, 19, 283, 293
Kristeva, Julia, 237, 253, 286-288, 291, 295-296, 301

La France, Marianne, 137
Lacan, Jacques, 254, 283, 288, 291, 294
Lanser, Susan, 293
Lawrence, D.H., 180-181, 294
Layton, Mrs., 140
Leavis, F.R., 294-295
Leavis, Q., 174
Lee, Hermione, 172
Lennox, Charlotte, 63
Lesage, Julia, 281
Lessing, Doris, 244, 253
Lévi-Strauss, Claude, 254
Lewis, W., 174
Lipking, Joanna, 164, 167
Little, Judy, 7, 8, 9, 14, 20, 181

Locke, John, 29
Lorenz, Konrad, 127
Love, Jean, 152, 154
Lowell, James Russell, 104
Lowell, Robert, 129-130
Lucy, I Love, 270

Macaulay, Thomas, 95
MacCarthy, Mary, 119
McCarthy, Mary, 126
McDowell, Deborah, 296
McGhee, Paul, 6, 136-137
McGinley, Phyllis, 219
McKay, Nellie, 296
Machiavelli, Niccolo, 50
Madonna, 281, 282
Malborough, Duchess of, 46
Malthus, T.R., 227
Manley, Delarivier, 43-55
Mansfield, Katherine, 62
Marcus, Jane, 9, 173
Marks, Elaine, 284
Martin, Robert, 175
Marx Brothers, 162, 164
Marx, Karl, 207
Mason, Mary G., 209
May, Betty, 140
Medusa, 16, 145-146
Meese, Elizabeth, 285
Mellor, George, 104
Melville, Herman, 194-195, 197-199
Meredith, George, 126, 156, 165, 171, 271
Merrill, Lisa, 15
Midler, Bette, 275
Miles, Rosalind, 13
Miller, Nancy K., 285, 287, 297
Millett, Kate, 150, 287, 291-292
Milton, John, 58
Mitchell, Juliete, 254, 291
Moers, Ellen, 292
Moi, Toril, 237, 284, 289, 291, 294-295
Montebello, Philipe de, 263
Monty Python, 138
Moore, Marianne, 126
Morrell, Ottoline, 175
Morrison, Toni, 298
Mott, Lucretia, 99
Muecke, D.C., 208, 218
Munich, Adrienne, 298, 304-305

Nemy, Enid, 163
Newman, Henry, 222
Nicolson, Nigel, 173
Nietzsche, Friedrich, 245, 253
Nightingale, Florence, 143-144
Norman, Marsha, 269

O'Connor, Flannery, 245
O'Donnell, Thomas, 102
Olsen, Tillie, 172-173, 293
Ostriker, Alice, 293
Otway, Thomas, 49
Ovid, 51

Pankhurst, Sylvia, 290
Patmore, Coventry, 168
Peck, Winifred, 142
Petrarch, Francesco, 51
Phaedra, 195
Piercy, Marge, 205-206
Plath, Sylvia, 128, 277
Plato, 136, 180
Polhemus, Robert, 127
Poovey, Mary, 58
Pope, Alexander, 43, 58, 156-157
Pownall, David, 71
Priestley, J.B., 4 7
Prior, Matthew, 58
Proust, Marcel, 249

Racine, Jean, 195
Rainer, Peter, 276
Raskin, Victor, 135-136
Reagan, Ronald, 267-268
Rhys, Jean, 301
Rich, Adrienne, 293, 303-304
Richardson, Samuel, 49
Ricoeur, Paul, 253
Ritchie, Anne Thackeray, 117-133, 285
Rivers, Joan, 273
Robinson, Lillian, 281, 289
Rochester, John, 43
Roethke, Theodore, 273
Rosenburg, Avis, 172
Rossner, Judith, 205-206
Roth, Philip, 59
Rousseau, Jean-Jacques, 198
Rowbotham, Sheila, 291
Rowe, Nicholas, 49
Rudnick, Paul, 265

Ruthven, K.K., 291, 303-305
Ryan, Mary, 102-103

Sand, George, 293
Sappho, 293
Sartre, Jean-Paul, 138
Scaldini, Richard, 19
Schenck, Celeste, 296
Schlack, Beverly, 165, 168
Schopenhauer, Arthur, 6, 135
Schweikart, Patsy, 285, 303-304
Searle, John, 253
Segal, Sondra, 274
Shakespeare, William, 119, 300
Shillaber, B.P., 104
Showalter, Elaine, 281, 283-298
Silver, Susan, 276
Simon, Neil, 259
Simpson, Carolyn, 18
Sinclair, May, 245
Sklar, Roberta, 274
Smith, Charlotte, 95
Smith, Emma, 140
Smith, Seba, 104
Smith, Stevie, 153
Smyth, Ethel, 289
Sorell, Walter, 272
Spacks, Patricia, 13
Spark, Muriel, 221-241, 243, 246-247, 249, 252-253
Spender, Dale, 172-173
Spillers, Hortense, 296
Spivak, Gayatri, 284-285, 290
Squier, Susan, 301
Staël, Germaine de, 293
Stanford, Derek, 224
Stanton, Domna, 245, 293
Stanton, Elizabeth Cady, 99
Steele, Elizabeth, 152
Steele, Richard, 44, 45, 46
Stein, Gertrude, 13-14, 18, 174, 196, 302-303, 306
Stephen, Leslie, 117-118
Stephens, Ann, 104
Sterne, Laurence, 58
Stillman, Deanne, 273, 275, 279
Stimpson, Catharine, 287, 290, 293, 297, 303
Strachey, Lytton, 143, 196-198
Strachey, Philippa, 174

Suls, Jerry, 136, 137
Swift, Jonathan, 10, 43-45, 61, 129, 172

Taylor, Elizabeth, 273
Tennyson, Alfred, 151, 158, 168
Thackeray, William Makepeace, 118-119, 122
Thatcher, Margaret, 267
Thorpe, Thomas B., 104
Tillery, Annie, 137
Tilly, John, 44
Toklas, Alice B., 196
Tomlin, Lily, 276, 277-278
Tootsie, 281
Tour, Georges de la, 228-229, 238, 240
Towner, Asburn, 104
Trilling, Lionel, 62
Trotter, Catherine, 27
Tune, Tommy, 262
Tuttle, Stephen, 104

Unkeless, Elaine, 189
Updike, John, 260

Vance, Danitra, 276, 277-278
Vita, 161, 196, 198
Vonnegut, Kurt, 126

Wagner, Jane, 277-278
Ward, Mrs. Humphry, 58

Washington, Mary Helen, 296
Weisstein, Naomi, 275, 280
Weldon, Fay, 7, 15, 204-208, 211-213, 219, 243-244, 248-250
West, Jane, 63
West, Rebecca, 293
Wharton, Edith, 205
Whitcher, Frances Miriam, 99-116
White, Antonia, 143
White, Kenneth, 152-154
Willis, Susan, 296-297
Wilson, Edmund, 302
Wilt, Judith, 7, 14-15, 18
Winnicott, D.W., 292
Wittig, Monique, 291
Wollstonecraft, Mary, 95
Woodward, Kathleen, 141
Woolf, Leonard, 173
Woolf, Virginia, 8, 23, 64-65, 117-118, 125, 138-140, 145, 149-177, 179-191, 196-197, 205, 284, 286, 288, 292, 294-305
Wyatt, Jean, 302
Wycherley, William, 29

Yeats, W.B., 180
Young, G.M., 174

Zillmann, Dolf, 136
Zimmerman, Bonnie, 291